Theology of a Diary

McMaster Divinity College Press
McMaster Theological Studies Series, Volume 10

Defining Issues in Pentecostalism (2008)

Pentecostalism and Globalization (2009)

You Mean I Don't Have to Tithe? (2009)

Baptism (2011)

Resurrection, Scripture, and Reformed Apologetics (2012)

The Globalization of Christianity (2014)

Salvation in the Flesh (2018)

The Empowering God (2018)

The Secularization of Baptism (2025)

Theology of a Diary
The 1949 St. Louis Exorcism

by
W. Brian Shelton

☙PICKWICK *Publications* · Eugene, Oregon

THEOLOGY OF A DIARY
The 1949 St. Louis Exorcism

McMaster Theological Studies Series 10

Copyright © 2025 W. Brian Shelton. All rights reserved. Except for brief quotations in critical publications or reviews, no part of this book may be reproduced in any manner without prior written permission from the publisher. Write: Permissions, Wipf and Stock Publishers, 199 W. 8th Ave., Suite 3, Eugene, OR 97401.

Pickwick Publications
An Imprint of Wipf and Stock Publishers
199 W. 8th Ave., Suite 3
Eugene, OR 97401

www.wipfandstock.com

PAPERBACK ISBN: 979-8-3852-5784-3
HARDCOVER ISBN: 979-8-3852-5785-0
EBOOK ISBN: 979-8-3852-5786-7

ISSN (PRINT): 2564-436X
ISSN (EBOOK): 2564-4378

Cataloguing-in-Publication data:

Names: Shelton, W. Brian, author.

Title: Theology of a diary : The 1949 St. Louis exorcism / by W. Brian Shelton.

Description: Eugene, OR: Pickwick Publications, 2025 | McMaster Theological Studies Series 10 | Includes bibliographical references and index.

Identifiers: ISBN 979-8-3852-5784-3 (paperback) | ISBN 979-8-3852-5785-0 (hardcover) | ISBN 979-8-3852-5786-7 (ebook)

Subjects: LCSH: Spiritual warfare--United States | Exorcism--St. Louis.

Classification: GR307.S54 2025 (paperback) | GR307 (ebook)

VERSION NUMBER 12/08/25

To C. John Collins, who labors to demonstrate the compatibility of a scientific frame of mind with a certainty of the metaphysical. As professor, he once graded my naturalistic approach to an assignment that claimed the sons of God and daughters of men to be descendants of Seth and Cain, replying: "You have helped me to see that the spirit beings interpretation really has the most going for it." This work salutes both his legacy upon his retirement and the potential for spirit beings in the world.

List of Tables

Table 1. Major Events and Locations
Table 2. Witnesses
Table 3. Claimants to Witness the Event

Contents

List of Tables | viii
List of Abbreviations | ix
Acknowledgments | xi
Introduction | xiii

1 The Event | 1
2 The *Diary* and the Witnesses | 41
3 Preternaturalism and its Critics | 77
4 Theology of the Demonization | 123
5 Theology of the Rite | 159
6 Theology of the Exorcism | 206
7 Appropriating the Event | 239

Bibliography | 263
Index of Authors | 273
Index of Subjects | 277

List of Abbreviations

ABD	*Anchor Bible Dictionary*
ACW	Ancient Christian Writers
ANF	Ante-Nicene Fathers
BAG	William F. Arndt and F. Wilbur Gingrich, *A Greek–English Lexicon of the New Testament and Other Early Christian Literature* (Chicago: University of Chicago Press, 1957)
BECNT	Baker Exegetical Commentary on the New Testament
BBR	*Bulletin for Biblical Research*
CBQ	*Catholic Biblical Quarterly*
CD	Karl Barth's *Church Dogmatics*. 14 vols. Published by T&T Clark, 1936–1977.
FC	Fathers of the Church
IBC	Interpretation: A Bible Commentary for Teaching and Preaching
JGRChJ	*Journal of Greco-Roman Christianity and Judaism*
NAC	New American Commentary
NASA	National Aeronautics and Space Administration
NIBCNT	New International Biblical Commentary on the New Testament
PNTCS	Pillar New Testament Commentary Series
SymS	Symposium Series

List of Abbreviations

TNTC   Tyndale New Testament Commentaries
WBC   Word Biblical Commentary

Acknowledgments

A RESOUNDING THANKS TO several who supported this project. The Office of the Provost at Asbury University helped to fund this endeavor. Paul Thigpen provided precision of insights into Catholic theology. Paul Nesselroade offered clarity to social science concepts. Joy Vaughan was a source of scholarship and encouragement. Tom Schmidt offered valuable manuscript feedback and project appreciation. For decades, Mr. John Waide unwittingly found himself to be a SLU legacy resource to many inquirers on the 1949 exorcism, providing one more interview for me. Bethany Groves in the Kinlaw Library deserves credit for obtaining rare sources on numerous occasions. Research assistance for the manuscript came from Isaiah Friedeman. All of these scholars offered friendship, without which research projects remain lonely enterprises. Sally Shelton perpetually offers support to such enterprises of mine.

Introduction

"For still our ancient foe does seek to work us woe; his craft and power are great, and armed with cruel hate, on earth is not his equal."

—Martin Luther, "A Mighty Fortress"

In 1976, the city of St. Louis began replacing a hospital complex in its southside urban community. The 110-year-old Alexian Brothers Hospital was slated to be razed.[1] Far from the public consciousness, one room on the old psychiatric wing of the fifth floor held a secret, locked behind its door since 1949. Within that decade, this wing had given way to storage rooms, abandoning this one space to unimportance. For the few hospital workers who recalled, it was said that an exorcism had once taken place here. The Catholic brothers occasionally spoke of the event when they reported haunting laughter and banging noises inside the aged facility.

Before the final phase of demolition in October 1978, an ordinary worker went about the wing removing furniture from the vacated rooms. Finding this one room surprisingly closed off but fully intact, he checked a dresser drawer that produced a stack of papers comprising a sort of diary. The volume had rested there for almost thirty years, with its contents ready to offer a firsthand account of an historic event that had inspired a blockbuster film.[2] The 1949 St. Louis exorcism, combined with its early

---

1. Faherty, *To Rest in Charity*, 119.
2. Allen, *Possessed*, 222–26, 322–23. The copy of the diary was reported as delivered to the hospital administrator, who handed it over to a lawyer, who placed it in a safety deposit box.

xiii

Introduction

phase in the Washington, DC, suburbs of Georgetown, had inspired the 1971 instant bestseller by William Peter Blatty and the 1973 blockbuster film directed by William Friedkin. Both were titled *The Exorcist*. As the second-highest grossing film that year, it was nominated for ten Academy Awards, with producer Blatty winning for Best Writing (Adapted Screenplay). With an original budget of $11 million, the film has grossed $500 million in sales in the last five decades.[3] One cinematic source claims that the contemporary equivalent would be $900 million in gross income.[4]

The 1978 discovery of the exorcist's *Diary* would eventually breathe new life into the curiosity of all who wondered about the events of that year. When Thomas Allen wrote his first edition of the most comprehensive treatment of the proceedings of the exorcism, he lacked a copy of the mysterious diary. Then he reached out to Father Walter Halloran, a Jesuit eyewitness and participant in the ordeal. The priest acquired the rediscovered papers from a safety deposit box and verified it as the daily diary of Father Raymond Bishop, the most prominent participant in the event next to the exorcist himself. Halloran copied the diary, returned the original to its vault, and then surprisingly offered to share his copy with Allen and agreed to allow its use as a primary source for the book.[5] This generosity offered knowledge and credibility for Allen to expand his interviews in the second edition of a work. It would also release the diary to the public for the first time.

Cultural Value of the Event

The 1949 exorcism event carries a life of its own in contemporary culture. It served as the backstory for a pioneering cinematic enterprise, contributing significantly to the genre of the horror film industry. It led the *Washington Post* to feature the event on its front page in 1949, calling it "one of the most remarkable experiences of its kind in recent religious history."[6] *Time* magazine claimed that ticket lines for the original film release reached 5,000 people, while one theater manager reported that each showing had an average of four patrons fainting, six vomiting, and several

---

3. Rueda, *Diabolical Possession*, 1.
4. LaChance, *Confrontation*, 183.
5. Allen, *Possessed*, 224–25. Cooperman tells this story: "When Allen interviewed him [Halloran], he said, almost casually, 'Oh, by the way, there was a diary kept. Do you want a copy of it?'" ("Touched by Evil").
6. Brinkley, "Priest Frees Mt. Rainier Boy."

Introduction

walkouts.⁷ The story has served as a milestone in public conversation about demons, demonology, demonization, possession, and exorcism. It still serves the historical identity point for one St. Louis university that unknowingly staffed the team of exorcists. Its story can also serve as a case study in the tension between science and faith, as notions of what is natural and explainable are confronted by the bizarre and inexplicable. Father John Nicola depicted its effect well in 1974: "With the publication of *The Exorcist* came a goading of the public conscience, an inquisitiveness about the reality of the hair-raising phenomenon identified as diabolical possession and, granted the reality of such a syndrome, a gnawing desire to know whether there exists a world of devil and demons who could so attack a human being."⁸

Fifty years after the exorcism event, as a graduate student at Saint Louis University in 1999, I observed how the legend still crept its way into the wonder and discourse of campus life. As a rumor from the past, it fostered a curiosity in the present. The theology department of my own doctoral studies was housed in Dubourg Hall, an imposing building with Gothic architectural style, old wooden floors, and an aura of age. Professors related how undergraduates would seek out any senior Jesuit priest teaching in this hallowed hall to inquire if he himself were the legendary exorcist. Then professor Father Francis X. Cleary claimed expertise on the event in only one way: "The tall tales and mythology that have arisen among the students and faculty . . . I guess every school has its ghost stories. Ours just happened to become a best-selling book and movie."⁹ Former university archivist John Waide remarked, "Without a doubt, the topic I'm asked about most frequently is the exorcism."¹⁰ In those days, St. Louis radio would phone in Father Walter Halloran from Nebraska, eyewitness to the events, each Halloween to revive the event in the consciousness of the city. Saint Louis University periodically and comfortably highlights the event in its publications. As recent as 2020, Saint Louis University proudly reprofiled the exorcism from a 2014 article in its alumni communications.¹¹ Back in Georgetown, in the Washington, DC, suburb, the iconic steps that centered prominently in

---

7. MacLeod, "*Exorcist, The*," 122.
8. Nicola, *Diabolical Possession*, 105.
9. McGuire, "St. Louis Exorcism."
10. Garland, "Exorcism Exposé," 13; John Waide, interview by W. Brian Shelton, October 30, 2024.
11. Garland, "Exorcism Exposé," 12–15.

Introduction

the film still stand, and the Hitchcock steps are now affectionately known as "The Exorcist Steps." This exorcism event has a living memory of its own, lingering in the identity of a university community and in public consciousness. Yet few know the details of the story behind the cinematic phenomenon.

A Christian Historiography

This book is about that event. It is not a journalistic report that summarizes the events, although it offers such a summary. It is not a press release with a newly discovered detail, although it highlights some recent developments around the victim. It is instead a theological examination of the events of the 1949 exorcism, the first treatment of its type. In tandem, it is also a historical evaluation of the overall interpretation of the events, framed from a Christian worldview and weighed theologically. This history and theology combine into a treatment of historical theology. While the 1949 exorcism has received journalistic, sociological, and psychological attention, it has received no comprehensive theological assessment. John McGuire captures its significance for Roman Catholic theology: "By some accounts, this exorcism that took place here in 1949 was considered by church officials to be the most significant reported and documented case in 300 years."[12] The hope is that this treatment might register with Christians as a historically credible illustration to a biblical theology which they claim to hold.

Yet the story of the exorcism of a young boy in 1949 is not congruent with the thinking of many people. The church, the Christian academy, and individual believers are generally skittish about demon stories, preferring to leave it to the ranks of the extremists. The association makes for an easy dismissal by many in the church. Meanwhile, the psychology guild, the secular academy, and the modern mind are skeptical of any such unnatural phenomena, preferring to offer a psychological or sociological explanation. For example, Henry Kelly remarks, "The story of *The Exorcist* manifests a diabolical mythomania." He posits that the documentary evidence is exaggerated, the facts have been distorted, and the event "seems to have been a pseudo-possession induced by the rite of exorcism itself."[13] Like tales of ghosts, specters, and leprechauns,

12. McGuire, "St. Louis Exorcism."
13. Kelly, *Devil*, 94.

Introduction

the story is the material of cinema and a naïve, premodern mind. The unexplainable manifestations of demonization simply serve to make for scary screen images, with their shrieks of terror and floating furniture. The superstitious citizen of a medieval village might believe that a demon had infected his cow because he lived in an era where misconception of unexplained occurrences found explanation in the spirit world. Now, however, the scientific cast of minds would attribute, for example, a psychosomatic cause to the mysterious behavior of any demonization victim. Even some religious experts will balk, as Graham Twelftree competently describes: "For the vast majority of biblical scholars and theologians this is tantamount to belief in such entities as elves, dragons, or a flat earth."[14]

As a result, the challenges to any evaluation of a supposedly supernatural event related to a suspicious category seventy-five years later are many. Yet the situation is not so dire that history and theology cannot worthily appropriate its testimony. These many decades are not very long for many historians, so long as appropriate sources of the event are available and proper methodology is honored.[15] At the same time, a biblical worldview that recognizes the potential for even unique supernatural events, that believes in spirit beings, and that is willing to recognize any measure of demonic activity, can find itself making religious room for such an event. Herein lies the need for such a book as this: Christians could use sounder, more historical examples of supernatural events to begin to bridge the disparity between biblical testimony and their everyday reality. Christians need such events to shoulder against claims of philosophical naturalism that would deny all supernaturalism. Christians who maintain any possibility of demonization need an historically credible case study. This book aims to meet such needs. In fact, it aims to recover the most popular, best-documented case of exorcism in the twentieth century available to the public for appropriation by the church. With a kindred spirit, this work hopes to attend to the same hope that the exorcist himself expressed: "Our diary would be most helpful to anyone placed in a similar position as an exorcist in any future case."[16] The 1949 event can offer such a case.

---

14. Twelftree, *In the Name of Jesus*, 1–2.

15. For a discussion on the problem of historical knowability from a lack of direct access, see Craig, *Reasonable Faith*, 222–34.

16. Bowdern, "Letter to Peter Blatty," October 17, 1968 (cited in Blatty, *On The Exorcist*, 20–21).

Introduction

The hypothesis of the enterprise here is that if the theology in the *Diary* is credible—sustained by similar biblical accounts and Christian orthodox thought—then its historical claim to veracity is more likely to be credible. As the claim rises to a higher threshold of likelihood, its explanation of preternatural and supernatural situation becomes more likely. Behan McCullagh remarks, "Although historical descriptions cannot be proved true beyond all possibility of error, they can often be proved probably true, given empirical assumptions."[17] In this study, the *Diary* and other witnesses are evaluated for their historical potential. While traditional canons of historiography are employed, one positive bias is also employed in the methodology of the book. Christian thought perpetuates a conviction that the metaphysical can have a place in the historical retrieval process. For the Christian historian, retrieval of an immaterial explanation ought to accompany the canons of historiography and offer a legitimate expansion to them. Recognizing that historical descriptions like the *Diary* are subject to the judgments of its author and to the historian's interpretations, if history is indeed characterized by the activity of a providential God, then the preternatural and supernatural belong in the evaluation. A critical realism is thus at work here, employing empirical standards while employing a theology of a supernatural God as the means for one possible element of judgment about the historical record. William Lane Craig hypothesizes how a thorough investigation of the historicity of an event can in fact see the supernatural as "best or most probable explanation of these facts."[18] Should the theology of the record reinforce its historicity, then the historical account can potentially rise to a threshold of reasonability. Should the hypothesis of a case in demonization and exorcism prove reasonably true, then the case of 1949 exorcism can illustrate the biblical testimony of the preternatural in a contemporary realm. In so doing, this historical case can referee how philosophical naturalism wrongly dismisses the preternatural and disallow social science explanations to excuse the existence of spirit beings automatically.

This book is more than merely theological appraisal of a historical event, however. It is a fascinating story of a boy, a priest, and a terrifying enigma that brought them together. The *Diary* of the exorcist offers

---

17. McCullagh, *Justifying Historical Descriptions*, 4. He further remarks, "To make a claim about an historical description being 'probably true,' one must adopt an approach that is 'partly descriptive and partly critical'" (11).

18. Craig, *Reasonable Faith*, 350.

Introduction

a striking account of their encounter with the frightening unknown in a physically and spiritually grueling experience of faith. Reality became blurred as a boy's behavior evaded natural explanation, and demonic manifestations confused the judgment of the clergy and physicians. In a Catholic culture that avoided reading the rite of exorcism and with priests that had no evidenced proclivity to administer the rite, involuntary parties were drawn into a drama that brought a crisis of faith. The story can captivate a reader with wonder about the demonic and the divine, but it inevitably prompts and calls for an accompanying explanation of probability and cause. For Christians, *The Exorcist* is not merely another horror film; it is a fictional profile of the biblical possibility of demonization. Its profile is not entirely fictional.

Summary of Contents

The book hosts the intersection of history, philosophy, and theology around the 1949 exorcism account. First, in historical review, the story of the three-month event receives a summative narrative in chapter 1, "The Event." Here, a Washington, DC, youth is ensnared by the hope that occultic practices will restore his aunt to him when erratic and unexplainable behavior ensues. Medical, psychiatric, and psychological testing did not provide a cause or a solution to the violence marking the boy's life. When a Catholic priest imagined a spiritual cause, exorcism ensued as an act of pastoral ministry and spiritual conflict. While the name of the boy has been released as Ronald Edwin Hunkeler with his passing in 2020, the historic pseudonym of "Robbie" continues to be used throughout this book. This will offer continuity with the numerous sources that have employed this name over time. Chapter 2 presents the history and contents of the *Diary*, complemented by its participants and witnesses, to give voice in the recovery of the events. Their collective perspective provides a timeline with essential theological elements to be evaluated in three theological chapters below. The philosophical framing begins here and continues in chapter 3, "Preternaturalism and its Critics." This section profiles the nature of demons from a biblical and theological perspective, a category called the "preternatural." The challenges to the preternatural and supernatural require a brief recognition of its objectors and their alternative views, introduced here while proffering the risks to their assumptions.

Introduction

At the core of the book, three chapters evaluate the theology of the *Diary* and other sources around the 1949 exorcism. Chapter 4, "Theology of the Demonization," examines and analyzes the possession interests of the early phase up to the moment of exorcism, from its cause to its manifestations. Chapter 5, "Theology of the Rite," explores the intersection of the Catholic rite of exorcism with the demonized boy. The ecclesiastical nature of sacraments and sacramentals are evaluated, such as the Eucharist, relics, and the rite itself. Chapter 6, "Theology of the Exorcism," focuses on the theology around the climactic success of the ordeal in the life of the young boy, including the Catholic claims to authoritative, spiritual efficacy. Finally, the application and conclusion to the study come in chapter 7, "Appropriating the Event," closing with thoughts towards relating elements of this case study for the church and the academy. This all begins with the story inaugurated in January 1949.

1

The Event

"Permission was granted by the Most Reverend Joseph E. Ritter that Father William S. Bowdern, S. J., Pastor of the College Church in St. Louis might read the prayers of exorcism according to the Roman Ritual."

—*Diary*, Wednesday, March 16

IN 1949, FATHER WILLIAM Bowdern, a member of a Jesuit community at Saint Louis University, engaged in an extensive and exhausting experience with a demonized boy. Under the rare approval of the archdiocese, he applied the rite of exorcism over four and a half weeks. He assessed and confronted demonic activity, he coached the boy spiritually, he prayed fervently, he read the rite forcefully, and he lay claim to biblical and ecclesiastical authority over the demon. A diary of the events that lay dormant for decades preserves the episodes of the exorcism for us. This source is this record of Father Raymond Bishop, a priest ministering to the boy and serving in the exorcism for the boy's entire St. Louis stay, and it becomes the primary source of its summary narrative provided here.[1]

---

1. This book cites the *Diary* with the entry date according to Bishop and Booth, *Exorcist Diary*. Note that, as the original diarist, Bishop's name is added posthumously. For "Background to the Case" notes, the Saint Booth edition page numbers are provided. Additional cross-references to the historical narrative of Allen's book sometimes accompany the diary entries, especially because his narrative version factors multiple sources together with a flare towards a readable story. Ruickbie remarks that Allen's account is censored. While this censorship applies primarily to names, at times spelling corrections and minor variations to the *Diary* appear in Allen (Ruickbie, "Hunkeler," 156).

The events find treatment in five books devoted almost exclusively to the exorcism, the best-known being Thomas Allen's *Possessed: The True Story of an Exorcism*.[2] Various elements of the story also find representation in brief summaries that populate many books dealing with exorcism.[3]

For this chapter, the *Diary* is followed precisely. As the demonization lasted a long and wearisome three months, it breaks effortlessly into Georgetown and St. Louis phases. Some information about the Georgetown phase comes in the "Background" section of the St. Louis *Diary* report, finding additional contribution from the interviews of first-hand witnesses, as well as the testimony of second-hand witnesses and news reports. The St. Louis phase comes primarily from the daily entries of the *Diary*, in addition to the testimony of witnesses for years to follow. In the narrative below, this latter phase is broken into a diagnosis period of nine days and an exorcism of thirty-four days. An overview of the 1949 exorcism comes here, but the narrative is revisited in the *Diary* chapter below to highlight its theological themes. A consideration on the after-phase and the legacy phase of the exorcism closes out this story.

Georgetown Phase

The story begins in Cottage City, Maryland, in the Washington, DC, suburbs with a nominal Lutheran couple and their thirteen-year-old son.[4] *The Washington Post* that year would name him Robbie Mannheim.[5] The names Roland Doe, Robbie Doe, and Douglas Deen have also been used

---

2. See Allen, *Possessed*; Blatty, *On The Exorcist*; Opsasnick, *Real Story*; Rueda, *Diabolical Possession*; Travers and Reiff, *Story*; Taylor, *Devil Came to St. Louis*.

3. See Kelly, *Devil*, 94–102; Hallowell, *Playing with Fire*, 3–10; Laycock, ed., *Penguin Book of Exorcisms*, 244–47; Laycock and Harrelson, *Exorcist Effect*, 51–64; Masters, *Devil's Dominion*, 207–9; Roland, *Complete Book of Ghosts*, 225–26; Wiggins, *Nightmares with the Bible*, 10–12, 169–82; Young, *History of Exorcism*, 200–202.

4. Traditionally, the address with city was identified as 3210 Bunker Hill Road, Mt. Rainier, MD, either as a mistake or as a redirecting pseudo-location. Perhaps a deflection by an original participant resulted in a mistaken perpetuation of Mt. Rainier. Mark Opsasnick has shown with impressive research that the actual address is 3807 40th Avenue, Cottage City, MD, following a street name change in 1942. The family resided there until 1958. Opsasnick, *Real Story*, 9–10, 21–44; Ruickbie, "Hunkeler," 156.

5. Brinkley, "Priest Frees Mt. Rainier Boy." His father has been identified as Edwin Hunkeler; Rueda, *Diabolical Possession*, 162. His mother had been identified as Odell Hunkeler; Ruickbie, "Hunkeler," 156. Opsasnick has recognized that Robbie's birthday of June 1, 1935, revealing him to be thirteen years old at the time of the exorcism. Opsasnick, "Haunted Boy," 7–8.

The Event

as pseudonyms.[6] In December 2021, the *New York Post* and *The Guardian* released the actual name of Ronald Edwin Hunkeler as the victim, one who died in 2020 with his identity secured throughout his life.[7] This was headline news. However, unrecognized by popular culture was the revelation of the real name in a 2015 encyclopedia entry by scholar Leo Ruickbie and intermittently in books to follow.[8] The Georgetown phase represents the period of January 15 to March 8, 1949, prior to the beginning of the exorcism.

As an only child, Robbie often played with his aunt who was a paranormal spiritist that introduced him to the Ouija board, while she herself participated in other forms of communication with the dead. Aunt Tillie is often called Aunt Harriet when pseudonyms are used, but she has been identified as Mathilda Hendricks.[9] She freely shared her belief with Robbie that spirits sometimes rapped on walls and fused their energies with mediums in seances as modes of communication. These were a slower and inferior way of communicating than the Ouija board. Although no documentation of formal occultic interests by the family are recorded beyond Aunt Tillie, they will soon be engaging occultic spirit manifestations. Aunt Tillie's loss to the family on January 26, 1949, in St. Louis, seems to have emotionally impacted Robbie. He initiated communication efforts with his Aunt by using the planchette of the Ouija board. Just before her passing, unexplainable events around the house ensued.[10]

---

6. For example, Robbie Mannheim is employed in Taylor, *Devil Came to St. Louis*, 67–153; Roland Doe is employed in Erdmann, "Truth" and Brian, *Enchanted Voyager*, 179–84; Robbie Doe is employed in Opsasnick, *Real Story*, 29–43; Douglas(s) Deen is employed in Masters, *Devil's Dominion*, 207–11 and Linson, "Washington's Haunted Boy."

7. Vincent and Morphet, "What Really Happened"; Yang, "Boy Whose Case Inspired *The Exorcist*."

8. Ruickbie, "Hunkeler," 156–57.

9. Ruickbie, "Hunkeler," 156. Allen employs the pseudonym "Harriet" for the diary; Saint Booth changes the text to read "Auntie." Tillie is an abbreviation for Mathilda; her maiden name Hunkeler reveals her to be the sister of Ronald's father.

10. Allen, *Possessed*, 6, where he claims Robbie spent hours on the Ouija board in dealing with his grief; Flood, "SLU Legends and Lore"; Hallowell, *Playing with Fire*, 6, who observantly posits, "Chaos erupted after he tried to use the board to reach Tillie in the afterlife." Allen recognizes seances as "a form of possession" (*Possessed*, 3, 5).

Theology of a Diary

January 15–Mid-February

Beginning on Saturday, January 15, 1949, Robbie and his grandmother heard a dripping sound in the house. Seeking its origins, they entered her bedroom to the sight of a painting of Christ shaking "as if the wall back of it had been thumped."[11] Unexplainable scratching sounds in the floor began that night. The next day, an exterminator treated for potential rodents. For ten nights, the scratching sounds continued. Around the time of Aunt Tillie's death eight hundred miles away, the *Diary* reports, they stopped.[12] Then the sound of squeaking shoes was heard alongside Robbie's bed, continuing for six nights, when the scratching sounds re-emerged. As Robbie lay with his mother and grandmother on the bed, they heard the walking sounds like "the rhythm marching feet and the beat of drums."[13] It repeated itself until the mother asked the sound if it were Aunt Tillie, inviting her spirit to knock three times and then four times, with response knocks faithfully following. Waves of air were also reported with the knocking. That night the scratches began again, this time inside Robbie's mattress. It was as if the manifested sounds came closer to the boy. The mattress began to shake. The corners of the bedspread levitated upward over the bed, stiff and curled in form. Father John Nicola, who had access to the archival report, claims that this night the parents also saw the bed levitate with the boy: "Then slowly the mattress, with the boy on it, levitated off the bed and floated in the air."[14] The scratching sounds continued each night for three weeks.

Any of these abnormal events could be imagined with a boy screaming and family members rushing to his aid. Anticipation of the next fearful shriek to break the peaceful silence of a home was likely chilling. The terror of arriving to see a trembling boy or a moving object was equally petrifying. On February 26, the scratching moved from the mattress to the boy's body. In the words of Spitzer, "The spirit then began to invade Robbie himself."[15] For four successive nights, scratches began to appear on his body like claw marks. On the fifth night, the scratches

---

11. *Diary*, "Background"; Bishop and Saint Booth, *Exorcist Diary*, 13.

12. *Diary*, "March 11"; Bishop and Saint Booth, *Exorcist Diary*, 21, for a similar supposed *telekinesis*.

13. *Diary*, "Background"; Bishop and Saint Booth, *Exorcist Diary*, 13.

14. Nicola, *Diabolical Possession*, 109. He particularly aims to refute any fraud hypothesis about the demonization with his testimony of this event.

15. Spitzer, *Christ Versus Satan*, 158.

formed words. The boy screamed from his bathroom, and the rushing Mannheim mother encountered her son trembling before the mirror with the word "Louis" scratched out in blood across his chest.[16] Allen describes the scratches to be like "the kind a cat makes, long and shallow, the marks of claws."[17]

Robbie's mother began to imagine that this communication from Aunt Tillie advised them to leave for St. Louis—whether actively communicating with the spirit or assuming that the spirit overheard her—as the word "Saturday" appeared and "3 1/2 weeks" supposedly could be read. One source adds that she inquired if "Louis" meant "St. Louis," and the scratched "Yes" appeared on his belly.[18] The source for the diarist's background case reported, "The printing always appeared without any motion on the part of the boy's hand." Likewise, the diarist describes, "The boy could not have done the markings for the added reason that on one occasion there was writing on his back."[19] With the parents' weariness of the forces of their own Georgetown house, this communication motivated them to transition to St. Louis in March. While there is no early evidence that the screaming was heard by the neighbors, Spitzer reports neighborhood rumors began and the mother sought to escape the local attention.[20]

One night in the Georgetown era, the parents responded to Robbie's scream to witness a heavy dresser moving across the bedroom floor, blocking the door as the drawers opened and closed, seemingly on their own. During this time, Robbie's desk at school would scoot across the rows in the classroom, without explanation, so that the *Diary* compares it to moving "similar to the plate [planchette] on a Ouija board."[21] Later, in St. Louis, one of the body scratches appearing on the boy was an answer to his mother's wonder if he should return to school. "No" appeared on his wrists and an "N" on both legs. The diarist's comment, "The mother feared disobeying this order," suggests that the parents were the source

16. *Diary*, "Background"; Bishop and Saint Booth, *Exorcist Diary*, 14–15; Allen, *Possessed*, 40–41. Authors such as Schulze, Brian, and Kelly might be paraphrasing the word "Louis" towards its interpretation when they say the words "Go St. Louis" were welted on Robbie's body. Brian, *Enchanted Voyager*, 182; Kelly, *Devil*, 96, who attributes it to the thigh rather than the chest.

17. Allen, *Possessed*, 23.

18. Cooper and Epperson, *Evil*, 25.

19. *Diary*, "Background"; Bishop and Saint Booth, *Exorcist Diary*, 15.

20. Spitzer, *Christ Versus Satan*, 160.

21. *Diary*, "Background"; Bishop and Saint Booth, *Exorcist Diary*, 15.

for this background information there, a logical cause given the diarist's proximity with the family and their home when the background was recorded. He also remarks how this embarrassment discouraged the boy from wanting to attend school.[22]

A coat hanger flew from a closet; a Bible moved from the bookcase over to Robbie. Fruit flew across the room. Food and drink flew from the table and stove. The kitchen table flipped over without explanation. A breadboard slid by itself off the counter. He placed his clothes in his bedroom, but they would be found scattered across the kitchen floor. A large lounge chair flipped over with Robbie in it, but even the men in the room could not flip it over when they tried sitting in it. A vase levitated before shattering against the wall. Robbie would thrash on and off for hours, seemingly partially asleep and partially awake, screaming and mumbling in restlessness. Allen describes the effect: "The incidents of those weeks entered the memories of witnesses not as a narrative but as shards of a mosaic."[23]

The parents' belief that these activities were prompted by the now-deceased Aunt Harriet led to numerous occultic activities. In the background entry of the *Diary*, Bishop reported when the family heard the footsteps in a marching and drum rhythm, they asked the sound, "Is that you, Aunt Harriet?" This was when they proceeded to invite the dead to knock three times in confirmation, with another four time knock to ensure it.[24] Even up through March 16, the first day of the reading of the rite of exorcism over Robbie by the Jesuit priest, their attempt to process the cause was accompanied by occasional attempts to communicate with Harriet. On one early occasion, at least Robbie and his mother used the Ouija board believing they were receiving messages from the aunt.[25] On another occasion in Georgetown, the family invited a spiritualist to rid the boy of an evil spirit.[26] Later in St. Louis, a séance was held by several family members using an alphabet on paper, underlining letters when the table moved. The result was a determination that the spirit was not

---

22. *Diary*, "Background"; Bishop and Saint Booth, *Exorcist Diary*, 15.
23. Allen, *Possessed*, 11.
24. *Diary*, "Background"; Allen, *Possessed*, 7, 246.
25. Allen, *Possessed*, 151.
26. The diary states, "A Spiritualist was called in to use his formulae for ridding people of spirits but he had no success" (*Diary*, "Background"; Bishop and Saint Booth, *Exorcist Diary*, 16).

The Event

a demon but their aunt.[27] A séance was held in response to the moving bookcase, a moving stool, the flipping stool, the migration of a relic across the bed, and rhythmic shaking and scratching of the bed. They concluded from the spirit of the aunt that a map would guide them to money in a metal box in the attic of her home. Only the father could retrieve it, and it was dedicated to her daughter. Appeals to make the bed stop in the aunt's name were effective.[28] The family was further convinced that the mysterious spirit of Aunt Harriet was concerned about a moneybox left in the house rather than a demon responding to occultic invitations.

The connection between bizarre activities and their aunt would have been reinforced by one occasion when she rode with the family on a Sunday afternoon. A blanket in the back seat began to curl on its own. An unexplained force pushed the boy and his mother against the seat. The key was not found in the ignition upon arrival, but it was found under the front seat during the drive.[29]

Meanwhile, in Georgetown, something was happening to Robbie: uncontrollable fits of behavior, anxiety, and withdrawal may have been fueled by his parents' accusation of trickery and magic surrounding the inexplicable phenomena. If this is indeed the parental response, their care for the boy is questionable. Early events were either unexplainable around the house or atypical of Robbie, including the scratching, footsteps, and knockings that filled the walls and floors. Furniture moving on its own made the blame difficult. Robbie was irritable and reclusive, or he was frightened of an impending presence. All of this led the parents to pursue a more spiritual solution. The invitation for clergy to help saw the consultation by two Lutheran pastors, a rabbi, and a Catholic priest in Georgetown. Alongside these consultations, this phase saw a stay at a local research hospital. The timeline is difficult to lay out with accuracy, but a best attempt to reconcile the sources comes here.

---

27. *Diary*, "March 7."

28. *Diary*, "March 11."

29. Rueda, *Diabolical Possession*, 30. He does not report the source for this event, but given the author's critical stance, his time frame for participation, and his reliance on Schulze, it is reasonable to assume it the family reported the incident to their Lutheran pastor.

Mid-February–March 4: Schulze

In mid-February that year, the family invited their Lutheran pastor, Rev. Luther Schulze, to investigate the conditions around Robbie.[30] His own account provides a record of the activities prior to his own arrival and prior to Father Bowdern's exorcism.[31] As an Enlightened figure, the minister was not initially amenable to the concept of demonization. Meanwhile, he also showed a unique interest in the psychokinetic quality of moving items about the house—a semi-supernatural element in an otherwise natural mind. In the occasions of his visit to the house, he witnessed flying dishes and a shaking bed. According to Allen, this led the family to forsake any theory of sleepwalking or pranks by Robbie. Then was when they began to wonder about demonization.[32]

The faith and belief of Luther Schulze receive important attention in scholars' analysis of his role in the Georgetown phase. Allen describes him as skeptical of demonization; committed to an Enlightenment perspective; showing fascination with spiritism and parapsychology, such as psychokinesis, telekinesis, telepathy, and clairvoyance; and preferring to confront the spiritual conflict with prayer.[33] He describes how the Lutheran pastor "turned towards another belief, an amalgam of the Spiritualism practiced by Aunt Harriet and one of Schulze's interests, parapsychology."[34] This interest is evidenced by Schulze himself in his letter to the director of Duke's parapsychology lab: "We have in our congregation a family who are being disturbed by Poltergeist phenomena."[35]

---

30. Rev. Schulze is identified as Luther Miles Schulze, age forty-three at the time of his arrival, serving as pastor of St. Stephen's Evangelical Lutheran Church just across the Maryland state line. See Allen, *Possessed*, 12–13; Ruickbie, "Hunkeler," 156. He receives the pseudonym Rev. Winston in Linson, "Washington's Haunted Boy."

31. See "Appendix A: The Letters between the Rev. Luther Miles Schulze and Dr. J. B. Rhine" in Rueda, *Diabolical Possession*, 161–69; Laycock, ed., *Penguin Book of Exorcisms*, 244–47. This testimony comes from the report given by Schulze to Joseph B. Rhine, Director of the Parapsychology Lab at Duke University; Laycock, ed., *Penguin Book of Exorcisms*, 244. They shared an interest in the paranormal, leading parapsychologist R. P. Rhine to his interview of Schulze, where psychokinetic explanation of the events find introduction; Brian, *Enchanted Voyager*, 183.

32. Allen, *Possessed*, 15.

33. Allen, *Possessed*, 15–19.

34. Allen, *Possessed*, 17.

35. See "Appendix A: The Letters between the Rev. Luther Miles Schulze and Dr. J. B. Rhine" in Rueda, *Diabolical Possession*, 161.

The Event

In an interview years later, Schulze described how he tried prayer for the boy and the house, while exhorting the Lutheran family to communion, only once ordering "whatever it was disturbing him, in the name of the Father, Son, and Holy Spirit, to get out and let him alone."[36] Thus, his interest in the paranormal, evidenced by his letters to J. B. Rhine of the Duke Parapsychology Laboratory, is amalgamated with this Christian faith. Furthermore, his public address to the Society for Parapsychology on August 9 of that year in his own city identifies an audience that he finds compatible with his paranormal interpretation of the events.[37]

On February 17, Schulze brought the boy to his own home to separate him from any possibility of a haunted space. Allen surmises that this was in part motivated by the minister's belief that poltergeists would not follow their victims to another location, but stay centralized in one house.[38] Terry Cooper recognizes that any suspicion of pranking underway would be neutralized in a new environment.[39] In his own home, Schulze witnessed similar inexplicable unnatural events: the shaking bed, scratching in the walls, a moving lounge chair, a sliding pallet, and a repeated slamming of the boy's own head while under the bed.[40] A 1949 interview with Schulze reported the pastor's observation this way: "The armchair was extremely heavy, yet it moved as if in the grip of a malevolent and massive force or several strong invisible individuals that tipped it sideways in a slow motion. It moved as though the air was made of treacle [molasses]."[41] The pastor made a floor pallet for the boy instead, but watched it move across the room to a wall, testifying that he could see the boy's hands above the blankets and his legs stretched out under the blankets. This "ruled out normal propulsion with hands or feet."[42]

36. Brian, *Enchanted Voyager*, 180; Allen, *Possessed*, 15–16.

37. Linson, "Washington's Haunted Boy," 32; Opsasnick, "Haunted Boy," 8–9.

38. Allen, *Possessed*, 20.

39. Cooper and Epperson, *Evil*, 24. This point is overlooked by Opsasnick, who suggests that much of the manifestations can be explained by the boy's trickery and stunts (see Opsasnick, "Haunted Boy," 20–22). In fact, given Schultze's unwillingness to concede demonic causes easily makes his testimony of the unexplainable even more convincing of something beyond the natural.

40. Schulze, "Luther Schulze Case Report," 246–47; "Appendix A: The Letters between the Rev. Luther Miles Schulze and Dr. J. B. Rhine" in Rueda, *Diabolical Possession*, 161–62. Spitzer elaborates that the ordeal caused the boy's head to be cut (*Christ Versus Satan*, 158).

41. Brian, *Enchanted Voyager*, 181–82.

42. Brian, *Enchanted Voyager*, 182. Ruickbie describes the events of February 17 as his defining moment of recognition for Schulze, or at least that potentially poltergeist

Theology of a Diary

Schulze was ministering to the boy and his family around the occasions that scratch marks changed to scratched words. In his letter to Rhine, he testifies as witness to the events in his own home but attributes scratches to the first-hand witness of the parents rather than his own.[43] He reinforces the testimony of the parents that "a blood-red message was scratched on his skin: 'Go to St. Louis.'"[44] It becomes evident that the attempt of the family to call upon their Lutheran pastor revealed a skeptical, Enlightenment minister whose prayers and exercised spiritual authority seemed to have no effect on Robbie or his condition. The *Diary* states that he had no success in aiding Robbie.[45] The boy's bizarre behavior, the inexplicable events in his own home, and his preference for a poltergeist explanation would be followed by the arrival of a Georgetown Catholic priest on the scene. These unexplainable scratch marks from inside the body, coupled with Robbie's agonizing condition and the priest's powerlessness, may have resulted in Schulze's recommendation to consult a Washington, DC, parish priest for the rite of exorcism. Thomas Allen claims as much.[46] Somehow, one Father Albert Hughes is about to encounter bizarre happenings.

About this time, Schulze himself claims that he recommended a physician, but the family first opted for the spiritualist mentioned above.[47] Questions about Robbie's mental health resulted in physical, psychological, and psychiatric testing. Georgetown University Hospital is the primary host to these examinations from February 28 to March

---

activities where not of the boy's contriving. See Ruickbie, "Hunkeler," 156. Likewise, he is cited early by a Washington, DC, newspaper conceding that the moving chair and pallet were "inexplicable phenomena . . . the clergyman had no explanation for what he had seen" (see "Minister Tells Parapsychologists").

43. See Letter A in "Appendix A: The Letters between the Rev. Luther Miles Schulze and Dr. J. B. Rhine" in Rueda, *Diabolical Possession*, 161–62.

44. Brian, *Enchanted Voyager*, 182.

45. *Diary*, "Witnesses"; Bishop and Saint Booth, *Exorcist Diary*, 16.

46. Allen, *Possessed*, 27, 308–9. Allen captures the quote from Schulze: "You have to see a Catholic priest. The Catholics know something about things like this" (*Possessed*, 24). McGuire corroborates this (see "St. Louis Exorcism").

47. See Letters A and B in "Appendix A: The Letters between the Rev. Luther Miles Schulze and Dr. J. B. Rhine" in Rueda, *Diabolical Possession*, 162–63; Rueda, *Diabolical Possession*, 33–35; Stevenson, "Possession and Exorcism," 69. Faherty places the recommendation to a family minister in St. Louis, who personally met with Bishop, Kenny, and other Jesuit priests, but this part of the history seems to be disordered (*To Rest in Charity*, 81).

The Event

3, 1949.[48] The *Diary* references a visit to a physician, reporting only his observation that the boy was "somewhat high-strung."[49] The psychiatrist stated him to be "normal" but admitted his own disbelief in the paranormal reports. He added that the boy seemed annoyed by the exam.[50] John Nicola claims to have found one doctor, who found Robbie to be in good health except for a nervous tension about him—likely the same events.[51] Speculations have followed about a psychological and neurobiological diagnoses, including conversion disorder, automatism, obsessive-compulsive disorder, and Tourette syndrome, as well as a response to sexual abuse.[52] However, in the end, the medical examinations and treatments seemed to show little results. One might have expected at least one of these diagnoses to be postulated by medical professionals and circulating among the popular news reports. This makes the confidence of contemporary diagnostic professionals imply incompetence to the 1949 medical examiners. The absence of any evidence led the *St. Louis Post-Dispatch* to report "Curiously, during these convulsions, the doctors attending him could find no change in his pulse rate or blood pressure."[53]

This Catholic hospital venue could possibly host the physician and the psychiatric examinations cited in the *Diary*. Here, both various medical testing and a possible first exorcism attempt could have taken place. A visit to a University of Maryland psychologist who worked at a nearby clinic finds additional medical testing. Schultze reports that the boy went to the County Mental Hygiene Clinic, visited for two appointments, and did not report for the third.[54] He states here that his

---

48. "Priest Freed Boy of Possession by Devil" states that "the boy's affliction was studied exhaustively" at Georgetown University Hospital. Opsasnick claims an uncited source confirming the dates of stay at this hospital, providing even the check in and check out times. Given the precision of his historical research and his scrutiny on unsubstantiated facts, there is reason to trust the claim of his unnamed source. Opsasnick, "Haunted Boy," 23. See also Opsasnick, *Real Story*, 37; Allen, *Possessed*, 11–12, 248; Taylor, *Devil Came to St. Louis*, 64.

49. *Diary*, "Witnesses"; Bishop and Saint Booth, *Exorcist Diary*, 16.

50. *Diary*, "Witnesses"; Bishop and Saint Booth, *Exorcist Diary*, 16.

51. Nicola, *Diabolical Possession*, 108.

52. Rueda, *Diabolical Possession*, 151–59; Cooperman, "Touched by Evil"; Roland, *Complete Book of Ghosts*, 225.

53. McGuire, "St. Louis Exorcism."

54. See Letter A in "Appendix A: The Letters between the Rev. Luther Miles Schulze and Dr. J. B. Rhine" in Rueda, *Diabolical Possession*, 161. For the two clinical visits, see "Minister Tells Parapsychologists" and "New Details." Rueda can somehow be certain that a clinical diagnosis would have been rendered on the third visit (*Diabolical*

witness of the scratches did not show words, but he surmised a nerve reaction rash. Meanwhile, in a 1949 interview, Luther Schulze wrote that a hospital report described how Robbie "could expectorate in a steady stream," seemingly of spit or vomit.[55] After testifying to scratches in the form of words like, "Spite," and a primitive shape of the devil, Schulze's biographer observed, "Twentieth-century medicine had no more effect on his condition than prayer."[56] Travers and Reiff also imply that Robbie was examined at Saint Louis University Hospital, but the claim appears nowhere else.[57]

If the teenage boy had shown signs of mental illness or neurological disorder, then there is a likelihood that this would have extended beyond the exorcism experience. While mental illness can be modified with counseling and medication, and while epilepsy and Tourette's does not necessarily prevent a relatively normal life, the fact remains that severe expressions of these could prevent a recognizable career as a signature of health. Yet the recent announcement of the boy's actual identity evidences that he was married, had children, and went on to work as a NASA engineer in support of the Apollo space endeavors of the 1960s. That he gained a patent on space shuttle panels make it more difficult to speak against a chronic psychological disorder as the cause of the events of 1949.[58] All evidence suggests that winter and spring of 1949 were an undiagnosable anomaly in the life of Ronald Hunkeler.

Late-February–Early March: Hughes

Sometime in late February, a request to the nearby Catholic rectory of St. James Church saw a consultation by the family with Father Albert Hughes. He was a forty-year-old who served this local congregation for twelve years.[59] At least one parent met with the priest to discuss the situation. One account, sustained by Allen, reports that Robbie also visited the church office, where Hughes saw Robbie harangue the priest with

---

Possession, 153). Cf. "Minister Tells Parapsychologists," cited in Opsasnick, "Haunted Boy," 8.

55. Brian, *Enchanted Voyager*, 182.
56. Brian, *Enchanted Voyager*, 182.
57. Travers and Reiff, *Story*, 18.
58. Vincent and Morphet, "What Really Happened"; Yang, "Boy Whose Case Inspired *The Exorcist*."
59. Opsasnick, "Haunted Boy," 23–24.

The Event

cursing before the room grew cold. His desk phone supposedly moved by itself.[60] Hughes's observations were enough for him to send home a bottle of holy water with some blessed candles for the family. Later that night, the bottle would be mysteriously thrown and broken, while the candle flame was seen climbing to the ceiling.

Some uncertainty surrounds the details of Hughes's interaction with Robbie. There would be no official record of a ministry encounter and the testimonies of Schulze, Bober, and the news releases are difficult to harmonize. The "Background of the Case" material in the *Diary* explicitly states that Hughes did not meet with Robbie in person. It also claims that Hughes was seeking bishop approval for an exorcism.[61] These two elements are difficult to reconcile, as a report case with priestly evidence would be required for such a request. The difficulty of the exorcism approval process, including the need to demonstrate marks of demonization cited in the *Roman Ritual*, would mark either a frivolous and naïve priest or else suggest that the background material reported to Bishop for the case study background was not precise. The details of the background were likely jotted down as the weary parents summarized its relevant events. Allen surmises that the family may not have wanted to relate the suffering of Father Hughes on the inaugural visit of Father Bishop.[62] LaChance postulates, "Perhaps Father Bishop was extending a professional courtesy toward Father Hughes by excluding this information from the diary."[63] The meeting between priest and boy becomes more likely. Nonetheless, Opsasnick insists that there was no home visit and cites Bober in interview saying the same.[64] This interaction at Georgetown Hospital holds possibility; Father Hughes would likely have been called in to the hospital based on this prior consultation, even with the parents.

---

60. Allen, *Possessed*, 28. Bober denies that Hughes ever visited the home but confirms that he entertained a visit by the boy in his office; Opsasnick, "Haunted Boy," 24. Cooper and Epperson also report the temperature and telephone incidents; Cooper and Epperson, *Evil*, 24.

61. *Diary*, "Witnesses"; Bishop and Saint Booth, *Exorcist Diary*, 16–17; Ruickbie, "Hunkeler," 157.

62. "Whatever the reason, Bishop did not learn of the abortive hospital exorcism" (Allen, *Possessed*, 56–57).

63. LaChance, *Confrontation*, 60, 94, 139–140. LaChance, *Confrontation*, 139–40.

64. Opsasnick, "Haunted Boy," 23–24. The only liability of Opsasnick's work is the posture of disproving as many details as he can, evidenced by his citations throughout this book. Bober claims both the office visit and the tragic exorcism attempt in *In the Grip of Evil*; Allen, *Possessed*, 308–9.

Theology of a Diary

Sources claim that Hughes intended to engage in an exorcism of Robbie that never occurred. Cooper claims that Hughes arranged a room at Georgetown University Hospital while personally preparing for an exorcism.[65] The timing of hospitalization and the potential exorcism align perfectly, and a Catholic priest could have had the latitude for such an initiative in a Catholic hospital. An appeal for the rite of exorcism may have been made to the archbishop, Patrick O'Boyle. Many speculate that the high-profile career of O'Boyle would avoid such approval. One source claimed that Father Hughes applied the rite of exorcism after gaining approval from O'Boyle, who instructed, "'You investigate, and if you think it needs to be done, go ahead and do it.' So, he went ahead."[66] Another source claims that an appointment of the young Father Hughes would be irregular.[67] While the *Diary* claims Hughes's intention and initiative for an exorcism, he was either unable to gain diocesan approval or execute the permission before the family moved.[68]

Other sources claim that Hughes did engage in an exorcism of Robbie that was not successful. Among scholars, Sergio Rueda takes special care to provide historical details behind the Georgetown phase, and he claims its legitimacy, as well as Hughes's identification of signs in preparation of a report and his initiation in fasting and praying in preparation for the event.[69] Without citation, Taylor reports conflict between the priest and demon, including unexplainable violent events of room artifacts and furniture.[70] LaChance reports that a Father Joe Jenkins received in confession one of Hughes's assistants from the exorcism who witnessed spitting, slugging, Aramaic, Latin, and the bed spring incident.[71] Spitzer claims that when Hughes began to read the rite of exorcism, the bed moved across the room to slam into a wall, witnessed by hospital nuns.[72] This occasion would likely have taken place during

---

65. Cooper and Epperson, *Evil*, 25. Cf. Stevenson, "Possession and Exorcism," 69.

66. The quotation was provided by Father Nicola. See Brisbane, "Youth's Bizarre Symptoms."

67. Taylor, *Devil Came to St. Louis*, 61. This account also claims that the archbishop instructed Father Hughes not to record any of his observances or activities.

68. *Diary*, "Background"; Bishop and Saint Booth, *Exorcist Diary*, 16–17. Cf. Ruickbie, "Hunkeler," 157.

69. Rueda, *Diabolical Possession*, 36, 39.

70. Taylor, *Devil Came to St. Louis*, 60–61.

71. LaChance, *Confrontation*, 137–39.

72. Spitzer, *Christ Versus Satan*, 160.

Robbie's stay at Georgetown University Hospital. The possibility of such a manifestation or even the foundation for a myth would more likely be elicited if Hughes at least delivered the rite of exorcism, as some sources claim. It becomes somewhat circular, but exorcism provides the venue for manifestations while these manifestations also reinforce exorcism. The testimonies of an attempted Catholic baptism would support priestly activity during this stay in a Georgetown hospital.[73] The intersection with a Seattle University Jesuit priest is afforded at this Catholic hospital.[74] Likewise, this would provide an historical opportunity for the legend to arise around his injury sustained in an exorcism attempt, introduced below. The ability to construct such a legend would be precarious if there were not even an attempt to read the rite of exorcism.

A story exists that during a failed exorcism attempt, Father Hughes suffered greatly from the preternatural strength of the boy. *The Prince George's Sentinel* claims that the boy was in the Georgetown University Hospital during the event.[75] Father Hughes was praying from the rite next to the boy's bed when the boy slipped a hand from the straps, reached under the bed, worked loose a bedspring, and cut the priest in his left arm from his shoulder to his wrist. A hundred stitches were required. Legend maintains that he suffered permanent damage and even a nervous breakdown that impacted his ministerial service. Arthur Brisbane even names two parishioners who testified to this.[76] Father John Nicola interviewed Hughes, who along with Thomas Allen, Robert Spitzer, and Terry Cooper, maintains an attempted exorcist event as factual.[77]

Mark Opsasnick convincingly tries to evidence that no exorcism and no suffering attempt ever took place with Father Hughes, who faithfully served St. James Church until 1960 and then 1973 to 1980. Likewise, newspapers evidence his speaking engagements without a hitch in the calendar days to follow.[78] While the boy was checked into the hospital

73. Erdmann, "Truth," 55; Taylor, *Devil Came to St. Louis*, 65.

74. Head, "Interview."

75. Gordon, "*The Exorcist*" (cited in Opsasnick, "Haunted Boy," 12).

76. Brisbane, "Youth's Bizarre Symptoms." Hughes's long-term suffering is first referenced by a journalist (Gordon, "*The Exorcist*"). The story is then perpetuated, as in Taylor, *Devil Came to St. Louis*, 63.

77. The event of the spring slashing finds an origin in John H. Nicola, and it is first offered by Dobson, "Luncheon." Nicola, *Diabolical Possession*, 112; Allen, *Possessed*, 36–38, 308–9; Spitzer, *Christ Versus Satan*, 152–53, 159–60; Cooper, *Evil*, 25. Spitzer claims that 140 stitches were required (*Christ Versus Satan*, 160).

78. For a list of the public activities of Hughes posted in the *Prince George's Sentinel*

Theology of a Diary

during this time with only clinical records of medical and psychological evaluations, no eyewitness record relates this story and no such report is cited by Bishop in the *Diary*, along with no written evidence that Father Hughes visited the boy at home.

This seemingly apocalyptic account of the attack on Father Hughes is attributed to Frank Bober, who served as his assistant pastor. Bober is reported as the last person to whom Hughes related his Georgetown part of the story.[79] Supposedly, Hughes and Bober shared a private dinner when the exorcist shared part of the story with his assistant, pledging to talk more on it before he died days later. Allen calls Bober "extremely reliable" as a source.[80] Taylor claims that some feel that he was prone to dramatize Hughes's testimony by appearing in "literally dozens of articles, books, and documentaries" around the case.[81] As a result, Bober's credibility for precision is at times suspect.

Independent of the bedspring incident, the numerous testimonies suggest that some exorcism attempt was engaged at the hospital, matching Hughes's intention stated in the *Diary* while omitting his lack of success in the *Diary*. Yet, when the family returned to Washington, DC, in March, Bowdern then seems informed about their former experience with Hughes. The best explanation is that the background case of the *Diary* was not amended as the facts later unfolded, and Bishop did not update the *Diary* to contain the knowledge of the Georgetown experience. Numerous details are not contained in the *Diary*, whose function is a day-by-day report of the experience with a provisional background section.

---

from February to June 1949, see Opsasnick, *Real Story*, 37–38.

79. Opsasnick, "Haunted Boy," 12, 24; Allen, *Possessed*, 302; Brisbane, "Youth's Bizarre Symptoms."

80. Allen, *Possessed*, 302. The first historical discrepancies enter with the events around Father Hughes. The testimony of these events is mediated by Frank Bober, in his dialog with Hughes; Allen, *Possessed*, 308–9; Opsasnick, "Haunted Boy," 12. Allen claims to follow Reppetti, who took notes on a lecture given by Hughes which are supposedly found in the Georgetown University archives. Allen calls Reppetti "the source closest to the eyewitness" (*Possessed*, 309).

81. Taylor, *Devil Came to St. Louis*, 64. He also reports that this episode was "passed along to author Thomas Allen from a friend of Father Hughes, making it third-hand information at best" (60). Cf. Opsasnick, "Haunted Boy," 12.

The Event

Other Georgetown Phase Elements

Another opportunist may be Luther Miles Schulze, who offered speaking appointments on his encounter with the demonized boy. He is the unnamed minister relating such an event to the Society of Parapsychology in Washington, DC, that summer, leading to articles in the nearby *The Washington Post,* the *Evening Star,* and the *Times-Herald,* before being named in the *Parapsychology Bulletin*.[82]

Troy Taylor adds another unnamed eyewitness account who saw the boy during an infirmary stay along with other neighborhood boys, gathered for observation during a flu epidemic in February 1949. Both the witness and a room of boys were frightened by a boy that "glared into the eyes" in a fashion scary enough that other children began to pray.[83] Noteworthy alongside the testimonies of preternatural manifestations are the interviews conducted by Mark Opsasnick among the family friends, including Robbie's childhood friend from this time. His explanation was of a troubled boy whom he regularly joined in mischief.[84]

Ida Mae Donley provides a first-hand account of her own intersection with the family in Georgetown. The Lutheran Church organized prayers for the family, with whom she shared a friendship. In early 1949, she served as personal assistant to Reverend Schulze.[85] The circles of prayer occurred both at the church and at the family home. She recollected one occasion when Robbie was lying on the bed as the prayers began. He screamed and cursed, seeming to speak in another language, as one person attributed it to Latin. "I was standing in front of him and noticed that his body, lying flat on the bed, began to rise slowly from it. His body seemed to be completely separated from the bed about two inches and then fell back."[86] This is not the only eyewitness report of levitation by the child. Halloran testified that the bed also levitated: "The first night I was there I was kneeling at the bed on which the boy was lying and the bed

---

82. His identity as the unnamed pastor in these news articles was revealed in "Report of a Poltergeist" in *Parapsychology Bulletin* 14 (August 1949) according to Opsasnick, "Haunted Boy," 8–9.

83. Taylor, *Devil Came to St. Louis*, 65–66.

84. Opsasnick, "Haunted Boy," 21–22.

85. See "Appendix C: Interview with Ida Mae, the Leader of the Circle of Prayers" in Rueda, *Diabolical Possession*, 190–94.

86. Rueda, *Diabolical Possession*, 32, 245n6. While he took the interview and while he also confirms that Schulze heard of levitation occasions, Rueda dismisses the testimony entirely (see 97, 137).

started going up and down." When asked how high, he responded, "Oh, I'd say, eight inches."[87] William Peter Blatty adds that a professor from the Jesuit-founded Seattle University witnessed the levitation.[88]

Finally, the popular opinion that the boy manifested knowledge of Latin and Aramaic finds its anchor in the newspaper and magazine reports during the Georgetown phase. According to a 1975 account, a manifestation occurred in which the boy spoke in two foreign languages. First, supposedly, to the shock of a rabbi, the boy spoke in Hebrew unfamiliar to the boy. Upon observation, a professor of Oriental languages from Catholic University cited that the boy spoke in Aramaic.[89] Secondly, the use of articulate Latin emerges in the Washington newspapers within months of the events. The legend appears early after the event in Washington, DC, newspaper articles.[90] Thomas Allen makes the claim that Father Hughes witnessed this in Georgetown. Supposedly, the Catholic priest was stunned to hear this Lutheran boy speak skilled Latin: "O Priest of Christ, you know that I am the devil. Why do you keep bothering me?"[91] Father Eugene Gallagher claimed that exorcism participant Father O'Hara described how every language proffered resulted in a fluent response in the same: "He was able to understand the Latin questions."[92] Eyewitness Ida Mae Donley claims the prayer circle heard an unknown language and one suspected it to be Latin.[93] Faherty claims that many occasions saw that the boy "displayed a clear understanding of Latin phrases and sentences, although the young man had never had a day's class in Latin."[94] Spitzer remarks that his responses with "No!" and a disdaining laugher at the *dicas mihi* in the reading of the rite evidence a

---

87. Brown, "Interview."

88. Head, "Interview."

89. Erdmann, "Truth," 53.

90. "Priest Freed Boy of Possession by Devil"; "New Details"; Brinkley, "Priest Frees Mt. Rainier Boy."

91. Allen, *Possessed*, 29. William Faherty provides the same quote but implies it occurred in the St. Louis phase (*To Rest in Charity*, 82). Spitzer claims the event as true (*Christ Versus Satan*, 159).

92. This is a story told by Eugene B. Gallagher as reported in *National Enquirer* (March 17, 1974) (cited in Kelly, *Devil*, 95n60). Father John Nicola is similar: "Many times the boy had manifested in various ways a clear understanding of Latin phrases and sentences, although the boy had never learned a word of Latin" (*Diabolical Possession*, 114).

93. Rueda, *Diabolical Possession*, 32.

94. Faherty, *To Rest in Charity*, 82.

seeming understanding of the Latin on his part.⁹⁵ However, these events are not recorded in the background of the diary. The *Diary* makes its own affirmation of xenolalia during the St. Louis phase, while also eliciting surprise once when the mimicked Latin seemingly came with a precise accent.⁹⁶ Linson attributes the preternatural knowledge of Latin to the St. Louis phase.⁹⁷

The nightmare consuming the family in Washington, DC, would soon come to an end there. It would go with them to St. Louis. As the native city of Robbie's mother, it was coincidentally where Aunt Harriet had died. When the family of necromancy and séances witnessed the message "Louis" scratched across the boy's body like a planchette moving across a Ouija board, they were convinced. They departed two days after his hospital discharge.

St. Louis Pre-Exorcism Phase

The family travelled by train on March 7 to St. Louis, intending to stay with family. After one night in the suburb of Normandy, the mother's sister's home, they settled in the Bel-Nor neighborhood, where they would stay until their return to Georgetown in the late spring.⁹⁸ The Normandy family was Lutheran; the Bel-Nor family was Catholic.

March 7–15

Consultations with a second Lutheran pastor and an Episcopal priest seem to have taken place here.⁹⁹ Even in their Lutheran relatives' home here, the bed shook, loud knockings sounded, and the boy's violent and irregular behavior continued. According to Spitzer, the family continued to interpret these as communications from their aunt before moving to

---

95. Spitzer, *Christ Versus Satan*, 167.
96. *Diary*, "April 13."
97. Linson, "Washington's Haunted Boy," 34.

98. Taylor, *Devil Came to St. Louis*, 67; Allen, *Possessed*, 43–45; Spitzer, *Christ Versus Satan*, 160–61. The address of this extended stay is 8435 Roanoke Drive. See Ruickbie, "Hunkeler," 157; See Letter A in "Appendix A: The Letters between the Rev. Luther Miles Schulze and Dr. J. B. Rhine" in Rueda, *Diabolical Possession*, 162.

99. See Letter D in "Appendix A: The Letters between the Rev. Luther Miles Schulze and Dr. J. B. Rhine" in Rueda, *Diabolical Possession*, 164; "Minister Tells Parapsychologists"; Brian, *Enchanted Voyager*, 183; Spitzer, *Christ Versus Satan*, 160.

their Catholic relatives in St. Louis on March 8.[100] Here came the scratch marks reading "no school" when the peace Robbie experienced led his mother to speak of possibly returning him to school.[101] This means that now the manifestations took place in four different homes.

The story of a Jesuit exorcism develops because the Hunkelers had a niece at Saint Louis University, studying under a Jesuit professor. Amidst these manifestations, she would be the one to contact her professor for spiritual assistance, Father Raymond Bishop. One writer claims that Robbie's shaking bed—while sharing a room with his cousin Marty—led the parents to approve a priestly consultation.[102]

Father Raymond J. Bishop was head of the Department of Education at Saint Louis University when his student, named or pseudonymized Elizabeth in the reports, approached him about her concern. He was forty-three years old and noted as a good professor.[103] The story goes that one history professor Father Laurence J. Kenny, and the university president Father Paul Reinert, were part of his confidential dialog in processing of her testimonial claims. Allen reports that Bishop felt that he "knew that he had let his intuition eclipse his reason" as Kenny was keen to medieval thinking and Reinert was a practical administrator.[104]

Father Bishop first came to the house on Wednesday, March 9. He offered a blessing to the bed as well as the room. The relic of St. Margaret Mary was pinned to the bed pillow. For fifteen minutes, the mattress intermittently moved head to foot in three-inch increments, Bishop recorded. Holy water led the motion to stop, but six observers would see scratch marks appear on Robbie's abdomen. Spitzer remarks that from this event Bishop was convinced of a demonization.[105]

On Thursday, March 10, Bishop sought counsel from Father William Bowdern, rector of the University's St. Francis Xavier Church on campus. He was pastor to a university of students through the ministry of the church, as well as to local parishioners. During the rigorous exorcism ahead, the fifty-two-year-old priest still had to fulfill his duties by day

---

100. Spitzer, *Christ Versus Satan*, 160.
101. *Diary*, "Background"; Spitzer, *Christ Versus Satan*, 161.
102. Spitzer, *Christ Versus Satan*, 161.
103. Allen, *Possessed*, 48.
104. Allen, *Possessed*, 50. Allen offers insightful speculation on the sense of thought that may have characterized the tensions and consequences for all three men if they sustained a case of demonization (see 49–55).
105. Spitzer, *Christ Versus Satan*, 162.

while visiting the Mannheim house, sometimes deep into the night. Allen describes him as "short, stocky, black-haired and square-jawed with a reputation for cool, decisive action. He smoked Camels incessantly."[106] He had been principal of a high school in Kansas and then in St. Louis. He served as a US Army chaplain during World War II in both European and Pacific campaigns before becoming pastor of the College Church. Allen reports further that one Jesuit peer described him as "totally fearless" and that Bishop likely viewed him as a holy priest.[107] Another colleague describes him as "a marvelous man, an old shoe, Irishman, and storyteller. . . . he was just a great guy, a quiet man, with a wonderful smile, and a very modest man."[108] A Saint Louis University High School student describes him: "A kindly old man, seemed so gentle. In fact, he didn't seem like he could control the class, let alone a demon."[109]

That night, scratching and rhythmic marching continued in the Mannheim home. The safety pin holding the relic offered by Bishop came unpinned from the pillow and the relic of St. Margaret Mary seemed as if tossed to the floor.[110] Following Elizabeth's report, the two priests visited on Friday, March 11, to a house that had just conducted a séance. Bowdern brought with him both first-class and second-class relics.[111] He visited and talked gently with Robbie, who proceeded to go to bed. As the priests reviewed details with the family downstairs, they heard him yell. Robbie reported that a force had come into the room, the relic of St. Margaret Mary had flown across the room, and a scratched cross appeared on his left forearm. Bowdern proceeded to bless the boy with the relic whose identity was not recognizable by the boy, allowing for a spiritual discernment beyond his normal means. Gathered downstairs anew, Father Bishop then collected the background information contained in the case study of the *Diary*. A crash from Robbie's room brought them up again, where he claimed the holy water bottle had flown across the room. The *Diary* is unclear about the timing of several objects thrown and moved in the room here, but Halloran would later testify about that first

---

106. Allen, *Possessed*, 63. Cf. Faherty, *To Rest in Charity*, 81–82.

107. Allen, *Possessed*, 65.

108. Interview with Father Dan O'Connell (cited in Rueda, *Diabolical Possession*, 211). O'Connell comments on the silence around the event: "Bill Bowdern was keen on that; he didn't want to talk about it."

109. Richard Novosak excerpt (cited in Bishop and Saint Booth, *Exorcist Diary*, 5).

110. *Diary*, "March 10."

111. *Diary*, "March 11."

Theology of a Diary

night: "I just about got hit with a holy water bottle that was sitting on the dresser and came flying across the room and just missed me by an inch or two."[112] Bowdern proceeded to pray the rosary and the Lord's Prayer over the boy, as well as relate the story of the children who had a vision of Our Lady of Fatima. The evening ended peacefully for the priests.[113]

Sergio Rueda points out that many of these reported activities were not actually witnessed by the family.[114] Before the exorcism began, the family or even the priests would rush to the boy's room in response to some crash or a scream. The sounds of the marching footsteps and the testimony to a powerful presence did not always find testimony or witness outside of Robbie. This second-hand effect would later prove to augment the difficulty of Bowdern's proposal to the archbishop for the rite of exorcism.

However, it certainly seems that turmoil consistently broke out in Robbie's room. Here, family members and Robbie combined to claim a bookcase moved to block the entrance, a stool moved and turned over, relics moved, and one was lost, scratching was heard, and shaking of the mattress ensued. This was when the family decided to ask questions about the spirit they now imagined was haunting their house. This was when they developed a theory that necromancing Aunt Harriet was now communicating with them. They hypothesized that she had left a box of money somewhere in the house and sought to offer its location to them. Bishop records in the *Diary*, likely from Elizabeth's later testimony, that "the five people in the home then decided to ask questions of the spirit."[115] Amidst all of these activities, the examination of Robbie's signs by the priests were convincing enough to characterize those defined by the Catholic Church as true demonization: uncharacteristic familiarity with a foreign language, secret or future information, or unnatural power.[116]

In response to their own witness and the report of the family members, Bishop and Bowdern began to prepare an official recommendation for the rite of exorcism. Allen describes how they had to treat

---

112. Brown, "Interview."

113. *Diary*, "March 11"; Allen, *Possessed*, 68–70.

114. Rueda, *Diabolical Possession*, 126. This same basis for challenging a legitimate demonization comes in Cortés and Gatti, *Case against Possessions and Exorcisms*, 70–84.

115. *Diary*, "March 11"; Bishop and Saint Booth, *Exorcist Diary*, 25.

116. "Exorcism of the Possessed" 2 (Weller, ed., *Roman Ritual: Volume 2*, 169).

the testimony of the family as hearsay, even if the witnesses to events totaled fourteen at that time.[117] Their wonder around the events would have led them to the qualifications in the *Roman Ritual*, but otherwise Bowdern had little precedence to guide him. Sunday through Tuesday, March 13–15, the *Diary* shows that the priests did not visit the house, likely in preparation of the exorcism recommendation to Archbishop Joseph Ritter. Allen suggests that the archbishop would not have liked this proposal, especially in the wake of the Iowa exorcism of 1928 and due to his political acumen, evidenced by his appointment to cardinal in 1961. Despite the predicted reticence on the part of the St. Louis archdiocese to commission a priest for the formal rite of exorcism, permission came. Allen supposes that for Ritter, "He was duty-bound to challenge the evil and struggle against it. However, he would fight as a general; the exorcist would fight in the trenches."[118] Finally, and only under the command of secrecy, the *Diary* reports that Bowdern was appointed by the Most Reverend Archbishop Joseph Ritter to "read the prayers of exorcism according to the Roman Ritual."[119] Halloran relates the moment that many consider to be Jesuit lore. When the archbishop assigned the rite to Bowdern, the priest responded, "Nothing doing." The archbishop in authority answered, "You got it."[120]

ST. LOUIS EXORCISM PHASE

Numerous bizarre details characterize the work of the seemingly diabolical on, in, or through the room or the body of the demonized Robbie during the four-and-a-half-week exorcism period. Some of the details are graphic: cursing, phallic motions, and regular vomiting, including ballistic regurgitation with poignant accuracy. There were usually periods of crisis: mania, hysteria, violence, or seizures. Then Robbie would experience periods of calm: restfulness, peace, or even consciousness. Allen speculates about the emotional calm: "Exorcists explain this feeling as the touch of evil: Satan, while remaining hidden, projects a sinister aura that engulfs the victim."[121]

117. Allen, *Possessed*, 76.
118. Allen, *Possessed*, 89.
119. *Diary*, "March 16."
120. McGuire, "St. Louis Exorcism"; Allen, *Possessed*, 90.
121. Allen, *Possessed*, 170.

March 16–31

Father Walter Halloran was a twenty-six-year-old Jesuit scholastic who had been a student in the boarding school operated by Father Bowdern. Eight years into a friendship and now a Saint Louis University history graduate student, he often served as driver to his Jesuit superior.[122] The first night of the exorcism Halloran was not even aware of Bowdern's intentions when he was asked to drive him to the Mannheim house, then to come inside. Halloran becomes an important eyewitness who would stand for radio and book interviews in the years ahead but still honored the confidential details of the event. As an assistant who had played high school football and later served in the Vietnam War, his lending hand might provide an athleticism and strength to the physical restraint necessary for the situation.[123]

Wednesday, March 16, marks the date of the rite of exorcism first administered to Robbie Mannheim. At about 10:30 pm, Father William Bowdern met with Robbie in his room, likely to explain the sacramental experience ahead. The priest led him in the sacrament confession, as a spiritual coach would do for a middle-school boy who was not Catholic. They prayed together. Returning downstairs, Bowdern and the other priests dressed in surplices and purple stoles, they combined to carry the *Roman Ritual* and holy water. They prayed together, and the exorcist would have reminded them of the rules, such as not engaging the demon in dialog and remaining focused on their part in the responsive prayers. Adult members of the family joined them in prayer in the room.[124] Meanwhile, Allen describes from pieces of testimony, including that of Walter Halloran, that when Bowdern worked with Robbie, he "drew upon his years as teacher and counselor of adolescent boys to probe Robbie's heart."[125]

The priests began reading the rite of exorcism over the demonized boy. Bishop writes in the *Diary*, "On the *Praecipio* there was immediate action. Three large parallel bars were scratched on the boy's stomach."[126] More scratches would appear at the reading of the names of Jesus, Mary, and Michael the archangel in the liturgy. The deepest of brands occurred

---

122. Garland, "Exorcism Exposé," 13.
123. Silvers, "Jesuit Helped."
124. *Diary*, "March 16."
125. Allen, *Possessed*, 93.
126. *Diary*, "March 16."

The Event

like thorn scratches, and at least four heavy marks formed an "X." Once across his chest the letters "hell" appeared in the texture of thorn scratches.[127] An imprint like the devil also appeared on his leg at the reading of the *praecipio*, with its arms above its head and webbed like a bat. The letters "go" with a seemingly third letter pointed away from the groin. These signs led to some interpretative speculation as obligatory communication from the demon in response to the *praecipio*, which demands its name and departure date. The "X" was interpreted as a possible exodus prediction of ten days or one day at 10:00. The direction of "go" led Bishop to write, "An indication which might have meant that the devil would leave by way of urination or excrement."[128] Before the night was over, the boy would suffer the pain of more than twenty-five different scratchings.

For the nights of March 16 and 17, Bishop would remark in the *Diary*, "The family had not seen such violent reaction as was shown on this night and the following. Evidently the exorcism prayers had stirred up the devil."[129] The boy's reactions ranged: he smiled and laughed cynically, setting into singing of "Suwanee River" and "Old Man River" in a high-pitch and extreme volume. The boy offered violent threats, he struck the bed board with his fist, he punched the pillow, and threw unordinary strong blows with his fists, requiring two men to hold him down. Yet, even during these struggles, Robbie would doze and wake, often in fitful, struggling sleeps. Sometimes he was conscious enough to report that he saw multiple devils while recognizing that he was himself fighting against them. The night of March 16 ended at 7:30 am on March 17.

The nights became routine insofar as the rite of exorcism was read over the demonized boy. No two nights were alike, and no sense of mundane regularity accompanied the experiences of the exorcist. Prayers would be read, and the family often prayed the rosary. Thrashing and vulgar comments regularly came from the boy. Sometimes singing or humming sometimes filled the room. March 17 saw the introduction of systematic spitting, here in the face of both parents and his uncle. Like so many other entries in the *Diary*, the boy did not seem to be conscious during much of these activities. Like so many other entries in the *Diary*, the boy fell asleep, exhausted after the ordeal.

---

127. *Diary*, "March 16."

128. *Diary*, "March 16." The journal misspells "leave" as "leavy," earning a [*sic*]. This location was a medieval means of exit for the demon.

129. *Diary*, "March 16."

March 18 marked one of the most hopeful and some of the most curiously severe responses. The evening saw spitting at the relics, the mattress shaking, super-human strength against those restraining him, and screaming "in a diabolical, high-pitched voice."[130] While the shaking stopped when holy water was applied, Robbie also thrashed when it was applied to him. On this night, he seemed to break free of his restrainers, jumping up, swinging fists, and "snapping his teeth in fury . . . He bit those who held him."[131] His feet moved in a rhythm, and as Bowdern placed the Blessed Sacrament near one foot, it would stop, suggesting a correlation between the sacramental materials and the inferiority of the demon.

Before the night episode, Robbie had prayed the rosary and prayed to the Lady of Fatima. At a later calm, he stood up on the bed, dropped on his knees, and prayed the salaams, to the Lady of Fatima and to Mary. The boy seemed to be participating in the liturgical battle against his own demon. When *Diary* writer Bishop described Robbie's attempt to fight for the exorcism, the boy would also gyrate his body and pull up part of his clothes while also raising his hands in supplication. Signs of demonic exit include his attempts to vomit and the request for an open window. The voice was pleasant that declared, "He's going, he's going . . . There he goes," before the boy fell calmly onto the bed. "Everything seemed to indicate conquest," the *Diary* reads.[132] As the family gathered in prayer around the bed for thanksgiving, Robbie testified that a black cloud passed from him. "A figure in black robes, cowl, and white XXXX walked away in the cloud."[133]

At 1:30 am, Robbie helped to see the priests leave. By 3:15 am, Father Bowdern and three others were called back. About 2:00 am, the boy was declaring with fear, "He's coming back! He's coming back!" The exorcism activities that night ended at 7:30 am.

The next night of the reading of the exorcism, March 19, Robbie made violent shouts, diabolical laughter, dog barking sounds, and snapping of his teeth. The diarist notes here how the violence corresponds to the exorcism reading, qualities absent before the first night of March 16.

As the priest commanded a sign of departure from the demon at the *praecipio*, the boy urinated in pain. He sang "Blue Danube" with

---

130. *Diary*, "March 18."
131. *Diary*, "March 18."
132. *Diary*, "March 18."
133. *Diary*, "March 18." The "X" marks in the record offer no clue to its omission.

The Event

impressive skill and "The Old Rugged Cross" sounded professional. When the boy was calmed, he could not repeat the melody of "Blue Danube" on his own when Bishop hummed it to him. On the other hand, spoken words were equally profane. This evening also would hear the taunting of one unnamed priest. Calling first in a pleasant voice, it turned to a demanding voice, "Father, you stink," it declared. Curses marked the occasion, with graphic language about the priests recorded in the *Diary*.

The family was growing exhausted. Robbie was admitted to the Alexian Brothers hospital in St. Louis on Monday, March 21, to the psychiatric wing on the fifth floor. Here, screams and restraints against violence would be more commonplace. Robbie showed fear of the new surroundings. The rite of exorcism was administered in its entirety, seemingly without resistance. The diarist seems moved that Robbie's father, who had prayed alongside the exorcist this day, continued to read prayers for him for half an hour. Robbie was taken home the next day. That night saw the shaking bed three times, but the rite and the rosary prayers were completed peacefully.

On March 23, Bowdern set up two beds in the St. Xavier College Church rectory on the Saint Louis University campus. This was in accordance with the Catholic rite of exorcism: "The possessed person should be led to church or to some sacred and worthy place, where the exorcism will be held."[134] The exorcism would continue here for two nights, the *Diary* suggests. The first night, the boy revisited his catechetical instruction. Upon the beginning of the rite, Robbie fought, kicked, and spit against the men. Father Halloran's nose was broken and Father Roo's nose bled. The boy flatulated and urinated, as well as offered phallic references about himself. He taunted one priest by saying the year was 1957 and that the demon was surprised to meet him in hell. While Robbie supposedly would not employ such language as a boy, the *Diary* reads that "the vile and filthy talk, which followed, makes anyone shudder."[135]

The following day, Bowdern began to show a sense of hopeful immediacy of the exorcism. Perhaps the recent assumption of departure and return of the demon fueled this hope. Certainly, the Catholic liturgical calendar made him optimistic. The forthcoming feast of St. Gabriel on March 24 and the feast of the angelic Annunciation to Mary on March 25 corresponded in days to the "X" mark on Robbie from March 16, if that

---

134. "Exorcism of the Possessed" 11 (Weller, ed., *Roman Ritual: Volume 2*, 171).
135. *Diary*, "March 23."

"X" were interpreted as the number ten. March 24 saw another round of display of physical strength by the boy. Similar incidents were repeated, including mocking the priests, excretion, swearing, yelling, barking, and singing, with the addition of puerile rhymes. The degree of sexual and mocking language reached its apex, described in detail in the *Diary*. The diarist also declared that the Blessed Sacrament seemed to show no influence on the boy on this night.

Some irregular bodily movements marked March 25. Robbie spit at and cursed his father; he kicked at the priests. The three nights to follow were not notable, leading Bowdern surely to hope that day 10 might have been a night of exorcism. No signs typical of success were evidenced in the diary, however, and no entries were made for the next five days.

When Robbie felt sick and when the bed had shaken, Robbie provided another peculiar event on March 31. He started writing on the bed using his finger what he claimed to be read from a blackboard in his mind. The *Diary* says that his cousin—assumedly Elizabeth—recorded the following message in the absence of the priests, provided it is original despite its errors:

> I will stay 10 days but will return in 4 days. If Robbie stays (gone to lunch), If you stay and become a Catholic it will stay away. God will take it away 4 days after it has gone 10 days. God is getting powerful. The last day when it quits it will leave a sign on my front. Father Bishop all people that mangle (*sic*) with me will die a terrible death.[136]

When a pencil was provided to Robbie, he began to write on the bed board. Similar messages to those recorded above are provided in the *Diary*, written from the first person seemingly from the demon about Robbie and others. The eight messages include references to the "X" and the repeat timing of 10 and four days. The messages also pontificate on the use of language, refusing to use the priestly Latin while defying the liturgical use of English. Something like a map was drawn, which the diarist associates with a comment about what came from the Ouija board. Finally, one remarks around identity includes, "I am the devil himself. You will have to pray for a month in the Catholic Church," and "You may not believe me. Then R will suffer forever."[137]

---

136. *Diary*, "March 31."
137. *Diary*, "March 31."

The Event

April 1–17

The *Diary* pauses on Friday, April 1, to review how Robbie was undergoing catechetical training to become Catholic. The parents consented to this path for their son, while they had previously expected a Lutheran confirmation for him. The reversion of any progress led to the corporate decision to see Robbie baptized Catholic. The boy's response was resistant as they drove again to St. Xavier College Church on the campus of Saint Louis University. The voice mocked the idea of baptism and Holy Communion before Robbie grabbed the steering wheel of the vehicle and his uncle pulled over to defend against the violence. Supposedly the boy "suddenly glared at the priest, grabbed him by the throat and shouted, 'You son of a bitch, you think I'm going to be baptized but you are going to be fooled!'"[138] With stiffening resistance, the boy was transferred to the back seat where he was held down. With his aunt now driving, Robbie even outfought his uncle and father in the back to grab at her. The *Diary* also reports how the car radio supposedly would not operate during this car ride, yet it worked before and after the trip.[139] The return trip was no less violent, Spitzer states, as three men were required in the back seat with the boy.[140]

The battle ensued upon arrival before Robbie could be placed on a bed in the rectory. A worker nearby was enlisted for yet another adult man hand. The thrashing required Bowdern to instill a briefer version of the baptism liturgy. Especially at the point of renunciation of Satan, "Do you renounce Satan and all his ways?"[141] the demon in the boy resisted before the boy declared that he renounced him: "Finally R was normal long enough to give the answers."[142] Resistance continued at the priestly declaration, "I baptize you in the name of the Father, the Son, and the Holy Spirit."[143] They proceeded with the baptism attempt for hours, against the physical resistance by the demonized boy. The diarist speculates that the

---

138. Erdmann, "Truth," 55; Taylor, *Devil Came to St. Louis*, 65.

139. *Diary*, "April 1." Halloran offers additional details of the struggle in the car (see Brown, "Interview").

140. Spitzer, *Christ Versus Satan*, 167.

141. Weller, ed., *Roman Ritual: Volume 1*, 71, 113.

142. *Diary*, "April 1."

143. Weller, ed., *Roman Ritual: Volume 1*, 115. The Trinitarian declaration is made several times in the baptism of adults in the rite. Weller, ed., *Roman Ritual: Volume 1*, 75, 79, 85, 87, 93, 95, 99, 103, and 115, in addition to the salt and the exorcism components.

original Lutheran baptism was not effective, and reports that "the usual spitting, gyrating, cursing and physical violence continued until 11:30 pm."[144]

The diarist also reports that the baptism led to a peaceful confession on April 2 before the occasion of Robbie's first Holy Communion. However, as the Eucharist prayer began, the boy shut his eyes and mouth to resist the sacrament. Application of the bread into his mouth resulted in its expulsion, carefully caught by the priest each time. Two hours of failed attempts led Father O'Flaherty to suggest the prayer of the Rosary in honor of Fatima, after which Robbie took communion "under extraordinary opposition."[145] The ride home saw Robbie suddenly jump from his seat to seize onto O'Flaherty before being contained. Observing him rest much of the day, the diarist imagines, "The Sacraments had stirred up Satan more than any other Priestly administration."[146] In one of the tensest of diary descriptions, the same evening captures a feeling that marked recent months—at any given moment, demonic manifestations could surface with startling abruptness. The evening began with ice cream. Robbie retired upstairs "in boyish fashion, turned into his bedroom and ran straight for the reliquary of the Holy Cross," was stopped by O'Flaherty, and "with lightning speed" ripped four pages from the ritual book among the rite of exorcism pages. In the exorcism rite to follow, Bowdern commanded the demon to give its name, day, and hour of departure per the *praecipio*, which he would have given in Latin: *dicas mihi nomen tuum, diem, et horam exitus tui cum aliquo signo.*[147] "Stick it up your ass" was the response, along with the declarations, "'No!' or by a laugh of ridicule."[148] Mockery continued at the command as "Go," three parallel scratches, an "X," and three "18" figures arose on his body. These numbers would confuse the priests expecting a communication on the departure date, imagining the April 17 Easter date to have been a worthy exorcism date. Robbie moved from the bed to a chair, "his hands trembled in a nervous frenzy," and he requested of his father to return to Washington, DC, before sleep overcame him.

Playing baseball in the yard that day evidenced odd staggering behavior by Robbie, and he showed a fixation of wrapping his legs around

---

144. *Diary*, "April 1."
145. *Diary*, "April 2."
146. *Diary*, "April 2."
147. "Rite of Exorcism" (Weller, ed., *Roman Ritual: Volume 2*, 178–79).
148. *Diary*, "April 2." Cf. similar quoted language on April 12 and 13.

The Event

the kitchen table on the day of April 3. On a rare evening in the *Diary*, all assisting priests were named: Bowdern, Van Roo, Bishop, and O'Flaherty. Upon the administration of the rite on this Passion Sunday, two weeks before Easter, Robbie communicated what the *Diary* calls "a kind of devilish prophecy" about his cousin, Neil. "You will die tonight," he said repeatedly for ten minutes.[149] Restlessness and violence characterized the remainder of the night.

At this point of the ordeal, the family senses their St. Louis stay should end. The *Diary* references the father's work obligations and the tax laid on their host.[150] On April 4, Robbie, his parents, and Fathers Bowdern and Van Roo returned to Cottage City, Maryland. One undescribed event of behavior occurred on the train, but otherwise the family seemed fortunate. The priest may have thought that family regional diocesan authorities in Washington, DC, should oversee this case because he immediately networked upon their arrival. However, attempts to enroll Robbie in Catholic hospitals failed.[151] According to Henry Kelly, a rare interviewer of Father Bowdern, a local Catholic mental hospital refused to admit him because "their mission was to care for the mentally ill, not the diabolically possessed, of whom they wanted no part."[152] The Archdiocesan approval for the exorcism could easily have been the basis for their declinations. One bright spot had to be Bowdern's conference with Father Hughes, linking the Georgetown and St. Louis phases for that day. This encounter offers justification for Hughes to later report details of the 1949 exorcism from the St. Louis phase as second hand from Bowdern. However, anything learned from Hughes's pastoral effort in the Georgetown phase did not see the *Diary* background edited to include him. At the start of this trip, the *Diary* uniquely names nine Jesuits who served as record witnesses to Robbie's demonization. The declination by so many facilities in Maryland led Bowdern to phone Brother Rector Cornelius at the Alexian Brothers Hospital, who invited Robbie to return anytime. From April 4 to April 9, the family was gone from St. Louis.

In seems to have been at the family home in Cottage City that the extreme events of April 7 took place. At the point of the *praecipio* in the

---

149. *Diary*, "April 3." Cf. prophetic attempts by the demon on April 13.

150. *Diary*, "April 4."

151. *Diary*, "April 4–9"; see Letter E in "Appendix A: The Letters between the Rev. Luther Miles Schulze and Dr. J. B. Rhine" in Rueda, *Diabolical Possession*, 165.

152. Kelly, *Devil*, 99. *Diary* ("April 6") names the XXXXX Institute Daughters of Charity in Baltimore as the hospital.

reading of the rite, more than twenty scratch brands came to Robbie's body. The number 4, single and double strokes, a fork, and claw marks are named in the *Diary* as occurring without Robbie's cause. The words "hell" and "Christ" also appeared on Robbie. Violence, spitting, defecation, and foul language marked the night. The demon offered his own prophecy and sign by declaring he would fight with the priests until 6:00 am—four hours ahead of their current weariness—and declared that Robbie would awaken suddenly to evidence it. He did. And he slept for hours, well before the stated time.

Similar manifestation and the reading of the rite continued the next evening. Physical resistance, spitting, jumbling of Latin, and singing "Blue Danube" and "Ave Maria" mark the *Diary* narrative. Foul remarks about masturbation, contraceptives, and sexual activities among priests and nuns seem to be an attempt to defy Catholic values. He resisted Holy Communion. Noteworthy in this entry is the return of Father Hughes and another Father Canning to the exorcism event.

The April 10 Palm Sunday return trip saw Robbie return directly to the fifth floor of the Alexian Brothers Hospital to his former room. Faherty depicts the moment: "The hospital room became a chamber of horrors." The room held a chill that required Bowdern to wear an overcoat over his cassock and surplice.[153] Yet, for the weary Jesuits, the *Diary* exemplifies a sense of home stretch at this point, reporting that Robbie allowed rosaries, Holy Communion, and other prayers without resistance. Sleep came quickly in his fatigue. Being awoken for the sacrament, the diarist remarks, "The Blessed Sacrament brought peace to R."[154] Alexian Brother Emmet is named as a new encourager to Robbie, allowing him to serve the hospital in tasks and developing a friendship. On April 11, the word "exit" appeared three places on Robbie's body. Urination caused pain. Around midnight, during the institution of the rite, long scratches appeared from his ankle to his hip, imagined by the priest to be in opposition to the successful Holy Communion. Such remarks evidence how Bishop viewed a sacerdotal influence in the application of exorcism. The battle over the administration of the sacrament marked these times, including Robbie's request to receive it and the onset of a seizure preventing it. "The attempts to administer the Sacrament of the Eucharist roused the devil more than ordinarily." The Alexian Brothers

---

153. Faherty, *To Rest in Charity*, 82; Nicola, *Diabolical Possession*, 112.
154. *Diary*, "April 10."

joined in prayer as Robbie barked, cursed, spit, and shouted at the exorcists. April 12 saw singing and cacophony during the reading of the rite. Like many other entries, the diarist reports the response of Robbie during the *praecipio*, often pointing out the lack of response and showing obvious expectation of the command authority over the entity. Instead, once again, the response, "Stick it up your ass" was proffered. The demon declared that Robbie would awaken pleasantly but then reawaken aggressively; the boy did. The demon also declared, "I will not let R receive Holy Communion."[155] However, the next day he did. Halloran seems to be speaking of this occasion when the boy would "take a swing at Father Bowdern in the groin and say, 'How's that for a nutcracker?'"[156] Clearly the demon is taunting the priests by showing his control of Robbie through clustering, reinforcing the dramatic battle taking place between them with Robbie as the victim.

Likewise, April 13 heard another confession of a time of departure, that God had commanded the demon to leave at 11:00 pm, but only following a prophesy of resistance. The diarist affirmed its fulfilment: the boy displayed "relatively more physical power than at any previous time."[157] On a rare occasion, the length of a violent episode is named as twenty minutes. Coarse language characterized the night, as well as the resistance to the Eucharist. The boy cried "Fire" from his room to disrupt the environment. Yet when the boy began to mimic the church bell at 11:00 am, the diarist reports that they realized that the demon had lied in its prophetic claim.

Earlier that day held another memorable event in the 1949 exorcism story. Halloran remembers when Robbie accompanied him to the White House, a Jesuit retreat center outside St. Louis. While the *Diary* mentions this occasion briefly, saying that the boy had to be carried back to the car following a spell, he elaborates in an interview. Walking around the grounds there, the boy wondered at its displays of the stations of the cross. Halloran explained each one to the boy's interest, until the twelfth station commemorating Christ's death. "With that he took off and ran toward the edge of a bluff that dropped down about 150, 200 feet down to the tracks and I hollered at him and nothing happened, so I ran and for once in my life I made a decent tackle."[158]

155. *Diary*, "April 12."
156. Brown, "Interview."
157. *Diary*, "April 13."
158. Brown, "Interview."

The Holy Week surely fostered hope that the commemoration of resurrection to come at Easter would be a powerful force of timing against the demonization. New statues were placed in the hospital: Our Lady of Fatima in the lobby and St. Michael the archangel in the room. Yet Easter Sunday began with Robbie refusing the Eucharist. The fourth attempt succeeded by waiting out the smacking away of the elements. The seizures and spells prevented his advancement to the chapel, as he grabbed the *Roman Ritual* and a scapular garment, stomping on them. "I will not let him go to mass. Everything thinks it will he [sic] good for him," the demon declared.[159] In fact, the day seemed extra eerie. Allen imagines it as he reports it:

> The voice, the devil's voice, as Bishop called it, now spoke more frequently and authoritatively, that was sure. And there was something in the air, something that touched each man in a different way. Witnesses did not agree on what they saw and heard and felt and smelled. When they entered the room, they seemed to conjure up horrors that simultaneously exited in their minds and in the room itself. Witnesses told of feeling a chill go through them when they were in the room.[160]

During the severe episode to follow later in the day, the demon prophesied that Robbie would awaken to ask for a knife to kill those holding him down. When he awakened, his justification was to cut an Easter egg. Another prediction was that he would awaken and ask for water, which he did. The priests exited at 12:45 am.

April 18

On this day, for the first time, the *Diary* makes its entries in hours, foreshowing the unfolding drama ahead. Robbie awoke on April 18 to kick his attendant, grab the Holy Water, threatened to throw it at them, sprinkled them with water and finally dashed it against the wall over their heads. The lunch plate suffered the same fate. Communion attempts were resisted until one was taken. The demon declared that one of them had left, the speaker unwilling to depart until Robbie had received nine

---

159. *Diary*, "April 17."
160. Allen, *Possessed*, 207.

The Event

Holy Communions. The *Diary* remarks parenthetically, "Sacramental or spiritual apparently."[161]

It was decided that for the evening liturgy, the *praecipio* would be demanded for answers in English. This evidences the Latin application of the rite prior to this point. Likewise, the spiritual "medals" or relics would rest on Robbie, and a crucifix would be in his hand during his resistance episodes. "These resolutions were discussed and carried out because of the information gathered from the reading concerning several other cases of possession."[162] The diarist also comments that "the signs of the Cross and the Crucifix were very effective," revealing a theological optimism of their efficacy.[163] Once on April 18, the boy threw the crucifix from his hand, rejecting the holy object. Robbie was coached to learn the "Ave Maria" in Latin, and he asked for a Catholic reader. The medals bore hot on the boy's neck, but the priests would not honor the request to remove them. The diary notes that the day was marked by violence, urination, and more singing. Most importantly on this day, at one *dicas mihi* command after the offer of communion, the demon declared in its awful voice: "That isn't enough. He has to say one more word, one little word, I mean one BIG word. He'll never say it say it. He has to make nine Communions. He'll never say that word. I am always in him. I may not have much power always, but I am in him. He will never say that word."[164]

Amidst all of the tension of resistance and the passivity of rest, the diarist remarks, "Robbie was more co-operative this night than he had ever been before" and "the reaction to the medals and cross was exceptional."[165] After a mention that Father Bishop repeatedly prayed the exorcism prayer of St. Michael, the *Diary* reaches its climax: "At 10:45 pm, the most striking event of the evening occurred." After a seizure came a speech from a different source: "In clear, commanding tones, and with dignity, a voice broke into the prayers . . . 'Satan! Satan! I am Saint Michael, and I command you, Satan, and the other evil spirits to leave the body in the name of Dominus, immediately—Now! NOW! NOW!'" Violent contortions unseen prior to this evening was called by the diarist "the fight to the finish." Almost eight minutes of this violence

---

161. *Diary*, "April 18." There seems to be some narrative overlap between the 8:30 am and 10:00 am entries.

162. *Diary*, "April 18."

163. *Diary*, "April 18."

164. *Diary*, "April 18."

165. *Diary*, "April 18."

Theology of a Diary

heard Robbie declared with relief, "He's gone!"[166] Allen imagines how the countenance of the demonized boy lifted, and his mother wept for joy at his deliverance.[167]

With a sense of relief, the boy explained how a radiant while light emanated from a robed man described as beautiful, with flowing hair and a fiery sword in his right hand. The other hand pointed to a cave. The boy witnessed the devil inside the cave, where he could see heat and feel flames. While the devil at first laughed, at the declaration of "Dominus" he and ten demons fled into the cave. As they did, the boy reported feeling a pulling in his stomach that felt like a snap. Then Robbie relaxed. The word "spite" appeared above the cave, corresponding to the name supposedly given in one of the scratchings. He testified feeling the most relaxed since January.[168]

At last, the demonic influence departed from the child in a violent but dramatic affair. Father Bowdern received his sign of final discharge: an explosion like a gunshot reverberated through the hospital.[169] This instructive sign was important for Bowdern, who witnessed on a prior occasion how the demon seemed to depart when Robbie became calm and showed relief.

The final entry of the ordeal, April 19, describes the following day. Robbie arose from a good sleep, he attended mass for the first time, and he received Holy Communion without resistance. "No indications of the presence of the devil" closes the entry, recorded on the Feast of St. Mark, April 25, 1949.[170] One follow up entry of August 19, 1951, is provided. Robbie and his parents visited the Alexian Brothers. "Robbie now 16 is a fine young man." His parents also became Catholic.[171]

THE AFTER PHASE

Thomas Allen reports that Robbie went on to live a peaceful life. Allen passed away in 2020—the same year as Ronald Edwin Hunkeler—never to see the name announced publicly with much recognition. Father

---

166. *Diary*, "April 18."
167. Allen, *Possessed*, 124–25.
168. *Diary*, "April 18"; Brian, *Enchanted Voyager*, 182.
169. Dobson, "Luncheon"; Gallagher, *Demonic Foes*, 25; Cooper and Epperson, *Evil*, 26; Faherty, *To Rest in Charity*, 82; Brown, "Interview."
170. *Diary*, "April 19."
171. *Diary*, "April 19."

Bowdern had promised his diocesan superiors that he would keep the record of the exorcism case undisclosed, despite his certainty that the exorcism story could help people understand the reality of evil. The archbishop had instructed that the case be kept secret because he feared the emotional harm on the boy.[172] Bowdern thus felt compelled to decline any elaboration about the event for Blatty's book project *The Exorcist* based on the event.[173] The result was a display of fidelity among the exorcism participants, with only Luther Schulze initiating discussion of the details among the first hand witnesses and Walter Halloran being drawn into interviews as the sole primary participant survivor for decades to follow. Schulze reported in September 1949 that the boy was growing in a healthy manner. He also explained that the family did fear a resurgence of the activities, while also concerned about the attention to the event in the press.[174]

In 1973, Walter Halloran remembers attending the release of the film *The Exorcist* in the theater with Bowdern. Both were disappointed. Halloran says of Bowdern: "He gave sort of a running negative commentary throughout the whole movie. I thought the two of us were going to be thrown out of the theatre."[175] He reported upon their exit of the theater, "Billy came out shaking his head." He describes that the exorcist remarked, "'There is a good message that can be given by this thing' . . . the message was the fact that evil spirits operate in our world."[176]

The Legacy Phase

In the years to follow, the story of the 1949 exorcism gained a life of its own, but never deserting the original narrative. William Peter Blatty brought the most prominence to the event with his 1971 horror novel *The Exorcist* before joining director William Friedkin in production of the 1973 film. Mark Opsasnick remarks of its effect: "*The Exorcist* is a disturbing 121-minute film that leaves its audience pained, drained, and

---

172. Allen, *Possessed*, x, 220.

173. Allen, *Possessed*, 220.

174. See Letter I in "Appendix A: The Letters between the Rev. Luther Miles Schulze and Dr. J. B. Rhine" in Rueda, *Diabolical Possession*, 169.

175. Brown, "Interview." McGuire cites that Bowdern's brother, Edward, claimed that the exorcist did not like the book. McGuire, "St. Louis Exorcism."

176. Allen, *Possessed*, x, 220.

entertained."[177] There were rumors of cinema walks-outs, ambulances being stationed outside of theaters, and consequential psychiatric cases.[178] A common rumor was that heart attacks concentrated around the moment that the grotesque head of the demonized girl slowly rotated 360 degrees while remaining intact. One researcher cited how theater managers claimed it rare if at least one person failed to faint or feel nauseated.[179] On another front, Edward Fisk has suggested that filmgoers immediately expressed pastoral needs that Catholic priests found surprising, disoriented, and difficult. These encounters centered either on a sudden fear of demons or inquiries about demonization by parishioners who had seen *The Exorcist*.[180]

For the book and the screenplay, Blatty honored Bowdern's request to fictionalize the exorcism.[181] He made the demonized child a girl and embellished the psychological cause more than the occultic cause. The girl has an imaginary friend named Capt. Howdy, which echoes the divination element of the story. The girl and her mother play one round with a Ouija in their basement, where the planchette moved on its own, in séance fashion. Yet the premise, the settings, the demonization activities, and the exorcism activities remain quite similar. The plot develops quite unhurriedly before it sets into the graphic and intense scenes of the exorcism. The plot shifts the main character role from the demonized child, from her mother who struggles to care for the child, and even from the exorcist himself, although each has their own deep contribution. The focus ultimately lands on one Father Damien Karras, a Jesuit priest and an entirely fictional character, who struggles to maintain his scientific worldview in the face of the preternatural. With no final Alexian Brothers Hospital episode, the rite is administered entirely at the family home in Georgetown, ending with Father Karras's frustration and dangerous invitation to deliver the child by inviting the demon to enter him instead. He throws himself headfirst out the window, freeing the victim and portraying a sacrificial role for her.

Blatty's own experience of the book and the film are noteworthy for understanding the phenomenon of its cultural and shadowy effect.

177. Opsasnick, "Haunted Boy," 6.
178. Rueda, *Diabolical Possession*, 6.
179. Fiske, "'Exorcist,'" 15.
180. Fiske, "'Exorcist.'" The effect is also explored in Laycock and Harrelson, *Exorcist Effect*, 53–64.
181. Blatty, *On The Exorcist*, 22, 28n24.

The Event

The story first came to his attention as a Georgetown University student in 1950, studying under Father Eugene B. Gallagher. Blatty regularly requested to see the *Diary*, and when Gallagher lent it to the university dean, 7 pages went missing. Erdman wonders if Blatty was finally able to get a copy of the work.[182] On writing the novel, he said afterwards, "I thought I was writing a supernatural detective story that was filled with suspense with theological overtones. To this day, I have zero recollection of even a moment when I was writing that I was trying to frighten anyone."[183] Afterwards, he authored the book *On The Exorcist from Novel to Film*.[184] It includes his testimony of dialoging with Father William Bowdern, disclosing the first mention about a diary.[185]

Also mentionable is the documentary about the event *In the Grip of Evil*, a sixty-minute 1997 Henninger Media video. Thomas Allen was a consultant, and his material seems to be represented. This documentary includes interviews from different psychological, theological, and historical perspectives. Catholic clergy interviewed include Father Walter Halloran, Father Frank Bober, and Father Dan O'Connell. Additional interviews are with psychiatrist Elizabeth S. Bowman, behavior psychologist and theologian Sergio A. Rueda, and a historical theologian Jeffrey Burton Russell.[186]

The cultural effect cannot be overstated. Arnold Blumberg has recognized how *The Exorcist* redefined the horror genre by providing a permanent fixture to pop culture and spawning a subgenre of horror films. The themes offered by *The Exorcist* are evidenced in the now timeless interests around spirits, science and religion, and the dark recesses of the soul.[187] The legacy impact on cinematography is captured by one researcher: "Pastiched and parodied in countless similar novels and films ever since, *The Exorcist* defined a subgenre of horror and made iconic (and marketable) the personal and spiritual trials entailed in fighting evil

---

182. Erdman, "Truth," 51.
183. King, "Speaking of the Devil."
184. Blatty, *On The Exorcist*.
185. Blatty, *On The Exorcist*, 20–21.
186. More elaborate interviews with some of these participants from the video are contained in "Appendix D: In the Grip of What? Interviews with Experts on Demonic Possession" in Rueda, *Diabolical Possession*, 195–240.
187. Blumberg, "How 'The Exorcist' Redefined the Horror Genre."

entities."[188] Hollywood has invested and profited immensely from the legacy of the film through the genre to follow.

Perhaps the most important cultural effect this case and its film offer is a reconsideration of the place of demonology in the modern era. It confronts the Enlightenment and scientism of our generation by presenting a spiritual crisis to which science cannot attend. Rueda describes this effect that *The Exorcist* had on the mind of the culture: "The film gave new life to Satan and his legions, the Devil now acquired a tangible existence, the demons became real, they spoke and interacted with humans and had to be fought and driven out of a possess individual."[189] Arnold Blumberg speaks similarly:

> Despite taking viewers on a nerve-wracking roller-coaster ride of demonic proportions, the film manages to convey an extremely positive message for those with spiritual conviction. After all, the very idea that the Catholic rite of exorcism could work against an actual demon attempting to gain control of a girl's soul confirms that these things are true; therefore, God too must be real. The result is a film that, while horrific, tells they faithful that they are right.[190]

One journalist concluded from interviews with priests in 1974 that the film popularity stems from a desire for heroes and myths, a chance to address questions concerning human nature, and an inspired revival of personal religion.[191] These initiatives share an interest in spiritual matters and a longing for something beyond the natural, beyond the programmed and predictable. The film captures an important dimension for both the public and the reader of this book: a visual representation of the imagination of demonization and exorcism. When Gabriel Amorth was asked how his experience with actual exorcisms compared to the film *The Exorcist*, he responds: "The film was made with much seriousness, but it is not without exaggeration: most of the time, the cases that exorcists treat are not as serious."[192] However, "most of the time" has exceptions, and the witnesses to the 1949 exorcism testify to one of them.

188. MacLeod, "Exorcist, The," 122.

189. Rueda, *Diabolical Possession*, 5.

190. Blumberg, "How 'The Exorcist' Redefined the Horror Genre."

191. Fiske, "'Exorcist,'" 15. A related evaluation can be found in Wiggins, *Nightmare with the Bible*, 169–82.

192. Amorth, *Exorcist*, 103.

2

The *Diary* and the Witnesses

"Accordingly, we (a priest with me) kept a minute account each day of the happenings each preceding day and night... Our diary would be most helpful to anyone placed in a similar position as an exorcist in any future date."

—William Bowdern, *Letter to William Peter Blatty*

A daily record of observations and events around an exorcism in 1949 is a deeply valuable resource for study of the exorcism. With this document, the historian possesses a rare and unique primary source. Likewise, anyone who wonders about the events has an observation record of a seeming demonization. Lying dormant for decades, this irreplaceable primary source is a *sine qua non* for any historical retrieval and understanding of these happenings.

The journal author is Father Raymond Bishop, who participated in the rite of exorcism for most of the St. Louis phase and was an early friend to the family upon their arrival. It seems that Father Bowdern so ordered a record of the daily events, a practice expected for an activity under archdiocese oversight. The *Diary* begins with a case study summarizing background information and events prior to the St. Louis confrontation. This section contains Bishop's personal interview with the family and with Robbie, dated March 7–10. Beginning on March 11, 1949, the priest Father Bowdern went to the house to meet Robbie personally. Here the exorcist enters the journal; on this date he began his encounter with the demonized boy and the demon, even before any exorcism was approved. The shared experiences of Bowdern and other priests are recorded in the diary, leading to an exorcism on April 18. Father Bishop submitted his report to the Archbishop chancery on May 3,[1] and it can only be presumed that the diary was included. The *Diary* is supposedly preserved by the Jesuit Provincial of the Missouri Province, the Archdiocese of St. Louis, and the Archdiocese of Washington, DC.

Beginning from that day of discovery in 1978 through its current accessibility, the *Diary* is central to understanding the events of 1949. This chapter offers an examination of this primary source, first around its historical retrieval and its plausibility for belief. Then, it explores the *Diary* narrative for a theological reading of its contents as an essential component of its historicity. Finally, it surveys other primary sources and testimonies from the period to establish the best possible understanding of the events.

The *Diary*

The many legends around this historic event centralize the role of the *Diary* in recovering the 1949 exorcism. This diary is a priest's journal accounting daily activities of liturgical practices, ministry to the boy, encounters with the demonic, and fortuitous response of the priests.

The *Diary* is distinctively a first-hand account of Bishop's personal and collective Jesuit experience before and during the exorcism. Examination of his theology in his historical report reveals what he witnessed or believed he witnessed, getting us closer to what happened. Later, Halloran's recognition of the *Diary* and his own testimony become a second to the *Diary* testimony of the events.[2] Likewise, the testimony of other witnesses serves our examination. The historian's task in this case is as follows: "He has to discover what the person who wrote those words meant by them. This means discovering the thought (in the widest sense of the word . . .) which he expressed by them. To discover what this thought was, the historian must think it again for himself."[3] Any eyewitness testimony of the demonization and exorcism necessitates a theological discovery as part of the historical recovery, assessing the religious motivations behind the historical witness. Still, the *Diary* is front and center of our theological treatment of the exorcism.

---

1. Faherty, *To Rest in Charity*, 82.
2. Allen, *Possessed*, xiii, 225, 243.
3. Collingwood, *Idea of History*, 282–83.

The Diary and the Witnesses

The journal spans forty-seven pages in the Allen printing and may be twenty-six pages in its original form.[4] As a source, it takes priority over the numerous popular narratives that surround the event. This approach would please historian Benedetto Croce: "History is never constructed from [secondary] narratives, but always from documents."[5] As the central aim of this book is to evaluate the theological coherence of the event, the *Diary* offers deeper credibility to the history around the event. Croce would be further pleased: "A history without relation to the document would be an unverifiable history; and the narrative in which it is given concrete form is historical narrative only in so far as it is a *critical exposition* of the document."[6]

The *Diary* thus offers a unique bridge to the past event. By itself, it will not have the empirical power expected to satisfy a scientific bent of mind that narrowly construes naturalistic boundaries. Historian R. G. Collingwood establishes this in the enterprise of history: "Wars and revolutions, and the other events with which it deals, are not deliberately produced by historians under laboratory conditions in order to be studied with scientific precision. Nor are they even observed by historians, in the sense in which events are observed by natural scientists."[7] With this different observation culture, the theological nature of the report becomes a sort of judge in the subject of our historical study.

Finally, the historical value of the *Diary* is predicated on its preternatural content in a uniquely difficult way. For forty days in 1949, Father Raymond Bishop made a daily record of inexplicable observations of a demonized boy and an attempted exorcism. Pastoral counseling coaches the boy, who responds with physical tantrums, violent barking, unexplainable scratches spelling words, and visions of hell. A team of Jesuits participate in shock and horror that convince them that the preternatural is at work. As a primary source, the *Diary* provides essential details of a boy seemingly torn between demonic control and an exorcism to expel it. The difficulty becomes augmented when the record comes with an interpretative Catholic theology at work. For example, they believe the liturgy of the rite of exorcism has compelled a message from the demon about its time of departure in the form of a riddle which they dramatically attempt to solve in the battle to free the boy. With events such as

4. Allen, *Possessed*, xiii, 225, 243; Hallowell, *Playing with Fire*, 7.
5. Croce, *History*, 12.
6. Croce, *History*, 14 (italics original).
7. Collingwood, *Idea of History*, 249.

this, a study of the *Diary* obviously requires a theological reading that shapes a methodology for historical retrieval. It begins with seeing this important source in the larger 1949 story.

Historical Access

From 1949 to 1978, the *Diary* lay forgotten in the drawer of one room of the Alexian Brothers Hospital in south St. Louis.[8] Like a time capsule buried in the earth, the journal sat unmolested for almost thirty years. A routine sweep of the building before its destruction unveiled the journal in the dresser of the room that had been sealed off before the closure of the wing. The finding of this copy eventually came into the hands of Thomas Allen, who would publish it in 2000, and a copy came to William Peter Blatty soon after authoring *The Exorcist* in 1971.

When Blatty was a Georgetown University student in 1950, he sought to obtain the diary from his professor, Father Eugene Gallagher. While Gallagher refused, the diary's partial disappearance from the office of the dean allows for its contents to be available.[9] When Blatty was writing the 1971 book *The Exorcist* that would become a 1973 box office success, he penned Father Bowdern a request to dialog about the event. The priest declined, having been directed to discretion by Archbishop Ritter and out of concern for the boy. He wrote back to Blatty: "Accordingly, we (a priest with me) kept a minute account each day of the happenings each preceding day and night . . . Our diary would be most helpful to anyone placed in a similar position as an exorcist in any future date."[10] The correspondence of Father Bowdern to Blatty affirms the legitimacy of the *Diary* that would later be affirmed by Father Walter Halloran. Another possible motive for making a journal of the events is suggested here by Bowdern, mainly as an instructional aid to demonization and exorcism. Blatty also claimed that Bowdern requested a copy of the diary for him from the Cardinal of St. Louis, but they declined him for the same reason of privacy and to avoid its sensationalism. After

---

8. For a summary of this discovery, see Allen, *Possessed*, 222–26; Faherty, *To Rest in Charity*, 199–222.

9. Erdman's source for this story is identified as Gallagher, who claims to have gained his details from eyewitness Father Charles O'Hara. A diary copy seems to have been available to Blatty's professor through their collegiality. See Erdman, "Truth," 50–51, 56; cf. Kelly, *Devil*, 95n60.

10. Allen, *Possessed*, xi (cf. 305).

The Diary and the Witnesses

the novel was written, Blatty explained that he received a copy from the Alexian Brothers.[11] As Father Bowdern would contact him regularly in years to follow, Blatty showed a sense of integrity and did not publicly reveal the name of the boy. In fact, in the advising of the screenplay, this author claims he changed the story of a demonized boy to a girl to honor the exorcist but also to protect the identity of the historical figure.[12] In a letter from Bowdern quoted in interview, Blatty gains the closest thing to an admission ever yielded by the exorcist: "I'm sorry. But I want to help you. I think a lot of good could be done for a lot of people if they knew what happened. But I can't . . . I can tell you one thing . . . The case I was involved with was the real thing. I had no doubt about it then. I have no doubt about it now. Good luck with your apostolate pursuits."[13]

In the early 1990s, Thomas Allen sought to uncover the primary source in his research around the 1949 exorcism. Allen could only point Father Walter Halloran, a Jesuit participant in the exorcism, to the inaccessible diary in a bank vault. Halloran authenticated it for him and idiosyncratically offered Allen a copy. Allen also claimed to have authenticated the journal through other sources, including one who provided pages 25–26 that were missing from the original 24-page discovery.[14] Up to five copies of the *Diary* have been kept confidential in two archdioceses, a Jesuit archive, at the Alexian Brothers Hospital, and one at a Washington, DC, hospital, likely Georgetown University Hospital.[15] Opsasnick recognizes that "there are several other copies floating around out there among private collectors."[16] In ecclesiastical procedure, Archbishop

---

11. Head, "Interview"; Blatty, *On The Exorcist*, 22.

12. Blatty, *On The Exorcist*, 22.

13. Head, "Interview"; Blatty's interview quoted here is an accurate paraphrase of the letter found in Blatty, *On The Exorcist*, 20–21.

14. Allen, *Possessed*, xiii, 225, 243.

15. Blatty, *On The Exorcist*, 20–21. Allen locates the copies more specifically in the Jesuit Provincial of the Missouri Province archive, the St. Louis Archdiocese archive, the Washington DC Archdiocese archive, the Alexian Brothers archives, and the final copy discovered. Allen, *Possessed*, xii–xiv, 299–300. It might be that one of the two copies held by the Alexian Brothers ended up in the drawer in the original room. Spitzer supports this claim, naming the provincial of the Missouri province of the Jesuits and the Archdiocese of St. Louis as receiving Bowdern's report. Spitzer, *Christ Versus Satan*, 153–54.

16. Opsasnick, "Haunted Boy," 6. Allen concurs how the diary had a habit of being copied (*Possessed*, 299).

Theology of a Diary

Ritter appointed an examiner to investigate and report on the case before formally closing it.[17]

Finally, the journal contains a further testimony of its evidence by including a letter dated April 29, 1949, from Father Bishop himself to the rector of the hospital, Brother Cornelius. "The inclosed [sic] report is a summary of the case which you have known for the past several weeks." The letter includes rationale for appealing to its confidentiality and an expressed appreciation for the ministry of the Alexian Brothers. It also identifies "the prayerful assistance of your [Alexian Brothers] Community was certainly a strong factor in winning a battle against Satan."[18] The protection of the manuscript and the substantiation of witnesses offers an impressive testimony that its recorded contents are authentic. Of course, the authenticity of the document does not guarantee the authentic nature of the event.

This book references this original diary penned by Father Bishop, citing *Diary* with the entry date of the primary source. Bishop was the assisting exorcist, and he spans the entire St. Louis phase of the exorcism. Allen calls it "Bowdern's diary" but clarifies that Bishop is the author of the record of events. He cites Father Walter Halloran as saying, "The diary was seen and approved by Father Bowdern."[19] Not released to the public until 2000 in the Thomas Allen story above, the diary now finds publication in three notable print works. Thomas B. Allen's *Possessed: The True Story of an Exorcism* contains the diary while the entire book offers a summary and analysis based on it. His story form of the event draws from the *Diary*, followed by the text itself with notes of additional sources that construct his narrative account.[20] The Christopher Saint Booth edition *The Exorcist Diary* is published with a posthumous co-author attribution to Raymond Bishop. The journal comprises the entire book besides a lengthy forward of other testimonies.[21] Sergio Rueda calls his own edition "The Jesuit Report," which is included in his analysis of the events in *Diabolical Possession and the Case Behind* The Exorcist.[22] The *Diary* is now available online in multiple locations.

17. John Waide, interview by W. Brian Shelton, October 30, 2024.
18. See "Letter from Father Bishop to Brother Cornelius" (April 29, 1949) in Allen, *Possessed*, 243–44.
19. Allen, *Possessed*, xii, 299.
20. Allen, *Possessed*, 245–91.
21. Bishop and Saint Booth, *Exorcist Diary*, 12–58.
22. Rueda, *Diabolical Possession*, 41–68.

HISTORICAL RETRIEVAL

The access to the *Diary* provides the historian an opportunity to evaluate the daily events of 1949 as they were reported by one exorcist priest. Additional information for evaluation comes from source history, living history, and mythical history. The *Diary* is complemented by interviews with other witnesses, second-hand testimonies, reports offered in historical periodicals, journalists on fact-finding missions, and finally scholars and specialists interpreting these data. Claims are credible, and they require comparison and continuity in the reconstruction of the event. Many of the other witnesses and second-hand reports share a Catholic perspective of the event. The theological element that is inseparable from the historical record deserves to be extensively explored for its contribution to the interpretation of events offered by the *Diary*.

The Primary Source and Its Primary Challenge

The significant historical challenge of this event is its preternatural nature. Research can plot the actions of people and locations of places in the story, but this case study inevitably is confronted by a faith element—a view of demons and exorcism—habitually viewed as ineligible for historical study. Dennis Kinlaw once remarked about the difficult topic of demons, "Objectivity is needed but the subjective character of the search complicates our problem."[23] For a case of demonization and exorcism to be researched and eligible for acceptance, the inquiry into its historicity and the truth claims of the diarist inevitably requires a worldview that allows for spirit beings. Skeptics will immediately identify *prima facie* belief in the events as prejudicing any interpretation of the occasion beyond the scope of normal historical inquiry. However, the enterprise of history aims for a genuine discovery and recovery of the past to give meaning to the event. Where natural philosophy and social-scientific solutions cannot satisfy a full explanation of events, the faith element fills the gaps of the inexplicable. This faith is not merely a "possibility," but religious faith permits eligibility beyond the natural like that of a Christian system of belief. This book thus examines a historiography *in faith*. Such a recognition of an interpretive worldview can provide a more authentic approach

---

23. Kinlaw, "Demythologization," 29.

to the past in cases like this, suspending any abrupt dismissal of evidence on the grounds of metaphysical ineligibility.

Access to the historical event goes through the *Diary*, preserved as a testimony of its author's belief. In turn, the historian must evaluate and interpret the recorded testimony of the priest, processing and framing the actions attributed to the demon and a Catholic understanding that characterized the priests. This study certainly recognizes that the priests recorded the events as they perceived them, and no false motive emerges to disqualify *their* interpretation of what they saw. Our interest lies in the theological understanding of their observation: diagnosing demonization, envisioning an authoritative exorcism, applying the liturgy of the rite and holy objects, and other Catholic qualities. A recognizable historical method is necessary to treat such a bizarre past event, and it begins with recognizing the standards employed in handling historical writings.

Canons of Historiography

Accessing the diary requires a recognizable historiography. Historians operate under certain canons for historical inquiry and writing. These are standards for historical projects, acceptable and expected methods for evaluating the past. For example, a historian is expected to identify the author and occasion of a diary like this one, seek to understand the author's viewpoint reported in the text, and identify favored interpretations of the events. History too often stops here, unwilling to offer a judgment on the veracity of the claims from the text. William Lane Craig identifies this halt characterizing as the critical historical method: "The historian *qua* historian cannot tell us whether God is the cause of some event; he can at best tell us that certain people regarded an event as miraculous."[24] It is a different canon of historiography to consider whether the historian can identify the textual claims to be accurate accounts of a past event. This project seeks to do just this.[25]

Any issues of the theological validity of the 1949 exorcism, including the invasion of a demon or the deliverance of a God, would normally be considered a project *independent* of historical inquiry. Una Cadegan

---

24. Craig, *Reasonable Faith*, 350 (for elaboration on this critical approach leading to the inability to acknowledge miracles through historical writings, see esp. 247–81).

25. This section is indebted to William Katerberg, who helped shape the "public evidence" and "limit experience" dimensions of the historical method presented here (William Katerberg, correspondence with author, November 15, 2007).

typifies this norm: "Mending the breach between philosophy and theology is not part of an historian's job description."[26] She instead seeks neutrality in agreeing or disagreeing with the past participants, objectively avoiding it by not posing a question of reality or judging for historical fact. However, historian R. G. Collingwood describes the unfair attempts sometimes made by such perspectives, as he maintains that history cannot be scientific like a scientist would expect: "The scientific historian reads them [texts] with a question in his mind, having taken the initiative by deciding for himself what he wants to find out from them . . . the scientific historian puts them to the torture, twisting a passage ostensibly about something quite different into an answer to the question he has decided to ask."[27] Even more divergent from Cadegan is Peter Berger, who insists that sometimes "ordinary reality is 'abolished' and something terrifyingly other shines through." Such a moment he calls *der andere Zustand* ("the other condition") that pushes normal canons of historiography a step beyond standard limits.[28] This project challenges a certain status quo when it permits the scientific and the physical to be joined with the metaphysical, broadening its sphere of limitations to allow for the possibility of demonization and actual exorcism as historical events. Standard methodology is kept, but it is now accompanied with elements of the Christian faith. Such a historical method operates *from* a Christian faith.

    A burden of proof lies with any historian that takes the risk of allowing a primary source like the *Diary* to make its claim to the preternatural. Such a position does not deny that the diary by its private and past nature still risks isolated reflection or idiosyncrasy that could have shaped the historical record, mainly that descriptions merely represent what was understood by the recorder. However, it affirms neither that the potential subjective interpretation of the events by the *Diary* author must be accepted nor that the non-natural causes must be rejected. For the Christian, theology is an expression of historical supernaturalism joining the natural world. As a project in Christian inquiry, this attempt at historical recovery centers on the issue of theological credibility to inform historical credibility. The theology reported in the *Diary* can serve as a litmus test to its historical claims. Two essentials are thus at work as we

---

26. Cadegan, "Not All Autobiography is Scholarship," 53.
27. Collingwood, *Idea of History*, 269–70.
28. Berger, *Far Glory*, 128–29; Taylor, *Secular Age*, 5–6.

approach the *Diary*: the first is the theological means for judgment and the second is the plausibility for belief.

The Measure of Theology

In this theological enterprise, theology becomes a jurist. While history and science bear on the interpretation of the event, theology also judges the plausibility of the historical record. If the theology of the event proves "good," then a theological support joins other historical criteria in making judgment on its veracity. The theology that interlaces with the historical testimony can strengthen the evidentiary power of the event or it can discredit the credibility of the claims to the event.

The primary interest of this book is theological and even spiritual, asking how incidents of preternaturalism and supernaturalism can be judged as real and what they mean for the Christian faith. Similarly, the Catholic nature of the record is evaluated for the context of the claims in the *Diary*. This approach makes the book the first theological treatment of the 1949 exorcism. As this book uniquely examines and evaluates the Catholic theology that surrounds the priest's report, at times it filters the sacerdotal through an evangelical Protestant and more biblical critique in an irenic and balanced fashion.

This considerable approach presses the limits of historiography by hinging its veracity on the credibility of its theology. The strategy for this attempt employs an historical method typical of Christian thought. The epistemological source of Scripture serves as a standard for evaluating similar demonizations. The Catholic elements of ecclesiology are weighed to inform the efficacy of the exorcism. The role of medical tests is weighed to consider a mental illness alternative. The witnesses are interviewed to establish corroborating testimony. The newspapers, claimants, third-hand testimonies, and influential cultural paradigms are also weighed for accuracy. Major incongruence between standards for theology and the observations of theology would detract from the reasonability of the historical record. In other words, this study posits that historical methods can be used to deal with historical events related to the metaphysical if a reasonable doubt can be established for a naturalistic alternative to this event. The preternatural and supernatural elements are thus incorporated into the measures of historicity. Noteworthy here is that this study does not engage popular evangelical spiritual warfare trends and does not establish a favorite method of exorcism practice. Yet this is an enterprise in faith, not believing that it is reasonable to understand creation without the help of the Creator and a corresponding revelation.[29]

Through this process, the linking of the theological to the historical pulls the events closer to us through its scrutiny. Christians are commonly caught with an overarching, theoretical belief in the preternatural or the supernatural but display a tendency to dismiss the supernatural in any specific case. Then, case after case could be natural in their minds, so that no case of the inexplicable can be deemed supernatural. Craig Keener describes his own journey from unbelief to the authoring of a book on miracles: "When I was an atheist, I didn't believe in miracles. After I was converted through a dramatic encounter with the Holy Spirit, I understood that God did spiritual things, but I still didn't expect him to do anything *visible*. That is, as a Christian, I now believed in miracles *in principle*, but I did not really expect to see one."[30]

If theologians cannot articulate metaphysical appreciation of historical events, then a risk develops that our belief system is separated from our historical method or our religious practices. If theology is our focus then the church is our beneficiary. The victims of demonization have been subjected to a force inimical to their own welfare, suffering in the theater of God and Satan. For Catholicism, this is entirely a pastoral and ecclesial enterprise, a ministry of the priest to one who may or may not even be Catholic. The hope is study of this event will reinforce their supernatural, biblical worldview by offering one healthy, well-documented, and theologically sound case of exorcism. In this case, it would be the best documented case in the twentieth century. If the theology proves sound enough, and if the evidence proves plausible enough, then the profit comes to the church and its Christian academy. In fact, by taking a theological approach to the 1949 exorcism with an eye to the alternative approaches and conclusions to cause and effect, this book fills a void. After all, Malachi Martin remarks, "The Church is the only element in society with the authority and the availing remedy to counteract such manifest evil." If the church denies its legacy, if its leaders turn their backs to cases, or if they discount the claims, "Then actual victims of true demonic activity are left with no hope."[31]

29. Collins, *Science and Faith*, 28, where this is posited with similar rhetoric.
30. Keener, *Miracles Today*, xi.
31. Martin, *Hostage to the Devil*, xvi.

Plausibility for Belief

A working goal for this theological enterprise is a criterion of possibility based on a threshold of plausibility. The comprehensive judgments about veracity are based on a level of reasonableness. The attempt here is to pose the question of whether the testimony of preternatural and supernatural events, accompanied by their contemporary medical and scientific inexplicability of the events, can rise to a convincing wonder to call it real.

Philosopher and mathematician Pierre Simon LaPlace suggests that determining the probability of an event requires that stranger events require more evidence: "The more extraordinary the event, the greater the need of its being supported by strong proofs."[32] While LaPlace addresses probability of chance, his set of principles can apply to evidence that support the chance of possibility of events. This book takes on the challenge of the extraordinary necessity to evidence with reasonability—suspending philosophical naturalism and its material explanations to entertain the biblical claims of demons as a competing alternative. To do so, it must rise to the threshold of the evidentiary—in a sense, to offer enough proof—that the orthodox view of the preternatural can find support.

Plausibility requires a threshold of the evidentiary. The unfolding research seeks a judgment about the reasonableness of the historicity of this event, mainly the possibility that this occurrence was one of demonic invasion and successful exorcism. Behan McCullagh calls this threshold of the evidentiary "justification conditions." He remarks: "Justification conditions are reasons which we have at present for thinking historical descriptions are true." Granted, they "cannot be appealed to as evidence justifying historical descriptions," but they can serve as evidence towards veracity but without proving it.[33] While we might limit what can be known about the original event, we can still recognize that a possible belief in this demonization and exorcism to be justified. Thus, it allows for plausibility when taken at its value, including after comparison of other alternative explanations. This same approach is taken by William Lane Craig here. He describes that if the "facts can be historically established with a reasonable degree of confidence and if alternative naturalistic

---

32. LaPlace, *Philosophical Essay*, 17.

33. McCullagh, *Justifying Historical Descriptions*, 10. Likewise, "Although historical descriptions cannot be proved true beyond all possibility of error, they can often be proved probably true, given empirical assumptions" (4).

The Diary and the Witnesses

explanations for these facts can be shown to be implausible . . . then the preferred explanation ought to be the one given in the documents themselves."[34] This objectivity includes confronting the claim around any inability to acknowledge preternatural or supernatural events from historical writings, as seen below in philosophical naturalism: "The objective facts can lead a historian to abandon his naturalistic hypothesis in fulfilling the conditions of a best explanation."[35]

Evidence and its corresponding plausibility mature in layers in this study. The bottom layer is a phenomenal story of the preternatural and the supernatural come from the *Diary* of a priest, the other priestly eyewitnesses, the collective priestly silence that suppresses motives beyond genuineness, and the public eyewitnesses. A second layer of private, second-hand testimonies of the priests emerge alongside the newspaper reports from the era. A third layer of researchers engaged in fact-finding efforts in the decades to follow, including Blatty in the writing of *The Exorcist* and Allen in releasing the *Diary*. The outer layer is that of the legends surrounding the event in popular culture.

Discernment comes at each layer to distinguish a set of believable possibilities. Sometimes belief is suspended at key junctures to allow the historical voices to speak in their context with a measure of equity and possibility. In this vein of integrity, Grant Wacker calls for a moral consistency that requires the historian to present the historical information and offer interpretation with justice, shouldering the responsibility of a "heightened accountability" to present a "fairness to the data and fairness to the reader."[36] Great effort has been made to organize the events for clarity, to qualify the events where stipulations might govern, and to permit the testimony of the participants to declare their witness.

One central element that might detract from plausibility includes the religious positions of the witnesses. Yet our examination ahead reveals that Allen was a professed agnostic, a mainline Lutheran prayer meeting would not expect manifestations, Catholic culture resisted demonic cases, and Bowdern maintained lifelong confidentiality surrounding the events. At every turn when the exorcist had an opportunity to profit from the story, his remarks were few, a silent integrity persisted, and historical plausibility finds reinforcement.

---

34. Craig, *Reasonable Faith*, 360.
35. Craig, *Reasonable Faith*, 240.
36. Wacker, "Understanding the Past," 173–74.

Seventy-five years later, a corresponding element of plausibility is our commitment to the Christian faith as an admitted bias. For Christians, the supernatural and the spiritual are legitimate variables in the equation of historical events and our understanding of those events. These introduce set of principles which run contrary the solely scientific or Enlightenment paradigm of cause and effect are feely admitted. Craig Keener remarks, "Beliefs are not only a matter of evidence but also a matter of the interpretive grids through which we read the evidence."[37] While Scripture informs a Christian theology of demons, this book does not propose a "sole authority model" of Scripture naïvely placed above scientific evidence or historical possibility. It also seeks to avoid a "separate authority model" in which Scripture fails to intersect fully with science or history.[38] Instead, a "foundational authority" or worldview model is employed, which claims that "the major contribution of the Bible to our academic pursuits is that it gives us a worldview foundation from which to do our studies in science, social science, and the arts. This *worldview* approach acknowledges that beliefs do make a difference in academic pursuits. One's faith or worldview does matter when one engages in the learning process."[39] Similarly, paradigms like the Wesleyan Quadrilateral afford us the opportunity to evaluate phenomena like demonization through Scripture, tradition, reason, and experience. For example, Don Thorsen writes, "If a person's testimony is experimentally investigated and sufficiently verified in accordance with Scripture, tradition, and reason, it is reasonable to judge such witness as true and worthy of consideration as evidence of the truth of Christianity."[40] The faith element shapes our interpretation of this story just as it shaped the observations of the Jesuit priests who performed the exorcism seventy years ago.

In conclusion, historical retrieval involves first the suspension of naturalism in an opportunity to judge the preternatural. Timothy Keller posits it this way: "We come to every individual evaluation with all sorts of experiences and background beliefs that strongly influence our thinking and the way our reason works. It is not fair, then, to demand

---

37. Keener, *Miracles Today*, 1.

38. Both of these models are identified and discussed as integrative faith and learning models, as is the third arrived at next, in Beers and Jane Beers, "Integration of Faith and Learning."

39. Cosgrove, *Foundations of Christian Thought*, 57.

40. Thorsen, *Wesleyan Quadrilateral*, 209.

an argument that all rational people would have to bow to."[41] In turn, historical retrieval offers a call for integrity of historical inquiry means that our study cannot demand an outcome, either. An attempt is made to be accurate, fair, and researched, pursuing an historical objectivity while neither denying a Christian worldview nor slanting interpretation to support it. In fact, the requirement to suspend naturalistic explanation works the other way, too. The historical analysis of an event like the 1949 exorcism requires a bridle on hasty belief about the preternatural. As landmark historian R. G. Collingwood distinguishes scientific history from a host of other philosophical approaches, he promotes an awareness of limitations in historical inquiry: even a convincing perception of the past does not make the events real, and the historian must realize that uncontestable proof is ultimately impossible.[42] Historical retrieval can then see canons of historiography have room to explore, explain, and make judgment about what is written in the *Diary* and from the sources beyond it. Theology becomes the central way to evaluate the historical report in our enterprise. The resultant data can then have opportunity to rise to a level of plausibility, realizing that "proof" is a variable term, conditioned by culture measured in scientific, historical, sociological, and ecclesiastical ways. Yet, with faith underlying our interpretation of the evidence, plausibility becomes attainable.

DIARY CONTENTS

The *Diary* is a daily journal of the St. Louis phase of the demonization, augmented by a background section of the Georgetown phase. Its entries come by date beginning Monday, March 7, and ending Tuesday, April 19. Daily entries make up the core of the journal, with thirty-six entries comprising a diagnosis phase of nine entries and an exorcism phase of twenty-seven entries. Information about the prior Georgetown phase and the early St. Louis days comes in the "Background" section to start the *Diary* report, events that the family likely related to Father Bishop. Included in the count is one daily entry with a positive follow-up to the exorcism that comes at the end of the diary. Occasionally, the diary skips a day. For example, Friday, March 25 briefly describes Robbie first restless, then resisting the priests, before stating in that entry how Monday,

---

41. Keller, *Reason for God*, 118.
42. Collingwood, *Idea of History*, 134–204.

Tuesday, and Wednesday night were uneventful. The detailed entries begin again on Thursday, March 31. The Saturday and Sunday nights are not mentioned.

While an overview of the events comprising the 1949 exorcism came above in chapter 1, this section gives special attention to the theological elements from the *Diary* entries. Daily activities display the priests' ecclesiastical values in action, while key junctures in the narrative reveal their theological mindset from the encounters. When the weeks of exorcism involve numerous reoccurring manifestations, the rhythm of the entries lessen the preternatural effects and overshadow the developmental aspects of the demonization. Almost every day has environmental, physical, behavioral, and knowledge manifestations; they are sometimes reported as matter of fact. Theological elements in these collective events make up a timeline here as a basis for theological evaluation in the three chapters to follow: demonization, the rite, and exorcism. For this section, whenever the narrative offers the obvious *Diary* entry date, those footnotes are omitted.

Background Section

A "Case Study" launches the diary with biographical information on the family and background developments to the case. Robbie is identified as born in 1935, now an Evangelical Lutheran, who was baptized Lutheran six months after birth. The baptismal record and faith practices of his father, mother, maternal grandmother, and paternal grandfather are listed. These notes frame the family culture and any influence of the Christian faith surrounding Robbie. The priests would have recognized that not one of the individuals were practicing Catholics, depriving their efforts of minor compatibility with the faith expressed in their exorcism efforts. This incompatibility is mitigated by April 1 when Robbie begins his conversion to Catholicism and can participate as an insider in the exorcism effort.

The case background also identifies the events beginning on January 15, 1949, in Cottage City, Maryland. A dripping noise, a shaking picture of Christ, and scratching in the floorboards marked this first night. The latter comes as a key symptom, moving from under the grandmother's bed the first night to under Robbie's bed by the thirteenth night. They would eventually mark his flesh as a demonized victim. Next, the movement was recognized as "the sound of squeaking shoes," heard whenever Robbie went to bed. The march of the sound to his bed seems to foreshadow the demonization of Robbie.

On February 26, scratches first appeared on Robbie "for about four successive nights," becoming clearer and seemingly "to have been scratched on the body by claws." The family then decided that taking the boy to St. Louis would "avoid some of these strange manifestations." The word "Louis" appeared on the body's ribs, "Saturday" on his hip, and "3½ weeks" on his chest. Realizing later séance activities, especially by Robbie's mother, the length of time might have been prompted by the family inquiry of the spirit for guidance. Amidst these scratches, the background insists, "The printing always appeared without any motion on the part of the boy's hands," and "the markings could not have been done by the boy," especially because of the one on his back. The writing continued after the relocation, with "No" and "N" appearing when the mother seemed to inquire about his return to school, as she "feared disobeying this order."

A section of the background includes other manifestations. Here, various items moved or flew across the room: fruit, food, the kitchen table, a breadbox, a comb that extinguished candles, a Bible, a rocker, and his desk at school. Interestingly, "R's desk at school moved about on the floor similar to the place on a Ouija board," connecting this manifestation to the occultic activity of the boy and the family.

Another section of the background includes a list of witnesses mixed with additional demonic indicators. It claims fourteen different witnesses "to testify and verify different phenomena." Two Lutheran ministers are cited, with one matching the events of Father Schulze. A psychiatrist examined Robbie "but declared that he did not believe the phenomena," reporting how "the boy was quite normal." A physician examined him, finding him to be "a normal boy, but somewhat high-strung." A spiritist was called to dispel the spirit without success. Here, the aunt is named as participating in spiritism. Here the journal claims that Father Hughes was consulted, did not meet with the boy, but had proposed exorcism to the bishop. Recognized the narrative above, this reminds readers that the background to the case was an oral narrative, likely offered by the parents to Father Bishop and likely under a measure of duress.

A final section of the background summarizes activities since the family's arrival in St. Louis but before the daily entries begin. Witnesses are cited: two aunts, four uncles, and four cousins. This witness count matches the two lodgings of their first few nights.[43] The scratching "no school" was seen by four people, it claims. Many saw the moving mattress, moving bedroom furniture, and scratching on the mattress on two occasions. This St. Louis narrative reveals a sequence of events whereby the demonization rose to the level of the President of Saint Louis University, Father Paul Reinert, after Father Bishop consulted with him and Father Kenny. Prayers and a priestly blessing were the priests' application of choice up to this point.

Major Events Shaping Theology

January 15 marks the first manifestations in the house. The death of Robbie's aunt on January 26 would provide elements of timing and activities for communication between the family and the spirit. February 17 Father Schulze hosted Robbie in his home and himself witnessed manifestations suggesting that the boy, and not the home, was the source of these activities. From February 28 to March 3, Robbie was in the hospital for medical and psychiatric evaluation. On March 5, the family departed from Maryland to St. Louis.[44]

The *Diary* then sets into the daily entries of the St. Louis phase. The entries are sometimes brief, especially when no demonic resistance was evidenced by the priests. Some entries are long, with cycles of resistance, manifestations, and peace. The contents are descriptive yet somewhat matter-of-fact, reported free of emotional or melodramatic commentary. Revisited here from these entries are the events instrumental to the theological assessment in the chapters to follow.

---

43. The *Diary* remarks how their first St. Louis night was at the home of Robbie's non-Catholic aunt and uncle, while the second night at Robbie's Catholic aunt and non-Catholic uncle. These were in the Normandy and Bel-Nor neighborhoods, respectively (see *Diary*, "March 7"; "March 8"; Taylor, *Devil Came to St. Louis*, 67; Allen, *Possessed*, 43–45).

44. The *Diary* background does not report the travel date. This timeline follows Allen, *Possessed*, 41.

The Diary and the Witnesses

Robbie's Manifestations by Date and Place		Greater City Area
1/15–2/16	Cottage City House	
2/17	Schulze home	
2/18–26	Cottage City House	Georgetown
2/28–3/3	Georgetown Hospital	
3/4–6(?)	Cottage City House	
3/7	Normandy House	
3/8–20	Bel-Nor House	
3/21–22	Alexian Brothers Hospital	
3/22	Bel-Nor House	
3/23–25(?)	St. Xavier College Church	St. Louis
3/28–31	Bel-Nor House	
4/1–2	St. Xavier College Church	
4/3–4	Bel-Nor House	
4/5–9	Cottage City House	Georgetown
4/10–19	Alexian Brothers Hospital	St. Louis

Table 1. Major Events and Locations

Within two days of the family's arrival in St. Louis, they hold a séance with the extended family using "an alphabetical medium," either a Ouija board or something akin to it, with a likely anticipation of gaining direction from the spirit towards procuring the hidden treasure. "A code of messages became evident," as the spirit claimed to be the deceased aunt.[45] Around March 9, one of Robbie's cousins asks her Saint Louis University professor Father Bishop for clerical assistance. The *Diary* of that day has Bishop blessing the house for the first time, employing a relic of St. Margaret Mary and holy water, which were met by a shaking mattress and scratches on Robbie's body. The *Diary* claims credibility as it records, "It should be remarked that during the fifteen minutes the boy was not out of view of six observers," testifying to the impossibility of manufactured manifestations. Two days later, Father Bowdern visits the house for the first time, bringing relics and administering prayer. Observers were noted as going downstairs "to review some of the history of the case," likely the conversation in which Bishop gathered data for the Background to the case.[46] A loud crash interrupted them, and upon return to

45. *Diary*, "March 7."
46. *Diary*, "March 11."

Robbie's bedroom they discovered a relocated bookcase, the unexplained movement of a stool, and the relocation of a crucifix and relics. An exit of the priests must have taken place without *Diary* notation, because that night a séance—or at least a dialog with the spirit—took place by the family with explicit references to the location of the money. It then harkens back to the timing of the aunt's death with a parallel of the shaking mattress. Such inquiry of the spirit's intention surely happened without the priests, as this entry sees a combination of soothsaying with historical connections. The priests have found themselves in a position of pastoral ministry to a boy that could be demonized, surrounded by a family that experiments with the occult. At this point, the *Diary* is a combination of reporting of the family experiences and the priest's experiences.

Early March in St. Louis was marked by the shaking mattress, movement of relics, scratching in the bed or on Robbie's body, and peculiar family attempts to communicate with the spirit. The dynamics abruptly change on March 16 as the *Diary* reports, "Permission was granted by the Most Reverend Archbishop Joseph E. Ritter that Father William S. Bowdern, S. J., Pastor of the College Church in St. Louis might read the prayers of exorcism according to the *Roman Ritual*." Father Walter Halloran is introduced as attending with Fathers Bowdern and Bishop to the home that night. He will be an important witness in the decades to follow. Beginning at 10:30 pm, Robbie was invited to make contrition. It is an epic moment when the *Diary* reports, "Next Father Bowdern in surplice and stole began the prayers of exorcism." Immediately the *praecipio* of the liturgy becomes instrumental, as the first responses to the exorcism were scratches on Robbie's stomach, then his "legs, thighs, stomach, back, chest, face and throat." The repeated *praecipio* demanding the demon's name saw an imprint of the devil, the word "hell," and the word "go" with a mark pointing to the crotch, "An indication which might have meant that the devil would leave by way of urination or excrement." The speculation of the meaning of the messages prompted by the *praecipio* had begun. Foreshadowing seems to be at work when, at the mention of St. Michael in the liturgy, extreme resistance took place:

> R began sparring. He struck the board back of his bed strong blows with his fist, and then began punching, the pillow with more than ordinary force. As he swung his arms in violence he spoke of the conflict which appeared to him in all the manifestations since the beginning in January there were no words spoken by R. when he seemed to be under the influence of the devil.

The Diary and the Witnesses

> The family had not seen such violent reaction as was shown on this night and the following. Evidently the exorcism prayers had stirred up the devil.[47]

Noteworthy here is the violent reaction at the *praecipio* and to the mention of St. Michael, a distinction offered between Robbie's voice and the voice of the demon, and the recognition by the exorcists that "the exorcism prayers had stirred up the devil."

March 18 hosts the next significant event that introduces elements of theology. During the reading of the rite, "He writhed under the sprinkling of Holy Water. He fought and screamed in a diabolical, high-pitched voice . . . He shouted, jumped, and swung his fists. His face was devilish, and he snapped his teeth in fury." As the priests persisted, just after midnight, Robbie "held his arms high above himself in supplication. Then he made as though he were trying to vomit from his stomach." This moment proffered signs of exorcism—worship and expulsion. "'He's going, going, . . .' and finally, 'There he goes.' His body fell limp upon (unintelligible) bed in a perfectly relaxed condition." The boy also reported a vision of "a huge, dark cloud of black vapor" walking away into a cloud. Yet the exorcism proved to be a ruse. About 2:00 am, Robbie cried, "He's coming back! He's coming back!" Bowdern returned an hour later with priests to read the rite, not leaving until 7:00 am that morning. The next night was one occasion in which Robbie sang "Blue Danube" and "The Old Rugged Cross" in random fashion, later accompanied by demonic mockery. The singing was noted as "very beautifully in a clear voice and with real finesse."

Monday, March 21 saw Robbie admitted to the Alexian Brother Hospital, returning home the next day. On March 23, Father Bowdern escorted the boy to the St. Xavier College Church rectory, where he received instruction of a Catholic catechumen. Resistance to the liturgy included violence to Fathers Halloran and Roo's nose. Robbie urinated at the *praecipio*, complaining of a burning pain. He proffered sexually explicated language and gestures to the priests, while the *Diary* notes he was not prone to such behavior. Convulsions, barking, and singing marked the night until 2:30 am. March 24 saw similar resistance, adding "kindly expressions" and "passing foul air" to the list. His strength was impressive, noting how four men were required to hold him down. The *Diary* records how Father Bowdern calculated the "X" of the first night to

---

47. *Diary*, "March 16."

mean "10," predicting this to be the night before expulsion. The demon expressed revulsion to the use of Latin while also testifying to seeing one priest in hell in eight years. Again, the evening ended at 2:30 am. March 25 saw more of the same, noting that a priest blessed the house where Robbie would soon return. At this point, the forces of Catholic ecclesiology are underway to meet an enemy of the church, with the victim Robbie right at the center of this battle. The sacramentals of the rite and the relics met with mocking, taunting, convulsions, and violence as programmatic for the diary entries.

After some days of solace, the night of March 31 began with the shaking of the bed. Then a remarkable event took place in the communication of the demon around the *praecipio*. Robbie began writing with his finger on the sheet, which he explained was what he saw on a blackboard. Notes taken by a cousin were recorded in the *Diary*. It begins with a timeframe: "I will stay ten days, but will return in four days," with additional details listed above in "The Event." The subject of Latin and English, as well as references to leaving in ten days, are cited. Among the written remarks is, "I will answer in the name of Spite." A seemingly replication of a map and a claim, "Yeah, this is what I got on the Ouija board," were listed. Of particular note were the claims, "I am the devil himself" and "You will have to pray for a month in the Catholic Church." At the same time, the boy who was writing was beginning to hope that God was becoming stronger and that the Catholic Church could be instrumental in the success of any exorcism. The *Diary* does not comment on the priestly reflection on the timing here, but the details about the mechanics of Robbie's recording are precise. Such an entry describes how the *praecipio* command for the demon to identify the day and hour of its departure elicited a potential timeline that would be interpreted by the priests, often with uncertainty.

On April 1, Robbie's parents felt that his conversion to Catholicism was important. His baptismal sponsors drove Robbie to St. Xavier College Church when he complained of his feet burning. This is when he grabbed the steering wheel before being constrained. The *Diary* notes how the car radio would not work when Robbie was in convulsions. The attempt at baptism was heavily resisted, particularly when asked if Robbie renounced the devil and his ways. A worker named Michael is named for his assistance as a mark of credibility. However, Robbie was conscious enough for the rite to advance and he was baptized. The diarist reflects that the Lutheran baptism must not have been effective. The episode highlights the role that the Catholic faith will play in this exorcism—both the boy's belief and the priests' authority. At 11:30 pm, the family seems to have returned home.

The next day saw more resistance at the administration of the Eucharist. "R rallied for brief moments yet whenever Father Bowdern brought the Eucharistic particle near R, the boy went into his spell." Five times he spit it out. After praying the rosary and to Our Lady of Fatima, he received communion. Yet, on the ride back home, Robbie grabbed Father O'Flaherty as he drove before being contained. In a seemingly destructive manner, at home he grabbed for the reliquary of the Holy Cross before turning to the ritual book, tearing out four pages of the rite of exorcism which "he grasped with lightning speed." The exorcist commanded the *praecipio* in response, leading to "'Stick it up your ass,' or by 'No!' or by a laugh of ridicule." An hour later, jumbled Latin would be another response to the prompt. Yet "go" and "X" were scratched amid unfriendly responses. Similar activities followed on April 3, where the priests Bowdern, Van Roo, and O'Flaherty were named. The *Diary* reports "a kind of devilish prophecy concerning R's little cousin" was proffered. While behaving in rhythmic fashion while singing, the demon declared, "You will die tonight. You will die tonight." The violence led the priests to bind his arms and gloves his hands before quiet came at 3:30 am. The lists of participating priests during these entries expands, an important element in the witness list and later testimonies. The *praecipio* remains central in the liturgy and drama of the exorcism.

On Monday, April 4, the family returned to Washington, DC. The next day, Bowdern met with Hughes, who had arranged with the Chancellor of the Archdiocese of Washington for the exorcism to continue. However, their ability to land him in a Catholic hospital was unsuccessful. By April 6, Father Bowdern had relented that the Alexian Brothers Hospital in St. Louis would be required. Despite the explicit statement that all parties felt Robbie should not be at home,[48] two more days mark the return to Cottage City to an unnamed place. April 7 hosted several brands on Robbie's skin at the *praecipio*, while a Hail Mary saw the number "4" and several other undisguisable marks. The demon claimed control over Robbie by predicting at 2:00 am that it would wake him and that it would keep the priests until 6:00 am. While he effectively woke

---

48. *Diary*, "April 5."

the boy, sleep ensued soon to end the night. A list of nine witnesses was offered in this entry.

Throughout these entries, the *Diary* contains dozens of details of singing, humming, screaming, stiffening, convulsions, vulgarity, spitting, violence, and disgust of holy objects, with lapses in and out of consciousness. Many of these mark classic cases of demonization and corresponding manifestations. April 8 lists such a range of resistance to serve as one sample from the *Diary*: "This continued with shorter spells until 1:20 am: violence, spitting, nonsense jumbling of Latin questions, singing 'Blue Danube,' 'Ave Maria,' and so fourth [sic]. There was filthy talk and movements and filthy attacks on those at the bedside concerning masturbation and contraceptives, sexual relations of Priests and Nuns."

On April 9, the party returned to St. Louis without incident named. By April 10, Robbie entered the Alexian Brothers Hospital for the final haul of the exorcism. To the surprise of the priests, he received communion without resistance. On the 11th, the scratching "exit" seemed to point to his crotch, possibly suggesting the medium of exit for the demon. His crotch and urination burned painfully. The word "Hell" was scratched on his chest and thigh. Communion resulted in seizures at the boy's liturgical response of the word "communion." The administration of the Eucharist by the priest to his parishioner became a regular act of worship, a spiritual complement to the reading of the rite of exorcism. It became its own battleground in the fight against the demon, leading the diarist to write this night: "It seemed that the attempts to administer the Sacrament of the Eucharist roused the devil more than ordinarily."[49]

The April 13 trip to the Jesuit retreat center, the Little White House, exemplifies the competition between the awareness of Robbie and the dominant potential of the demon. The boy witnessed the Stations of the Cross, perhaps having a spiritually reflective experience on the path of Christ to Calvary. Halloran explained the boy's interest: "Not many 11-year-old [sic] would say they were interested in finding out about the Stations of the Cross, but he was."[50] However, the demon drove the boy towards the edge of a cliff before Halloran caught him. This day also heard another confession of a time of departure at 11:00 pm, but when it did not come the diarist comments on their consciousness of the false

---

49. *Diary*, "April 11."

50. Some details of this event are not contained in the *Diary*, but only an abbreviated experience including resistance. Brown, "Interview"; Flood, "SLU Legends and Lore."

The Diary and the Witnesses

claim. The boy displayed "relatively more physical power than at any previous time."[51] In response to the Latin *praecipio*, the demon responded in pig Latin. Noteworthy is that diarist recognized the imitation of the Latin was "clear and distinct."[52] The boy cried "Fire" to disrupt the reading of the rite. This week is a period of seemingly escalated physical violence, coarse language, and resistance to the Eucharist. The diary commends the Alexian Brothers for praying for hours this day, as well as constant adoration of the Blessed Sacrament to start Holy Week.

The story enters Holy Week with a sense of anticipation. The resistance to exorcism continues, but now the victim has become Catholic, at times he receives holy communion, the hospital provides a spiritually dynamic and safe environment, and the significance of Easter looms on the calendar. The detail of the rector placing a statue of Michael the archangel in Robbie's room seems minimal in the narrative alongside features like the placement of a statue of Our Lady of Fatima and the programmatic adoration of the Blessed Sacrament. Like foreshadowing in a novel, this seemingly minor element would be emblematic of the exorcism of 1949. The *Diary* even remarks how "one of the most effective prayers of exorcism was that dedicated to St. Michael."[53] The only other mention of Michael in the *Diary* came on March 16, when Robbie "began sparring" at his mention in the rite prayer.

When Robbie refused the Eucharist on Easter Sunday, it began a day that likely discouraged the Easter optimism of the priests. After stomping on the priest's scapular like a demeaning of the office it symbolized, Robbie resisted the chapel as the demon spoke, "I will not let him go to Mass. Everyone thinks it will be good for him." Confrontation through symbols seems to continue as Robbie asks for a knife "that he might cut an Easter egg," while the request was in the context of having threatened that he would "kill those who molested him," seeming these exorcist priests. In the quote above in "The Event" from this day, Thomas Allen suggested an eerier mood than usual, with an increased frequency of the demon's voice and witnesses claiming a chill passing through them when in the room with the boy.[54]

51. *Diary*, "April 13."
52. *Diary*, "April 13." The remark, "In no instance up to this point in the case has the devil answered in Latin" realizes how Bowdern had expected the demonic response at the *praecipio* to be in Latin. This is explicitly stated in the entry of April 2.
53. *Diary*, "Holy Thursday–Good Friday–Holy Saturday, April 14, 15, 16."
54. Allen, *Possessed*, 207.

In a rare occasion, the priests exited at 12:45 pm.

Monday, April 18, is the climax of the exorcism. It also offers a climax of theological elements, spanning the range of both demonic manifestations and Catholic ecclesiastical authority. The boy smashes the holy water vial and throws the crucifix placed in his hand. The medals seemed to cause a burning sensation to the boy's skin. Violence, urination, a seizure, singing, and mocking marked the interactions of the boy with the priests. In response to the *praecipio*, the demon insists that one word must be said by the boy but that it would never happen. Meanwhile, a statue of St. Michael rested in Robbie's room. Attempts at communion were eventually successful; the sign of the cross and the crucifix were called "very effective." Most of all, the prayer to St. Michael precipitated an intervention, the *Diary* claims, by the archangel himself. Rebuking Satan in the name of *dominus* ("Lord"), he laid claim to Robbie and the demon was expulsed. Afterwards, Robbie testified to a vision of a radiantly robed man and the flight of a devil into a cave bearing the name "Spite," formerly spelled out on Robbie's skin.[55] The April 19 entry reports that all was well, engaging in Mass, the rosary, and prayers to Our Lady of Fatima.

The *Diary* is not the only primary source available, but it is certainly the most attentive and thorough. Another set of sources comes from the rare occasions in which these Jesuits and other witnesses testified of their experience. Additionally, some second-hand testimony comes from those in a rare position to hear a Jesuit participant talk about the experience. Since Bishop penned the *Diary* and Bowdern offered his approval of it, these other voices become witnesses to what they saw.

THE WITNESSES

The diarist is the great witness to the 1949 exorcism. This section hears from other first-hand witnesses, as well as second-hand witnesses who heard the participants describe the events later. Rarely do the reported events lack two to six onlookers each time, combining for more than forty witnesses in total.

---

55. *Diary*, "March 31."

The Diary and the Witnesses

THE WITNESS LIST

By the beginning of the reading of the rite of exorcism, the *Diary* numbers the witnesses to be fourteen.[56] In various singular episodes, it names some of these Jesuit witness as Fathers William Bowdern, Raymond Bishop, Walter Halloran, George Bischofberger, Joseph Boland, Edmund Burke, John O'Flaherty, Albert Schell, and William Van Roo.[57] Noteworthy is Father Walter Halloran, who lived decades beyond the event and participated in reserved dialogs about the events through interviews.[58] Halloran's provision of the copy to Allen functions as a witness to the authenticity of the report. Father Canning assisted Father Hughes on the return trip to Georgetown.[59] Father McMahon is recognized for coaching Robbie as catechumen after March 23.[60] Additional witnesses among the Alexian Brothers staff include the nurse, Ernest Schaffer; the chaplain Father Widman; workers named Emmet and Theophane.[61] A worker at St. Xavier's College Church named Michael stood as proxy at Robbie's tumultuous baptism.[62]

Others may have been actively involved around the exorcism but not listed in the *Diary*. Saint Booth names Jesuit William Faherty as an eyewitness and consultant; Faherty's book on the Alexian Brothers Hospital with its description of the 1949 event bears the imprimatur of the archdiocese to evidence that he had access to the archdiocese archives.[63] Laurence Kenny was confessor to Saint Louis University Jesuit priests, but he is not named as a participant in the exorcism or first-hand witness.[64] McGuire names Edmond F. Sassin as the Alexian Brothers psychiatrist

---

56. *Diary*, "Background"; Bishop and Saint Booth, *Exorcist Diary*, 16 ("Since the beginning of the above-enumerated incidents, there have been fourteen different witnesses to testify and verify different phenomena.").

57. *Diary*, "Background"; "March 16"; "April 4"; "April 10"; "April 11."

58. Silvers, "Jesuit Helped"; Allen, *Possessed*, xiii–xiv; Opsasnick, "Haunted Boy," 25; Opsasnick, *Real Story*, 40–42. For a discussion on Halloran's flexible vow of confidentiality, see Cooperman ("Touched by Evil") below.

59. *Diary*, "April 8."

60. *Diary*, "April 1, 13."

61. *Diary*, "April 4–8, 13, 17, 18"; Erdman, "Truth," 56.

62. *Diary*, "April 1."

63. Bishop and Saint Booth, *Exorcist Diary*, 60; Faherty, *To Rest in Charity*, copyright page.

64. Allen, *Possessed*, 49; *Diary*, "March 9."

overseeing the case of Robbie.[65] Allen claims that by the time the event was over, more than forty witnesses was claimed by an unnamed observer of the archive report in the Archdiocese of St. Louis.[66]

From the Georgetown phase are extensive reports from Lutheran minister Rev. Luther Schulze, particularly in correspondence with notable Duke University parapsychologist J. B. Rhine.[67] Ida Mae Donley served as Schulze's assistant and provides a first-hand account of her experience, including witnessing levitation and the use of Latin.[68] The testimony of parish priest Fr. Albert Hughes finds minor representation through secondary sources, but among important names in the literature: Fathers Frank Bober, John Nicola, and William Reppetti.[69] Blatty claims that a Seattle University professor witnessed the levitation.[70] Additional interviews or public presentations by other St. Louis participants,[71] including reserved interviews with the exorcist William Bowdern.[72] These witnesses reinforce the contents of the *Diary* and sometimes provide insight beyond it.

Included among the witness list should the immediate and extended family members, who play an integral role especially in the early months of demonization and exorcism. The *Diary* takes care to mention them, especially in the "St. Louis" section of the "Background": "The violent moving of the mattress and the scratching on the boy's body was observed by the mother, an aunt, an uncle, a cousin of college age, a friend

---

65. McGuire, "Diary of an Exorcism."

66. Allen, *Possessed*, 300.

67. Schulze testimony is found in Schulze, "Luther Schulze Case Report" and in "Appendix A: The Letters between the Rev. Luther Miles Schulze and Dr. J. B. Rhine" in Rueda, *Diabolical Possession*, 161–69. Additionally, newspaper articles were based on his public speaking events in "Minister Tells Parapsychologists" (cited in Opsasnick, "Haunted Boy," 9).

68. See "Appendix C: Interview with Ida Mae, the Leader of the Circle of Prayers" in Rueda, *Diabolical Possession*, 190–94.

69. The Thomas Allen interviews best represent three priests who talked with Hughes (Allen, *Possessed*, 302–3). Frank Bober, who claims to have shared a disclosing meal with Hughes and offers it in various sources, including Opsasnick, "Haunted Boy," 24–25; John Nicola dialogued with Hughes and speaks of the event in *Diabolical Possession* (95, 105–16), as well as Dobson, "Luncheon"; William C. Reppetti, who made notes from a lecture by Hughes on May 10, 1950, at Georgetown University.

70. Head, "Interview."

71. For example, Kelly interviews two other Jesuit participants besides Bowdern, naming William Van Roo (see *Devil*, 98).

72. Kelly, *Devil*, 94–102 (from his 1960 interview with Bowdern); Blatty, *On The Exorcist*, 20–21.

The Diary and the Witnesses

of the family, and by Father Bishop."[73] The diarist makes an effort in the Background to list Georgetown ministers, a psychiatrist, a physician, and a spiritist in its witness list. Two attempts to interview the victim, Ronald Hunkeler, are recorded externally to the *Diary*, but both report his lack of memory of the events and his refusal to dialog on it.[74]

Noteworthy in the timeline is the intersection between William Bowdern and Albert Hughes when Robbie was brought from St. Louis back to Washington, DC, in April 1949. Upon arrival there, Bowdern conferred with Hughes, linking the Georgetown and St. Louis phases for that day. Additionally, Father Hughes participated in the exorcism events during this return to Washington, DC.[75] This encounter offers justification for Hughes to later report details of the 1949 exorcism from the St. Louis phase as second hand from Bowdern, along with his own testimony from the Georgetown phase.[76] Any early insights gained by Bowdern during this Catholic intersection, however, was not recorded in or edited into the diary, as the background to the case had already been penned.

Witness Confidentiality

Many of these witnesses maintained an authoritative silence about the event. Perhaps there was limited opportunity to comment beyond their own circle of peers, now lost to our generation. The participating priests, however, offer the most impressive confidentiality. Their spirit of pastoral care and the requirement of the Archdiocese not to disclose the information both governed the participating priests' ability to share publicly about the 1949 exorcism. From the beginning, trust was part of the pastoral relationship between priest and boy, and the priests' faithful confidence is now an impressive mark of credibility. The *Diary* itself was privately chronicled, likely to serve in the report to the Catholic Church that would perpetuate its secrecy. This confidentiality provides integrity

---

73. Similarly, "March 7" remarks, "Five or six relatives present" and "March 8" states, "R's Catholic aunt, two cousins and non-Catholic uncle" as witnesses to a moving bed, a shaking mattress, and scratching.

74. These conversations are still recorded by the three interviewers (see Rueda, *Diabolical Possession*, 190–91; Opsasnick, "Haunted Boy," 25–26).

75. He is named as blessing the house and administering the Eucharist alongside Father Canning (*Diary*, "April 8").

76. The same broadening of the narrative is seen in J. B. Rhine's interview of Rev. Schulze, mixing in generalizations about the whole exorcism experience with his own specific witness of experience (see Brian, *Enchanted Voyager*, 179–84).

to the priestly testimony contained in it. While affectionate or satirical biographies expect to be read by the public, a diary by its very nature is not. The pledge and successful practice to keep the events anonymous and protect the privacy of the victim diminishes other false motives on their part.

Bowdern's interview record best demonstrates the exorcist's unwillingness to divulge information beyond the presence of the diary. This is evident in Bowdern's letter to Blatty: "My hesitancy in giving you the details of the case of possession is due to two facts. First, ____ [Archbishop Ritter], who delegated me as the exorcist, instructed me not to publicize the case. I have been faithful to his instructions."[77] Henry Kelly remarks about his interview of Bowdern eleven years after the event: "His concern for privacy and the avoidance of notoriety was exemplary, and his determination to hold the facts manifests a rare virtue in this area."[78] Faherty reports that, "Father Bowdern and his associates made a promise of silence on the subject" to the Archbishop. Such silence cannot be interpreted as unbelief, as Bowdern was willing to declare: "I believe this one was the real thing."[79] Likewise, when John Cardinal Carberry succeeded Ritter, he renewed his pledge of silence on the event.[80] Cooperman suggests that Halloran was exempt from the vow, which would explain his ability to offer a diary copy to Allen and his willingness to dialog about the event with a measure of restrained freedom.[81]

The confidentiality of the priests is thus a mark of credibility that reinforces historical plausibility. Father Bowdern is obligated to maintain privacy through holy orders, disqualifying any suspicion of opportunistic embellishment from his experience. The release of the book and film *The Exorcist* certainly afforded him the chance to capitalize on the attention to the event, but he begged off the opportunity. In the years to follow, Blatty reports that Bowdern continued to plead not to reveal the

---

77. Blatty, *On The Exorcist*, 21. The second reason for discretion was the embarrassment and attention to the boy.

78. Kelly, *Devil*, 99.

79. McGuire, "St. Louis Exorcism."

80. Faherty, *To Rest in Charity*, 83.

81. Cooperman, "Touched by Evil." All six references to Halloran in the *Diary* uniquely employ the title "Mr." rather than "Father," even when listed alongside all other priests titled "Father." He was not ordained a priest until 1954, probably explaining his interview comments that he did not feel qualified to make judgments as much as to report what he witnessed. See Opsasnick, "Haunted Boy," 25.

identity of the boy.[82] In contrast, Rev. Luther Schulze was not bound to the same confidentiality standard as Bowdern, evidenced by his public lectures following his experience. Only when Halloran sat for interviews decades later was the simplest of remarks made, but his great disclosure was the provision of a diary copy to Thomas Allen. It would appear in the second edition of *Possessed* in 2000, while still unavailable in the first edition of 1994.[83]

WITNESS CREDIBILITY

The witnesses offer a kind of mediation between the exorcism and the contemporary era. They testify to what they saw, or at least what they thought they saw with their interpretation of it. With their testimony, the threshold for reasonable belief is more attainable, should the reasonability of their testimony be evaluated and recognized. This begins with realizing that testimony *of* what was believed to be seen is a testimony *towards* what was seen. Their testimony can still be scrutinized as Collingwood requires: "He [the historian] is aware that what he does to his so-called authorities is not to believe them but to criticize them."[84] Our theological enterprise is one way of critiquing the so-called authorities known as witnesses. The chart below offers a list of the witnesses, primarily from the *Diary*, and a list of those who claimed to hear from the witnesses first-hand.

Witnesses	Credibility
William Bowdern, SJ	Exorcist
Raymond Bishop, SJ	Diarist, exorcism participant
Reverend Luther Schulze	Georgetown minister
Father Albert Hughes	Georgetown priest
Father Canning	Georgetown priest
Walter Halloran, SJ	Exorcism participant
George Bischofberger, SJ	Exorcism participant

82. Head, "Interview."
83. Allen, *Possessed*, 225.
84. Collingwood, *Idea of History*, 282.

Joseph Boland, SJ	Exorcism participant
Edmund Burke, SJ	Exorcism participant
John O'Flaherty, SJ	Exorcism participant
William Van Roo, SJ	Exorcism participant
Albert Schell, SJ	Exorcism participant
Michael	St. Xavier's College Church worker
Ernest Schaffer	Alexian Brother nurse
Father Widman	Alexian chaplain
Emmet	Alexian Brother worker
Theophane	Alexian Brother worker
Edmond F. Sassin	Alexian Brother psychiatrist

Table 2. Witnesses

Claimants	Credibility
William Peter Blatty	Bowdern testimony
William Faherty, SJ	Bowdern testimony; Archdiocese archives
Father Frank Bober	Hughes testimony
John Nicola	Hughes testimony, Georgetown physician testimony
William Reppetti	Hughes public lecture
Thomas Allen	Halloran testimony

Table 3. Claimants to Witness the Event

For a moment, it is appropriate to recognize the limitations of their testimony. Our appreciation for witnesses to the event inside and outside the journal does not mean that the testimonies are necessarily true. Collingwood states this well: "The historian does not know the past by simply believing a witness who saw the events in question and has left his evidence on record. That kind of mediation would give at most not

The Diary and the Witnesses

knowledge but belief, and ill-founded and improbable belief."[85] Just as witnesses to a traffic accident provide their limited accounts to the police, so independent voices contribute to a comprehensive testimony of irregular activities in 1949. Since the very topic is religious in nature, the opportunity for an a priori set of presuppositions and subjective interpretation immediately could bias their testimonies.

It is also recognized that testimonies can be valid, even if based on personal belief of what was seen or experienced. They still offer a perspective on past reality beyond the historical idealism promoted by Collingwood. He is pressing beyond public evidence to more real evidence; this is not available to us. Additionally, since the venue for many events was private, every sign and episode does not necessarily find validation, even among other witnesses. They are introduced individually in this book at times as factual, while always ultimately subject to belief or elimination.

However, to the credit of the witnesses, they generally do not have access to one another to synchronize their stories like conspirators questioned by police. The diary disappears against any opportunity for public view, remaining confidential in diocese and hospital offices. The witnesses do not work in groupthink in the decade to follow. The priests themselves do not have any history of interest in exorcism to start the ordeal. Ida Mae Donley's mainline Lutheran prayer meeting had no expectation of the preternatural when they visited the Hunkeler home. While occasional figures like Luther Schulze pursued his paranormal interests to explain some events, most reveal no motive or agenda to the unexplainable events they witnessed. Of course, the most untainted witness is the primary source of the *Diary* itself. A private journal unintended for public access and lost to history for decades combines with former living witnesses to find no pressure to conform.

Furthermore, the most notable chronicler of the witness testimonies is marked by religious disinterest. The first narrator and publisher of the exorcist's journal, Thomas Allen, was suspected to be a professing agnostic.[86] He had no religious motivation to promote or overreach the spiritual or preternatural elements of this event. Perceptional psychologist Ian Stevenson commends his methodology: "Allen acknowledges the limitations of the evidence he deploys and shows that he tried to corroborate statements as much as possible. His attention to details pleases

---

85. Collingwood, *Idea of History*, 282.
86. McGuire, "Diary of an Exorcism."

me . . . I believe that his account is sufficiently reliable so that we can take the case seriously and consider alternative interpretations for it."[87]

William Peter Blatty was not committed to the Christian faith when wrote *The Exorcist* or advised the screenplay for the movie, but he was searching with a hope of the supernatural potential of the original story: "If there were demons, there were angels and probably a God and a life everlasting."[88] The testimony of the *Diary* and the witnesses augment his hope in God through the testimony of this encounter with a spirit being.[89] The only set of confident believers—beyond the team of Jesuit exorcists—seems to be paranormal specialists and ghost hunters who like to include the event among their stories, chronicled alongside episodes from an unbiblical worldview. This book is careful not to prioritize this type of specialists as historical sources or this field as particularly informational.[90]

The witnesses offer an opportunity for the retrieval of history through the inquiry of their testimony of events. From this, we make inferences about its historicity. Collingwood rejoins our enterprise here: "History is a science whose business is to study events not accessible to our observation, and to study these events inferentially, arguing to them from something else which is accessible to our observation, and which the historian calls 'evidence' for the events in which he is interested."[91] A sufficiency of evidence is a subjective standard, but the multiple testimonies and the nature of those testimonies through its documentary sources, witnesses, and historical probability can serve as an unheralded testimony to the evidence of preternatural events in 1949. This evidence makes this the best documented case of exorcism in the twentieth century. Only its theology remains to be tested.

---

87. Stevenson, "Possession and Exorcism," 69.
88. Blatty, *On The Exorcist*, 6.
89. Kelly, *Devil*, 7–8.
90. Exceptions to this elimination criterion are Roland, *Complete Book of Ghosts*, 225–26, for its sample portrayal of the 1949 event; Taylor, *Devil Came to St. Louis*, for its comprehensive treatment of the event with some noticeably worthy journalism around it; and LaChance, *Confrontation*, for his objective study of the event before relating his séance at Bowdern's tomb in the appendix.
91. Collingwood, *Idea of History*, 251.

CONCLUSION

A daily diary of an exorcism and a list of witnesses from the demonization comprise a vigorous range of historical testimony around the pseudonymous Robbie in 1949. The elusive but eventual access to that diary squares the historian to be in a rare position of discovery of those events. The complexity of this recovery includes an honorable use of historical testimony that discerns its limitations and concedes its conflicting sources, while not preventing forces beyond the natural from participating in history. Yes, canons of public evidence for historians lack an official line for adjudication on the supernatural. Yet the demonization of a boy and the exorcism by a priest can neither be accepted as fact nor can they be ignored as beyond the category of facts.

Noteworthy to our objective attempts to a fair historical method in this examination of the 1949 exorcism events is the confessional component that cannot be deserted. This book is written from a Christian worldview, a Judeo-Christian framework that recognizes Scripture with the authority to posit claims and that subjects its approach to the reality of spiritual beings. This book does not seek to prove the existence of demons, but it assumes it. Yet it can buttress this belief in demons by focusing on an historical event with significant testimony to establish the veracity of the event. New Testament theologian Craig Keener offers a historical measure to the supernatural while identifying the critical historiographical problem:

> Historians offer historical reconstructions on the basis of testimony, sometimes artifacts, and frequently additional critical evaluation based on context, intrinsic probability, and the weighing of evidence . . . the probability argument must engage the long-standing albeit declining Western philosophic assumption that miracles do not occur, or at least must be evaluated with a bar of skepticism so high that no individual miracle claim could ever be accepted as valid.[92]

The confession of confessionalism being made, this book reaches the historical without overreaching in its historical claims nor ignoring any historical method. Jack Collins calls for acknowledgement of a deeper promise of the supernatural: "Christian belief is not simply an acceptance of certain things as factual: it goes beyond that to personal

---

92. Keener, *Miracles*, 1:21–22.

commitment."[93] To quote one film historian about *The Exorcist*, the case study requires us to confront our fears, "The ones we have shoved aside."[94] The *Diary* and the witnesses provide a testimony to that theory shoved aside, to that conceivable explanation beyond the natural, as they serve as those necessary observers or agents of redemption. The theological analysis of their testimony, particularly the diarist, can provide a central, critical, and determining factor in establishing a confident measure of veracity around the event.

An analysis of the 1949 exorcism event is almost before us. For those who seek to understand the overall theology and philosophy of preternaturalism and supernaturalism, chapter 3 provides this overview before it confronts the dissenters against the case for them in the 1949 exorcism.

---

93. Collins, *God of Miracles*, 145.

94. Travers and Reiff, *Story*, 13–14. Like the audience who witnesses the miracles of Jesus narrated in the Gospels, audience members must marvel at them, or they must disqualify them (Matt 28:17). Its conclusion ultimately invites a decision of belief or unbelief in the story.

3
Preternaturalism and its Critics

"We need to know what faith and science are, how they relate to one another, and what claims either has a right to make about the truth.... good science and good faith both need sound critical thinking."

—C. John Collins, *Science and Faith*

THE LITERATURE AROUND THE events of the 1949 exorcism surprisingly lacks theological evaluation. Yet this Christian discipline offers a theory of a potential mysterious, supernatural dimension grounded in its foundational beliefs concerning demonization and exorcism. This foundation rests on the Christian view of creation, the divine working in creation, the drama of good and evil, and the authority of Christians in Christ's inaugurated kingdom. The biblical story first describes the first man and woman, Adam and Eve, encountering the serpent in the Garden of Eden as a first human/preternatural encounter. Their fall from grace, Satan's deceitful role, the place of angels and demons, the ministry of Christ, the phenomenon of exorcism, and the liturgy of the Catholic Church all contribute to provide a backdrop to our episode. Any study of this sort also sees an inevitable intersection between faith and science, as the doctrines of creation and ecclesiology traverse natural and social sciences. This chapter offers a theological baseline for understanding the events around a boy and a priest in St. Louis.

An analysis of the events of the 1949 exorcism also faces cultural challenges. Contemporary ideologies resist a theological assessment and explanation of the event, challenging religious claims as a reliable interpretation of the event. The modern mind is quick to claim that the mysterious must have a rational explanation, even if it is often beyond our understanding. In these interests the natural and the extra-natural seem to compete, clash, or counteract each other. Ghost stories and horror movies challenge this avoidance in a frightening format, as average families encounter preternatural terror on the screen. Off the screen, our rational and scientific minds seek to dismiss or explain these mysterious entities, while some mock the unintelligent minds as easily believing the superstitious. Science, social science, history, and ecclesiology, as well as their cultural patterns of thinking, are introduced here in brief ideological ways for the interpretive challenges they offer. Their objectivity and methodology are still valued here, stated well by Behan McCullagh: "Empiricism is a part of our cultural inheritance which has been of such spectacular value in helping us to understand and control nature that it would seem foolish to abandon it. There is no better framework of beliefs about the world which we could adopt instead."[1] However, natural empiricism alone reduces the story to medical and psychological explanations, necessitating a theological complement to its efforts. Sometimes even non-Christians and materialists are forced to imagine the ostensibly real worldview proposed by Christians: there is more to life than the physical.

The contents of this chapter are remarkably brief. The necessity of providing a framework to interpret this historical event is matched by the necessity of reigning in the vast literature on the preternatural. First, the chapter profiles a systematic theology of demons corresponding to a biblical theology of God's relationship to creation. Next, it presents medical, social, and ecclesiastical opinions around supernatural and preternatural events. A study of this kind must intersect theology and science to prevent the risk of a naturalistic reductionism.

Introduction to Demons and the Preternatural

A Christian understanding of the cause and effects of demons unfolds in the Old Testament discretely before finding more obvious descriptions in the New Testament. A more comprehensive treatment of these explanations is readily available.[2]

1. McCullagh, *Justifying Historical Descriptions*, 7.
2. For a survey of the demonic in the Bible, see Kuemmerlin-McLean, "Demons"; Reese, "Demons"; Heiser, *Demons*, 59–235; Walton and Walton, *Demons and Spirits*, 99–274; Twelftree, *Jesus the Exorcist*, 53–129; *In the Name of Jesus*, 57–182; Hallowell,

Grasping the Preternatural

In Christian theology, demons are creatures who are unclean, evil, and malignant spirits who work against the divine enterprise.[3] This resistance causes harm to people, both spiritually and physically by tormenting them—oppressing and possessing them.[4] In turn, exorcism is the expressed power over this manifested power in which the demon is cast out.[5] The term and the concept finds its basis in authority, with the affiliated *exorkizō* meaning "cause some to swear," adjure, or charge under oath.[6] The act of expulsion, *ekballō*, means "drive out," "expel," or cast out.[7] Sometimes the exit of the demon is simply described, *exerchomai*, "come or go out.[8] This language is based in the kingdom authority inaugurated by Jesus.

In Christian theology, this phenomenon of the advance of Satan in demonization and the counter advance of Christ in exorcism are viewed as part of a larger drama, a cosmic battle between God and Satan, between good and evil. In the fourth century, Tyconius framed the place of the church in this ancient battle: "He [Satan] fights in heaven with Christ, but in the church with [Christ] clothed with man."[9] This drama brings us to the first of terms to be explained. The term "conflict theology" is used here to expand the popular term "spiritual warfare" to the larger biblical drama, as used by John and Harvey Walton: "Its emphasis [is] on an ongoing conflict between God and Satan and their respective servants or underlings."[10]

The term "demonization" is employed throughout the book to identify the phenomenon of demonic influence commonly distinguished as "infestation," "oppression," or "possession." This single term is the New Testament verb to identify such phenomena, and it better generalizes the

---

Playing with Fire, 37–85.

3. For example, Matt 8:16; 12:43; Mark 1:23; 3:11, 30, 5:2, 13; 7:25; 9:17; Luke 6:18; 7:21; 8:2; Acts 5:16; 8:7.

4. For example, Matt 12:22; Mark 9:20; Luke 9:39.

5. Generally, this is seen in Matt 4:24 and Mark 1:34. Specifically, this is seen in Matt 17:18, Mark 1:25, and Luke 4:35. Likewise, it is seen in Paul's ministry in Acts 18:18.

6. BAG 277.

7. BAG 236–37.

8. BAG 274.

9. Tyconius, *Exposition*, 127.

10. Walton and Walton, *Demons and Spirits*, 1.

condition without requiring an identified degree of influence, control, or ownership.[11] The 1949 episode clearly shows the element of possession in this configuration. In turn, the term "exorcism" is the expressed power of God through by prayer, fasting, and the liturgical rite in which the person is freed from demonization.

The word "preternatural" has historically been used for the manifestations of spirit beings, although its usage has declined on the vernacular in the last century. From its Latin root *preter*, it simply means "beyond the natural." Activities called "supernatural" are usually attributed to the divine, so preternatural is employed for the beyond-natural work of demons. Thus, preternatural causes are not of this material world but are still in the material world.[12]

Theological Understanding of the Preternatural

This section will survey some Old Testament material related to demons, six episodes of exorcism in the Gospels and Acts, Jesus' teaching on demons, and other biblical passages foundational to a Christian understanding of demonization and exorcism. A theology of demons and exorcism will be developed along the way, highlighting elemental features of the 1949 exorcism events for comparison.

Biblical Origin of Demons

The origin and work of demons are intricately linked in the biblical story. In its theology of creation and the fall, the Christian tradition has viewed demons as spirit beings who are fallen angels.[13] This requires a creation of angels potentially independent to the material creation, but its immaterial matter need not be excluded in the creation story.[14] The timing

---

11. Reese, "Demons," 140; Keener, "Crooked Spirits," 346. Use of this term is not meant to be an alignment with those who seek to avoid of the issue of the possession of Christians—an issue not in priority for this book. For such an avoidance approach, consider Wimber and Springer, *Power Healing*, 109, 114.

12. Martin, *Hostage to the Devil*, 9, 422–23.

13. For an historical theological summary of this tradition, see Allison, *Historical Theology*, 298–318.

14. Even the material creation has a spiritual dimension. For example, the Holy Spirit breathes into Adam to make him a "living creature" (Gen 2:7), with the *nephesh* ("creature" or "being") associated with life animation or a living spirit (see Collins, *Genesis 1–4*, 47n33).

with the creation story and the Garden of Eden story provide a reference point for consigning the origins of spirit beings. Following the six days of creation, Adam and Eve are established in the garden when the serpent appears on the scene. Despite the lack of specific identity of the serpent, its ability to talk and its intention to tempt the first couple reveal more than another created being here. The book of Revelation refers to this enemy of God as "the old snake, who is called the devil and Satan, the deceiver of the whole world" (Rev 12:9), and "the dragon, that ancient serpent, who is the devil and Satan" (Rev 20:2). The serpent here is Satan; it is not a mere snake. It acts against the will of God, it acts to destroy humankind, and it deceives. Desmond Alexander can thus say: "Given the earth-shattering consequences of the serpent's actions and the peculiar nature of the punishment meted out to it, a case can be marshalled in favor of the claim in Revelation 20:2 that the 'ancient serpent' is Satan and the devil."[15]

Additional elements are noteworthy to a theology of Satan that leads to our understanding of demons. The creation of people in the image of God (Gen 1:26–27) establishes a connection between the Creator and his creatures who are called "good" in the Genesis narrative (1:31). This relationship between the divine and human becomes the axis of the biblical story. Meanwhile, God punishes disobedience to all three participants in Eden, establishing a tension between humankind and Satan: "I will put enmity between you and the woman, and between your offspring and her offspring; he shall bruise your head, and you shall bruise his heel" (Gen 3:15). This anticipates the work of Christ. The impetus for Satan to abuse humankind follows, from the destruction of Job's livelihood in the hopes he will curse God (Job 1:11) to the execution of the infants at Bethlehem (Matt 2:16) to thwart the prophecy. Satan seeks to upset the relational wholeness intended by God for his people.

While Satan is introduced as the source of evil in the world, the appearance of demons is more obscured. As early as Irenaeus in the late second century, Christian theology has sought to explain demons as fallen angels, with Satan the "chief of the apostasy" along with "those angels who became apostates along with him."[16] The leader is typed by the descriptions of ancient kings in Old Testament prophetic literature. Isaiah

---

15. Alexander, *From Eden to the New Jerusalem*, 100.

16. Irenaeus, *Haer.* 3.23.3 (*ANF* 1:456). This continues to be advanced, next most explicitly by Origen, *Princ.* 1.5.4 ("Some superior power which had fallen away . . . and was hurled to the earth" [*ANF* 4:258–59]).

describes one who declared that he would ascend to the heavens to set up his throne above God but whose splendor has been "brought down" and who has "fallen from the heavens" (14:9–13). Ezekiel describes one blameless, "anointed guardian cherub" in whom "wickedness was found" and "your heart became proud." As a result, the Lord says, "I dispelled in disgrace from the mountain of God" and "I threw you down to the ground." Essential to this description of Satan is that he is identified as being in Eden, "the garden of God" (28:11–17).

When these descriptions of fallenness encounter Rev 12, the rebellion and its inclusion of other angels takes form in a systematic theological way. War in heaven saw Michael the Archangel and his angels defeat Satan and his angels, so that "there was no place for them in heaven any longer" (vv. 7–8). The one who deceives the nations "was thrown to earth and his angels with him" (v. 9). The language of Satan's fall in the prophets is expanded to include other angels. Ladd recognizes: "It is this conflict in heaven between the Dragon and the woman that explains the evil the church experiences throughout its entire history."[17]

Biblical Activities of Demons

The Old Testament understanding of demons is limited, and developing a complete theology is problematic. There is no single word for demon in this era of events and writing, and the variety of terms imagine both evil spirits and the spirits associated with gods. Even as interest in spirit beings escalated during Second Temple Judaism, scholars lack agreement on the developmental understanding of demons in intertestamental Israel, ranging from a seminal Jewish theology to late theology. Evil spirits often occur in poetic texts; the book of Job is a worthy example as Satan appears in heaven to accuse Job before God (Job 1:6–12; 2:1–7). Much of the Old Testament language is comparative language of the Ancient Near East, grounded in magic, witchcraft, rituals, and popular religion.[18]

Yet there are important passages that offer even a basic view of demons as a sporadic part of the life of Israel. For example, in explaining how God's spirit was the basis for his relationship with King Saul and King David, God's spirit rested on Saul (1 Sam 11:6) before it was

17. Ladd, *Theology*, 626. This reading requires a recognition that sometimes Scripture uses an event to also foreshadow another event, in this case a past defeat and fall typed by a potentially future defeat and fall.

18. Kuemmerlin-McLean, "Demons," 138–39.

removed from Saul (1 Sam 16:14). It came to rest on David all his days (1 Sam 16:13), while it exits Saul's reign with an evil spirit from God replacing his own spirit. Thus, this distressful spirit haunts Saul (1 Sam 18:10; 19:9) as it was consoled by the harp of David.

The term *daimonion* is used by Jewish writers of the post-exilic age and Christians in the New Testament period, a loan word from Greek philosophers to describe good or bad intermediate semi-divine beings.[19] This is the language characterizing the theological culture of Judaism at the emergence of Jesus' ministry and the early church. Gruenthaner summarizes demonology in the Old Testament with its limits: "The story of the fall supplied the Israelites with all the elements requisite for the development of a demonology analogous to that of the New Testament."[20] While there are allusions to the rebellion of some angels, Satan and demons are not explicitly called fallen angels. Yet, in all of this, evil spirits are noted in the Old Testament text.

Activities of demons are more recognizable in the New Testament. Four specific Gospel episodes and two Acts episodes attribute uncontrollable or suffering behavior to demonization. This led to exorcism being a significant mark of the ministry of Christ and the apostles.[21] Noteworthy is the link between some suffering and demonization, presented as an overlap of the spiritual and physical realms. Certainly, Gospel episodes describe healing without mention of any demonization. For example, Jesus healed a leper simply of his illness (Matt 8:1–4). Several such examples occur in the New Testament.[22] However, some passages combine demonization and illness.[23] The distinction offered by biblical authors can help to counter the argument that the ancient world framed its mental illness as demonic. There was a woman with a deformed back "who for eighteen years had a sickness caused by a spirit; and she was

19. Gruenthaner, "Demonology," 6.

20. Gruenthaner, "Demonology," 27. In a radical statement, Karl Barth even insists of angels and demons: "They have no common denominator. They do not grow from a common root" (*CD* 3/3:520).

21. Twelftree remarks, "Not only does the conducting of miracles appear to dominate the activity of the historical Jesus, the exorcisms in particular loom large as one of the most obvious and important aspects of his ministry" (*In the Name of Jesus*, 46; see also 25–205). See also *Jesus the Miracle Worker*; *Jesus the Exorcist*; 53–174; Walton and Walton, *Demons and Spirits*, 229–74.

22. Matt 8:1–13; 9:1–7, 18–25; 20:29–34; Luke 17:11–19; John 5:1–15; 9:1–12; Acts 3:2–9; 14:8–10.

23. Luke 11:14; 13:11; Mark 1:21–28 and Luke 4:31–37; Matt 8:28–34; Mark 5:1–20 and Luke 8:26–39; Matt 17:14–20; Mark 9:14–29 and Luke 9:37–43.

bent double and could not straighten up at all" (Luke 13:11). Following Jesus' transfiguration, the father of the demonized boy describes his son's condition: "He has a spirit that makes him unable to speak." This leads Jesus to address the demon: "You deaf and dumb spirit" (Mark 9:17, 25), linking the possession activity to the illness. Jesus acted against the one cause that led to a solution to both causes: "He was casting out a demon that was mute, when the demon had gone out, the mute man spoke, and the crowds were amazed" (Luke 11:14). It is fair to recognize how these texts imply that the illnesses were secondary effects, as the demon is addressed but the whole person is healed. This is exactly the case evidenced in the 1949 case, as the chapters ahead display physical manifestations and secondary physical effects from demonization.

These links between demonization and illness reinforce the healing dimension of these stories. These pairs accompany one another for a complex but wholistic theory of suffering and healing. Matthew 12:22 sees demonization and illness linked in a single verse: "Then a demon-oppressed man who was blind and mute was brought to him, and he healed him, so that the man spoke and saw." Peter is described as one who "went about doing good and healing all who were oppressed by the devil" (Acts 10:38). A medical specialist who claims that 1949 science was inadequate to diagnose mental illness along contemporary lines either overlooks or discards the dual claim in the New Testament of both a spiritual dimension and related physical suffering. The biblical episodes of exorcism will illustrate this pairing.

Biblical Exorcism of Demons

As the work of demons becomes more explicit in the New Testament, so does the introduction of exorcism. Four Gospel episodes of exorcism at the hands of Jesus and one in Acts by the apostles are instructive, along with several teaching passages about demons found in the Gospels. Jesus' ministry was marked generally by mention of exorcism activities, such as: "And he went throughout all Galilee, preaching in their synagogues and casting out demons" (Mark 1:39), as well as "Go tell that fox [Herod] for me, 'Listen, I am casting out demons and performing cures'" (Luke 13:32). This was also continued as a general characteristic of the apostolic ministries (Acts 5:16; 10:35–38). The disciples had already participated in an exorcism ministry when they were commissioned on one occasion:

Preternaturalism and its Critics

"And he called to him his twelve disciples and gave them authority over unclean spirits, to cast them out, and to heal every disease and every affliction" (Matt 10:1; Luke 9:1; Mark 3:14–15).

First, Jesus entered the synagogue in Capernaum, he encountered a man with "an unclean spirit." After silencing the demon in rebuke, he exorcised it (Mark 1:21–28; Luke 4:31–37) as the man convulsed and emitted cries. Second, Jesus crossed into the Gadarene region, where a demon-possessed man dwelt among the tombs—unrestrainable, regularly crying out, and committing self-harm. After rebuke and dialog, the demons begged not to be sent into "the abyss" before leaving to enter a swineherd (Matt 8:28–34; Mark 5:1–20; Luke 8:26–39). Noteworthy in this episode is how Jesus asked the demon its name, and "Legion—for we are many" was offered. Third, as Jesus crossed into the region of Tyre and Sidon, he encountered a woman who begged for healing for her demonized daughter. Her expression of faith so impressed Jesus that he healed the daughter from afar (Matt 15:21–28; Mark 7:24–30), although the passage emphasizes the dynamic between an impure gentile making a faith request of the Jewish Messiah more than addressing exorcism. Finally, Jesus descended the mount of transfiguration to encounter his disciples unable to cast a demon from a boy marked with inability to speak, being seized as in epilepsy, being thrown down, foaming of the mouth with grinding of teeth, and made rigid. Jesus rebukes his disciples for their inability to exorcise the demon before doing so himself (Matt 17:14–20; Mark 9:14–29; Luke 9:37–43).

The book of Acts contains two other demonization encounters around the ministry of the apostle Paul. First, he came to Philippi where an enslaved girl was used as a soothsayer to profit traders. Her disturbances to his ministry led him to be "greatly annoyed" until he finally turned to command the spirit to come out and it exited right away (Acts 16:16–19). Evidentiary here is the association of the demonic with the occult and supposed knowledge beyond normal means, as well as an annoyance and interfering factor that comes from the oracular engagement of the demon. Second, as Paul ministered around Ephesus, some itinerant Jewish exorcists, the sons Sceva, attempted to cast out demons by the use of the name of Jesus. Magic in the day was often characterized by incantations with an authoritative declaration of a name. Commanding exorcism in Paul's and Jesus' names, their attempts met resistance when one evil spirit answered, "I know Jesus, and I recognize Paul—but who are you?" before it leaped on the men, stripping and beating them (Acts 19:13–20).

There is much contained in these passages to inform a theology of exorcism. Important for our study of the 1949 exorcism are several features in these passages.

- The Capernaum, Gadarene, and Sceva passages hear the demons speak to the exorcist. When Jesus is involved, they acknowledge his authority and express concern for their expulsion from the demonized person.

- The demonic speech often centers on authority. The Capernaum, Gadarene, and Philippi episodes hear the demon acknowledge God and the power of the exorcist. The concept of authority over the demon occurs in each expulsion story, with ineffective authority in the case of the Sceva episode. The occult variable of the Philippi episode implies demonic authority over the occultic participant.

- The use of name is instrumental in the Gadarene and Sceva passages. Only in the Gadarene passage does Jesus ask its name, likely stemming from how the exorcism itself seemed to be prolonged: "For Jesus had said to him, 'Come out'" (Mark 5:8). A plurality of demons was at work, prompting Jesus to demand the demonic name and revealing, "My name is Legion," he replied, "for we are many" (Mark 5:9; Luke 8:30). Name is associated with being, distinction, and essence of a person; to know the name is to know the one better. Twelftree remarks about religious movements, "The 'name' was part of the prescription used in preternatural control."[24]

- Jesus explicitly silences and rebukes the demon in its speech in the Capernaum and Gadarene passages. This is a form of engagement with the demon before expulsion, perhaps limiting its expression for effective exorcism. Likewise, Jesus silences the testimony of demons against those who would cast doubt on his work: "Even true testimony from satanic beings could only discredit Jesus in the eyes of most."[25]

24. Twelftree, *Jesus the Miracle Worker*, 284–85. See also Twelftree, *Jesus the Exorcist*, 61–62, where this position represents the perspective of the history of religions movement.

25. Brooks, *Mark*, 51. Levine and Witherington say it this way: "This news of Jesus' authority and power may not have been entirely positive (gossip and hearsay, of any sort, rarely are)" (*Gospel of Luke*, 125).

- There is a mixture of singularity and plurality with the demons in the same possessed victim at Capernaum and the Gadarenes. In the Mark 1 synagogue, there is a mixture of singularity of the demon (vv. 33, 35) and the plurality of the demons (vv. 24, 26) in the same possessed victim. In the Gadarene field, the name given by the demon is, "Legion, for we are many" (Mark 5:9). As noted above, this one occasion suggests multiple possible exorcisms.

- Remarkable strength marks the Gadarene and Sceva demoniacs, while similar control by the demon over the person in the Capernaum and Transfiguration passages. The strength is expressed as violence, including hurting the victim or the exorcist.

- The expulsion is met and marked by violence. The victim shows convulsions and upon exorcism in Capernaum. The transfiguration exorcism includes shrieking and convulsions as it came out (Mark 9:26). The demons in the Gadarenes are not described with violence upon exiting, but upon transfer into a pig herd, they led it over a cliff to destruction.

- The theological imagery of clean and unclean is at work in the Syrophoenician and the Gadarene accounts and more subtly in the Capernaum accounts. The gentile woman reports that her daughter "is severely tormented by a demon" (Matt 15:22) because "she has an unclean spirit" (Mark 7:26). In seeking mercy, the Gadarene demon is out of place in the man while more appropriately at home in a Jewishly unclean swine of pigs. The uncleanness of the demon stands in contrast to the cleanness expected in Jewish sabbath and dietary laws. Victor Hamilton describes the central book of the law: "Leviticus summons Israel to a holy life."[26] The gentile quality finds contrast with the Jewish quality, although faith transcends race in both cases. The Capernaum account likely reflects imagery of uncleanness in the synagogue, highlighting the need and purpose of Jesus' ministry.[27]

- Faith is instrumental in the Syrophoenician and transfiguration episodes. In the first, Jesus heals from a distance: "Great is your faith! Be it done for you as you desire" (Matt 15:28). In the latter, Jesus explains that the disciples were thwarted by the demon "because

---

26. Hamilton, *Handbook on the Pentateuch*, 246.
27. Klutz, *Exorcism Stories*, 125–29.

of your little faith" (Matt 17:20). Prayer is then cited as instrumental in the spiritual conflict in which disciples will engage through exorcism. "This type only goes out by prayer [and fasting]" (Mark 9:28–29).[28] Likewise, the father and Jesus dialog about belief and its condition for divine possibility.

Biblical Discourse on Demons and Exorcism

On several occasions, Jesus offered additional theology about demonization and exorcism that make their way into the 1949 exorcism narrative. First, after Jesus healed a demonized man marked by blindness and an inability to speak, it led to a discourse about exorcism before the crowd as the strong man parable (Matt 12:22–32; Luke 11:14–23; Mark 3:23–27). The Pharisees had accused Jesus of successful exorcism because he employed the power of Satan: "It is only by Beelzebul, the prince of demons, that this man casts out demons" (Matt 12:24). In Jesus' response, he challenged the logic of the claim that he defeats Satan by the power of Satan. For that matter, this same accusation could be levelled at their own exorcism activities. Then a vague illustration comes: "How can someone enter a strong man's house and plunder his goods, unless he first binds the strong man? Then indeed he may plunder his house" (v. 29). Not only is the spatial metaphor at work, but also the possession of a house (the space) by one strong man who must be bound. Since the immediate context is exorcism, it seems appropriate this description as one of demonization. Jesus depicts his own authority with a strength superior to the demon he cast out of the blind and mute man that began the discourse (v. 22). This strength is foundational to a biblical theology that established him as messianic and missional against the powers of darkness.

Second is an employed metaphor of the finger of God (Luke 11:20; cf. Matt 12:28). Continuing his line of thinking against the rationale of the Pharisees, Jesus remarks, "If I drive out demons by the finger of God,

---

28. There is a question of textual originality here, as two of the earliest Markan manuscripts do not contain "and fasting," leading to its omission in many translations. While the instruction of prayer seems appropriate, the narrative does not report Jesus engaging in prayer for this exorcism to be effective. The lack of Jesus modeling prayer before teaching on the importance of prayer reinforces the historical legitimacy of the story for Twelftree (*Jesus the Miracle Worker*, 291): "If the story had its origin in the life of the [later] early church, we could expect it would have reflected this conclusion, with, for example, Jesus being shown to pray as part of his technique."

then the kingdom of God has come upon you." The finger of God finds reference in Aaron's miracle (Exod 8:19) and the writing on the Sinai tablets (Deut 9:10). By relating his own ministry to these activities of God, Christ posited his authority before the skeptical religious leaders.[29] France goes to the heart of the biblical theology here: "Jesus thus claims the arrival in his ministry of that to which the Old Testament and Judaism had looked forward."[30] This finger brings hope of deliverance, healing, and a new victorious life marking the inaugurated kingdom of God.

Third is another element from this discourse, the explanation of an evil spirit returning to a clean house (Matt 12:43–45; Luke 11:24–26). Jesus identifies a special dynamic of demonization when he describes how an exorcized demon "passes through waterless places seeking rest but finds none" (Matt 12:43). So, it returns to find the "house" that is the victim clean, inviting more evil spirits to "enter and dwell there, and the last state of that person is worse than the first" (v. 45). The *Roman Ritual* emphasizes the discipleship of the victim, that he or she should continue in sacramental and spiritual fidelity: "Finally, after the possessed one has been freed, let him be admonished to guard himself carefully against falling into sin, so as to afford no opportunity to the evil spirit of returning, lest the last state of that man become worse than the former."[31]

Central to this work is how a spiritual healing intersects with the physical realm. Theologically, at the heart of an exorcism is a healing, a New Testament kingdom solution to the consequence of suffering rooted in the fall. The healing vision offered by the kingdom was evident in Jesus' opposition to illness.[32] Meanwhile, both illness and demonization were part of Satan's perversion of creation, and both are overcome by the emerging kingdom of God in a conflict theology. Like an intruder in the Garden of Eden, illness is alien to the design of creation. Gregory Boyd remarks, "Every exorcism and every healing marked an advance toward establishing the kingdom of God over and against the kingdom of Satan."[33] Concerning the intersection of disease and demonization, Boyd

---

29. Levine and Witherington, *Gospel of Luke*, 319.

30. France, *Matthew*, 209.

31. "Exorcism of the Possessed" (Weller, ed., *Roman Ritual: Volume 2*, 175). The Earling, Iowa demonization story with its re-experienced exorcisms seems to represent this logistic.

32. Boyd, *Satan and the Problem of Evil*, 37, who writes, "Jesus opposed the illness as something that was not part of God's kingdom."

33. Boyd, *Satan and the Problem of Evil*, 36.

also remarks, "Jesus *never* treated such phenomenon as anything other than the work of the enemy."[34] Augmenting the theology constructed here is the element of mercy. Adam Blai remarks, "Mercy is at the heart of deliverance ministry and exorcisms." Amidst the confusion of the enemy, only God can accomplish this protection to our spiritual selves, as "in this spiritual warfare, we know, and we are known."[35]

Finally, on another occasion the disciple John inquired of Jesus about the validity of an unnamed exorcist who was operating under their auspices (Mark 9:38–39; Luke 9:49–50). Jesus affirmed this other's ministry, saying that no one can do the miracle in his name without affirming him: "For he that is not against us is for us" (Luke 9:50). The passage offers the basic reinforcement of a delegated power to all of Jesus' disciples, including the power of 1949 exorcists to cast out demons. Amy-Jill Levine declares, "Given their own failures, this is a point they, and those who claim today to be their heirs and therefore have a lock on discipleship, need to take seriously."[36]

This authority demonstrated by a believer beyond the twelve anticipates a divine power available to all believers. This power was displayed in the ministry of Jesus and the apostles. While many of the elements of demonization above will be witnessed in the 1949 exorcism, the subject of authority is essential.

Conflict Theology and Kingdom Authority

Conflict theology is the basis of the Christian reading of *Diary* ahead. In Christian thought, this greater drama in which an exorcist participates is part of a larger battle between Christ and Satan, between good and evil. This work of Christ is evident when Jesus goes immediately into the wilderness upon his baptism. Tempted by Satan as Adam was tempted, Christ resists the temptation (Matt 4:1–11; Luke 4:1–13). Here the name "Satan" is first given to describe the *enemy* of God and his grand purposes.[37]

Thousands of years after Eden, with sin now characterizing the fallen human condition, Christ enters the temporal theater of conflict

---

34. Boyd, *Satan and the Problem of Evil*, 36.
35. Blai, *Hauntings*, xi.
36. Levine and Witherington, *Gospel of Luke*, 268.
37. France, *Matthew*, 100.

in a divine-human fashion for humanity. The presence of God on earth, incarnated and participating in the fallen creation in a new way, brings the cosmic drama to a climactic head here in the wilderness. It is no coincidence that natural creation is the venue for Jesus' temptation by Satan. Yet rather than a plush garden with provision for life, it is now a barren desert.[38] From the goodness of creation to the forsakenness of the wilderness, creation is about to be bounce back to a condition before the enemy of God guided its corruption. Following the wilderness, Jesus engages in three plus years of healing, teaching, and miracles to overturn the effects of sin. Greg Boyd remarks, "Creation has been seized by a cosmic force and God is now battling this force to rescue it."[39] Exorcism is one expression of this battle, an eschatological element to his healing ministry. Ben Witherington posits it this way: "He had already defeated Satan at the Temptation; the exorcisms are part of the mop-up operations."[40]

This conflict between Satan and humanity—prototyped by Adam and anti-typed in Christ—becomes the basis for the Christian's participation in kingdom victory over the power of evil. This is the basis for understanding exorcism. The exorcist attends to the demonized victim by marshalling the power of Christ against the oppressor. The authority of Christ is employed, through prayer and through a ritual of prayer, against one weaker and wicked. As it was in the time of Jesus, so the conflict continues for people dealing against the power of sin. Clinton Arnold sets up the worldview for conflict theology: "We live at a time when the present evil age overlaps the age to come. The kingdom of God coexists with the kingdom of darkness, but it is not a peaceful coexistence; there is tension."[41] The Roman Catholic Church augments this confrontation of God's representative to the demon through its sacramental life.[42]

Noteworthy around the biblical passages are displays of authority over demons. Joshua the High Priest is accused by Satan when an angel rebukes the accuser (Zech 3:1–2). Possession of Moses' body was in dispute when the archangel rebuked Satan (Jude 9). These episodes further illustrate the conflict theology at work in the world and demonstrate heavenly authority against the accuser.

---

38. Heiser reinforces this wilderness association with destruction, wildness, and forsakenness associated with demons in ancient thought (*Demons*, 24–30, 214–19).

39. Boyd, *Satan and the Problem of Evil*, 35.

40. Levine and Witherington, *Gospel of Luke*, 126.

41. Arnold, *3 Crucial Questions*, 21.

42. See *Catechism* §§1667–69, 1673; Allison, *Roman Catholic Theology*, 230–38.

This ministry of Jesus in turn shapes the ecclesiology of the church. Ladd remarks, "This messianic struggle with the powers of death, which had been raging in Jesus' ministry and had been shared by his disciples, will be continued in the future, and the church will be the instrument of God's kingdom in the struggle."[43] Conflict theology can be framed as violent and combative in its effort to restore creation and humanity, to bring about a closer reality that anticipates a fuller, eschatological reality. Conflict theology cries, "Thy kingdom come," to God against the forces of darkness that compete with Jesus' inauguration of that kingdom. This power that comes to a Christian, endowed by God in a redeeming arrangement of fallen creation by the Sprit through the Son, foreshadows Satan's final defeat. It is anticipated and claimed throughout the Catholic rite of exorcism, one sample illustration of conflict theology. God is described in the Catholic rite of exorcism as the one "who didst one time consign that fugitive and fallen tyrant to everlasting hell fire," implored by the rite to "strike terror into the beast that lays waste thy vineyard."[44] The conflict within creation is seen at the rationale for the command to be cast out there: "He it is Who commands thee, Who once ordered the sea and the wind and the storm to obey."[45]

Historical Affirmation of the Preternatural

A glance at the understanding and experiences of demons by Christians in history provides insights into the experience of the 1949 exorcism. In an overall effect, such a survey evidences how the church has viewed demons as spirit beings working contrary to the sanctification and ministries of believers. To that end, a brief sampling is provided here for continuity between the New Testament and today, retrieving elements of demonization and exorcism that is instructive for our study.

Ancient and Medieval Thought

The premodern era of the church thought and wrote more comfortably the spiritual dimensions in conflict theology. In the centuries to follow the New Testament period, the legends of the apostles present exorcism

---

43. Ladd, *Theology*, 116.
44. Weller, ed., *Roman Ritual: Volume 2*, 177.
45. Weller, ed., *Roman Ritual: Volume 2*, 185.

at the forefront of their encounters.[46] They evidence an association of demonic activity around pagan idolatry, akin to the testimony of the apostle Paul (1 Cor 10:20), as well as deceitful bondage of people and cultures. The violent resistance to exorcists parallels the 1949 case. The patristic period continued its attention to demons as a genuine and active presence in the world.[47] For example, Justin Martyr wrote how "we do continually beseech God by Jesus Christ to preserve us from the demons."[48] Origen recognizes the place of Christ's name and his victorious testimony for efficacy:

> For it is not by incantations that Christians seem to prevail [over evil spirits], but by the name of Jesus, accompanied by the announcement of the narratives which relate to him; for the repetition of these has frequently been the means of driving demons out of men, especially when those who repeated them did so in a sound and genuinely believing spirit.[49]

Tertullian gives attention to two dynamics of exorcism in his *Apologeticus* that relate to our case study. First, he describes a compulsion for the demon to speak: "The wicked spirit, bidden to speak by a follower of Christ, will as readily make the truthful confession that he is a demon, as elsewhere he has falsely asserted that he is a god." Second, he describes a semi-sacramental conflict leading to exorcism: "Let there be produced one of the god-possessed, as they are supposed, who, inhaling at the altar, conceive divinity from the fumes, who are delivered of it by retching, who vent it forth in agonies of gasping." The effect is that "fearing Christ in God, and God in Christ, they become subject to the servants of God and Christ. So, at our touch and breathing, overwhelmed by the thought and realization of those judgment fires, they leave at our command the bodies they have entered."[50]

One other patristic resource informs our study of the 1949 exorcism that contains liturgical practices around church ceremonies. As baptismal candidates prepared spiritually, Hippolytus's *Traditio apostolica*

---

46. Exorcism activities are especially common in the early apocryphal stories of Bartholomew, Simon, and Jude (see Shelton, *Quest*, 165–68, 215–20, 227).

47. Ferguson, *Demonology*; Sorensen, *Possession and Exorcism*; Bradnick, *Evil, Spirits, and Possession*, 18–53.

48. Justin Martyr, *Dial.* 30 (*ANF* 1:209).

49. Origen, *Cels.* 1.6 (*ANF* 4:398).

50. Tertullian, *Apol.* 23 (*ANF* 3:37–38). All citations in this paragraph are found in this chapter of *Apologeticus*.

reports the practice of laying on hands for exorcism daily. At the moment of baptism, the bishop confronts spiritual forces in a climactic manner: "And laying his hand on them he shall exorcise every evil spirit to flee away from them and never to return to them henceforth. And when he has finished exorcising, let him breathe on their faces and seal their foreheads and ears and noses and let him raise them up."[51] Breath and wind find biblical association with the Holy Spirit (Gen 2:7; John 3:8; Acts 2:2), so the priest symbolically breathes new life into the candidate to replace the old life, the demonic presence, and the sinful quality to be deserted by a Christian. The act harkens back to Jesus' breathing on his disciples, saying, "Receive the Holy Spirit" (John 21:22). Thus, the priest stands in a position to exercise authority towards purification from sin, association with the Satanic, and an infilling of the Holy Spirit.

Graham Twelftree concludes that the early church by and large saw preaching and teaching as primary prongs of its mission rather than deliverance from demon possession, where they relied on Christ more than they emulated him.[52] This Christ-centered authority becomes important in the theology of exorcism. The medieval era perpetuated a powerful premodern worldview that was readily accepting supernatural and preternatural explanations for unexplainable experiences. Francis Young even recognizes a tendency to be "trivial" about exorcism in the era.[53] The habits of the era are instructive when it comes to contemporary accusations of exorcism as being "medieval."

The staple book about the supposed work of Satan in the era was published in 1486 in the city of Speyer, Germany, entitled *The Hammer of Witches*, well-known by its Latin name *Malleus Maleficarum*. From this work, inexplicable forces and tragic events found causal explanation. One excerpt posits its mentality: "The devil attacks us from without and from within. Therefore, Holy Water is ordained against his attacks without; but exorcism against those from within."[54] Germany also strengthened the liturgy of baptismal exorcism in the Catholic West. A monk in the Abbey of St. Alban at Mainz during the tenth century incorporated a priestly exorcism of pre-baptized children where Satan was renounced in association to the candidate's sin. It would remain unchanged until the sixteenth century, reinforcing the culture of demonic awareness and

---

51. Hippolytus, *Trad. ap.* 20.8 (Dix and Chadwick).
52. Twelftree, *In the Name of Jesus*, 29, 281–84.
53. Young, *History of Exorcism*, 61.
54. *The Hammer of Witches* (cited in Nauman, *Exorcism*, 73).

overemphasis. It would also shape the notion of the rite of exorcism as a sacramental of the church. By the early twentieth century, German theologian Adolph Franz offered three essentials for a Catholic sacramental as cultic in use, apotropaic in function, and a welfare for believers.[55]

Intellectual endeavors also participated in demonology. For example, the thirteenth century philosopher Thomas Aquinas says about the feats performed by spirit beings: "Although these works of demons which appear marvelous to us are not real miracles, they are none the less sometimes real happenings" (*Summa Theologiae* [Part 1; Question 115]).[56] Demons cannot do miracles, Aquinas insists, because supernatural works are attributed only to the divine. When demonic operations seem to provide the semblance of a miracle it happens "internally as when demons can effect a change in a man's imagination and even on his bodily senses, so that something appears to be other than it is" (*Summa Theologiae* [Part 1; Question 115]).[57] Likewise, this can happen "externally . . . he can clothe any material thing in a material form, so that is appears in the guise of the latter" (*Summa Theologiae* [Part 1; Question 115]).[58]

Modern Thought

A survey of the modern world finds Christians continuing in this premodern, biblical worldview. The great Reformer Martin Luther showed a penchant towards opposing the devil in his theology. He could not help but frame his thwarted efforts as demonic in cause. "Following him [God] means being initiated into life between God and the Devil,"[59] Oberman describes. This quality is seen most obviously in Luther's hymn "A Mighty Fortress is Our God": "And though this world with devils filled should threaten to undo us, we will not fear, for God hath willed his truth to triumph through us." In a 1576 handbook for exorcists endorsed by the Vatican, *Flagellum Daemonum* or *The Devils Scourge*, Father Girolamo Menghi offered a list of manifestations, including unknown language, superhuman knowledge, superhuman strength, aversion to holy things,

---

55. Young, *History of Exorcism*, 64–65.
56. Aquinas, *Summa Theologiae*, 83 (Charlesworth).
57. Aquinas, *Summa Theologiae*, 85 (Charlesworth).
58. Aquinas, *Summa Theologiae*, 85 (Charlesworth).
59. Oberman, *Luther*, 225 (cf. 179, 212).

deep melancholy, appeal to demonic help, and vomiting of objects. This is virtually the same list that Catholic exorcists use today, Wilkinson explains.[60] The 1626 *Treasury of Exorcisms*, with a provenance in Cologne, demonstrates the tenacity of the exorcist and contains demeaning humiliating language against the demon:

> Thou lustful and stupid one, . . . thou lean sow, famine-stricken and filthiest, thou wrinkled beast, thou mangy beast, thou beast of all beasts the most beastly, . . . thou mad spirit . . . thou bestial and foolish drunkard, . . . most greedy wolf, . . . most abominable whisperer, . . . thou sooty spirit from Tartarus! . . . Loathsome cobbler, . . . dingy collier, . . . filthy sow, . . . perfidious boar, . . . envious crocodile, . . . stinking drudge, . . . rust-colored asp, . . . swollen toad, . . . lousy swineherd, . . . lowest of the low, . . . cudgeled ass![61]

Such disdain and loathsome deprecation of the demon and its reciprocation will be important in the 1949 exorcism event.

With the solidification of the modern era in the eighteenth and nineteenth centuries, and with newfound natural explanations for causes normally attributed to witchcraft, Levack reports the continuation of reported exorcisms alongside a decrease in witch trials. Both Protestants and Catholics perpetuated a belief in demonization, while the Catholic Church recognized the scriptural support for interpreting demonization as a conflict theology.[62]

The late twentieth century saw an explosion of interest in conflict theology, giving rise to the popular category of "spiritual warfare." This era joins the rise in the popular interest around the film *The Exorcist*. This period took various interests, from counseling to theology to popular literature. Some of these trends cost demonization and exorcism credibility. For example, Frank and Ida Mae Hammond's *Pigs in the Parlor* made demonology systematic and demons ubiquitous.[63] Rebecca Brown in *Prepare for War* contends that demons cling to familiar objects as

---

60. Wilkinson, *Vatican's Exorcists*, 41.

61. Nauman, *Exorcism*, 82

62. Levack, *Devil Within*, 215–17, 229–30.

63. Hammond and Hammond, *Pigs in the Parlor*. James Collins describes the tendency: "Predominantly anecdotal, exegetically naïve and simplistic in outlook. It sold like hot cakes and proved profoundly influential. It, and others like it, fueled the already burgeoning interest in the exorcism of evil spirits . . . this represents only the crudest analysis of the debate" (*Exorcism and Deliverance Ministry*, 1).

common as rock-and-roll T-shirts, crucifixes, or pictures of Catholic saints, while insisting that demons transfer between people through sexual activity.[64]

The culture of the church associates these activities with a fringe element. Such works served to create a field of itinerant exorcism ministry that was enthusiastic and hyperbolic, as ministers and laity adopted a suspicious belief in demonic causes for all sorts of ailments and unexplained phenomena. On the other hand, Protestant writings around conflict theology during this time also provided better efforts towards biblical and systematic theology, such Clinton Arnold and Gregory Boyd, although critics offer their challenges.[65]

The next two decades saw new developments and several examples illustrate a new complexity. John Wimber offered a "power" themed approach.[66] David Powlison emphasized a personal confession of sin as repentance, prayer, reading Scripture, and devotion to Christ as central to deliverance.[67] Collins remarks that "the equation of Charismatic deliverance with minor exorcism was the theological bridge over which mutual acceptance of sacramental exorcism and Charismatic deliverance could pass."[68] The fictional work of Frank Peretti, *This Present Darkness* and its sequels, rose to national popularity to promote a prayerful consciousness of demons and a corresponding oversensitivity to the topic.[69]

Within Roman Catholicism, there remains a continuous line of belief that the manifestations witnessed from biblical through historical to contemporary encounters with preternatural spirit beings are real. The *Roman Ritual*, essentially unchanged since 1614, contains characteristics of demonic manifestation that the exorcist should expect to encounter. These are commonly cited manifestations in the testimonies of those

---

64. Brown, *Prepare for War*, 59, 108.

65. Boyd, "Ground-Level Model"; *God at War*; *Satan and the Problem of Evil*; Arnold, *3 Crucial Questions*, 19–58. For a range of contrasting positions, see Beilby and Eddy, eds., *Understanding Spiritual Warfare*.

66. Wimber and Springer, *Power Healing*, 125.

67. Powlison, "Classical Model"; *Power Encounters*. He calls his approach the "classic mode" based on biblical teaching of discipleship. He distinguishes this from the "ekballistic mode of ministry" (EMM), which centers on demon identification, demonic binding, and authoritative casting out. The classic mode shows a superior "reliance on the power and protection of God, embracing the word of God, specific obedience, fervent and focused prayer, and the aid of fellow believer" (*Power Encounters*, 36).

68. James Collins, *Exorcism and Deliverance Ministry*, 191.

69. Peretti, *This Present Darkness*.

who witness demonization and exorcism. The 1949 exorcism shows a continuity with these same characteristics. There is much variety and much subjective interpretation across Catholicism, however, ranging from over-belief to belief to unbelief. For example, Romolo Rossi insists that common manifestation lists of the rite of exorcism have an entirely psychological explanation. Adrenaline can explain the superhuman strength. A foreign language might be informed gibberish, and glossolalia can be a soothing expression for the victim. Aversion to sacred symbols can be merely suggestive or obsessive-compulsive behavior.[70] Even Gabriele Amorth, the former Chief Exorcist of the Vatican, is viewed suspiciously, as Laycock describes his reputation: "Some Catholic authorities regards his work as an embarrassment. Even priests who are sympathetic to claims of possession have dismissed Amorth's claims as unbelievable and sensationalistic and have questioned whether Amorth's approach to exorcism is consistent with Catholic theology and canon law."[71]

Still, the presence and office of formal exorcists in the Catholic Church evidences this priority for the ministry of exorcism. Yet the number of such ministers is proportionately low, given the 64 million Catholic registered in the US. In 2020, Lampert reports 125 officially appointed Catholic exorcists in America, with those numbers greater including many who remain anonymous.[72] For perspective, in 2007, Wilkinson reports that Italy had about 350 exorcists.[73] She also claims that one of them, Monsignor Andrea Gamma, has performed five exorcisms a week for thirteen years.[74]

Contemporary Exorcism Accounts

Alongside historical theological trends are oral legends, primary sources, and secondary literature on recent exorcisms. More popular examples that lack a sound theology in the primary source testimony include the 1877 Wateska case and the 1977 Basa case. While one might imagine demons at work in the legends, the stories lack the credibility of other cases. For example, in Wateska, IL, Lurancy Vennum allowed the gentle

---

70. Romolo Rossi, "Italian Society of Psychopathology 11th Annual Congress, Rome (Feb 2006)" (cited in Wilkinson, *Vatican's Exorcists*, 157–59).
71. Laycock, "Amorth, Gabriele," 9.
72. Lampert, *Exorcism*, 8.
73. Wilkinson, *Vatican's Exorcists*, xiii.
74. Wilkinson, *Vatican's Exorcists*, 86.

spirit of the daughter of spiritist Asa Roff to possess her. The Roff parents even allowed Lurancy to live with them for fifteen weeks, believing her to be their daughter reincarnated. Eventually, the spirit departed and Lurancy was healed.[75] Although Troy Taylor chronicles this event among his demonization cases and calls it a "benevolent possession,"[76] there is no theological motivation to imagine a demon to foster such benevolence. In the Basa case, one Remy Chua began to have visions of the murder of her coworker, Teresita Basa, as well as a sense of disturbance by another male coworker. Remy began to display odd behavior in which she acted, talked, and sounded like Teresita herself, leading her husband to believe her possessed. However, she supposedly provided communication from Teresita to the police, that leading the arrest of the perpetrator, the other coworker.[77] Again, the pleasant result of the potential demonization lacks theological congruency and neither episode here informs the 1949 exorcism.

Other examples offer a more preternatural and theological explanation that inform a study like ours. The 1906 Cele case tells of a girl in Umzinto, South Africa, engaged in occultic activity who manifested demonization. Uncontrollable violent behavior, unprecedented and impossible strength, beast-like behavior, recognition of the difference between holy water and objects, and violence against exorcists were evidenced.[78] Comparatively well-documented is the 1928 Iowa case of Emma Schmidt,[79] where a twenty-three-day exorcism was marked by two responses: her slumbering into unconsciousness and her sudden burst of alternative energy, strength, and voices. Schmidt offered atypical obscenities and laughing in church; unexplainable strength and violence; screams, howls, and growls with witness testimony that her mouth did not open; ability to distinguish between holy objects and feigned holy objects; inexplicable knowledge of people and another language; and dung as a sign of expulsion.[80] A published pamphlet in 1935 by Carl Vogl brought the story to popular attention in America.[81] The 1937 Wu case relates how a diabolical Nanking killer named Thomas Wu, charged with

75. Taylor, *Devil Came to St. Louis*, 31–37; Roland, *Complete Book of Ghosts*, 236–40.
76. Taylor, *Devil Came to St. Louis*, 32.
77. Taylor, *Devil Came to St. Louis*, 37–44.
78. Taylor, *Devil Came to St. Louis*, 22–26; Levack, *Devil Within*, 240–41.
79. The pseudonyms of Anna Ecklund and Mary X are sometimes used.
80. Bunse, "Earling Possession Case"; Young, *History of Exorcism*, 199–200.
81. Carl Vogl, *Begone Satan!*

killing and eating at least five women, was confronted by missionary priest Father Michael Strong. The attempted exorcism saw a resistance of the demon to yield its name upon command of the rite, demonic mocking of the exorcist, and emergence of flames that required the priest to be pulled from the burning building, living in regret for his defeat at the resistance of Satan that night.[82] Additional cases worthy of comparison to the 1949 exorcism are the 1865 demonization of twin boys in Illfurt, Germany, sometimes considered the first modern account,[83] and the 2014 demonization of the children of Latoya Ammons in Gary, IN.[84] The recognition of such reports to evidence a demonic-centered approach to the exorcism offer better theology and allow a biblical assessment to their contents.

Perhaps the most interesting and the best documented case beyond the 1949 exorcism is the 1975–1976 Klingenberg case of Anneliese Michel of Klingenberg am Main, Germany. Years of unsuccessful medical treatments were accompanied by horrific visions and voices that led her parents to believe she was possessed. Physical and psychological symptoms abound: epilepsy, severe headaches, walking around stiffly, displaying unexplainable strength, displaying claw-like hand positions, paralysis, trance-like states, depression, feelings of internal condemnation, guttural screams, irregular profanity, or violent language. Spiritual symptoms accompanied these: numerous aversions to religious symbols, testimony of mysterious presences, citing the demons as prohibiting food while eating spiders and flies while sleeping on the basement floor, and unexplained supernatural experiences. Anneliese began to improve before she worsened, cycling in and out over the years, and the demons were thought to be exorcised in October 1975 as she retched and vomited. Goodman suggests that another demon entered until she eventually wore down physically, including starvation, so that she died in July 1976.[85] There are claims that the episodes were audio taped over forty-two episodes, providing an immense volume of historical details of application of the rite and manifestations of the demonic.[86] Two years later, civil court saw

---

82. Martin, *Hostage to the Devil*, 3–7, 447–57; Roland, *Complete Book of Ghosts*, 222–25.

83. Masters, *Devil's Dominion*, 186–89.

84. Hallowell, *Playing with Fire*, 11–22.

85. Goodman, *Exorcism*, 114–22; Odle, "Ethnography of the Devil," 177; Taylor, *Devil Came to St. Louis*, 44–49; and Levack, *Devil Within*, 240–41.

86. Goodman, *How about Demons?* 114.

the priests and parents defending against negligent homicide. The intellectual tension between the physical and spiritual causes led to the 2005 American film *The Exorcism of Emily Rose*, where the girl was renamed and the plot offered enough uncertainty about her condition for viewers to make their own judgment.

Even this brief survey should demonstrate that the 1949 exorcism is hardly a historical anomaly. It introduces the consistent belief within the church that demons are fallen spirits at work in the world to thwart the work of God by causing suffering to his creation. While the early modern church continued its beliefs in demons and demonization, the late seventeenth to early nineteenth century Enlightenment era reinterpreted the world through more natural means than the premodern worldview. Its thinkers recognized how easily the ancient world attributed inexplainable, natural effects to spiritual causes, giving rise to science, medicine, and social science. For example, Oesterreich felt that all accounts of demonization among the ancients should today find a diagnosis of some form of psychosis: "We are dealing throughout and always with parasitic psychic obsessions. There develops in the psyche a sort of secondary system of personality which directs the person's life against his will."[87] Appealing strongly to Enlightenment philosophy, he documents numerous cases in which he employs a psychosomatic explanation to eclipse the preternatural explanation. For him, ethnography shows how missionaries "inspire the natives with trust in God and free them from the fear of demons and their attacks on the souls of the living."[88] Thus, demonization and exorcism as religious concepts would likely thrive in regions without an Enlightenment perspective. Contemporary views inherit this worldview, framing conflict theology exclusively with medical, psychiatric, and psychological explanations. Since they bear directly on any interpretation of the 1949 exorcism, they are explored below as critiques to the traditional view of demonization and exorcism.

CRITICAL PERSPECTIVES ON THE PRETERNATURAL

Interpreting the 1949 exorcism along natural lines provides a fascinating set of justifications for causes beyond the preternatural. Three major spheres of alternative explanations mark the literature. The first sphere

---

87. Oesterreich, *Possession*, 65.
88. Oesterreich, *Possession*, 379.

is the scientific critiques, such as philosophical naturalism and clinical diagnoses. The second sphere is sociological critiques, such as cultural perceptions and political explanations. The third sphere is an ecclesiastical critique, marking those who disbelieve that a Catholic version of exorcism can be effective and reducing the exorcism to chance. After a summary of each critical perspective, a reasonable appeal for objectivity is offered.

Scientific Critiques

Perhaps one of the greatest achievements of the last three hundred years is the contribution of science to our understanding of the world. It explains the invisible more accurately than ever, providing powerful insights into the unseen world from our own DNA to the surface of Mars. As scientists are conditioned to seek naturalistic explanations for the world, philosophical naturalism often emerges to deny any non-natural explanation or to compel a hypothesized natural cause. In turn, this philosophy can foster a popular suspicion of manufactured religious experiences and gives a stigma to dramatic spiritual warfare.

Philosophical Naturalism

As the Enlightenment period in the West celebrated rational and explainable explanations for traditionally spiritual causes, many of its thinkers came to deny the supernatural work of a divine being and the preternatural works of spirit beings. An example of inconvincibility of miraculous testimony is philosopher David Hume, who wrote in 1748, "No testimony for any kind of miracle has ever amounted to a probability, much less a proof."[89] For an empiricist like Hume, the senses—particularly the observable—is the basis for positing belief: "It is experience only, which gives authority to human testimony; and it is the same experience, which assures us of the laws of nature."[90] Since Hume could not see the miracles of the New Testament and since readers could not witness an exorcism in 1949, such a skeptic has no commitment to faith of a supposed miracle: "Therefore we may establish it as a maxim that no human testimony can have such force as to prove a miracle, and make it a just foundation for

---

89. Hume, *Enquiry*, 183.
90. Hume, *Enquiry*, 184 (see §10.35).

any such system of religion."⁹¹ Contemporary science is marked by this same naturalistic empiricism. Bradnick describes the effect: "Naturalism would propose that there is only one type of causation—efficient causation—which is exclusively physically-based and can be explained by reducing events to their lowest-level ontological substrates."⁹²

The insistence on rational and natural explanations for all matters can be termed "philosophical naturalism." Jon Tal Murphree speaks of it this way: "Now a major portion of the scientific community refuses to allow itself to identify any pointers to God, no matter how strong the scientific evidence. That is the peril of naturalism speaking in the name of science."⁹³ Alvin Plantinga speaks similarly: "Science discovers and endorses natural laws; if God did miracles or acted specifically in the world, he would have to contravene these laws and miraculously intervene; and that is incompatible with science."⁹⁴

This pressure to explain spiritual causes in the world as naturalistic cannot be overstated. Charles Taylor recognizes this secularizing social condition in which religion is associated with mere belief but science with fact: "Science refutes and hence crowds out religious belief."⁹⁵ C. S. Lewis took great lengths to engage philosophical naturalism in his book *Miracles*, but his famous quote comes from *The Screwtape Letters*: "There are two equal and opposite errors into which our race can fall about the devils. One is to disbelieve in their existence. The other is to believe, and then feel and excessive and unhealthy interest in them. They themselves are equally pleased by both errors, and hail a materialist or a magician with the same delight."⁹⁶ Even a recent *New York Times* writer recognized how the film *The Exorcist* framed an "opposition of modernity and tradition" through the dramatization of the two priestly characters.⁹⁷

A Christian worldview expands the borders of the naturalist to include the supernatural, while philosophical naturalism reduces the soul to psychology, the spiritual to a metaphor, goodness to personal ethics, and hope for life beyond life to a fable. Meanwhile, religion is alive and well in the world to entertain and even realize causes beyond the natural.

91. Hume, *Enquiry*, 184 (see §10.35).
92. Bradnick, *Evil, Spirits, and Possession*, 67.
93. Murphree, *Science's Unscientific Claim*, 35.
94. Plantinga, *Where the Conflict Really Lie*, 75.
95. Taylor, *Secular Age*, 4.
96. Lewis, *Screwtape Letters*, 3.
97. Walther, "Spiritual Lessons."

Likewise, the rise of interest in magic, the occult, and even accounts of demonization and exorcism provide a re-enchantment of the preternatural.[98] Michael Green recognizes these particularly in the Western culture, where rationalism and skepticism eclipse even the miraculous essentials of the faith such as belief in the resurrection.[99] John Nicola recognizes the place of demonization in this situation: "There exists a gnawing inability to explain in purely human terms the origin of a complex web of evil which constantly seeks to engulf humanity."[100]

Critical readings of the Bible have crippled the church in its confidence about the supernatural. This is especially true outside conservative Protestant circles and outside conservative, pre-Vatican II Roman Catholic circles, where many secularists insist on explanation in the social, psychological, and scientific. Here, the traditional *supernaturalism* is filtered through a modern, natural explanation of phenomena. Theologically, Paul Tillich emphasized a *correlation* between truths that essentially called for an adjustment of the biblical or traditional to match philosophical and scientific truth, while Rudolph Bultmann called for "demythologizing" of Scripture from its record of supernatural events.[101] In the nineteenth and twentieth centuries, this purging of the supernatural sterilized the confidence, belief, and fundamental heart of the church's theology, reducing it in many ways—including its perception of the supernatural—to a reduced position that Berger calls a state of "cognitive minority." This represents the position of this book: "people whose view of the world differs significantly from the one generally taken for granted in their society."[102] Alvin Plantinga recognizes that classical science before modernism did not in fact view the world as causally closed to the divine but saw compatibility between "science and divine special action, including miracles."[103]

The scientific bent of our culture leans towards the scientification and demythologization of unexplainable events. Even biblical and theological studies had its era of scientific demythologization, deconstructing the biblical texts to explain certain spiritual matters, including demons.

---

98. Possamai and Giordan, "Introduction."

99. Green, *I Believe in Satan's Downfall*, 112–18.

100. Nicola, *Diabolical Possession*, 13.

101. For a good evaluation of Tillich and Bultmann, see Bradnick, *Evil, Spirits, and Possession*, 91–95 and 96–101, respectively.

102. Berger, *Rumor of Angels*, 7.

103. Plantinga, *Where the Conflict Really Lies*, 83.

Preternaturalism and its Critics

Critical New Testament scholar Rudolph Bultmann and social theologian Walter Wink are models of this approach. Bultmann evidences skepticism when he insists in this much-quoted citation: "It is impossible to use the electric light and the wireless and to avail ourselves of modern medical and surgical discoveries, and at the same time to believe in the New Testament world of spirits and miracles."[104] Similarly, Wink seeks to integrate biblical studies and social sciences in a way that recovers the Bible from preconceived attitudes for a contemporary society. Demons as spiritual beings in Scripture become "powers," and these powers are systems in society that oppress and possess people. Demonic powers are "the systems themselves, the institutions and structures that weave society into an intricate fabric of power and relationships." While he promotes these powers from their bondage of the spiritual world, he diminishes the ontology of evil spirit beings in a theology of conflict theology.[105] Wink's application of biblical criticism fits perfectly in the sociological critiques below.

For Christians who attempt this worldview, it is akin to a practicing deism in which God created the world supernaturally but ceases to continue to engage it as he transcends the created operative order. This is no more evident around the 1949 exorcism that when a physics professor in Washington, DC, supposedly witnessed preternatural activity when Robbi's bed stood levitated. He is noted as remarking, "There is much we have yet to discover concerning the nature of *electromagnetism*." William Peter Blatty, researcher and author of *The Exorcist*, recognizes how the remark crowns science and eliminates any merit for alternative responses. He rightly calls it "an observation impervious to challenge."[106] Instead, Christian thought invites a mysterious element, inexplicable and beyond the natural, as a cause for the preternatural and the supernatural. This study scrutinizes the natural while also permitting a place for the supernatural. Just as the exorcist functions as a pastor in the life of the demonized victim, he also enters the realm of the spiritual to confront the demon. After interviewing multiple seasoned exorcists in Rome,

---

104. Bultmann, "New Testament and Mythology," 5. For a precise evaluation of Bultmann's view along these lines, see Bradnick, *Evil, Spirits, and Possession*, 91–95.

105. Wink, *Powers that Be*, 1. For Wink's own representative view, see his "World Systems Model." For a precise evaluation of Wink's view, see Bradnick, *Evil, Spirits, and Possession*, 105–10.

106. Blatty, *On The Exorcist*, 24 (emphasis mine).

Matt Baglio reports that even exorcists speak about "thing that couldn't be known" around their exorcism experiences.[107]

Medical Explanations for Manifestations

The most common naturalistic approach to demonization is the attribution of mental illness. Medical professionals challenge the concept of demonization, attributing the condition to "hysteria, unconscious role-playing, high suggestibility on the part of patrons."[108] This attitude promotes the psychological attribution of epilepsy, psychosis, and hysteria to see any demonic activity as having an inevitable physical or psychological cause. This modern assessment extends to all supernatural and preternatural phenomena. For example, in John Kildahl's *The Psychology of Speaking in Tongues*, a behavioral scientist studied and interviewed individuals claiming the gift of tongues, or glossolalia, which is recognized biblically as a supernatural work. While this scientist recognized the potential community and individual benefits, along with its possibility of being a gift of God's providential care, he also asserts that glossolalia can be learned. "It is not uniquely spiritual; it is not uniquely the result of God's intervention in man's speech."[109]

The 1949 case is marked by inexplicable behavior and manifestations akin to delusions, paranoia, dissociation, manic depression, and hallucinations as marks of a possible mental illness. These are often assigned under the diagnostic rubric of schizophrenia, which is a common place holder for the uncertainty around the difficult diagnoses desired. Perhaps the most recognizable quality related to our case study might be the diagnosis of conversion disorder. Here, anxiety is converted to physical symptoms commonly shared with demonization accounts. A social scientist would immediately entertain an expression of mental illness, a starting point for a consideration of the sociological challenge. It is recognizable that the psychological initiative seeks the best explanation, sometimes working in theoretical concepts simply bearing the name of diagnosis.[110]

---

107. Baglio, *Rite*, 245.
108. Wilkinson, *Vatican's Exorcists*, 5.
109. Kildahl, *Psychology*, 86.
110. For one of the best summaries of challenges from psychology and its proponents, see Bradnick, *Evil, Spirits, and Possession*, 118–37.

The victim was a thirteen-year-old boy. His natural teenage emotional challenges may have been augmented by family dysfunction. So, when Robbie began to show irregular acts of violence, it would compete with any attempt to explain the shaking of his mattress following the sound of footsteps in the house. The appearance of words scratched from within his flesh confused the family even more. The diarist once referred to "whatever force" to describe the scratches, and he would ultimately link the force to the boy's behavior and the material aberrations as demonization.[111] Bowdern himself is noted as remarking in this case that a seven-year-old could have discerned the difference between the demonized Robbie and a mentally ill person.[112]

Like physicians, clinical psychologists offer a naturalistic explanation by attributing demonic behavior to cognitive activities of the subject. The psychological or psychiatric hypothesis is as old as Sigmund Freud himself, who proposes "states of [demonic] possession correspond to our neuroses . . . we regard them as having arisen in the patient's internal life, where they have their abode."[113] Tracy Wilkinson reports that many believe exorcism functions as a kind of hypnotic experience in itself, "creating the same state of consciousness that hypnosis would." She suggests that the rhythm of the liturgy, the inward reflection of the patient, the isolation of the experience, and the accompanying suggestion of demonization serve as a powerful proposition that the person is possessed. As a good hypnotist can make a patient bark like a dog, a good exorcist can make a patient speak like the devil.[114] The power of suggestion becomes a justification for behavior otherwise attributed to demonic manifestation. One Catholic bishop expressed how the rite of exorcism offers a calming effect to the subject that can reinforce a belief in a present demon: "Disturbances of this sort often are purely subjective. Yet the rite of exorcism often seems to quiet the persons' mind."[115]

Mainline biblical scholarship has partnered with medical and social science to ascribe mental and physical illness to the New Testament. For example, Lamar Williamson says of the Gadarene demoniac of Mark 5, "This element in the text parallels an insight of contemporary medicine

---

111. *Diary*, "Background."
112. Cooper and Epperson, *Evil*, 26.
113. Freud, "Seventeenth-Century Demonological Neurosis," 72.
114. Wilkinson, *Vatican's Exorcists*, 151.
115. Robert Mortimer (Bishop of Exeter) (cited in Masters, *Devil's Dominion*, 183–84).

and psychology: The causes of emotional disorder are often complex. Under any single diagnosis may lurk multiple causes, physical and psychic."[116] He remarks of the demoniac boy of Mark 9, "The symptoms described however, sound like the seizures we call 'epilepsy' ... *from the viewpoint of the text*, the boy is a victim of a hostile force which proves to be the subject to the authority and command of Jesus."[117] Rudolph Bultmann represents the medical causation well: "Now that the forces and the laws of nature have been discovered, we can no longer believe in *spirits, whether good or evil* . . . not daemonic beings which enslave mankind to their service."[118]

For example, the *Diary* from the 1949 exorcism reports how eyewitnesses saw scratches forming words from inside the boy's body into his skin. Scientists have sought to explain these phenomena in the 1949 events as angioneurotic edema, a swelling under the skin that can appear as red lumps or ridges. Cortés and Gatti argue, "All clinical psychologists know that in many cases of hysteria the skin becomes particularly sensitive."[119] Of interest in our event at hand is that all sources—both primary and secondary and faith-based and secular—make mention of attempts to identify a psychological and medical diagnosis. Yet these diagnoses seemed to have nothing to offer the demonized boy and his tormented family. In 1949, Robbie and his grandmother heard scratching noises on the floors of their home. The natural inclination of the father on the next morning was to call an exterminator to discover the locations of the imagined rats causing the infested noises.[120] Naturally, the notion of an evil spirit being present would have been presumptuous or even prosperous as a first explanation. When their Lutheran pastor heard the family reports of Robbie's nighttime manifestations, he reports a scientific approach to evaluating the reports: "I had him in my home on the night of February 17–18 to observe him for myself." After observing activities that he called "paranormal," Rev. Schulze saw the boy enter the County Medical Hygiene Clinic under a University doctor.[121] These were appropriate scientific approaches to phenomena that were tested along

---

116. Williamson, *Mark*, 106–7.

117. Williamson, *Mark*, 164.

118. Bultmann, "New Testament and Mythology," 4.

119. Cortés and Gatti, *Case against Possessions and Exorcisms*, 79, 83.

120. *Diary*, "Background."

121. See Letter A in "Appendix A: The Letters between the Rev. Luther Miles Schulze and Dr. J. B. Rhine" in Rueda, *Diabolical Possession*, 161.

natural explanations. The real test of the caretakers would follow, when natural and scientific explanations could not satisfy.

Yet behavioral specialist Melissa A. Bromwell recognizes that biology cannot explain many things related to supposed demonization. In particular, she names decreased room temperatures, unexplained writings and sounds, and unexplained movements like levitation. "One cannot dismiss the possibility that demonic possession is a real and true phenomenon."[122] For generations, Christian historians have also convincingly demonstrated an integrity of religious experiences—even those related to demonization and exorcism—in shaping our understanding of the faith. Not all experiences need to find naturalistic explanations, realizing an unexplainable nature of phenomena as well as the spiritual and emotional dimensions to our being. The science related to our case study comes as a powerful testimony to the inexplicable by scientific means alone. Even the *Roman Ritual*, which contains the rite of exorcism, recognizes the erroneous presumption that "Satan has no existence outside of the product of fable, superstition, or fragment," and it calls it "an error endemic in materialists of any age."[123]

Psychologists Terry Cooper and Cindy Epperson assess the potential for several mental illness diagnoses of the 1949 demonized boy, Robbie, based on the historical report: multiple personality disorder, schizophrenia, Tourette's Syndrome, sexual abuse, group hysteria, and paranormal behavior. While their analysis is brief, it does not overreach like many specialists reflecting on the event, and it posits logical challenges to a potential natural diagnosis. Their conclusion is that his behavior satisfies no classifiable psychological disorder. For example, for multiple personality disorder, they point out the lack of psychotherapy necessary for improvement and question how the boy's symptoms suddenly disappeared to end the ordeal. They also recognize how this disorder cannot explain the strange paranormal activities around the boy.[124] The explanatory option of mental health and psychological illness around the 1949 demonization

---

122. Melissa A. Bromley, "Demonic Possession" (cited in Rueda, *Diabolical Possession*, 158).

123. "Exorcism" (Weller, ed., *Roman Ritual: Volume 2*, 160). Since this section in integrally woven into the *Roman Ritual* without author familiarity to many, its citations will be "Exorcism" (*Roman Ritual*) henceforth.

124. Cooper and Epperson, *Evil*, 27–32. For a summary, see Spitzer, *Christ Versus Satan*, 171–73.

victim finds further explanation later. The spiritual option offers a balanced view of the historical event under consideration.

Sociological Critiques

Social scientists join natural scientists in a tendency to assign unexplainable behaviors to the realm of natural explanation. Social psychologists and sociologists are the relevant members here. Their critique participates in the demise of a supernatural worldview in our society. Peter Berger identified the state of things fifty years ago: "Today the supernatural as a meaningful reality is absent or remote from the horizons of everyday life of large numbers, very probably of the majority, of people in modern societies who seem to manage to get along without it quite well." The sociological consequence is that those who maintain supernatural explanations or even possibilities find themselves feeling unconventional, stressed by the realization that they are a "cognitive minority" in which their inferior value statements interfere with real "knowledge."[125] Such a popular attitude provides a foundation for suspicion around the preternatural. Sociological critiques here center on culture and cultural norms, having covered clinical psychology above.

Cultural Suspicion around the Demonic

Three intellectual forces shape suspicion around popular views against demons. First, philosophical naturalism described above conditions people to think in material and less metaphysical ways. Second, popular spiritual warfare can be theologically uncritical and can appear embarrassing for the church. This subpopulation has a reputation for being passionately interested advocates for demonic interests, ranging from mistrusted scholars to deliverance ministers to genuine fanatics. These voices sometimes exacerbate society's disdain of religion, and their hyperbole appears paranoid about the ubiquity of demonic influence. For example, Frank and Ida Mae Hammond open their book *Pigs in the Parlor* with this lead: "Demon spirits can invade and indwell human bodies. It is their objective to do so."[126] They go on to provide a list of fifty-three demon groupings across hundreds of named demons, like an objective

---

125. Berger, *Rumor of Angels*, 5–9.
126. Hammond and Hammond, *Pigs in the Parlor*, 1.

scientific taxonomy. In *Deliver Us from Evil*, Don Basham offers a sample test for self-diagnosing the presence of an evil spirit in two steps. If prayer, confession, submission, and discipline do not relieve a person of his or her sins, then "you may be dealing with a demon—and you should seek deliverance."[127] The instruction is offered in less than eighty words. While some of these provide testimonies and while their research may be credible, the culture of the church associates these activities with a fringe element. Spiritual warfare thinkers are often viewed suspiciously, as some theologians of this movement reinforce the axiom of seeing a demon behind every tree.

Third, the release of popular films featuring demonization muddies the water even further. These works include historical fiction, often with dramatic embellishments, like the 2005 film *The Exorcism of Emily Rose* introduced above. Based on a historical exorcism, this film guides the audience to decide for themselves whether the events were justifiably supernatural or merely natural but certainly engenders sympathy against priestly exorcism. While the prosecution argued from the physical and scientific, even psychological, the mother of Annaliese Michel is noted as exhausted that possession was subordinated to a mere mental disorder. The intense recordings were played during the trail, as screams, liturgical readings, and a recognizable third voice intermittently troubled the jury charged with a verdict. Priests and parents were found guilty of negligent manslaughter, yet sentences were rendered with a measure of leniency. Its exorcist Father Rodewyk would later write on exorcism, sustaining medical psychological explanations along with spiritual explanation with some balance. A later conference of German bishops would require the presence of a medical professional during future exorcisms.[128]

Popular films might also include invented fictions with dramatic embellishment rooted in theology, like the 1999 film *Stigmata* or the 2016 film *Incarnate*, where religion, demons, and creative situations intersect anew. Noteworthy in shaping popular opinion about demonization and exorcism is not only the classic forerunner to these movies *The Exorcist* (1973), which finds its basis in the 1949 exorcism at hand. It also spawned several films that claimed the same story line: *Exorcist II: The*

---

127. Basham, *Deliver Us from Evil*, 119. After the two-step formula, later this pastor does offer elaboration on self-assessment for demonization with self-exorcism steps (202–8). Still, this elaborative chapter is entitled, "Right Now, In your Own Room."

128. Goodman, *Exorcism; How about Demons?* 114–22; Taylor, *Devil Came to St. Louis*, 44–49; and Levack, *Devil Within*, 240–41.

Heretic (1977); *Exorcist III* (1990); *Exorcist: The Beginning* (2004); and *Dominion: Prequel to the Exorcist* (2005). It is obvious from the popularity of these films that demonization is a theme of horror movies that shape popular culture's view of the spiritual realm, usually without Christian witness or Scripture involved in the storyline. While this means the public is talking about demon possession, a dishonor is often committed against Christianity through film sensationalism. As a result, a vast section of the Christian academy is hesitant to be involved in the subject.

However, philosophical naturalism, spiritual warfare obsessions, and exaggerated popular films should not stand as the whole set of sociological influences in viewing demonization and exorcism. Sociologists are beginning to show that exorcism is "no longer as an atavistic [ancient] ritual in conflict with science and modernity."[129] While these interpretive readings of demonization and exorcism from the Bible by social psychologists and sociologists are attempts to explain what proves even to them to be unexplainable, one can maintain more. Anthony Masters remarks, "But of possession there is little knowledge, and explanations concerning hysteria and obsession are barely satisfactory in face of the mass of evidence for the inexplicable."[130]

Stepping beyond Western culture, which marks many readers of this book, reveals more cultural openness to metaphysical phenomena, which in turn helps repair the suspicion around the preternatural. Anthropological studies augment our cultural understanding as they provide insights from across the globe, showing similarities and varieties of demonization and its cultural interpretations.[131] While various cultures enjoy an independence of each other, they manifest the same types of phenomena akin to demonization that the Bible reports in the first century. Joy Vaughan has convincingly shown that the reports of demonization experiences in the biblical narrative of Luke–Acts are "characteristically analogous" to those "found in ethnographies and anthropological

---

129. Possamai and Giordan, "Introduction," 1.

130. Masters, *Devil's Dominion*, 211. Masters does not necessarily concede the unexplainable to the supernatural however: "Possession is a separate condition well removed from physical or mental illness, although both may play some small part in its makeup. If my argument is to be accepted and possession is seen as a separate and specific state of mind, then it is worth investigating in a separate and specific way. Everyone accepts that many of the secrets of the mind are as yet unrevealed to us. Surely this mystical and terrifying secret is a classic example" (232).

131. For a summary of challenges from anthropology and its proponents, see Bradnick, *Evil, Spirits, and Possession*, 137–48.

writings" across the globe.[132] The extent of this documentability is evidenced in Craig Keener who claims, "anthropologists have documented spirit possession or analogous experiences in a majority of cultures, although interpretations of the experiences vary."[133] Adam Possamai and Guiseppe Giordan have demonstrated how a social science evaluation of exorcism can find demonstration in cultures and times ranging from nineteenth-century France to the secularized Quebec. They seek to bridge science and faith, contending that for late modern society, "Science is no longer the dominant paradigm and must engage more and more with religions."[134]

Metaphor for Social Obstacles

The Enlightenment influenced mainline Protestant biblical and theological scholars to seek out philosophically natural explanations for supernatural and preternatural activities. Sociological alternatives became popular readings of the New Testament in the twentieth century. One relevant option is that biblical illnesses are viewed as socio-political obstructions from which the victim is liberated by the social healing of Jesus. Scholars like John Pilch and John Dominic Crossan maintain that Jesus did not cure any diseases—medical conditions, but that he did heal the illness of the person—sociocultural challenges framed metaphorically as physical illness.[135] At work in their theory is a "somatic symptom disorder," where a mental disorder is undiagnosable but can invite a cure that is equally undiagnosable, including a miraculous, a medical, or preferably a social solution. For example, Pilch remarks, "The concept and word 'illness' reflect a sociocultural perspective that depends entirely upon social and personal perception of certain socially disvalued states."[136] He accuses medical materialism for shaping expectations of a medical reading without regard for a cultural reading: "What is needed is a way to imagine Luke's language of sickness and healing in terms of his own culture, that is, a new scenario."[137] Similarly, Crossan remarks,

---

132. Vaughan, *Phenomenal Phenomena*, 206.
133. Keener, "Spiritual Possession," 215.
134. Possamai and Giordan, "Introduction," 5.
135. Pilch, *Healing in the New Testament*; Crossan, *Jesus*.
136. Pilch, "Sickness and Healing," 191.
137. Pilch, "Sickness and Healing," 182.

> I presume that Jesus, who did not and could not cure that disease [leprosy] or any other one, healed the poor man's illness by refusing to accept the disease's ritual uncleanness and social ostracization... By healing the illness without curing the disease, Jesus acted as an alternative boundary keeper in a way subversive to the established procedures of his society.[138]

Richard Horsley joins Crossan in believing that the accounts of demon possession represent social illnesses, especially that Jesus' exorcisms function as a symbolic defeat of Roman rule.[139] A mute person in the Gospels becomes one whose voice is socially suppressed; a blind person is one whose vision is thwarted by political obstacles. Ben Witherington describes this interpretation in the Gadarene exorcism passage: "One could conclude that the demons symbolize Roman authority; just as the demons possess the man and strip him of his resources, so do the Romans possess the lands and people and take what they want."[140]

Yet the new semantic distinction between "disease" and "illness," as well as "cure" and "heal," cannot reduce demonization to social-oriented obstacles to be overcome. Pieter Craffert renounces such a view: "The fallacious implication of this kind of reasoning is that if no laboratory is around, people cannot suffer from diseases... In this view, cross-cultural interpretation takes place when biomedical categories are avoided and local explanations are endorsed."[141] Likewise, Amanda Witmer has shown that social positions and marginality, commonality with other exorcists, the presence of witnesses, and the worldview of agrarian society do not require us to accept Jesus as a strategist who used exorcism to accomplish social improvement. Like his audience, she shares a belief in demons.[142] Such a methodological reading of the Bible finds a parallel in socially allegorical interpretations.

---

138. Crossan, *Jesus*, 82.

139. Horsley, *Jesus and Empire*, 102–9. Crossan (*Jesus*) mixes the psychology and the political oppression: "An occupied country has, as it were, a multiple-personality disorder" (89) and the citizens have a "split-personality position" (91).

140. Levine and Witherington, *Gospel of Luke*, 239.

141. Craffert, "Medical Anthropology," 11.

142. Witmer, *Jesus*, 203–7 (viz. 206).

Allegory for Life Challenges

Some interpreters of the New Testament reduce the difficulties of demonization to allegorical parallels of the difficulties of life. For example, concerning Jesus' description of demons returning to the victim to take up residence in the house now clean (Luke 11:24–26), Amy-Jill Levine hypothesizes:

> Perhaps the parable is a warning: compulsions to keep things neat and tidy can be problematic. The more we try to pick up every crumb, straighten every line, and avoid the untidiness that is human life, the less comfortable we are, the less able we are to offer hospitality or take a break in our schedule. Accepting a bit of messiness may be a good way of avoiding demons.[143]

Her commentary on Luke is marked by an either/or conjoining of spiritual/personal meanings to demonization and exorcism. The departure of demons through exorcism is qualified, "Whether spiritual powers or addictive behavior." The return of demons are akin to "the reality of the cancer or the depression returns with a crash."[144] Concerning Jesus' declaration that he casts out demons by the Spirit of God, they introduce more than spiritual possession: "This Kingdom is one of self-possession rather than demonic possession; it is one in which evil, of any sort, human or supernatural, is cast out."[145]

Like the other social readings of the Gospels exorcisms, these interpretations bring to the text what is not contained there. The claim is that meaning is contained in the cultural setting, but such a reading requires more generosity than believing in the spiritual beings consistently depicted in the testimony and theology of the Bible.

A similar separation of the claims of the biblical text from its historical value is the approach of John and Harvey Walton. Their historical hermeneutic sees spirit beings as a collective literary device in an ancient cosmological worldview, documented in the ancient Near Eastern and Greco-Roman sources. References to demons and spirits in the biblical text do not affirm the beliefs of the original audience as being true, nor does it affirm their cosmology, but the text reflects the original cultural setting where ancient readers understood God in their own "cognitive

---

143. Levine and Witherington, *Gospel of Luke*, 320–21.
144. Levine and Witherington, *Gospel of Luke*, 320.
145. Levine and Witherington, *Gospel of Luke*, 319.

environment."¹⁴⁶ Descriptions of demons become a literary device or a metaphor to reflect the culture's conception of evil divine forces, and "as such the portrayal fits well with other aspects of biblical theology."¹⁴⁷ Vincent Lampert accuses the position this way: "This reads too much into the sacred text. If Jesus makes the distinction between evil spirits and sickness, then we make the distinction as well and recognize the reality of these spiritual creatures."¹⁴⁸

Accepting the claims of the biblical text about demons as fallen spirit beings offers a more reasonable account of the stories and a more coherent theology. A fairer reading joins the momentum of historical voices above to reestablish a place for supernatural explanation in social and religious circles. However, a biblical, supernatural perspective nowadays still hangs in delicate balance with an overwhelming cultural scientific naturalism. As the church continues to live with the tension between the natural and supernatural, between modern and postmodern worldviews, this 1949 exorcism account has something important to offer. It provides a solid, historical event that evidences a documented hypothesis, observation, testing, and thus makes a claim to historical demonization and exorcism. Its credibility is enhanced when one considers that it comes from a day in which Catholicism was trying to forbid exorcisms, surely greatly influenced by the social stigma, but finally had to concede biblical demonization in this account. The activities that followed served to validate the decision, when a St. Louis priest devoted to prayer and characterized by humility found himself plunged into spiritual activity outside the normal, natural world. No metaphor for social obstacles nor allegory of life could suffice to explain what unfolded. This occasion longs for a supernatural explanation, at least one healthy, documented claim of exorcism in the modern era. One critical obstacle remains, which is the attitude towards Roman Catholicism that often quiets the testimony of the 1949 exorcism.

Ecclesiastical Critiques

Exorcízo te, immundíssime spíritus, omnis incúrsio adversárii, omne phantásma, omnis légio ("I cast thee out, thou unclean spirit, along with

---

146. Walton and Walton, *Demons and Spirits*, 297.
147. Walton and Walton, *Demons and Spirits*, 298.
148. Lampert, *Exorcism*, 18. See also Shelton, Review of *Demons and Spirits*.

the least encroachment of the wicked enemy, and every phantom and diabolical legion").[149] These are the words of the Roman Catholic rite of exorcism. While belief in demonization traverses all branches of Christianity, the differences with Protestant Christians can be enough to create an ecclesiastical challenge of suspicion around the Catholic ecclesiastical elements the 1949 account contains.

When Fathers Raymond Bishop and William Bowdern were invited in 1949 to evaluate a distraught relative of a parish family, they did not simply provide pastoral skills of their ecclesiastical service to a suffering young boy. They also brought a commitment to Catholic belief and practice—a formal technique based a specific theological worldview. From the approval of Archbishop Ritter to the reading of the rite, these Jesuits believed that the liturgical prayer of exorcism would confront and defeat the power of the demonic. They believed that the prayers of entreaty to Mary the Virgin and Michael the archangel would be heard, and in faith believed that their intercessory action would strengthen the cause of exorcism. They believed that the demon should not be engaged, being a presence capable of naming the sins of the priests before their colleagues. They believed the strength of the demon put them on guard against physical attacks, evidenced by the priests whose noses were cracked by the possessed boy. A range of beliefs governed their actions and their hope.

Catholic Ecclesiology

The Catholic rite of exorcism is an enactment of church authority over mundane competitors to the kingdom of God. The *Diary* reveals a belief in authority of the church over powers of darkness, a confidence of the application of a liturgical rite of exorcism, and an effective use of sacred objects and water. However, for some, this rite is a formulaic mechanism or a powerless script applied to a demonized victim. The Catholic approach to exorcism must be recognized as part of a sacerdotal worldview in which God dispenses his grace primarily through the church, empowering the ecclesiastical body of Christ on earth—through the office of priest—to be a means for the divine work among its people. While Catholicism recognizes seven sacraments as the primary means of grace, there are other elements of ecclesiology that are sacramental. Exorcism is one such element. Other secondary means of grace, or sacramentals,

---

149. Weller, ed., *Roman Ritual: Volume 2*, 184–85.

will abound in the story, such as the role of holy water and the prayerful invocation of the saints.

Non-Catholics will be suspicious or object to the merits of the Catholic qualities in the *Diary* for its ecclesiastical privilege, social positions, and theology.[150] For example, Geisler and Betancourt remark, "Even if Rome is judged not to be a cult, it is in many respects, nonetheless, cultic in its practices."[151] Leonardo di Chirico compares evangelical and Catholic thought: "The words may be similar, but Rome's theological world is different."[152] Often unrecognizable to Protestant critics is the shared theology of Christ's atoning work, demonic work, the potential for a divine work, and the authority of God's people. Despite commonalities and any potential for unity, Grant Wacker states the situation: "It is well to recognize that religious history stirs up more than its fair share of touchiness."[153]

In this case study, Catholic theology underlies the record in the *Diary*. All seem to pivot on sacerdotalism, or the ability of the priest to execute the liturgy of exorcism with Christological authority. The approach this book takes, with an invitation to readers for the same, is to recognize a core of faith common to both branches for the purpose of contextual understanding. A basic Christological confession underlies both, as do doctrines of the Trinity, the humanity and divinity of Jesus, the real resurrection of Jesus, an eschatological hope, created spirit beings, and a belief in the revelatory preeminence of the Bible.[154] These shared values cannot be understated. The priestly report reveals these very theological tenets in the faith of the exorcist Father Bowdern. He is to be commended for the promotion of a Christ-centered authority over a real spiritual enemy through spiritual disciplines and struggle. At points of disagreement, while the Protestant and Catholic differences are articulated and the interpretation comes from a Protestant perspective, these

---

150. For an understanding of anti-Catholic sentiment and its causes, see Jenkins, *New Anti-Catholicism*, 1–22; Stark, *Bearing False Witness*, esp. 1–8, 117–33; di Chirico, *Same Words, Different World*.

151. Geisler and Betancourt, *Is Rome the True Church?* 184. However, at the same time, they admit, "The truth is that Rome is many things to many people" (185).

152. di Chirico, *Same Words, Different World*, 120.

153. Wacker, "Understanding the Past," 167–68.

154. Allison summarizes the common core of both branches as no less than twenty major tenets (*40 Questions*, 69–74). His credibility towards this common foundation of theology is all the more evident, given that Allison is not particularly generous towards Catholicism.

theological differences can stand as relevant or tangential dissimilarities for the reader. In this sense, this work is not so tribal as to disregard Catholic testimony in toto and might even offer a moment of rapprochement between the two. After all, knowledge of an historic exorcism can reinforce the biblical worldview that is held by all Christians, and the greater concern is how it is held sheepishly by too many.

Likewise, those familiar with Catholic polity know its own limitations in delineating the logistics of demonization and exorcism. Mystery marks them both, despite the best systematic theology to explain it, making it easier to dismiss the liturgical approach to exorcism. Despite the theology contained in the *Catechism of the Church* and the *Rite of Exorcism*, Richard McBrien can say, "Demons do not occupy a significant place in the official teachings of the Church."[155]

The Abuse Predicament

Another complicating factor around the implementation of the rite of exorcism is the episodes of liturgical abuse around the rite. Forceful exorcists and obsessive demon seekers cast a lack of credibility on the integrity of demonization and the prayers of exorcism. For example, Italy has shown a high level of exorcist activity, viewed by some as "unnecessarily and perilously excessive."[156] These include a proliferation of idiosyncratic exorcisms, including from unauthorized exorcists.[157] The 1975–1976 Anneliese Michel exorcism controversy was brought to public consciousness in the popular 2005 film *The Exorcism of Emily Rose*. Brian Levack describes how an Australian woman was accidentally choked in 1993, a woman was pummeled to death by San Francisco Pentecostal ministers in 1995, three exorcists stomped a woman from Glendale, CA, to death in 1997, and a Romanian nun was gagged and lashed on a crucifix before she died in 2005.[158] Such cases make the Roman Catholic Church

---

155. McBrien, *Catholicism*, 2:1153.

156. Wilkinson, *Vatican's Exorcists*, 136. She describes the trend: "In Italy there is a bumper crop of exorcists . . . [these] embrace it and appear as nonchalant about conducting an exorcism as a pharmacist is about doling out aspirin" (60–61).

157. Levack, *Devil Within*, 243, who notes, "The Church faced a challenge from unofficial lay exorcists who were taking advantaged of troubled souls," including the charging of a fee. "Today the Italian population still provides a ready supply of people who are susceptible to overtures by such unauthorized exorcists, many of whom are hucksters."

158. Levack, *Devil Within*, 311n5.

concerned for their own rite of exorcism. Anthony Masters comments, "Indeed, the exorcist is more often the instrument of the Devil rather than the instrument of God."[159] C. S. Lewis was supposedly once asked if he believed in demons, to which he said, "Yes, I know lots of us."[160] This is a predicament for the reputation of Catholic exorcism.

While such abuses do not represent most exorcism attempts, poor judgment and bad theology—unrepresentative of formal Catholic policy and theology—leads to such abuse. A major concern among skeptics is the oversight of medical and psychological causes to the symptoms attributed to demonization. Sometimes, potential exorcists promote a subjective feeling or intuition-based assumption of a demonic presence over an objective diagnosis by professionals. Lavack describes the pattern in the late twentieth century: "A series of botched exorcisms, in most cases by amateur exorcists or family members, and even cruder and more violent efforts to drive demons from children who manifested signs of physical or emotional illness contributed to this heightened awareness."[161] Wilkinson concurs: "An exorcism can be highly suggestive, and a mentally unstable or otherwise susceptible patience could be convinced that he or she is possessed and could begin to display the symptoms."[162] Today, Catholic Church authorities require thorough examinations of potentially demonized individuals, in search of medical or psychiatric alternatives before any exorcism will be approved. A review of medical and psychological reports is standard protocol for any diocese considering the rite of exorcism.[163] The revision of the rite in 1999 was intended to curb the unstructured attempts taking place and to help to prevent the misapplication of the rite.

Individual and institutional abuse does not necessarily bear on the credibility of a phenomenon, of course. The fact that some exorcisms see the misappropriation of the rite or physical harm to the victim does not detract from the potential reality of demonization or the merit of the rite of exorcism. The Latin expression *abusus non tollit usum*, which means

---

159. Masters, *Devil's Dominion*, 225.

160. Masters, *Devil's Dominion*, 185. This quote could be apocryphal. Special thanks to Asbury University professor Devin Brown for his fruitless search of the quote that evidences its mythology.

161. Levack, *Devil Within*, 242.

162. Wilkinson, *Vatican's Exorcists*, 17.

163. *Catechism* §1673; Lampert, *Exorcism*, 103–7; Martin, *Hostage to the Devil*, 13; Wilkinson, *Vatican's Exorcists*, 16–18.

that the abuse of something does not nullify its use, can be applied here. Jack Collins remarks, "This form of argument is not sound, because the mere fact of *abuse* does not take away the possibility of *proper use*; but it does warn us to be wary of some common traps."[164] Here, facts can be distorted and slanted about the life of the church, but a death from an application of the rite leaves viewers justifiably conflicted.[165] While the abuse problem is real, it should not distract from the question of demonic and exorcism legitimacy, especially in the 1949 exorcism.

Approaching the *Diary*

The survey of scientific, sociological, and ecclesiastical challenges to an event like the 1949 exorcism leads to the approach of this book in its examination of the *Diary*. The study ahead will evidence the difficulty for even the best medical or social scientist to explain the phenomenon recognized across time and across cultures known as demonization with an alternative causation that accounts for the complexity of challenges it offers them. Instead, it recognizes that some situations cannot find full explanation through natural explanations, that the human body with its soul mystifies science, and that a spiritual dimension is a part of the created order. In that sense, the book joins the approach of David Bradnick in recognizing a demonic causation "beyond reductionist anthropological models or traditional supernaturalistic options."[166] Yet it continues to weigh these approaches, offering an approach that recognizes the value of the social sciences in tandem with a biblical worldview, as solutions to what Peter Berger calls the "crisis of credibility" in religion.[167] Christianity offers a complementary explanation to spiritual events to that of good science. The Christian faith contribution is essential. This book is not an attempt to be anti-modernist, but to allow for preternatural and supernatural activities in a Christian worldview that cannot be reduced to modernist or scientific explanations. It not an attempt to be dogmatic

---

164. C. John Collins, *Science and Faith*, 122. The context of Collins's quote is how monism is favored over dualism because of the abuses seen in distinguishing the body and the soul. "You can't refute Christianity, or Darwinism, or anything else, just by pointing to the buffoons who have used it for base purposes; you have to examine the ideas themselves" (*Science and Faith*, 25).

165. Keller, *Reason for God*, 51–67.

166. Bradnick, *Evil, Spirits, and Possession*, 16.

167. Berger, *Sacred Canopy*, 127.

rather than critical; it recognizes how the two need not be mutually exclusive.[168] A theology of spirit beings and the historicity of one event involving them come together here in evaluation and analysis. It begins with understanding the methodology and the value of studying the *Diary*.

---

168. Rueda particularly deals with the case and point as potentially being historical exorcism (*Diabolical Possession*, 159).

4

Theology of the Demonization

"This scratching continued for ten days and then stopped. There were waves of air striking the grandmother, mother and the boy, and three distinct knocks were heard on the floor. The mother asked again, 'If you are Harriet, tell me positively by knocking four times.' Four distinct knocks were heard. Then there followed claw scratchings on the mattress."

—*Diary*, "Background of the Case"

Our evaluation of the 1949 exorcism now turns to the nature, causes, and manifestations of the demonization that led to its dramatic event. Since the exorcist, the diarist, and several serving witnesses were Jesuit, this chapter naturally explores a distinctively Catholic theology of demonization. This theology is also the basis for many Catholic interpreters of these events in the generation to follow. This chapter specifically profiles the characteristics of the boy prior to the application of the rite of exorcism on Wednesday, March 16, 1949. A deeper evaluation into the exorcism experience is treated in chapter 6 below. Alternative theories to demonization are considered only when they intersect with the diary or other sources.

Theology of a Diary

Contributing Cause of the Demonization

Scripture does not systematically explain causes to demonization, but it does imply them. Views on various causes are available in scholarship.[1] Malachi Martin offers one of the most widely accepted Christian sources of demonization: "The voluntary collaboration of an individual, through his faculties of mind and will, with one or more of those bodiless, genderless creatures called demons."[2] Among the most obvious activities linked to a state of demonization are occultic activities. Even while demons may not be sought, a guilty collaboration in the practices associated with them is a common formula for demonization.

Occultic Activities

The Old Testament prohibitions abound against divination or communicating with spirits. It prescribes legislation not to practice divination or fortune-telling, not to seek omens or use witchcraft, and not to consult a soothsayer, sorcerer, or medium (Lev 19:26; 20:27; Deut 18:9–12; 32:15–18). When the Judah King Manasseh "practiced divination, sought omens, and consulted mediums and spiritists," the Bible declared, "He did much evil in the eyes of the Lord, arousing his anger" (2 Kgs 21:6; 2 Chr 33:6). The prophets perpetuate this value of disengaging from necromancy and pseudo-prophetic attempts (Isa 8:19; 19:3; Jer 27:9; Ezek 14:14). The apostle Peter condemns the magical practices of Simon Magus (Acts 8:20–23) and the practices of Elymas (Acts 13:6–11). For believers, these biblical commands functioned in worship of the covenantal God and provided spiritual health of God's people; binding oneself in the spirit realm to another was dangerous and justifiably prohibited.

New Testament stories present no evidence that the conjuring of demons or communication with the dead, intentionally or unintentionally through witchcraft, leads to demonization.[3] However, the Philippian soothsayer is confronted with an exorcism by Paul (Acts 16:16–19). Likewise, the apostle recognized that when pagans made idolatrous

---

1. Amorth, *Exorcist*, 63–81; Blai, *Hauntings*, 14–26; Gallagher, *Demonic Foes*, 74–89; Goodman, *How about Demons?* 1–5; Lampert, *Exorcism*, 31–40; Levack, *Devil Within*, 56–65; Nauman, *Exorcism*, 87–98; Arnold, *3 Crucial Questions*, 73–106; Thigpen, *Manual*, 63–67.

2. Martin, *Hostage to the Devil*, xx.

3. Sorensen, *Possession and Exorcism*, 126.

Theology of the Demonization

sacrifices to their gods, they made them to demons: "The things which the Gentiles sacrifice, they sacrifice to demons, and not to God; and I do not want you to become sharers in demons" (1 Cor 10:20). This phrase "sharers in demons" is particularly revealing. Gordon Fee notes that Paul draws from Old Testament revelation here, where Israel in the wilderness deserted the living God for idols (Exod 32:1–6). Israel realized that "'mute' gods of the pagans did in fact have supernatural powers." Since God alone is the true divinity, they developed a belief that the powers around idolatrous practices were in fact demonic.[4] While the meat from such worship might be sold in the marketplace to eat, a realization of demon worship established a relevant criterion that required the attention of the church at Corinth.

In the early church, Marcus Minucius Felix was among the majority who affirmed the demonic association with the occult. He made a comprehensive statement insisting that demons are behind the practice of all magic and occult practices.[5] Today, as in antiquity, the occult includes ancient and contemporary psychic activities like séances, Ouija boards, necromancy, soothsaying, fortunetelling, magic, spells, and curses, as well as consulting mediums for the same. The consensus is almost universal among historic Christian thinkers articulating a theory of the cause of demonization. Practice of the occult invites demonic activity. Concerning the 1949 event, Thomas Allen recognizes that even the séances of Aunt Tillie in themselves are "a form of possession."[6] Likewise, Steve Wiggins declares, "In its most basic form, the Ouija board is a form of divination."[7]

Gabriel Amorth describes modern spiritism as "the evocation of the dead through a medium." While some mediums fake the moving table or the sounds of the dead, there are some who indeed contact spiritual beings: "Often these voices announce beautiful things or leave edifying messages that are difficult to ignore."[8] Clients to the séance or Ouija board long for communication, making themselves vulnerable to the cooperation of a demon feigning the dead. Robert Spitzer remarks that "if you want to make use of occult powers, you must also subject yourselves

---

4. Fee, *First Epistle to the Corinthians*, 472. Cf. Ps 96:5 ("all the gods of the nations are idols"), which is translated as "are demons" by the Septuagint.

5. Marcus Minucius Felix, *Oct.* 26–27 (ACW 39:98–103).

6. Allen, *Possessed*, 3, 5.

7. Wiggins, *Nightmares with the Bible*, 30.

8. Amorth, *Exorcist*, 50.

to them . . . It is an endangerment to one's eternal salvation and may even entail pledging allegiance to the dark lord—Satan himself." The users of the Ouija board essentially serve as mediums: "The proponents of them have already, wittingly or unwittingly, subjected themselves to the power of unknowns spirits who can be deceitful and incredibly evil."[9]

In the 1949 case, the boy sought to communicate with the dead. The foundation for the contributing cause of demonization is noted in the *Diary*: "It should be remarked here that R's Aunt believed very much in Spiritualism and often consulted Spiritualists."[10] Robbie would follow her example, as would the family. Halloran would recognize this influence later in an interview: "In a way he was a victim to the frame of mind of the aunt."[11] Certainly, his use of the Ouija board with his aunt while alive and his practice of it after her death for communication is an occultic practice.[12] The family sitting around the kitchen table for a séance session is an occultic practice.[13] The family's attempt to dialog with the aunt through knockings on the wall is an occultic practice, along with their desperate inquiry of the location of the money box in conjunction with the shaking of the bed.[14] A theology of demonization recognizes that necromancy is not neutral or harmless, but its engagement with evil spirits leads to a relational effect that is psychological, emotional, and spiritual. One possible consequence of becoming "sharers in demons" can be demonization. One Catholic exorcist claims a thought-provoking relationship tendency: "Demons may offer companionship, usually during youth or old age . . . The victim often drops their guard because they long to interact with their loved one again."[15] This seems to be an application to Paul's message in 1 Cor 10:20, as one commentator remarks: "Idols can safely be treated as nothing more than so many blocks of wood and stone. The *demons* use people's readiness to worship idols."[16] Another commentator puts Paul's juxtaposed two powers of God and demons this way: "There is no room for other affiliations."[17]

9. Spitzer, *Christ Versus Satan*, 155–56.
10. *Diary*, "Witnesses"; Bishop and Saint Booth, *Exorcist Diary*, 16.
11. Brown, "Interview."
12. Allen, *Possessed*, 2, 6, 151.
13. *Diary*, "March 7."
14. *Diary*, "Background"; "March 11"; Allen, *Possessed*, 7, 73–75.
15. Blai, *Hauntings*, 20.
16. Morris, *First Epistle of Paul to the Corinthians*, 144.
17. Soards, *1 Corinthians*, 210.

Theology of the Demonization

Family Culture of Spiritism

The Hunkeler parents do not seem to understand this dynamic. They employ the Ouija board to contact the dead. They invite the ghost of Aunt Harriet to communicate with knocks on the walls. They invite a spirit medium to communicate with their dead loved one. At these times, they stand in contrast to one father and one mother who beg Jesus to free their child of a demon (Mark 9:23–24; Matt 15:28). Before the ordeal is over, the Hunkelers would be just as imploring as these desperate parents. While such activities can feel benign, they are spiritually powerful, and for those who deal with their consequences in demonization, these practices are universally recognized as dangerous. Meanwhile, James Collins suggests that demonic association with occult practices is a particular trend emphasized in the late twentieth century among some Protestant movements, but there is evidence of a perpetual trend within the Judeo-Christian tradition.[18]

Steven LaChance offers the most thorough analysis of the family participation in the occult, not just the boy and his aunt. The mother is at the center to episodes with séances, knocking communication, and the Ouija board. She asked questions of the branding "Louis" that led to the family move to St. Louis. She is at the table seeking to find out where Aunt Harriet hid the treasure. LaChance suggests she was a practicing spiritualist in a way that influenced Robbie.[19] "I would even make the accusation that the mother had become morbidly fascinated with the occult and was obsessed with finding the outcome in St. Louis."[20] His critique of her lack of care is scathing: "Her child was paying the price for her sin," "Roland's mother was a spiritual 'Mommie Dearest,' if you will," and "He was the human planchette to find where the aunt hid the money."[21] In contrast, LaChance sees the father displaying the opposite of selfish or greedy motivations.[22] He flies to St. Louis when Robbie was suffering, he is noted for his presence during the rite and even holding of his boy during the rosary, he slept in the same room, and he prays with Robbie to help him sleep through the night.[23]

18. James Collins, *Exorcism and Deliverance Ministry*, 139–49.
19. LaChance, *Confrontation*, 36–54, 72–75.
20. LaChance, *Confrontation*, 37.
21. LaChance, *Confrontation*, 42, 54, 72.
22. LaChance, *Confrontation*, 85–88, 104.
23. *Diary*, "March 17, 18, and 21." On March 25, his father joins the priests as being

While the family is Lutheran at the beginning of the story, their consultation with Jesuit priests leads to a Catholic version of confrontation to Robbie's condition. The perspective of the Catholic Church concerning spiritism is akin to the biblical stance of its prohibition and spiritual danger. One such exorcist, Charles Fraune, identifies this activity as a mortal sin for Catholics, related to making a pact with Satan, participation in Satan cults, or engaging in witchcraft. This would have been the perspective of the Bowdern exorcists as they tried to coach Robbie to faith as a competition to his commitment to the demonic. Framing this cause in the metaphor of space with the analogy of an open door, such activity for Fraune invites the demonic to have place in the life of the participating individual.[24] The apostle Paul's phrase "sharers with demons" corresponds to this notion of invitation. Hallowell can describe this development similarly: "When people flagrantly reject the call to resist evil and cling to God's standards."[25]

These dynamics embody the lifestyle of Robbie in 1948–1949 as a textbook case study. In seeming prophetic fashion, the parapsychologist of Duke University stated in correspondence with Schulze that the boy—although possibly self-creating his condition—is "being the victim of mysterious agencies or forces."[26] The boy displayed an affection for contacting his beloved aunt, even if done so naïvely and innocently. The family did no better by engaging in communication activities with the demon. However, the target of the boy seems to stem from his heart-felt commitment to believing in necromancy.

In this process, a noteworthy matter of the will is at work in the contributing causes of demonization. The victim dabbles with the demon in a way that is best recognized as intentional and invitational. Gregory Boyd posits it this way: "Moral responsibility is always shared broadly . . . All things being equal, the self-determining agent most directly involved in the behavior is more responsible than others . . . Though appeal to demonic influence can (and sometimes, I believe, must) at times help *explain* diabolic behavior, it rarely if ever excuses it."[27]

---

spit on by the boy.

24. Fraune, *Slaying Dragons*, 43.

25. Hallowell, *Playing with Fire*, 96.

26. See Letter C in "Appendix A: The Letters between the Rev. Luther Miles Schulze and Dr. J. B. Rhine" in Rueda, *Diabolical Possession*, 164.

27. Boyd, *Satan and the Problem of Evil*, 168–69.

Nature of the Demonization

The theological challenge to understanding demons and demonization is its unsystematic nature. This became evident in chapter 3. From the book of Job with its attention to Satan, Greg Boyd remarks that literature "teaches that evil must remain a mystery precisely because we are so small while the creation is so vast and complex . . . the main point of Yahweh's monologue from out of the whirlwind is to humble Job and all humans facing evil circumstances by pointing out *how little we know about the vast cosmos he has created*."[28] The *Catechism* provides a teleology of demonization: "The power of Satan is, nonetheless, not infinite. He is only a creature, powerful from the fact that he is pure spirit, but still a creature. He cannot prevent the building up of God's reign . . . It is a great mystery that providence should permit diabolical activity."[29] Narrowing in on the possibility of understanding this phenomenon, Karl Barth attributes Satan and demons to the category of *das Nichtige* ("the nothingness"), resultant from what God did not ordain, leading to falsehood and evil independent of divine actions. In that sense, their actions represent only what God permits.[30] Divine permission can be far from divine desire, though, and the Bible recognizes the effects of a willing participant in the occult in violation of the warnings in the Law. Much of this feels like speculation within systematic theology but some elements are discernable.

Given the limitations of Scripture in amplifying the nature of demonization, experiences inevitably play a role in shaping our understanding. This remains true even with the excessive value placed on experience in the spiritual warfare field. Methodological help is gained here from the Wesleyan Quadrilateral. Don Thorsen writes about one of its elements: "Experiential knowledge relies on understanding, insights, or information that derive from person or interpersonal sense experiences . . . Experiential knowledge derives from introspection, self-analysis, private conscious states, and other means."[31] Such empirical knowledge still requires Scripture, reason, and tradition in the Quadrilateral, but patterns of observation from experience in literature remain valuable. The section "Historical Affirmation of the Preternatural" in chapter 3

---

28. Boyd, *Satan and the Problem of Evil*, 220.
29. *Catechism* §395.
30. Boyd, *Satan and the Problem of Evil*, 284–85.
31. Thorsen, *Wesleyan Quadrilateral*, 204.

provided some patterns of behavior from experience which link to better theological understanding of these issues.

Free Will

Central to a conflict theology is the place of the will, of both the demon and the demonized. Concerning the will of the demon, numerous theologians take lengths to insist on the free will of fallen angels, both leading to and following their fall.[32] The demonic display personality and free will. Important in intercession for the victim can be a recognition of the cause leading to demonization, the human free will opportunity leading to possession. Concerning the will of the victim, the 1949 exorcism reveals a willing participant in necromancy. While the cause of the demonization is mostly eclipsed as the exorcism ensues, the converted will of Robbie became an important element in the battle against the demon. The priests would consistently foster spiritual care to him along Catholic discipleship, which will unfold in the analysis below.

One can witness the consequences of the occult activity advance in the condition of Robbie in a developmental fashion. Scratches in the wall precedes footsteps in the house. The steps led to the boy's bed, where scratches and shaking of the mattress ensued. Like a bus transfer, the centralization of the demonic activity moved to the boy himself, where violent convulsions, irregular behavior, and even scratches came from within. While medical and psychological solutions seemed limited, so did the efforts of a Lutheran pastor's prayers. The séances and the spiritist certainly did not provide any solutions. The force from within was alien, strong, and resistant. Allen infers a correlation between scratches and demonization: "Now the force seemed to be inside him, manifesting itself by emerging from his body in bloody lines. Possessing him."[33]

While Robbie was a vulnerable adolescent, his actions of necromancy had unfortunate consequences. As a creation of God, he exercises a free will that was misguided. In time, the effect was devastating. Nicola recognizes the dynamic interaction between the demon and the victim in the process of demonization. Free will and cooperation is essential for the relationship: "The devil can never usurp the personality of a possessed

---

32. Boyd, *Satan and the Problem of Evil*, 42; Powlison, "Response"; Thigpen, *Manual*, 7–17; Berkhof, *Systematic Theology*, 144–45; Grudem, *Systematic Theology*, 415–16; Allison, *Historical Theology*, 298–318.

33. Allen, *Possessed*, 24.

person. The person remains a rational creature with intelligence and free will. However, the use of these faculties can be suspended."[34] As the demonization advanced, eventually Robbie's faculties were usurped. As the 1949 story unfolds, his free will began to compete against the demonization process, especially as Robbie became genuinely tired of suffering. As a divine gift comprising the image of God, free will became an instrument for participation against the demon. The will can confront the alien nature, as the classic demonologist Don Basham remarks, "Evil which is not an integral element of our nature but [what] *has invaded us from the outside* must be evicted."[35] The victim's free will participates with spiritual initiatives towards resolving the demonization.

Physical Illness

While the New Testament data often linked illness to demonization, illness is not always a manifest quality. In the 1949 exorcism, the victim shows more irregular behavior than he shows physical illness. The most commonly related somatic phenomenon was the scratchings that began as bleeding welts to develop into words as messages. Scientists have sought to explain these phenomena in the 1949 events as angioneurotic edema, a swelling under the skin that can appear as red lumps or ridges. It is usually associated with an allergic reaction. Rueda takes great lengths to explain the nature of rashes around this event.[36] Elizabeth S. Bowman, in the documentary entitled *In the Grip of Evil*, suggests that dermatography—writing made under psychological stress—led to the brandings of words on his flesh.[37] The semi-skeptical pastor Luther Schulze also attributed the scratches to rashes, although he concedes he was not present when they emerged.[38] Cortés and Gatti argue similarly, as cited above: "All clinical psychologists know that in many cases of hysteria the skin becomes particularly sensitive."[39] For them, the combination of hysteria,

---

34. Nicola, *Diabolical Possession*, 115.
35. Basham, *Deliver Us from Evil*, 98.
36. Rueda, *Diabolical Possession*, 86–87, 92.
37. *In the Grip of Evil*.
38. See Letter A in "Appendix A: The Letters between the Rev. Luther Miles Schulze and Dr. J. B. Rhine" in Rueda, *Diabolical Possession*, 161.
39. Cortés and Gatti, *Case against Possessions and Exorcisms*, 79, 83.

Tourette's syndrome, and dermatography are required to sustain a natural theory, all brought on by the exorcism itself.[40]

The attempt to provide a psychosomatic explanation for the unexplainable is commendable. Of interest is Rueda's employment of Occam's Razor in his theory of a scientific economy around the 1949 event.[41] This principle suggests that when all things are judged to be equal, the simplest or least complex explanation is to be preferred. However, a dermatological explanation for written words on the flesh—when witnesses denied that he could have caused it—does not fulfill the principle. Furthermore, a burden of proof lies with the speculative cause of dermatography, an impossibility to prove. It becomes an alternative theory lacking evidence, a hope of a natural explanation that is empirically unnatural. Beyond the missing diagnosis of a skin disorder, the dermatological mechanism theory requires two explanations. One is this miraculous coincidence of rashes that spell relevant terms. Multiple rashes spelled words that matched the nature of a demon and the rite of exorcism: "spite," "hell," "go," and "exit." Another is an exaggeration of the phenomena by both the priests and the family, or an attribution of ignorance and suggestibility among the witnesses. The miraculous first theory ignores the preternatural criteria of demonization; the second theory dismisses the testimony of any historical witness when it does not fit. Either of these explanations arguably requires greater assumptions than the explanation of demonization. Occam's razor works towards preternatural causes, not against them.

At the same time, the ongoing psychological component of has led to attempts to diagnose episodes like the 1949 exorcism as mental illness. For example, Laura Hatchman describes "conversion disorder" as an occasion when symptoms of illness and uncontrollable behavior manifest without explanation. It is classified as a mental illness by the *Diagnostic and Statistical Manual of Mental Disorders*.[42] Anxiety is transformed or "converted" to physical symptoms like seizures, twitching, convulsions, and temperamental behavior—qualities which are commonly shared among demonization accounts. Occasions of unresponsiveness are eligible expressions. Sometimes the phenomenon can be contagious, spreading across populations. Yet she admits, "Because the supernatural is beyond the purview of historical inquiry; it has often been assumed that

---

40. Cortés and Gatti, *Case against Possessions and Exorcisms*, 70–84.
41. Rueda, *Diabolical Possession*, 70–71, 237.
42. *Diagnostic and Statistical Manual*, 318–21.

early modern people were simply feigning the symptoms of bewitchment or possession."[43] A possibility of attachment disorder could be underway for Robbie, contributing to demonization but without substituting for it. LaChance argues that maternal behavior seems dysfunctional during Robbie's early phases of demonization and Opsasnick gathers testimony of Robbie's troubled childhood from Cottage City residents.[44]

While affirming the clinical merit attributed to situations of demonization, our objection is to those who reduce demonization to mental illness, social oppression, or life metaphors. These efforts are reductionistic in their attempt to explain all phenomena naturally. However, the premodern worldview of New Testament writers does not mean that our modern recognition of mental illness or neurological disorders disqualifies the preternatural. Steve Wiggins summarizes it well: "Our view of ancients as unsophisticated rubes is unjustified."[45] The sufferers were subjects of healing power, and a divine act was necessary to accomplish it.

That suffering takes many forms but shows historical patterns. Charles Fraune posits that demonic oppression can appear as illness while characterized by no naturally explainable cause.[46] The physical and mental illnesses most associated with demonization are epilepsy and delusion. Falling down, convulsions, writhing, catatonic symptoms, and physical distress are cited as commonly reported symptoms, leading to the assumption of epilepsy. Behavior akin to hysteria or multiple personality disorder are commonly cited symptoms, leading to an assumption of delusion or some other mental illness.[47] Such characteristic manifestations are central to a quality of demonization. These are explored next.

Manifestation Phase

The introduction to some voices from Christian history above begins to illustrate a continuous witness of demonization across the ages that

---

43. Hatchman, "Conversion Disorder," 86–87.

44. LaChance, *Confrontation*, 36–54, 70, 72–75, 106; Opsasnick, "Haunted Boy," 20–21, 26.

45. Wiggins, *Nightmares with the Bible*, 29.

46. Fraune, *Slaying Dragons*, 39.

47. Taylor, *Devil Came to St. Louis*, 12–13; Masters, *Devil's Dominion*, 174; Cooper and Epperson, *Evil*, 27–33; Rueda, *Diabolical Possession*, 93.

is well-represented in literature.[48] From his experience in deliverance ministry, the influential Don Basham lists these witnessed manifestations: "Screams, shaking, convulsions, weeping, hysterical laughter, writhing, fainting, sighing, groaning, choking, gagging, retching, actual vomiting."[49] John Wimber suggests that demons attack people by gripping their person in three areas: physical, mental, and spiritual.[50] The moment that Malachi Martin describes as the turning point of the power struggle, the "breakpoint" depicted in more detail at the exorcism below, is particularly marked by sounds of penetrating horror. The 1949 exorcism shows a continuity with many of these same characteristics introduced here.

For Catholicism, the *Ritual* recognizes that manifestations should be expected as elementary to demonization during the exorcism experience. Such are foundational to establish diabolical possession:

> Signs of possession may be the following: ability to speak with some facility in a strange tongue or to understand it when spoken by another; the faculty of divulging future and hidden events; display of powers which are beyond the subject's age and natural condition; and various other indications which, when taken together as a whole, build up the evidence."[51]

The 1906 Cele case was marked by smells that were unnatural to a human being. The 1928 Iowa case showed a verbalized anticipation by the demon that Father Steiger would suffer soon, followed by the descent of a black cloud to cause his bridge accident. Each had their own share of what the *Roman Ritual* calls, "Various other indications to build up the evidence."

Personality and Behavior Alterations

Authors who testify from encounters of demonization describe how the victim will show changes in personality, character, and behavior. For example, Masters remarks, "Symptoms of acute demonic attack, as listed by some exorcists and theologians, begins with a change of personality both

---

48. Among the best sources are Laycock, ed., *Penguin Book of Exorcism*; Young, *History of Exorcism*; *History of Anglican Exorcism*; and Nauman, *Exorcism*.
49. Basham, *Deliver Us from Evil*, 137–38.
50. Wimber and Springer, *Power Healing*, 108.
51. "Exorcism of the Possessed" 3 (Weller, ed., *Roman Ritual: Volume 2*, 169).

in terms of intelligence and character."[52] Wimber remarks, "The severely demonized person frequently projects a new personality."[53] Violence is often association with this behavior, seen in the New Testament when the father describes his demonized son to Jesus: "He slams to ground, foams at mouth, grinds his teeth, stiffens out" (Mark 9:18).

The 1949 exorcism powerfully attests to significant alteration in Robbie's behavior. While this is not a direct qualification for exorcism in the rite, it confirms and reinforces the candidacy of the person for diagnosable demonization. By most accounts, he seems to be a mild-mannered boy characterized by youthful mischief, a naïvely curious boy on matters of the occult.[54] Paranormal type activity first centers around the boy, external to his behavior but likely contributing to its stress. Next, recalling the dynamic of space with its notion of a demon entering, internal forces modify his behavior. For example, involuntary and obsessive use of profanity is evidenced that is atypical for Robbie. At worst, this alternation can include self-harm, a demonic driving to action that hurts the victim. The Gospel narrative reports about the demonized, epileptic boy confronted by Jesus: "When he saw him, immediately the spirit threw him into a convulsion, and falling to the ground, he began rolling around and foaming at the mouth" (Mark 9:20). The Gadarene demoniac could not be bound or chained, he could not be subdued, he tore his clothes and cried strenuously, and he would cut himself with stones, leading to a life wearing tattered clothing among the tombstones (Mark 5:3–5; Luke 8:27). From his experiences, Vincent Lampert names foaming at the mouth and eyes rolling back in the head as symptoms.[55] The 1949 case did not see self-harm as a significant characteristic of the demonization.

Violent speech is commonly attested among those who have witnessed demonization events. The involuntary and obsessive use of profanity is called "coprolalia," and in a demonization context Wilkinson calls this "blasphemic rage."[56] In one of the more graphic records is the diary of Father Renz in the 1976 Klingenberg case, which records the victim howling like a dog before profaning expletive around the holy

---

52. Masters, *Devil's Dominion*, 174.

53. Wimber and Springer, *Power Healing*, 111.

54. For theories of cause by those engaging the *Diary* record beyond the occult, see LaChance *Confrontation*, 38, 43–44, 106; Opsasnick, *Real Story*, 33–36, 43–44.

55. Lampert, *Exorcism*, 40.

56. Wilkinson, *Vatican's Exorcists*, 25.

water.⁵⁷ The diary of Father Bishop in this 1949 case records graphic declarations illustrated in a sample list of one entry: "Get away from me"; "You assholes"; "Go to hell, you dirty sons of bitches. God damn you, sons of bitches"; and "You dirty assholes."⁵⁸ One entry summarized the pattern: "The usual spitting, gyrating, cursing and physical violence continued until 11:30 pm."⁵⁹ Robbie's swearing once extended to his biological father.⁶⁰

Fraune describes this behavior as one of obsession: "Obsession is an internal diabolical assault, involving a bombardment of thoughts into the person's mind."⁶¹ Likewise, Amorth designates this behavior for the victim: "He is subjected to a powerful force that creates mental activity in him that is repetitive, obsessive, and irresistible. Such representations of reality, even if foreign in his manner of thinking, become profoundly fixed in his psyche."⁶² The relationship between the demon and the demonization are recognized here in a conflict theology. The one holds power of the other, so that unholy activities exude from an otherwise unwilling victim. The atypical behavior is still a discouraging display of power by the possessor over the possessed. The effect is one aimed at witnesses more than it is some accomplishment against the one possessed. The violent, crude actions are a shock to the audience. As a result, a power play manifests to defeat attempts of exorcism. Vincent Lampert describes how "demonic obsessions are mental attacks that the devil uses to influence a person's external and internal senses." Various imaginations, nightmares, hallucinations, wicked thoughts, or fixations on demonic symbols are common.⁶³

Coprolalia is at times rampant in the *Diary* for a document of its length. The pattern leads Bishop to write, "His expressions were lowly and smacked of the abuse of sex."⁶⁴ Some of the behavior of the boy throughout the story has led to accusations of past sexual abuse, already described. While such an expression is fair when operating on a natural level, the preternatural element interferes with the scientific in this

---

57. Goodman, *How about Demons?* 120
58. *Diary*, "March 19."
59. *Diary*, "April 1."
60. *Diary*, "March 25."
61. Fraune, *Slaying Dragons*, 40.
62. Amorth, *Exorcist*, 72.
63. Lampert, *Exorcism*, 38.
64. *Diary*, "March 23."

Theology of the Demonization

case, preventing a controlled postulation of the behavior. Psychologists Cooper and Epperson deny the accusations, first pointing out the lack of evidence of abuse. It remains only a theory of reading a lack of evidence into the record. Next, they point out the unique behavior of Robbie in a society marked by regular sexual abuses. If this supposed demonization were merely a reaction against sexual abuse, the frequency of abuse should see more such events, not see a rare event like this.[65] Yet even if there was past sexual abuse, this could allow an exploitation by the demonic through a person's vulnerabilities without maintaining abuse as a cause.

Some haunted imagination is in play for Robbie that shapes his behavior. He is cited in the *Diary* as claiming to have been visually oppressed by threatening images made against him. Early on, the *Diary* states that he is frightened as objects are thrown across the room.[66] On the occasion of the faux expulsion, he said that he saw a dark cloud before him in a vision. A figure in hooded cloak walked away, into the cloud, as if to match the artificial departure of the demon.[67] On another occasion, he emerged from his unconsciousness to describe a vision that he was escaping from a deep, hot pit through its iron gate cover while the devil sought to prevent it in the presence of smaller devils. He showed confidence that his strength was enough to eventually overpower the enemy.[68] In a competitive fashion, at the end, Robbie claimed to see more light during his spells, even envisioning a light at the end of a tunnel for the first time.[69]

The 1949 exorcism also presents the bizarre behavior of the boy singing. The songs "Blue Danube," "Suwanee River," "Old Man River," and "The Old Rugged Cross" are specifically named.[70] The randomness of such a sudden act—singing in the midst of an exorcism—is an eerie and inexplicable behavior. Of interest in the development of the demonization and exorcism itself, Steven LaChance suggests that the sarcastic singing of religious songs is an indicator of the deepening of demonic control: "It becomes quite apparent with the entrance of the

---

65. Cooper and Epperson, *Evil*, 30.
66. *Diary*, "March 11."
67. *Diary*, "March 18."
68. *Diary*, "March 16."
69. *Diary*, "April 18."
70. *Diary*, "March 19"; "April 7"; "March 17"; "March 16"; "March 19," respectively.

song state that the boy was losing his battle."[71] The consciousness of the boy seems to be entirely lost at this point, reinforcing LaChance's theory that oppression had become possession. However, when the singing is beautiful, LaChance seems to miss the fact that it is not Robbie himself singing when he claims, "The singing at this point is a reassuring sign of the positive presence of good and the fact the demon is still in a transient state."[72] One is hard-pressed to systematize the singing as a manifestation of good on either occasion, especially when Robbie cannot reproduce the song at Bishop's urging on the latter occasion.

Oracular and Vocalic Alterations

Authors who testify from encounters with demonization describe how the subject's voice can alter in a range of vocalizations that sound terrifying. Speech is altered in demonized persons, including pitch, language, and other variations. Joy Vaughan has shown how these vocal characteristics—vocalic states, demonic speech, or oracular activity—are evident in both biblical narratives and ethnographical studies of demonization across cultures.[73] There is a story from one of the three occasions that Pope John Paul II applied a prayer for exorcism; in this case, the prayer seemed to fail. After he concluded with a pledge to say a mass for the demonized woman, she was examined by Father Gabriele Amorth in the following days. "A deep, booming voice" spoke from the woman to Amorth, boasting: 'Not even the pope was able to defeat me.'"[74]

Voice tone is often altered in a whole range of expressions, from high and childlike to deep and monstrous. One exorcist author describes the latter voice adoption as "deeper and louder in order to instill fear."[75] Nicola describes the 1949 case: "His soprano voice changed to a strident and deep bass."[76] The *Diary* records Robbie once screaming "in a diabolical, high-pitched voice." On the same day, the voice is expressed, "In a happy, victorious mood . . . said sweetly."[77] The next day, "fiendish laugh-

---

71. LaChance, *Confrontation*, 82; *Diary*, "March 16."
72. LaChance, *Confrontation*, 96; *Diary*, "March 19."
73. Vaughan, *Phenomenal Phenomena*, 175–203.
74. Wilkinson, *Vatican's Exorcists*, 49.
75. Lampert, *Exorcism*, 40.
76. Nicola, *Diabolical Possession*, 113.
77. *Diary*, "March 18."

Theology of the Demonization

ter" is named.[78] Allen describes one participant of the exorcism several years later, bristling when he heard the *Woody Woodpecker* theme, "With Woody's jangling, maniacal laugh: 'Ha-Ha-Ha-*Ha*-Ha.' Trembling and sweating, he described for the bystanders how his Alexian Brothers Hospital residency had been marked with himself and others "kept awake by wild, spine-chilling laughter coming from one of the rooms in an old wing."[79]

Growling and animal-like noises are cited as vocal activities among demonization accounts.[80] The 1949 *Diary* records how Robbie made dog barking sounds and snapping of his teeth amidst other primeval behavior.[81] The diarist states, "The shouting resembled the barking of a dog, and the snapping of R' teeth was truly diabolical."[82] While this characteristic fosters an effect of fear by the demon, it also finds a tie into ancient Near Eastern thought of demons as wild beasts. To a people who lives in or near the desert wilderness, beasts and phantom-like animals commonly find cause in their thinking.[83] Desert demons are associated with howling creatures, as the Amplified Bible promotes in translation: "The creatures of the desert will encounter jackals and the hairy goat will call to its kind; Indeed, Lilith (night demon) will settle there and find herself a place of rest" (Isa 34:14).

Lampert is among exorcists to identify uncontrollable laughter or screaming among the demonized.[84] This event was not marked by such uncontrollability, but shouting was a regular part of the activities. The demon in this case regularly laughed mockingly at the attempts of the exorcism, even fiendishly so.[85] Episodes of screaming abound.

In a similar experience, one exorcist claims to have witnessed the imitation of snake-like qualities as a manifestation of the demonic, including hissing and serpentine locomotion among the demonized.[86] The theology is significant: the demonized victim is dominated by a minion of the ancient serpent, Satan. The 1906 Cele case showed Clara slithering

78. *Diary*, "March 19."
79. Allen, *Possessed*, 222–23.
80. Blai, *Hauntings*, 42.
81. *Diary*, "March 19"; "March 23"; "March 24"; "April 11."
82. *Diary*, "March 19."
83. Heiser, *Demons*, 27–29.
84. Lampert, *Exorcism*, 41.
85. *Diary*, "March 19"; "April 2"; "April 12"; "April 13"; "April 18."
86. Lampert, *Exorcism*, 41.

in serpent-like behavior. The rite of exorcism makes the connection between the serpent Satan and the victim: "No longer dare, cunning serpent, to deceive the human race, to persecute God's Church, to strike God's elect and to sift them as wheat."[87] While the *Diary* reports no snake-like behavior, Father John Nicola states that the boy aimed his head like a cobra when he delivered some spit. An attendant would hold up a pillow between the exorcist and the boy to block the spitting. "The boy's tongue began to flick out and his head to move to and fro in the gliding fashion of a snake. Suddenly he would make a quick movement above, beneath or alongside of the pillow and spit mucous in the exorcist's eyes."[88] The film *The Exorcist* adopted this long-standing association for diabolical effect. The exorcist hears the victim hissing while following the reading of the rite and looks up to the victim: "She is sitting erect, the whites of her eyes exposed, while her tongue flicks in and out rapidly and her head weaves back and forth like a cobra's."[89]

These oracular manifestations include a superhuman knowledge of events or insights into personal histories. This dynamic explored below in "Preternatural Strength," including the dimension of speaking in unknown languages as an oracular communication. These oracular manifestations also reveal the combative relationship that can occur between the demon and the demonized victim in a clustered effect. As evidenced here, the wild, chaotic, and violent beast marks the behavior of the demon manifest in the victim.

Cluster Effect

The historical record of the 1949 exorcism is marked by a back-and-forth, in-and-out sense of consciousness for the boy. The rite anticipates this: "Molestation by the devil is manifested in various disturbances of the human body itself, where he has gained control over a man's sight, hearing, speech, or the physical organism in general."[90] Allen describes that for Robbie "a veil had divided his normal consciousness and the consciousness of possession."[91] On the whole, the boy may not have

---

87. "Rite of Exorcism" (Weller, ed., *Roman Ritual: Volume 2*, 227).
88. Nicola, *Diabolical Possession*, 113; Dobson, "Luncheon."
89. Blatty, *On The Exorcist*, 230, from the first draft screenplay.
90. "Exorcism of the Possessed" (Weller, ed., *Roman Ritual: Volume 2*, 163).
91. Allen, *Possessed*, 168.

Theology of the Demonization

been conscious of the events of demonization that occurred during the majority of the exorcism period. This surely contributes to the journalistic citations that he does not remember the events.

During possession, spirits display a measure of control over the body of the victim, causing the demonized person to act as they command and to speak on their own behalf. The victim can phase out during a stage of manifestations, while phasing back in when control is relinquished. In these periods of recession, the person becomes alert, capable of acting and speaking for himself or herself. This makes for confusion and surprise by advocates of deliverance. At times, one cannot know which person is really speaking, especially when the demonic deceive their spiritual perpetrators by imitating the willingness of the victim. Amorth says, "The obsessed goes into a trance and loses consciousness, leaving space for the evil spirit to speak."[92] Masters employs the phrase "clouding of the consciousness" to describe the eclipsing of the victim's mind by the demonic.[93] Lampert uses the term "clusters" to describe the combination of present demons, vacillating in singular and plural manifestation.[94] John Wimber remarks that the demonization sometimes extends to "even blotting out the person's consciousness." He elaborates on the effect: "The demon refers to itself in the first person, bystanders in the second person, and the person it is inhabiting in the third person."[95]

The Gospels and Acts demonstrate how spirits speak through a demonized person, as the narrative seems to distinguish between the voices of the victim and the demon in a way that evidences a condition of mutuality.[96] Perhaps the young girl in Philippi was an unconscious mouthpiece for soothsaying and fortune telling, although the spiritual dynamic cannot be discerned (Acts 16:16). This "in-and-out" effect is complicated further by the singular and plural effect of demonization. This is evident in the Gadarene passage, where the voice answered the question of name, declaring, "Legion, for we are many" (Mark 5:10; Luke 8:30). In the synagogue at Capernaum, a man is demonized "by an unclean spirit" in the singular, but the voice speaks in the plural twice before speaking the singular (Mark 1:23–24).

---

92. Amorth, *Exorcist*, 66.
93. Masters, *Devil's Dominion*, 174.
94. Lampert, *Exorcism*, 57.
95. Wimber and Springer, *Power Healing*, 111.
96. Luke 4:34; Mark 1:24; Luke 8:28; Mark 5:7; Matt 8:29; Acts 16:16; 19:15.

Theology of a Diary

Bizarre activities of personality and speech evidence demonization, while these activities indicate this cluster effect for Robbie. His bodily behavior such as writhing, seizures, mutilation, spitting, vomiting, urinating, and scratching, all mark the governance of the demon. The verbal expressions of profanity, prophecy, and xenolalia are also the expressions of the demon. The rite anticipates this: "To be possessed can mean that Satan has beclouded the intellect, so that the light of faith cannot illuminate it."[97] At the same time, the boy emerges from these spells, conscious of himself and capable of acting and speaking for himself. On one occasion, the demon sang, "Blue Danube," and afterwards Father Bishop hummed it only to be met by Robbie's unfamiliarity and inability to carry the tune. We can assume a limited consciousness by Robbie in his delirium, as the demonic singing of "Blue Danube" was a song unfamiliar to the boy who showed an inability to replicate it.[98] The other songs might also be beyond his familiarity, although they represented the hymnal and popular church culture.

This tension marked the battleground of deliverance, as the exorcist tried to appeal to the will of the boy for prayer, confession, and communion, sometimes successfully but sometimes confronted by the demon. The attempt to baptize, catechize, and administer the Eucharist represent the cultivation of positive spiritual activities during the victim's conscious phases of the cluster. While the demonic resistance increases toward the end of this demonization, so did the commitment of Robbie to join in the patient perseverance of the exorcist. Allen recognizes how Robbie became more aware of the battle toward the end as he seemed to be coming free of the demonization.[99] On the final day, Robbie claimed to see light during his spells, even envisioning a light at the end of a tunnel for the first time.[100]

The same wavering, in-and-out effect finds testimony in virtually all exorcism attempts. Taylor describes the report of the 1906 Cele case, "Alternating between states of diabolical possession and her normal personality, she was able to take part in confession and communion. However, this involved great spiritual risks, of which Father Horner quickly became aware."[101] He further describes, "In some cases, a self-dialogue

---

97. "Exorcism of the Possessed" (Weller, ed., *Roman Ritual: Volume 2*, 163).
98. *Diary*, "March 19."
99. Allen, *Possessed*, 168.
100. *Diary*, "April 18."
101. Taylor, *Devil Came to St. Louis*, 25.

Theology of the Demonization

seemed to be going on. It was as if two beings were speaking through Clara's mouth."[102] This in-and-out effect has been evidenced in longer phases, such as in the years of struggle in the Klingenberg Case. Fraune describes how manifestation came come "only once in a while," even to the point that demonized individuals can "hold down jobs and carry on a normal life, without anyone knowing they are possessed."[103]

Yet another expression of this "in-and-out" effect is the logistic of sleep. The *Ritual* warns, "During the exorcism they cause him to fall asleep, and dangle some illusion before him, while they seclude themselves, so that the afflicted one appears to be freed."[104] The diarist illustrates this for Robbie: "The next phase of the reaction took the appearance of quiet sleep" before a tantrum came seamlessly without the boy waking.[105] Allen speculates about the emotional calm: "Exorcists explain this feeling as the touch of evil: Satan, while remaining hidden, projects a sinister aura that engulfs the victim."[106]

Preternatural Strength

Experienced witnesses to demonization describe how the victim will show superhuman physical displays, such as heightened strength and anesthesia to pain.[107] In the New Testament, the Gadarene demoniac would break bonds and chains, surpassed the strength of those who tried to subdue him, and he cut himself with stones (Mark 5:3–5; Luke 8:27). Joy Vaughan evidences how both biblical narratives in Luke and Acts and modern anthropological observational studies show how demonization is a cause for illness as well as violence or extraordinary strength.[108] The rite of exorcism anticipates this as a sign of demonization: "Display of powers which are beyond the subject's age and natural condition."[109]

Violence is shared with superhuman strength manifestations as a commonly witnessed characteristic. The *Diary* of the 1949 exorcism

---

102. Taylor, *Devil Came to St. Louis*, 25.
103. Fraune, *Slaying Dragons*, 43.
104. Weller, ed., *Roman Ritual: Volume 2*, 171.
105. *Diary*, "March 16."
106. Allen, *Possessed*, 170.
107. Wimber and Springer, *Power Healing*, 111.
108. Vaughan, *Phenomenal Phenomena*, 175. For extensive illustrations, see esp. 175–203.
109. Weller, ed., *Roman Ritual: Volume 2*, 169.

mentions such strength on display. The *Diary* references how multiple priests attended the exorcism to offer physical support when only two readers comprise the liturgy. Other occasions witnessed the physical assistance of his father and his uncle. On one occasion marked with unprecedented violence, the boy felt himself fighting against a devil to escape from a pit. During the vision, he punched the bed board and the pillow "with more than ordinary force." The *Diary* described how "his blows were beyond the ordinary strength of the boy." While fighting against this devil, he also fought off the attendants seeking to hold him down. The *Diary* states, "exorcism stirred up the demon."[110] The next day saw his father and his uncle fighting to hold him down. Nicola claimed, "Four adult men could not contain him; he was able to get free," a count also cited in the *Diary*.[111] Once when he fought and kicked, Robbie successfully hit his attendants, breaking Halloran's nose and causing Van Roo's nose to bleed. The *Diary* describes the preternatural strength: "The first blows were accurate, quick, and deadly, although R's eyes were shut."[112] This manifestation is akin to the Georgetown rumor that the boy could remove a bed spring and slash the arm of Father Hughes. In contrast, one entry of the *Diary* highlights an occasion when he was not difficult to hold down.[113] The boy is only thirteen and not a sturdy youth, verifying the strength displayed against adult men when he resisted. Nicola comments that Robbie was naturally ninety-five pounds to start the ordeal.[114]

Experienced witnesses of demonization describe how an exorcist should expect wounds, cuts, burns, scrapes, scratches, bruises, and swelling from physical attacks.[115] The 1949 exorcism is unique in the elaborate markings that appeared on Robbie's body, testified in every phase of the demonization by the parents, by Rev. Schulze, and by Bishop in the *Diary*. Since these markings play such an important role in the interpretation of the demonic response to the *dicas mihi*, "What is your time of departure?" in the rite, it is considered below in the discussion of preternatural knowledge.

---

110. *Diary*, "March 16."

111. Dobson, "Luncheon"; *Diary*, "March 24."

112. *Diary*, "March 23." Cf. The athletic strength of two priests as former football players is cited by Faherty, *To Rest in Charity*, 82.

113. *Diary*, "April 2."

114. Nicola, *Diabolical Possession*, 111.

115. Lampert, *Exorcism*, 34; Blai, *Hauntings*, 43.

There are other physical expressions that take place in patterns of exorcism testimonies. The bending of the body in a semi-circular shape with entangled limbs, a position commonly called the "hysterical arch," is commonly cited outside of the *Diary*.[116] McGuire boldly claims about Robbie's alterations, "His body distorting and transforming, heels touching the back of his head, the body forming a loop."[117]

The activity of spitting is dominant in the 1949 record, listed here among the preternatural strengths as a measure of extraordinary dexterity. Faherty describes the spitting during prayers as landing between the priest's eyes.[118] Eyewitness Halloran remarked that during the exorcism: "Yeah, there was spitting, and when I think back on it, it amazes me, his accuracy. He'd spit right in your eye from about eight feet away."[119] McGuire claims that it could travel across the room with accuracy.[120]

Preternatural Knowledge

Authors who testify to demonic encounters describe how the demonized person will show new preternatural mental abilities, such as superhuman intelligence, advanced knowledge, clairvoyance, telepathy, predictive powers, occult powers, and a familiarity with unknown languages.[121] The rite anticipates also the "ability to speak with some facility in a strange tongue or to understand it when spoken by another; the faculty of divulging future and hidden events."[122] For the 1949 exorcism, two types of preternatural knowledge dot the landscape of the story.

Knowledge of Facts

This category is a display of information or mental skills that are witnessed and judged as beyond the means of the victim's experience or

---

116. Taylor, *Devil Came to St. Louis*, 13; Lampert, *Exorcism*, 40; LaChance, *Confrontation*, 149.
117. McGuire, "St. Louis Exorcism."
118. Faherty, *To Rest in Charity*, 82.
119. Brown, "Interview." Halloran also notes there that, contrary to the film adaptation, the spit was not projectile vomit.
120. McGuire, "St. Louis Exorcism."
121. Masters, *Devil's Dominion*, 174; Wimber and Springer, *Power Healing*, 112.
122. Weller, ed., *Roman Ritual: Volume 2*, 169.

exposure. This knowledge is not attributed to the victim in miraculous fashion, but to the demon in manifestation.

Included in this expressed knowledge is the demonic familiarity with the divine and biblical fate that awaits them. They seem to recognize and anticipate Jesus in the Gospel exorcisms, communicating familiarity of his identity that is always linked to his own judgment against them. This is seen in the Capernaum synagogue, the Gadarene, and the Sceva passages.[123] For example, "Let us alone! What have you to do with us, Jesus of Nazareth? Have you come to destroy us? I know who you are, the Holy One of God" (Luke 4:34). This is preternatural or superhuman knowledge, as the stranger to Jesus would not have been able to make a claim that his disciples themselves could rarely make (Matt 16:16). Likewise, the young girl in Ephesus was a mouthpiece for soothsaying and fortune telling (Acts 16:16), with some dynamic of either demonization or by communication with the demonic—either of which provides preternatural knowledge.

Preternatural knowledge is evident in the 1949 exorcism as the demon called out the priests' personal weaknesses. Nicola claims of Robbie, "On occasion he manifested an unfathomable knowledge of the sensitivities of the exorcist and others, attempting to create a feeling of distrust and hostility between them."[124] The demon attempts to show knowledge as intimidation, as the *Diary* reports it saying: "He met one of the Fathers in hell and stated the year as 1957. He indicated surprise at finding the Father in hell. The vile and filthy talk which followed makes anyone shudder."[125] Similarly, it stated as threat: "Fr. Bishop—all people that mangle (*sic*) with me will die a terrible death."[126] Such prophetic intimidation is not easily dismissed when heard.

Steven LaChance suggests that a knowledge of the significance of numbers is underway in communication from the demon. LaChance's thoughts are speculative and ultimately may simply show a theological coincidence. He suggests that three knocks on the wall by the supposed Aunt Harriet represents a mockery of the Trinity. He posits that Robbie's five-day respite on March 26–30 corresponds to a biblical meaning of "God's grace and favor towards humans" without citing a basis for this.

---

123. Matt 8:29; Mark 5:7, 10; Luke 8:28, 31; Mark 1:24 and Luke 4:34; Luke 4:41; 8:28; Acts 19:15.

124. Nicola, *Diabolical Possession*, 113.

125. *Diary*, "March 23."

126. *Diary*, "March 31."

He also notes that five in the occult is a number for light. He imagines that the "X" brand is the number ten that is biblically representative of a perfect number "that signifies testimony, law, responsibility, and completeness of order." He does not provide biblical thought around these interpretations but claims ten to have "the strongest occult pulls of all the Hebrew letters." He brings the number four as a creation number to accompany this karmic price to be paid.[127] LaChance's attempts are creative, suggesting preternatural knowledge of numerology by the demons that are unknown to Robbie and unrecognizable by the priests, but the biblical basis is limited, and the systematic operations of these numbers remains hypothetical.

Knowledge of Departure, Identity, and Scratches

Among the knowledge seemingly manifested in the 1949 case that intersects with the expectations of the rite of exorcism to illicit knowledge from the demon, is that of the scratching on Robbie's body. Scratches occurred for four consecutive nights, and by the end, they were seemingly printed as if scratched by claws.[128] His mother testified that the boy's hands were always visibly separated during the moments of the scratching. The *Diary* reports that a scratching occurred on his back, out of reach and without any witnessed use of his hands.[129] When asked about the most remarkable feature of the event, Halloran referenced the scratches. "I didn't think there was any way they could have been self-induced, the marks, the scratches, the words, the numbers and that sort of thing that appeared."[130]

One such word "Louis" was among the early scratched messages.[131] St. Louis was the city where Aunt Harriet had died, and somehow the mother surmised that a change in the boy's environment might offer relief by taking him to St. Louis. This episode was introduced above to reveal a suspicion of a motive that a treasure could be found there, deepening the link to an occultic aunt.

---

127. LaChance, *Confrontation*, 25, 116–17, 119–20.
128. *Diary*, "Background"; Bishop and Saint Booth, *Exorcist Diary*, 14.
129. *Diary*, "Background"; Bishop and Saint Booth, *Exorcist Diary*, 15.
130. Brown, "Interview."
131. *Diary*, "Background"; Bishop and Saint Booth, *Exorcist Diary*, 14–15.

Not only does the phenomenon of scratches characterize this case but also the frequency and variety of this means of expression. When the mother either spoke of Robbie returning to school, or if she inquired of the spirit whether he should, the scratched message, "No" came to her through his flesh.[132] After the beginning of the application of the rite, the imprint of a cross appeared on Robbi's left forearm.[133] Five days later came the imprint of "hell" on his chest.[134] The same day, a unique image of the devil with detail came on his body.[135] The surrender of a name was mixed in with the scratches of numbers. Markings reading "Hell" and a devil image are accompanied by the declaration of "spite" as the demon's name.[136] Denis Brian reports from his interview with Rhine from Schulze that the word "spite" was among the scratched messages.[137] This name returns at the event of the climax of the exorcism, marking the descent of the exorcized demon into an abyss. Meanwhile, the scratches frequently show a correspondence to the *dicas mihi* of the rite in which the time of departure is required to be given by the demon. This instruction by the priest ("Tell me") is part of the *praecipio* command of the *Diary*, which is to be explored in the next chapter.

Knowledge of Other Languages

The rite references a knowledge of other languages as one possible feature marking the speech of a demonized person. While the *Diary* only once hints at this characteristic, other witnesses and second-hand reporters claim that Robbie manifested a demonstration of Latin and Aramaic.[138] Meanwhile, the theme of Latin is an undercurrent of the exorcism event. The rite was read in Latin until the priest chose to select the *praecipio* to be read in English. A potentially apocryphal Georgetown episode of

132. *Diary*, "Background"; Bishop and Saint Booth, *Exorcist Diary*, 15.
133. *Diary*, "March 11."
134. *Diary*, "March 16."
135. *Diary*, "March 16."
136. *Diary*, "March 31"; cf. "April 18."
137. Brian, *Enchanted Voyager*, 182.
138. For Aramaic, see Erdmann, "Truth," 53; Taylor, *Devil Came to St. Louis*, 55; Brisbane, "Youth's Bizarre Symptoms"; LaChance, *Confrontation*, 138. For Latin, see "Priest Freed Boy of Possession by Devil"; "New Details"; Brinkley, "Priest Frees Mt. Rainier Boy"; Linson, "Washington's Haunted Boy," 34; Rueda, *Diabolical Possession*, 32; Nicola, *Diabolical Possession*, 114; Kelly, *Devil*, 95; Faherty, *To Rest in Charity*, 82; Spitzer, *Christ Versus Satan*, 167.

Theology of the Demonization

Robbie speaking in Latin appears in some testimonies. Likely without conscious intention, the diarist articulated a role for Latin as a metanarrative of authority in the exorcism record. It deserves elaboration.

Xenolalia, or xenoglossy, is the term for speaking in a foreign language, whether preternaturally or otherwise. It represents one type of glossolalia, or speaking in any form of tongues, and finds correlation to the New Testament spiritual gifts, signs, and wonders. Felicitas Goodman compares xenolalia among spiritual gifts tongues speakers and preternatural demonization cases across cultures to offer some natural explanation to this phenomenon.[139] An altered state or a trance-like state characterized her studies where the participant expresses "a rhythmic quality" and an "intonation and segmentation" quality, which she correlates to activities of the cardio and nervous systems. As an anthropologist, she recognizes that "when the functioning of the body is altered in this special way, namely, in ecstasy, that particular person gains the ability to come in contact with beings and events of another reality, with the sacred dimension."[140] This approach to understanding xenolalia becomes the scientific explanation for potentially all occasions of speaking in foreign tongues. Related to exorcism experiences specifically, Goodman says, "On the physiological level, there is the altered state of consciousness of ecstasy and the emergence of brain maps." Ritual acts connect the mind and the body into an experience "that ties in with healing, especially in our context with the cure of injurious possession by the ritual of exorcism."[141] In other words, the victim subconsciously can repeat and articulate a foreign language by suggestion. Writing about the 1949 case, Rueda is equally skeptical scientifically, stating that the brain can capture impressive amounts of information that emerge during abnormal conditions of the mind.[142]

The context of the rite being delivered in Latin is important for the 1949 exorcism. Until the Council of Vatican II in the 1960s, the standard application for all liturgical activities were in Latin. As a result, the ecclesiastical language of Roman Catholicism becomes the medium for engagement of the exorcist with the demon. It is presumed by the *Diary* writer that the reader will know this, obvious when the diarist makes a late note of a changed language logistic. It is a significant moment that

---

139. Goodman, *How about Demons?* 6–12.
140. Goodman, *How about Demons?* 12.
141. Goodman, *How about Demons?* 24.
142. Rueda, *Diabolical Possession*, 139.

illustrates the barrage of Latin that Robbie had been hearing from March 16 to April 18 when Bowdern decided to deliver the *praecipio* in English. This means that Robbie—a Lutheran nurtured adolescent—heard Latin for almost an hour and half each time the rite was read. This provides opportunity for particular words or phrases to fasten to his conscious mind, seeming to offer some justification to Goodman and Rueda above.

Meanwhile, the testimonies around the 1949 exorcism show historical confusion and uncorroborated documentation about Robbie Mannheim speaking in a foreign language. Governing all claims is the reality that the *Diary* does not specifically substantiate this phenomenon, including Robbie speaking in Latin or Aramaic. Surely such a sign would have been noticed and recorded by the diarist. Reflections on this lack of evidence occur in the scholarship. Henry Kelly claims that Bowdern rejected this happening in their 1960 interview together and Opsasnick claims that Halloran did the same.[143] *Dominus* was the only Latin word of significance spoken by the boy, which could easily be garnered from the liturgy.[144] While the evidence of the demon speaking these languages during the event is unsubstantiated by the *Diary*, one must recognize that its background report about the Georgetown phase is quite abbreviated. The parents seemed to offer a cursory report, including any deeper consultation of Father Hughes or the event of the prayer circle. Additionally, there is still discussion about xenolalia, found in secondhand reports and in one firsthand account from original witnesses. While the data among eyewitnesses is sometimes contradictory, realizing that not all witnessed all events, the possibility of a belief in the manifestation of Latin is not unreasonable if held tentative. The same elimination criteria must come twice, also to the Aramaic account.

However, there are two striking indications that something more may have been at work. First, given the fact that the rite is given in Latin, there is no explanation why Robbie or the demon would respond with a pattern of resistance at the moment of the *praecipio*. The boy would not be able to discern its significance. The priest's delivery of the *dicas mihi*, requiring a name and time of departure, was met with resistance, mockery, or urination on nine different occasions.[145] On these occasions in

---

143. Taylor, *Devil Came to St. Louis*, 63–64; Kelly, *Devil*, 95, 97–98; Opsasnick, "Haunted Boy," 9, 25.

144. Kelly, *Devil*, 95; Opsasnick, "Haunted Boy," 25 (citing Halloran's recognition of imitating Latin). Cf. Stevenson, "Possession and Exorcism," 69.

145. *Diary*, "Mar 16"; "Mar 19"; "Mar 23"; "April 2"; "April 7"; "April 12"; "April 13";

the rite of exorcism, seizures, profanity, derision, and rebellion regularly found a place in the commentary of the diary. Once the *Diary* records how the command in Latin for the demon to give its name, *nomen lingua Latina*, the demon answered in English, "I speak the language of the persons." On this occasion, there is additional commentary from the demon around the exclusive use of English.[146] One night saw the demon insist that "the exorcist cut out the damned Latin."[147] One another night, the demon answered in pig Latin, "playfully imitated the commands," or waited until the delivery of the Latin to respond by using the phrase, "Stick it up your ass."[148] In fact, the violent but engaging responses were enough for Bowdern to begin to center on it, including the decision to switch the *praecipio* to English.

A second indication that something special was at work led to a diarist comment on the mimicked Latin. This included singing in Latin an exact phrase of defiance and once employing pig Latin. Here there is a curious point in the *Diary*. The entry five days before the expulsion reads: "In no instance up to this point in the case has the devil answered in Latin."[149] This affirms the lack of xenolalia as a sign between March 16 and April 13 when the Jesuits began their effort and Bishop recorded his own observation in the diary. However, the narrative continues: "Although his imitation of Latin was clear and distinct."[150] Some drastic change is suddenly in place in the demonic mimicking of Latin that the diarist would record the wonder. Another consideration is the distracting nature of demons. It is rarely considered whether a demon might deceive evaluating priests by not playing into the signs required for exorcism. However, in the heat of battle, perhaps xenolalia might manifest itself. While an accent is not knowledge of a language, this dimension of language expressed here is noteworthy.

"April 17"; and "April 18." While "April 3" saw no response, "Mar 31" and "Apr 18" were marked by a sense of yielding by the demon.

146. *Diary*, "March 31." This was part of the writing incident. When asked to give a sign in the Latin language this day, Robbie wrote indiscernible marks until paper and pencil were placed on his writing area.

147. *Diary*, "March 24."

148. *Diary*, "April 13."

149. *Diary*, "April 13."

150. *Diary*, "April 13."

Theology of a Diary

Proximal Phenomena

Another type of manifestation associated with demonization are phenomena external to—but proximal to—the subject. Sounds are heard near the victim, objects in the room move on their own, or diverse irregular phenomena take place.

For the 1949 exorcism, proximal phenomena include initial footsteps and scratching in the walls, the shaking mattress, the flipping furniture, the gliding desk, the sliding pallet, and the casting away of religious objects. The examples are numerous in the background to the case. A pear and an orange fly across the room; milk and other food upset from the table and stove. The bread box was thrown to the floor. A coat on a hanger flew, a comb flew the air while extinguishing candles in its path, and a Bible sailed across the room.[151]

Among other exorcists are testimonies to mysterious, physical alterations to the environment. Both Hughes and Bowdern independently cited a drastically chilled room temperature.[152] Nicola cites that Bowdern once wore an overcoat over his cassock and surplice due to the "psychic chill."[153] Gallagher states this is not an uncommon feature among testimonies.[154] Foul and revolting odors are not uncommon, such as in the 1976 Klingenberg case.[155] Faherty describes Bowdern's Alexian Brothers Hospital stay: "The stench nauseated him."[156] Blai claims that black shadows gliding or walking on any of the four walls, floors, or ceilings have been cited by witnesses of other demonizations; in our event, Robbie is the only one to testify to such a presence.[157]

Two effects come from these activities. First, phenomena external to the boy initially define the demonic presence independent of the victim. These elements unfold proximally to Robbie, moving closer in a notion of space to center on the victim. The footsteps beginning in the grandmother's room moved to Robbie. The scratching in the wall eventually was like the scratching on his own body. Eventually, the scratches even

---

151. *Diary*, "Background"; Bishop and Saint Booth, *Exorcist Diary*, 13–15.

152. Allen, *Possessed*, 28; Faherty, *To Rest in Charity*, 82, respectively. Lampert (*Exorcism*, 41) says this "demonstrates their distance from God."

153. Nicola, *Diabolical Possession*, 112; cf. Faherty, *To Rest in Charity*, 82.

154. Gallagher, *Demonic Foes*, 25.

155. Lampert, *Exorcism*, 41; Blai, *Hauntings*, 42.

156. Faherty, *To Rest in Charity*, 82.

157. Blai, *Hauntings*, 42; *Diary*, "March 16"; "April 18."

Theology of the Demonization

seemed to come from within. Such phenomena can be interpreted as a haunted space, inviting an affinity with the paranormalists' worldview around this event. The random, proximal phenomena are so many that the collective sum is hard to dismiss, even if most of these reports come from family members reporting to the diarist.

Based on these proximal phenomena, perceptional psychology Ian Stevenson finds reason to reject the fraud theory for this event. The notion that Robbie was playing tricks this expansive in ways that fooled multiple adults is difficult to sustain. Although working from a belief in poltergeists not sustained here, he still remarks, "Poltergeist cases always require the careful elimination of fraud . . . There is, however, no evidence of trickery in the moving and flying around of objects, phenomena that numerous observers witnessed on different occasions."[158] An extensive commitment to fraud by a thirteen-year-old boy under lengthy and extreme duress is preposterous to maintain and presents the witnesses as foolish.

Second, the proximal phenomena illustrate a rejection of spiritual objects. If a heavy chair flipped, a bed shook, and a pallet slid without any religious association, then the proximal phenomena that come as a rejection of spiritual objects from the space of the victim are inevitable. For the 1949 exorcism, this list includes holy water, shaking Christ picture, relics moving across the bed and flying across the room, the extinguishing of candles, and the rejection by the victim for holding the crucifix. They are examined next as theological aversions to spiritual objects.

Spiritual Aversions

Experienced authors who witness demonization describe certain spiritual changes, such as reactive fear to Christ, blasphemy, and abhorrence to prayer.[159] Likewise, another physical alteration common to demonization includes the damaging, throwing, moving, or removing of sacred items or symbols.[160] Such aversion to religious things is a manifestation, a response to the rite, and a resistance to exorcism. The Catholic Gabriel Amorth remarks, "My exorcistical experience confirms that demons have

---

158. Stevenson, "Possession and Exorcism," 69.

159. Masters, *Devil's Dominion*, 174; Wimber and Springer, *Power Healing*, 112; Amorth, *Exorcist*, 67.

160. Blai, *Hauntings*, 44.

a natural repulsion toward all sacred objects . . . they extract all or part of their power."[161] While this theology is highlighted here, it reemerges at additional places in the story below.

In the 1949 exorcism, the relic of St. Margaret Mary was thrown onto the floor without identifiable agency.[162] The next day, Robbie claimed that a force threw the relic against a mirror. A crucifix and the same relic moved from under the pillow, close to Robbie's head, to the foot of the bed, the furthest point from him. The relic was lost in the room, seemingly temporarily, as it is thrown from the pillow four days later.[163] Later that night, the crucifix led the boy into a bout. On the day of the exorcism, the boy threw the crucifix that was placed in his hand, leading the diarist to remark, "The signs of the cross and the crucifix were very effective." One evening, when blocked by O'Flaherty from violently accessing a relic of the cross, he turned to rip pages from the rite of exorcism.[164] Similarly, the diarist remarked, "The reaction to the medals and the cross was exceptional."[165] Robbie was cited as dozing when the bottle of St. Ignatius holy water flew from a table.[166] On another occasion the boy threw the holy water across the room and twice its application was followed with a response of spitting.[167] Nicola reports that he would spit at the exorcist during the rite "with uncanny accuracy."[168]

The use of profanity by the demon around the blessed objects consistently characterizes the *Diary* record. On March 19 alone, for example, cursing against the priests, fiendish laughter, urination, and singing marked the reading of the rite. The diarist wrote, "The violent reactions always followed upon the prayers of the exorcism."[169] As early as the prayer circle in Georgetown, eyewitness Ida Mae Donley claims that the boy cursed those around him that read from the Bible.[170] Halloran remarked in an interview that aversion to religious speech was most

---

161. Amorth, *Exorcist*, 130.
162. *Diary*, "March 10."
163. *Diary*, "March 11"; "March 15."
164. *Diary*, "April 2."
165. *Diary*, "April 18."
166. *Diary*, "March 11."
167. *Diary*, "April 18"; "March 17"; "March 18", respectively.
168. Nicola, *Diabolical Possession*, 113.
169. *Diary*, "March 19."
170. Rueda, *Diabolical Possession*, 32.

Theology of the Demonization

concentrated at the naming of Mary and Jesus, as well as the application of holy water.[171]

Prayers and the rite themselves see the concentrated aversion to spiritual things. Halloran describes another occasion of resistance to religious initiatives: "On Holy Thursday that year, this phenomenon started occurring as I was reading the prayers. 'Don't talk about it anymore, this hurts too much,' the kid said. The markings were most visible, and there were many obscenities."[172] It was the administration of the rite itself that led to Halloran's broken nose and Van Roo's bloody nose. Spiritual aversion centered on the declaration of the *dicas mihi*. For example, once while it was read along with the saying of the Hail Mary, the *Diary* states that twenty brands occurred on the boy.[173] Almost every day of the *Diary* shows an aversion to the rite, if not relics, medals, or holy water.

Aversion also centered on the attempts to administer the sacraments to the demonized boy. Supposedly the trip to the Catholic rectory in Georgetown for baptism saw the demon counter attack, grabbing the priest by the throat. The resistance to baptism cost hours.[174] The *Diary* provides similar resistance in a car was experienced in a trip to baptism at the rectory in St. Louis.[175] On two occasions, the demon remarked, "I will not let R receive Holy Communion" and "I will not let him go to Mass."[176] On another date, the boy attempted to declare his intent for communion, but he could not complete the declaration at the word "communion."[177] Thrashing, violence, and swearing accompanied the sacramental attempt regularly. From April 2, the first but difficult administration and acceptance by Robbie, the battle ensued regularly on nine recorded attempts. Four were successful; five were unsuccessful. Two of the unsuccessful attempts see the *Diary* report an attempt at a "spiritual communion," an expression of intent for Catholicism when the physical communion is not possible.[178]

---

171. Brown, "Interview."
172. Silvers, "Jesuit Helped."
173. *Diary*, "April 7."
174. Erdmann, "Truth," 55; Taylor, *Devil Came to St. Louis*, 65.
175. *Diary*, "April 1."
176. *Diary*, "April 12" and "April 17" respectively. See also "April 11," where its administration saw a seizure and declaration of resistance by the demon.
177. *Diary*, "April 11."
178. Successful attempts on April 2, 10, 13, and 14; unsuccessful attempts on April 11, 12, 13, 17. The overlap of April 13 is because of the success morning administration

Theology of a Diary

Henry Kelly alleged that Bowdern's brother, also a Jesuit priest, claimed that the blessed host would show a measure of levitation during the exorcism. Yet this seems more reverential or haunting than destructive: "The eucharistic host would often fly violently out the hand and swirl about the room but would always fall back eventually on the gold paten in the priest's other hand." Kelly's interview of Bowdern himself denied this part of the stories of administering the Eucharist to Robbie. Kelly relates simply: "The boy would sometimes lapse into unconsciousness and spit the host onto the paten."[179] The latter description fits exactly with the *Diary* entry of April 2.

Functions of Manifestations

The manifestations evidence a theological element that counters the attempt or authority of the exorcist. In the battle between Christ and Satan, the demons mock and revolt to the presence of the Christian sacred. In an upcoming chapter, this role of manifestations becomes even more apparent when Malachi Martin describes the stages of resistance that the exorcist should expect to witness during the development of the exorcism.[180]

Besides the intention of resistance to exorcism, manifestations of demonization produce two other noteworthy effects. Distractions seem to be a main force of demonic resolve. The rite itself remarks about the encounter of the priest: "He will be on his guard against the arts and subterfuges which the evil spirits are wont to use in deceiving the exorcist. For oftentimes they give deceptive answers and make it difficult to understand them."[181] The demon will attempt to "hide behind" the one demonized, conflating the victim and his or her demonic presence.[182] In the account of the Bowdern exorcism, the demon once yelled "Fire! Fire!" and thus interrupted the priest's exorcism prayer when the hospital staff rushed in.[183] The command for a time and day of departure, analyzed

---

and a failed attempt later, just after midnight.
179. Kelly, *Devil*, 95.
180. Martin, *Hostage to the Devil*, 17–24.
181. Weller, ed., *Roman Ritual: Volume 2*, 169.
182. Martin, *Hostage to the Devil*, 18.
183. *Diary*, "April 13."

below, led to numeric communication that diverted and confounded the exorcists.

The fostering of fear evidences another function of manifestations: horror can infiltrate the exorcism process. This element goes to the terror and curiosity that make such events interesting to the public. In reference to Robbie's cousin in the house, the demon repeated "You will die tonight" for ten consecutive minutes.[184] Likewise, he drew a face when he declared, "Dead bishop," either referring to the priests or to Father Bishop himself.[185] Fiendish laughter, voice alternation, and animalistic behavior can instill fear in witnesses to demonization.[186]

Conclusion

The possible nature, causes, and manifestations of the demonization that led to the 1949 exorcism have been at the forefront of this chapter. The irregular, violent, profane, and resistant behavior of the victim marked the event. Whether a demonstration of the power of the demon over the victim, or the resistance of power by the demon to the exorcism attempt, manifestations of a preternatural nature fill the pages of the *Diary*.

Theologically, the recognizable contributing causes to Robbie's unbalanced behavior is his demonization, cultivated by his participation in the occultic activity of necromancy. A young boy is hurt and lonely at the loss of his aunt, so he employed the coping means he knew—that is, reconnecting with her as she had taught him. The family joined this initiative, revealing a potentially greedy motivation to communicate with the dead for hidden money. Marks of failed social attachments and conversion disorder seem to be in place here. Fraud by the boy has been entertained by some. However, these alone do not explain the length and duration of the irregular activities and the unexplainable nature of all the activities. The bold premise of demonization solely explains them all. The manifestations of personality and behavior alterations, oracular and vocalic alterations, the cluster effect, the preternatural strength, preternatural knowledge, related proximal phenomenon, and spiritual aversion justify this theological explanation. The characteristics of historical

---

184. *Diary*, "April 3."
185. *Diary*, "March 31."
186. *Diary*, "March 18"; "March 19"; "April 18."

demonization and exorcisms are congruent with this 1949 event, as are the brief snapshots of demonized behavior in the New Testament.

5
Theology of the Rite

"I cast you out, thou unclean spirit, along with the least encroachment of the wicked enemy, and every phantom and diabolical legion. In the name of our Lord Jesus Christ, depart and vanish from this creature of God."

—*Roman Ritual* 2:185

For four hundred years, Roman Catholic priests would be ordained as exorcists. This accolade came automatically and intentionally with holy orders taken by every priest. However, following the initiative of the Council of Vatican II, Pope Paul VI issued his *Ministeria Quaedam* in 1972 to remove four minor orders of priestly ordination. The office of exorcist joined that of the portent, lecturer, and acolyte as omitted offices for every priest.[1] These activities can still take place; exorcism requires special archdiocese approval, and some American dioceses make special appointments to the office of exorcist.

This chapter introduces the Catholic rite of exorcism, the means for Bowdern and the other priests to engage the demon in the 1949 exorcism. It considers the nature and use of the rite, as well as other liturgical elements instrumental to our event. For example, since one of its elemental requirements is the integrity and readiness of the exorcist, the relationship between the exorcist and the text is considered. It offers and evaluates a Catholic theological justification for their belief in spiritual

---

1. Nicola, *Diabolical Possession*, 98; Martin, *Hostage to the Devil*, xvii; Lampert, *Exorcism*, 8–10.

beings, work of rebellion against God and in deceit against the church, the authority of Christ, his exercise over demons, the historical nature of prayers for exorcism, and the nature and application of the rite. Anthony Masters remarks about the ritual, "It is a very interesting and, in many ways, enlightened document and is in no way a mere series of outdated incantations."[2]

Its role in the narrative of the *Diary* is instrumental. The anticipated time of departure especially becomes a feature of suspense in the narrative account, because the demon demonstrated its most frequent resistance to a section of the rite called the *praecipio*. This is the first of three parts of liturgy that delivers a message of power and command directly to the demon, requiring its response by all heavenly authority. Drama apexes during the reading of the rite at this point more than all others.

History and Nature of the Rite

The *Catechism* today reads, "Exorcism is directed at the expulsion of demons or to liberation from demonic possession through the spiritual authority which Jesus entrusted the Church."[3] In 1614, Pope Paul V updated the *Roman Ritual*, which still contains the liturgy for the rite of exorcism. However, stemming from changes in Catholicism at Vatican II, the 1999 *Of Exorcisms and Certain Prayers* revised the rite in a new 84-page document. This ritual continues in liturgical use today. While the pre-Vatican II form was the liturgical source for the 1949 exorcism, the contemporary rite is employed throughout this work as a Catholic primary source.[4] The theological elements of interest remain the same, such as the prayers and incitements, and a Latin text still accompanies the English translation approved by the Vatican in 2016.

Still, the change is important because of the care around the victimized person. A new section distinguishes between mental illness and demonization, now requiring bishop appointment for the rite of exorcism when medical alternatives have been exhausted. Amorth evidences the reason for this change:

> For more than three centuries, and with serious damage done to those who suffered from spiritual evils, exorcism was practically

---

2. Masters, *Devil's Dominion*, 175.
3. *Catechism* §1673.
4. Weller, ed., *Roman Ritual: Volume 2*.

Theology of the Rite

not practiced; moreover, in the seminaries the subject was practically ignored. The motive, favored by a rationalist mentality, was based on the furious rejection of the witch hunts, the persecutions of heretics, and the religious wars of the past centuries. And so the baby was thrown out with the bathwater.[5]

The assurance of a mental illness evaluation reinforces the justification that this sacramental must be read and implemented only by a priest, and only under approval of the bishop. The *Code of Canon Law* declares, "No one may lawfully exorcise the possessed without the special and express permission of the local Ordinary."[6] This means the bishop of the diocese. The *Catechism* states the same: the solemn exorcism "can be performed only by a priest and with the permission of the bishop."[7]

The 1999 document reinforced the spirit of the time from Vatican II, one marked by modernism when exorcism was somewhat embarrassing, abused, and undesirable for many in the church. Wilkinson recognizes the tension around the topic of exorcism at the progressive Second Vatican Council: "Emphasis was placed on good, hope, and compassion, and discussion of evil and demons was minimized . . . the *Roman Ritual* governing exorcism was shoved to a back burner" until Pope Paul VI restored its prominence.[8] Even while natural philosophy pressed on a traditional supernatural theology, Catholicism maintained its belief in spirit beings.

The necessity of priestly and not laity administration of the rite also stems from the ecclesiastical belief in the spiritual authority of the office of priest. The *Roman Ritual* remarks, "It is allowed at present only to priests, who ordinarily are obliged to seek the authorization of the bishop before exorcism is resorted to."[9] For Roman Catholicism, the rite of exorcism is a sacramental. According to the *Catechism*, sacramentals are "sacred signs which bear a resemblance to the sacraments." As such, they always include prayer and a sign, such as the laying on of hands, the sign of the cross, sprinkling with holy water, or anointing with oil. While sacramentals do not confer the same grace as sacraments, "They prepare us to receive grace and dispose us to cooperate with it."[10]

---

5. Amorth, *Exorcism*, 99.
6. *Code* 1172§1; James Collins, *Exorcism and Deliverance Ministry*, 206.
7. *Catechism* §1673.
8. Wilkinson, *Vatican's Exorcists*, 46.
9. Weller, ed., *Roman Ritual: Volume 2*, 167.
10. *Catechism* §§1667, 1668, 1670.

The application of the rite is for major exorcisms, and it also bears the name "solemn exorcism." Meanwhile, minor exorcisms are simple prayers in any form, most available for laity, that appeal to God for freedom from demonization. These prayers are "intended for places there the activity of the Devil is suspected, not for possessed people."[11] Such prayer is used in liturgy for adult converts and baptized children, "Essentially uniform and standard theological fare for helping people protect against evil."[12] In different forms, exorcism prayers are available to Catholics and non-Catholics for prayer.[13] Meanwhile, for Protestants who emphasize the priesthood of all believers (1 Pet 2:5), the ecclesiology here appears limiting. Yet for sacerdotal Catholicism, the priest is viewed as more authoritative in ecclesiastical authority of spiritual matters by virtue of his office. Nicola recognizes this difference when he declares, "It would be extremely narrow and provincial to think that the interest of the devil and the demons is redistricted to Catholics, or to those to whom the Catholic Church's rite of exorcism is available."[14]

Contents of the Rite

The *Roman Ritual* contains three guiding sections for exorcism. A first section entitled "Exorcism" explains the Catholic perspective on the nature of demonization and exorcism. A second section entitled "Exorcism of the Possessed" provides specific rules for diagnosing and establishing the criteria for exorcism, as well as rules for preparation and behavior throughout it. A third section entitled "Rite of Exorcism" is the rite itself to be read and prayed.[15] Throughout the rite are readings of Scripture that support the authoritative claims and commands of the rite and its reader. Features related to the content of these three sections are dispersed throughout this chapter and explain the theology and actions of the priests in 1949.

A governing admonition to the exorcist comes as a preface in the first section:

---

11. Blai, *Hauntings*, 137.
12. Hallowell, *Playing with Fire*, 143.
13. Lampert, *Exorcism*, 55.
14. Nicola, *Diabolical Possession*, 100.
15. Weller, ed., *Roman Ritual: Volume 2*, 160–229. For an overview, see Masters, *Devil's Dominion*, 175–83.

> Man, above all Christians, must reckon with the realm of the prince of darkness and his legions, not presuming that Satan has no existence outside of the product of fable, superstition, or figment ... There is a world of demons, as revealed religion teaches, and even if revelation were not so absolute, we could conjecture that the devil is real person and that his sway is tremendous.[16]

This justification for the rite is provided at the outset, revealing the Roman Catholic perspective on spirit beings and framing preternatural expectations for any reader.

Readiness of the Exorcist

The rite itself is further preceded by a brief set of requirements in preparation for the one performing the exorcism. Since the celebrant is always a priest, the exclusive male pronoun is used for its requirements. For example, the opening requirement is that he "must be properly distinguished for his piety, prudence, and integrity of life." Commonly stated requirements include humility, age, study, integrity, and ability to suspend judgment that demonization is underway.[17] The emphasis on the moral integrity and constitutional strength of the exorcist is so valued that Chajes says that the administration of the rite is performed *ex opere operantis* ("by the work of the one who does") rather than the normal sacramental quality of *ex opere operato* ("by the work done by Christ").[18]

In 1949, Father William Bowdern accepted the appointment of exorcist with these full criteria in view. A biographer of the exorcist would likely mention that his pre-requisite humility was illustrated in a story considered to be Jesuit lore. Supposedly when the archbishop assigned the rite to Bowdern, the priest responded, "Nothing doing." The archbishop in authority ordered, "You've got it."[19]

Even the junior assistants should have a readiness about them. The exorcist, Martin states, should ensure that "his assistants will not be

---

16. Weller, ed., *Roman Ritual: Volume 2*, 160.

17. Weller, ed., *Roman Ritual: Volume 2*, 169. For parallel descriptions of the qualifications of the exorcist, see Taylor, *Devil Came to St. Louis*, 17–18; Lampert, *Exorcism*, 71–73; Amorth, *Exorcist*, 107–10; Fraune, *Slaying Dragons*, 99–131; Martin, *Hostage to the Devil*, 13–14.

18. Chajes, *Between Worlds*, 79.

19. Allen, *Possessed*, 90.

weakened or overcome by obscene behavior or by language foul beyond their imagining; they cannot blanch at blood, excrement, urine; they must be able to take awful personal insults and be prepared to have their darkest secrets screeched in public."[20]

The participants would take care to guard themselves spiritually in this process. Father Bowdern recognized his important role as the steward of God's power and grace against the personal demonic being and the power of Satan. It was neither a thankful nor easy task but one that involved self-examination and spiritual preparation, including prayer, confession, and fasting. Thomas Allen describes it this way:

> An exorcist has to touch evil, breathe it, focus on it.... To work against the devil, an exorcist enters the deep, clutching shadow of evil. When he appears, the demons turn their evil on him.... The exorcist priest, though he sees himself as an agent of good aided by an almighty God, simultaneously sees himself as a mere human being pitted against a powerful enemy with long experience in perpetrating evil.[21]

Allen claims that before his first application, Father Bowdern spent the day of the rite in prayer, in Mass, in confession, and in fasting, and he later called on his assistants to fast.[22] The ritual commentary advises the exorcist to exercise faith as a mustard seed—an instruction given by Jesus when the disciples could not exorcise a demon from a child (Matt 17:20). Two reports in 1949 and 1951 suggest that Bowdern took only bread and water with prayer during the day, while able to eat at night, for two and a half months. They cite that he lost fifty pounds in this fasting and stressful experience.[23] This is called a black fast, or a strict fast, like the kind taken during Lent. Halloran would remark on his own fast in an interview later that this Lenten period already saw a fasting underway. While he might take only coffee and toast as part of skipping a meal, Bowdern fasted "quite a bit, and sometimes he would go off because he was getting worn out."[24]

---

20. Martin, *Hostage to the Devil*, 16.
21. Allen, *Possessed*, 89.
22. Allen, *Possessed*, 96, 116, 186.
23. "New Details"; Linson, "Washington's Haunted Boy," 33–34.
24. Brown, "Interview."

Theology of the Rite

Prayers and Scripture

The rite of exorcism opens with prayer: "Remember not, O Lord, our offenses." It sets the tone of reliance on the divine for the reading of the rite, following instructions to have already "implored God's help in devout prayer." It sets into the Lord's prayer next, followed by Ps 53 that opens "Save me, O God, by thy name, and further my cause by thy power."[25] As the posture and rhetoric of prayer continue throughout the liturgy, one realizes that the entire reading of the rite is in fact a prayer. The exorcist appeals, implores, asks, petitions, and requests for divine intervention on behalf of the victim. Prayer pauses only when the exorcist commands the demon into submission with imperatives that lead to its expulsion. The contrast is stark: humble reliance on God and commanding authority against Satan.

The rite contains prayers that are laden with biblical rhetoric. It contains a variety of psalms and passages that can be read during the rite. Psalm 23 predominates with the verse, "Deliver us from evil." Psalm 51 deals with the issue of sin in an effort to correct spiritual quality. John 1:1–14 recognizes Christ's authority. Mark 16:15–18 commands the disciples to "drive out demons in my [Christ's] name." Luke 10:17–20 reports how Jesus saw "Satan fall from heaven" when the disciples returned from a mission of ministry. Luke 11:14–22 shows how Christ cast out a demon from a mute man and taught on the authority of the "strongman." Psalm 67 reveals how God's enemies flee from his power. The biblical attributes of God—mercy, lovingkindness, forgiving, and providence—flavor the rite. The liturgy employs additional theological and dogmatic statements—for example, referencing the Trinity and the Athanasian Creed that have biblical support and contain biblical rhetoric. Such data theologically evidence the authority of Scripture in the life of a believer, especially against the powers of Satan. These references make apparent both the authority of Scripture as well as the authority of the church.

The assistant exorcist plays an important role in supporting the activities of the exorcist, particularly in prayer and in responsive readings. At key junctions in the liturgy, the exorcist and the assistant read in tandem and in unison. This practice finds a measure of support in Matt 18:18–19, where the Gospel describes how two or three gathered in Christ's name can agree, bind, and loosen matters on earth and in heaven. Wilkinson describes the thought of Monsignor Andre Gemma,

---

25. Weller, ed., *Roman Ritual: Volume 2*, 175.

an Italian bishop and a rare exorcism officiant: "Unity and communion are important among men of God and people of faith, because such spirituality keeps evil away . . . That is why joint prayers and prayers of liberation recited in unison are particularly effective."[26]

Commanding Material

The rite has three principal exorcism prayers historically identified by Latin words that begin the prayers. These are imperative prayers, giving a command to the demon first to produce information or later to exit the victim. The rite that was read on this occasion and its component parts are introduced theologically here. As part of his narrative, Thomas Allen provides a dramatic imagination of the first reading of the rite, combining the testimonies, the *Diary*, and the rite into one sample exorcism experience.[27]

The Praecipio

The words *praecipio tibi* deliver the imperative "I command you." The demanding authority specifies not to harm the demonized victim as a creature of God and not to harm the participants providing the ministry of deliverance to the victim:

Praecipio tibi	I command you
Quicumque es, spiritus immunde	whoever you are, unclean spirit
Et omnibus sociis tuis	and all your associates
Neque hance creaturam Dei	neither shall you harm this creature of God
Vel circumstantes	nor the bystanders[28]

A second, essential directive is embedded here. Accompanying the command above lies the controversial authority of the exorcist to require "some sign or other thy name and the day and the hour of thy departure."[29]

---

26. Wilkinson, *Vatican's Exorcists*, 85.
27. Allen, *Possessed*, 95–111.
28. "Rite of Exorcism" 2 (Weller, ed., *Roman Ritual: Volume 2*, 178–79).
29. "Rite of Exorcism" 2 (Weller, ed., *Roman Ritual: Volume 2*, 178–79).

Theology of the Rite

Dicas mihi nomen tuum, diem, et horam exitus tui cum aliquo signo.	Thou shalt tell me by some sign or other thy name and the day and the hour of thy departure[30]

This element is known as the *dicas mihi* ("Tell me"). This phrase and its theology become central to the 1949 exorcism story. Time and time again in the *Diary*, the narrative centers on the priestly attempt to interpret the elusive answer to this mandate. In his ministry to Robbie, Father Bowdern sought to enlist his willful participation against the demon, which included shifting this one element from the Latin rite to English.[31] Since the combination *praecipio tibi . . . dicas mihi* is indispensable to our story and the exorcism moment, it finds special elaboration below.

The Exorcizo

The words *exorcizo te* mean "I cast you out." Here lies the central command of exorcism:

Exorcizo te, immundissime spiritus	I cast you out, you unclean spirit
omnis in cursio adversarii	along with the least encroachment of the wicked enemy
omne phantasma, omnis legio	[and] every phantom and diabolical legion
in nomine Domini nostri Jesu Christi	in the name of our Lord Jesus Christ[32]

While the exorcist speaks the *exorcizo*, Christ is the one who orders the demon. Jesus' past victories and his historic atoning work are reminders of the defeated humility suffered by the enemy. For example, the liturgy further names Israel and Joseph from the Old Testament, as well as the slain lamb, crucified man, and triumpher over hell from the New Testament.

The Adjuro

The words *adjuro te* mean "I adjure you," which is a charge or obligation. This command urges or solemnly demands the demon to surrender control by the power of Christ. It combines into a series of exclamatory

---

30. "Rite of Exorcism" 2 (Weller, ed., *Roman Ritual: Volume 2*, 178–79).
31. *Diary*, "April 18."
32. "Rite of Exorcism" 2 (Weller, ed., *Roman Ritual: Volume 2*, 184–85).

Theology of a Diary

commands of authority against the demon on the authority of Christ, the Trinity, the saints, the angels, and the martyrs. "Yield, therefore, yield, not to myself but to the minister of Christ!"[33]

Adjuro te, serpens antique	I adjure you, Ancient Serpent
Adjuro te iterum	I adjure once more
non mea infirmitate	not by my own weakness
sed virtute Spiritus Sancti	but by the might of the Holy Spirit
ut exeas ab hoc famulo Dei	be gone from this servant of God[34]

The section actually contains three *adjuro te* commands. "I adjure thee, thou ancient serpent" leads into biblical theology of the relationship between condemned fallen beings and the redeemed church. "I adjure thee, therefore, thou profligate dragon" sets the powers of the enemy against the army of God with its angels. Finally, *adjuro ergo te, omnis immundissime spiritus* is curiously translated as "I cast thee out, unclean spirit," as if it combines the *adjuro* and *exorcizo* in a finale before leading into the psalms of prayer.[35]

Typical of the appeal for God to hear the prayer of the exorcist throughout the rite is the appeal contained after the *praecipio* and the *exorcizo*. It affirms the authority of Jesus on earth to cast out demons and an appeal to have the faith and power to do the same. It follows the reading of the Great Commission (Mark 16:15–18), the apostles return from mission in which Satan falls from heaven (Luke 10:17–20), and the exorcism in which religious leaders accused Jesus of casting out demons by Satan's power (Luke 11:14–22). It also shows the dependence of the exorcist on the power of Christ.

Domine, exaudi orationem meum	O, Lord, hear my prayer
et clamor meus ad te veniat	and let my cry come to you
Domnus vobiscum	The Lord be with you
et cum spiritu tuo	And with your spirit
Oremus	Let us pray[36]

---

33. "Rite of Exorcism" 2 (Weller, ed., *Roman Ritual: Volume 2*, 189).
34. "Rite of Exorcism" 2 (Weller, ed., *Roman Ritual: Volume 2*, 186–87).
35. "Rite of Exorcism" 4 (Weller, ed., *Roman Ritual: Volume 2*, 187, 191, 192–93).
36. "Rite of Exorcism" 2 (Weller, ed., *Roman Ritual: Volume 2*, 178–79).

Ending with a call to prayer, the repeated intercession typifies the perpetual prayer dimension of the content of the rite of exorcism.

THE CENTRALITY OF THE *DICAS MIHI*

The *praecipio* would prove to play a central role in the drama that is the 1949 exorcism. Here, the command to the demon, *dicas mihi*, is to divulge information about itself and about its hold on the victim. From the first to the last day of the exorcism, as well as days in between, Bowdern looked at this section for particular communication about the nature of demonization. He listens for the demon's name so that he might name it back with authority. He listens for the predicted time of departure, that he might measure the strength of its hold. It became Bowdern's regular habit to demand the demon's name and departure, after which violence would follow. Toward the end of the exorcism period, Bowdern commanded the *dicas mihi* phrase more and more, believing that this command was most effective, as if he had discovered an Achilles's heel in the demon's grasp of Robbie. This instance in the liturgy is portrayed as the battleground between spiritual forces, the moment where ecclesiastical power should overwhelm the spiritual enemy.

Command Authority

Three primary pieces of information are sought at this point of the rite in command form. It reflects the Catholic belief that ecclesiastical authority mandates obedient response. Father Frederick Bunse, who offered an account of the 1928 Iowa exorcism, insists, "It is true that the evil spirits are liars by habit; but they are compelled to tell the truth by the exorcism of the Church when, under the ordeal of exorcism they attempt to lie, they feel great pain and soon cry out, 'I have told a lie.'"[37] Martin remarks, "To force as complete an identification as possible is perhaps a mark of domination of one will over another."[38] Basham claims that demons commanded to identify themselves will resist with protests and

---

37. Frederick Bunse's unpublished manuscript (cited in Laycock, "Secret History," 30).
38. Martin, *Hostage to the Devil*, 21.

arguments but when they were pressed, they "had to obey."[39] Bowdern seems to agree, searching the answer given to expedite the exorcism.

First, "The number and names of the spirits inhabiting the patient" are to be asked. This undoubtedly harkens back to the Gadarene passage, where Jesus asks the demoniac, "What is your name?" By answering, "Legion," the demons reveal, "For we are many," instructing the disciples on the nature of demonization (Mark 5:9; Luke 8:30). This command finds elaboration with the permitted question of the role of necromancy, amulets, or evil symbols in the life of the victim, whether concealed on or consumed by the person.[40] Eric Sorensen suggests that the demand for a name is part of the ancient mentality of gaining authority over the subject.[41] The significance of using another's name has already been demonstrated in the theology above. Interestingly, in a later interview, Halloran claims this legendary nomenclature: "During the rite when it was asked its name the only answer I can remember that was given was 'legion.'"[42]

In the 1949 exorcism, the day of Thursday, March 31 marks the unique event of Robbie writing mysteriously with his finger on the bed before he is given pencil and paper. The result is a lengthy communication about identity and time of departure for the demon. "Spite" was one recorded answer to the question of identity.[43] "Hell" also appeared among the scratches, associated the cause with Satan (Matt 25:41; Jude 6; Rev 20:10).[44] When Robbie was given a pencil to write messages when he seemed obsessed with writing, he recorded, "I am the devil."[45] "I am the devil himself" is one of the points Robbie provided.[46] The Iowa exorcism also offers a narrative in which Satan himself is the agent of demonization.[47] In this case, one is reminded of the hermeneutic of Tyconius in the early church, that Satan and his demons are used interchangeably, just as Christ and the church belong to one another.[48]

---

39. Basham, *Deliver Us from Evil*, 152.
40. "Exorcism of the Possessed" 4 (Weller, ed., *Roman Ritual: Volume 2*, 169).
41. Sorensen, *Possession and Exorcism*, 120.
42. Brown, "Interview."
43. *Diary*, "March 31."
44. *Diary*, "March 16"; "April 7"; "April 11."
45. *Diary*, "March 31."
46. *Diary*, "March 31."
47. Young, *History of Exorcism*, 202.
48. Robinson, "Introduction," 8–15.

Theology of the Rite

On the same *Diary* date, Robbie also wrote, "I will answer in the name of Spite." This association becomes important in the vision around the final exorcism moment, when Robbie testified that the word "spite" appeared above the cave where the demon descended.[49] This appeared in the *Diary* as a marked response to an occasion of the *praecipio*, when *dicas mihi . . . diem* ("tell me the day") of your departure was invoked. Brian reports from his interview with Rhine that the word "spite" was among the scratched messages.[50] Perhaps another intended answer to the question of identity is the scratches that read "hell."[51] Similarly, the image of the devil that appeared on the skin is an association of the identity of the demon.[52] Some will interpret these communications as individual demons, but the typology offered by Tyconius might suggest that they are names representing Satan by members of his body. The priests do not show any intention to act based on these names provided.

Second, "The time when they [the demons] entered into him, the cause thereof, and such like" should be asked.[53] This command is at best tied to the identity of the demon in the prior question, as "the cause thereof" anticipates an association with that demon. At worst, it is asking another question in engagement of the demon without a direct biblical precedent. While not all Christian practices necessarily have to be illustrated in the Scripture, a theological expansion of questioning here is dangerous.

Third, the question of the anticipated time of departure is embedded in the text of the rite. While not named in the introduction to the rite, another question occurs later in the text. "I command you . . . tell me by some sign your name, and the day and hour of your departure."[54] Why it is not named in the introductory guide alongside the other two questions is a mystery. One might make a case that it is within the spirit of the question around "the time when they entered into him" named earlier, but at the same time, it requires a measure of foreknowledge by the demon. The expectation that the demonic would know the temporal efficacy of the upcoming exorcism is problematic.

---

49. *Diary*, "April 18."

50. Brian, *Enchanted Voyager*, 182. This is based on the testimony of J. B. Rhine, informed by Schulze.

51. *Diary*, "March 16"; "April 7"; "April 11."

52. *Diary*, "March 16."

53. "Exorcism of the Possessed" 15 (Weller, ed., *Roman Ritual: Volume 2*, 173).

54. "Rite of Exorcism" 2 (Weller, ed., *Roman Ritual: Volume 2*, 179).

Chaos from Compulsion

As the rite was read, the demon would often scratch communications in the body of its victim, Robbie. On the first occasion, the "X" appeared twenty-five times.[55] As a reminder of the preternatural quality, the report claims, "The printing always appeared without any motion on the part of the boy's hands." Vincent Lampert names "incisions of letters that appear on the skin that persist for some time and then disappear" from his own experiences as an extraordinary activity of demonization.[56]

The compulsion for the demon to provide its identity and departure is mixed together in the communications. Even the diarist remarks that "at least during the first days of the exorcism the 'X' had no significance."[57] This mark was interpreted as the Roman number ten, understood by the priests as a possible prediction of an exit date, time, or number of days for demonic departure. The message only frustrated them because they never had a point of reference from which to calculate "ten." The diarist first postulated, "This impression [X] may have indicated that the exorcism would take ten days, or that the devil would depart at 10:00 o'clock."[58] Nine days later, the *Diary* reveals how Bishop anticipated an impending departure on the feast of St. Gabriel the archangel, a high figure in the litany of the saints. However, Bowdern was counting the tenth day as the feast of the Annunciation as a date for departure.[59] Fifteen days after the initial "X" branding, on the occasion of the writing episode of March 31, the communication came in a flat and eerie voice that the demon would stay ten days and return after four days. "I will stay 10 days and return after the 4 days are up." Additionally, "In 10 days I will give a sign on his chest he will have to have it covered to show my power." Finally, "You will have to pray for a month in the Catholic Church," along with, "You may not believe me. Then R will suffer forever."[60] A timing was delivered in response to the rite command, but it was couched in chiasm, riddles, and

---

55. *Diary*, "March 16."
56. Lampert, *Exorcism*, 34.
57. *Diary*, "March 16."
58. *Diary*, "March 16."
59. *Diary*, "March 24"; Allen, *Possessed*, 142. Allen also implies that Bowdern thought the time of 10:00 the next morning might be the communication of departure (103).
60. *Diary*, "March 31."

a death threat to the exorcist. The priestly calculations would continue in vain.[61]

Nicola curiously posits of the "X" scratch, "It was taken to be a sign of the unknown," an interpretation as unknown as the mark itself. He later claims that on the penultimate day at the *dicas mihi*, the diabolical voice responded with ten names. We might infer that Satan, Hell, and Spite were among them. He suggests that ten demons thus solved the mystery of the Roman number for ten.[62] LaChance connects four "X" scratches on one day as an indication of forty demons in the boy. He ties the number to the biblical significance to forty as suffering or tribulation, illustrated in Abraham and Jonah stories where cities are in judgment for this number of days. Likewise, Jesus is in the desert of temptation by Satan forty days.[63] Yet LaChance also here reminds his readers of demonic deceit and the distraction puzzling the Jesuits as he still suggests demonic coordination of this number: "The priests had made a very crucial error in thinking and they played directly into the demon's hand. Even Father Bishop does not mention the significance of the error in the diary. . . . A demon will often present a riddle to be solved, but at the same time, that riddle can easily be turned into a joke on those who try to solve it."[64]

In addition to the "X" brand, other marks and words dotted the response of the *dicas mihi*. Both the words "go" and "exit" appeared in different places as scratches, but it could not be interpreted as a communication of time.[65] Once, in response to the command, scratches communicated the Roman "X" but also the number "18." On another occasion of the *dicas mihi*, scratches communicated the names "hell" and "spite" and the numbers 4, 8, 10, 16.[66] The pattern developed as a response to the *dicas mihi*, leading the exorcist to continue the practice. On April 7, the point of the *praecipio*, more than twenty scratch brands came to Robbie's body. The number 4, single and double strokes, a fork, and claw marks are named in the *Diary* as occurring without Robbie's cause. The

---

61. Allen, *Possessed*, 154–55.

62. Nicola, *Diabolical Possession*, 113, 115. McGuire claims that both Blatty and Walsh believed that the event involved ten demons (see "St. Louis Exorcism").

63. LaChance, *Confrontation*, 109–10.

64. LaChance, *Confrontation*, 112.

65. *Diary*, "March 16," "April 1," and "April 11" respectively.

66. Allen, *Possessed*, 178, which he attributes to April 7. The *Diary* details are briefer, starting on the number 4. However, on this day, it notes that he wrote on his body with his own fingernail, "Christ" and "Hell."

words "hell" and "Christ" were produced on Robbie. Violence, spitting, defecation, and foul language marked the night. Almost in mimic of the *dicas mihi*, the demon offered his own prophecy and sign by declaring he would fight with the priests until 6:00 am—four hours ahead of their current weariness—and declared that Robbie would awaken suddenly to evidence it. He did. Then he slept for hours.[67] In all of these communications, it is noteworthy that at the *praecipio,* sometimes the demon does not appear under compulsion to give any name and departure time at all.[68]

Amidst the many numerical and alphabetical messages that came at the compulsion of the rite, one particular communication had to be tantalizing for the priests. When Robbie declared that he wanted to receive communion on the day of climax, the voice protested its effectiveness and asserted that one word must be spoken for expulsion: "That isn't enough. He has to say one more word, one little word, I mean one BIG word. He'll never say it say it. He has to make nine Communions. He'll never say that word. I am always in him. I may not have much power always, but I am in him. He will never say that word." Here is another riddle for the priests that also sound like the key to unlock the demonic hold. Yet to exacerbate the message, singing, urination, and violence surrounded the confession.

Theological Considerations

Several elements are worth addressing theologically about the Catholic perspective, both of the Jesuit priests in 1949 and the doctrine of the church historically.

Dialogical Engagement

For starters, the rite approves a measure of dialogical engagement with the demon. Ecclesiastical authority affords the exorcist to inquire about the demon, expecting verbal or written communication as a response. From the early church, Tertullian provides a precedent: "The wicked spirit, bidden to speak by a follower of Christ, will as readily make the truthful confession that he is a demon, as elsewhere he has falsely asserted

---

67. *Diary,* "April 7."
68. *Diary,* "April 2"; "April 3"; "April 12"; "April 17."

Theology of the Rite

that he is a god."[69] While Jesus models the nomenclature inquiry at the Gadarenes, this affordance is also balanced by Michael's unwillingness to engage Satan over the body of Moses: "But he simply said, 'The Lord rebuke you'" (Jude 9).

However, the rite also keeps this liberal engagement in check. At the *praecipio*, the rite sets into some of the most important elements of exorcism that were encountered in this unfolding historical case. In addition to the *dicas mihi* ("tell me") the name and time of departure, another inquiry into manifestation comes about the exorcist's efforts towards understanding:

> Let him inquire of the person possessed, following one or the other act of exorcism, what the latter experienced in his body or soul while the exorcism was being performed, and to learn also what particular words in the form had a more intimidating effect upon the devil, so that hereafter these words may be employed with greater stress and frequency.[70]

In the process of demanding communication from the demon, Catholic theology affords the exorcist the right to silence the deception and demand information. It makes exception to dialogical engagement on the three features: the name of the demon, the cause of the demon, and the anticipated departure date. In order to gain these, as well as to silent ancillary distractions, the command above is given to clear the cacophony that the demon offers. Robert Priest objects to the entire approach of such dialog: "While they claim that it is God's power which allows them to force the father of lies to tell the truth, the fact remains that the source of the revelation is demonic. It is not God speaking, but Satan."[71]

Knowledge of Time of Departure

Peculiar for one unfamiliar with the Catholic rite is the very expectation that the demon will have knowledge to express its time of departure. This attempt was central to the exorcism attempt by Bowdern, and the *Diary* often makes mention of the delivery of this feature and

---

69. Tertullian, *Apol.* 23 (*ANF* 3:37).

70. "Exorcism of the Possessed" 4 (Weller, ed., *Roman Ritual: Volume 2*, 169).

71. Priest, et al., "Missiological Syncretism," 30 (For a recent history and an objection to dialoging with demons, see esp. 26–31.).

the expected response of the demon. At this point of the rite, the most demonic resistance is portrayed. This is no more elaborate than on the entry of March 31, where Robbie is writing something with his fingers and then with a pencil and paper delivered to him. The Roman numeral X seems revealed as a stay of ten days before a return in four days. The identity of the spirit is given as Satan himself, along with an intimidating message: "I am the devil himself. You will have to pray for a month in the Catholic Church."[72] It concedes answers to the Latin command to give his name. It yields information that soon a sign on Robbie's chest will display its power, as well as other related material. This knowledge given is still accompanied by a power play by the demon. Most importantly, this knowledge assumes the demon will understand the efficacy of exorcism in anticipation of its expulsion. It must know a sense not only of the present but of the future, defined by various elements beyond its control. This requires a foreknowledge that only God might possess. Both the words "go" and "exit" appeared in different places as scratches, but it was not a communication of time.[73] Meanwhile, the demonic voice did insist there would be no exit until the boy says one important word, which he would never say.[74] That name of "Lord" ironically was not the name of the demon commanded by the *dicas mihi* but the name of its archenemy.

Knowledge of the Name

Expecting a demon to yield its name seems less precarious to a Protestant theologian, as a demon might bear an identity and because Jesus modeled this in the Gadarene passage. By way of analysis, one might argue that Christ's actions in the biblical account of the Gadarene demoniac do not necessarily become programmatic for all Christians, any more than his spitting on the blind man's eyes to heal him (Mark 8:23). Furthermore, the danger of dialoging with demons borders on occult practices and may be syncretizing faiths when done in the name of Jesus. It is appropriate to wonder if ecclesiological limits should apply to this risk of demonic dialogue. Concerning the communication of Roman numerals by the demon, perhaps the enemy deceived the exorcist by enticing him to persist in a trivial practice through the *dicas mihi*. At one point of the

---

72. *Diary*, "March 31."
73. *Diary*, "March 16," "April 1," and "April 11" respectively.
74. *Diary*, "April 18."

Diary, there is also the passing comment that the number of demons was demanded, which at best might be a form of its name.[75]

Furthermore, in the Gadarene passage, the name is not a sin but an expression of quantity. Perhaps it was a didactic technique by Jesus, showing the disciples the complexity of demonization when Jesus had been casting out demons as others lingered.[76] Perhaps more normative is the testimony of Jude, who remarks how Satan vied for the body of Moses, but Michael "dare not utter a slanderous condemnation against him but said, 'The Lord rebuke you'" (Jude 9). In fact, Jude seems to be saying that arguing the position of Satan was not necessary—only the declaration of authority against him. Jude's example should be just as informative as the Gadarene example. Biblical narrative can have an historical circumstance that is unique for that case.

Effectiveness and Distraction

As far as the timeline revealed in *Diary*, the dates and times provided by the demon never prove to have any correlation with actual departure when demanded by the *dicas mihi diem*. Experienced Catholic exorcist Amorth admits, "Rarely does the date given correspond to the real date."[77] Nor is a name obviously yielded as the *dicas mihi nomen*. In the words of psychologist Ian Stevenson about this case, "His 'devil' never named himself."[78] This means that the rite did not prove to be a simple formula for success for identity or departure data for the demonization.

Catholic ecclesiastical authority is at work when the command is delivered to require for a demon to give its name and time of departure. A theology of demonic compulsion, predicated on Christ giving keys to the kingdom to Peter in Matt 16, is underway in the rite. This the basis for divine authority now distributed to the church to do battle against Satan and his forces. First Peter 2:9 captures this: "You are a chosen race, a royal priesthood, a holy nation, God's own people, that you may declare the wonderful deeds of him who called you out of darkness into his marvelous light." For Catholicism, this is always a priest, as a major exorcism

---

75. *Diary*, "March 16."

76. Mark 8:8, where the pluperfect tense—Jesus "had said to him"—sets up the identity of the many, "Legion," and the explanation why the exorcism was not yet completed.

77. Amorth, *Exorcist*, 103.

78. Stevenson, "Possession and Exorcism," 69.

cannot be read by a lay person and the authority given to Peter in Matt 16 is viewed as a priestly appointment rather than a demonstrable authority for all Christians. The most generous conclusion to offer Catholicism here is that the demon complied by yielding vague references to its identity and undiscernible information about its departure time. John Nicola offers an alternative interpretation of the "X" as a response to the *dicas mihi*, based on the April 17 response to the command. The demon offered ten names, including Satan, in a diabolical voice. Beyond the record of the *Diary*, for Nicola this offered a final meaning to the "X" branding.

These scratching manifestations might have served as a demonic distraction, a teasing and confusing message about the St. Louis connection of the aunt and the family or the time of departure. Perhaps the demonic entity did not like the ecclesiastical path being advanced by the parents with the invitation to clergy in the Washington, DC, phase. Perhaps the demon simply pretended to be under compulsion to reveal the time of departure. Yet, for the Catholic priests, these messages were prophetic data stemming from a mandate to communicate. The imprint of "3 ½ weeks" reported in the background to the case study might be the demon casting horror or randomly choosing a period for continued communication, in this case not concerning an exit date but a length of time to stay in St. Louis. The problem of demonic deceit needs consideration to get to this disconnect between ecclesial authority and the fruitless data gathered.

Problem of Deceit

Meanwhile, the problem of deceit accompanies any answer that the demon may offer in response. Theologically, demons are characterized by deceit and fraud (1 Tim 4:1; John 8:44). An inherent problem exists in conversing with a liar. Logically, a demon might intentionally feign suffering or comfort when an opposite effect might be at work. The cleverness of the demonic is evidenced when Satan used Scripture to tempt Jesus and Satan's ability to appear as an angel of light (2 Cor 11:14). In the account of the Bowdern exorcism, the demon once yelled "Fire!" and thus interrupted the priest's exorcism prayer when the hospital staff rushed in.[79] Yet this deceit factor seems to be ignored by Bishop as he

---

79. *Diary*, "April 13."

Theology of the Rite

records both the responses for time and day of departure, as well as their reported analysis of the meanings of the messages.

Deception should be expected from the demon and the rite offers examples of deception, including confusing answers, natural causes, fake departures, revelations of sins, and sudden sleep or a peaceful participation by the victim. This deception accompanies and even overlaps the acts of distraction and delay analyzed in the next chapter. Thus, Catholic doctrine warns that the exorcist should be careful not to engage in chatter with the demon, even when curiosity of hidden matters is revealed. The *Roman Ritual* gives special precaution against engaging the demonic during the application of the rite:

> The exorcist must not digress into senseless prattle nor ask superfluous questions or such as are prompted by curiosity, particularly if they pertain to future and hidden matters, all of which have nothing to do with his office. Instead, he will bid the unclean spirit keep silence and answer only when asked. Neither ought he to give any credence to the devil if the latter maintains that he is the spirit of some saint or of a deceased party, or even claims to be a good angel.[80]

The 1949 exorcist interprets aspects of the episode in a presumptuous manner when he fails to consider the demonic deception factor. Bowdern is driven to interpret the demonic response to the *dicas mihi* as an act of sacerdotal compulsion, but no indication suggests a critical potential for deceit in the response. It almost seems like a naïve expectation of compelled truth in the narrative. Yet, like a hostile witness in court can give information and claim veracity, so a demon would be expected to maintain falsehoods and communicate with deceitful signs through manifestations. In the 1928 Iowa exorcism, Father Riesenger's interrogation of demons in exorcism was so extensive that Laycock declares he was essentially a necromancer.[81] This is the same error of Ed Murphy, the author of a popular spiritual warfare book, in which he approves of the viability of demonic communication. Murphy trusts the testimony of demons that surrender spiritual insights while under compulsion, while conceding that they are capable of perjury.[82] Murphy insists that he has proved demonic claims as true on several occasions so as to validate their

---

80. "Exorcism of the Possessed" 14 (Weller, ed., *Roman Ritual: Volume 2*, 171).
81. Laycock, "Secret History," 30.
82. Murphy, *Handbook*, 53.

statements. He does not deny the deceit factor, but finds himself superior in judgment to it, claiming, "I have learned how to keep demons from lying to me."[83] Unfortunately, Murphy's task is unscientific, subjective, and anecdotally conditioned. He ignores the simple biblical precept that Satan also fosters pride—even to make us think that he temporarily is not deceitful or that we can supersede it.

THE RITE IN LARGER CONTEXT

Other considerations guided by the rite—both in and outside of the text—are worth considering. This includes protocols for the application of the rite that shape the background and some elements of the 1949 exorcism event. Any priest who finds approval from his archdiocese may apply the major rite of exorcism. While the sections below will reveal that this approval does not come easy, the eligibility of any priest through a special appointment by the bishop is universal, contingent upon fulfilled criteria. This potentiality is supported by the historic ordination to the priesthood to include his membership in a minor order of exorcism until Vatican II.

Approval for Application

It is indisputable that bishop approval is required for the application of the rite of exorcism. Two sets of criteria come into view for the established approval for an exorcism: criteria of evidence and criteria of the celebrant.

Evidence of demonization according to the *Roman Ritual* involves a distinction between possession and another illness. A priest should inquire of the demonization person to ascertain certain signs to function as proof. These include, firstly, the "ability to speak with some facility in a strange tongue or to understand it when spoken by another." The evidence of the demon speaking Latin or Aramaic is unsubstantiated by the diary of the exorcist. However, it is still claimed by former witnesses on later occasions. Secondly, "The faculty of divulging future and hidden events." Thirdly, "display of powers which are beyond the subject's age

---

83. Murphy, *Handbook*, 53.

Theology of the Rite

and natural condition." Fourthly, "various other indications which, when taken together as a whole, pile up the evidence."[84]

In all of these, Henry Kelly takes a dismissive approach, claiming that none of them were evident according to William Bowdern. "There had been no reported or observed signs of diabolical possession nor even of 'natural' possession before the exorcisms began."[85] Yet the same interview showed Bowdern testifying to strange events that would have qualified for approval by the criteria of the *Roman Ritual*. It seems that Kelly declares that first-hand priestly observation of the criteria prior to approval was lacking. The most obvious explanation for the approval was that the archbishop allowed the testimony of the parents and the backstory, in combination with the early explainable events while the priests were in another room of the house, to compound the case for demonization. This remains a hypothesis with the file closed to the public. Yet Kelly's interview of Bowdern minimizes the bizarre even further when he claims that the exorcist was of the opinion that "none of this could be taken as a preternatural sign of demonic activity."[86] The exception was the scratching within the boy's body which often came as a response to the liturgical references to Mary and Jesus. This was the convincing verification for Bowdern that demonization was underway. In the end, plenty of criteria fulfilment would ensue to validate exorcism once the exorcism began.

Additionally, clerical qualification for the administration of the rite is necessary for church approval. The *Code of Canon Law* captures this: "The permission is to be granted by the local Ordinary only to a priest who is endowed with piety, knowledge, prudence, and integrity of life."[87] Since exorcism is a matter of spiritual conflict, the priest must be spiritually and constitutionally healthy. Likewise, the rite repeats this.[88] Lampert suggests that the appointed priest "needs to have a strong priestly identity, be at peace in his priesthood, and not do this ministry full-time."[89] The qualified choice for exorcist should continue in the sac-

---

84. "Exorcism of the Possessed" 3 (Weller, ed., *Roman Ritual: Volume 2*, 169).
85. Kelly, *Devil*, 95, 97–98.
86. Kelly, *Devil*, 98.
87. *Code* 1172§2; James Collins, *Exorcism and Deliverance Ministry*, 207.
88. "Exorcism of the Possessed" (Weller, ed., *Roman Ritual: Volume 2*, 169).
89. Lampert, *Exorcism*, 48.

ramental and spiritual practices expected of one dedicated to God. This includes prayer, attending Mass, praying the rosary and fasting.[90]

The rite makes specific mention of the medical sphere of exorcism when it says, "The exorcist should guard against giving or recommending any medicine to the patient but should leave this care to physicians."[91] Likewise, the *Catechism* makes clear that "illness, especially psychological illness is a very different matter; treating this is the concern of medical science. Therefore, before an exorcism is performed, it is important to ascertain that one is dealing with the presence of the Evil One, and not an illness."[92]

In the case of the 1949 exorcism, Archbishop Ritter appoints Father William Bowdern as the celebrant of the sacramental. Even this choice involves theology. The Society of Jesus was founded with the principle that it reports directly and solely to the pope, not to the bishop or archbishop of the diocese where its working priests may be found. However, Father Bowdern was appointed as a parish priest, making him a rare Jesuit under the jurisdiction of the archbishop.[93]

Hesitancy for Approval of the Rite

It is well known that the Roman Catholic Church requirement for archdiocese approval does not come easy. A strict protocol for examination with a minimum set of requirements must be fulfilled before a requested case qualifies to be an official case.[94] The rite itself declares about any priest that "He should not believe too readily that a person is possessed by an evil spirit."[95] Vincent Lampert remarks, "The exorcist, in many ways, is trained to be a skeptic."[96] He offers an extensive familiarity with the process of archdiocese approval of any exorcism activities.[97]

---

90. Blai, *Hauntings*, 33.

91. "Exorcism of the Possessed" (Weller, ed., *Roman Ritual: Volume 2*, 173).

92. *Catechism* §1673.

93. Kelly, *Devil*, 96. Kelly is one of the few writers who show awareness of this ecclesiastical dynamic.

94. Lampert, *Exorcism*, 101–16; Taylor, *Devil Came to St. Louis*, 21.

95. "Exorcism of the Possessed" (Weller, ed., *Roman Ritual: Volume 2*, 169).

96. Lampert, *Exorcism*, 101.

97. Lampert, *Exorcism*, 101–16. This includes his own intake questionnaire for one believed to be suffering from demonic activity.

Theology of the Rite

Many prominent Catholic exorcists share a common position that the church does not take seriously the need for exorcism ministry. It is reasonable that the medical approach offers a buffer for postponing the application of the rite, not merely for ensuring demonization but to avoid the attention of exorcism. For example, Amorth describes Catholicism's own negligence of the use of rite and attention to demonization. He remarks: "The motive, favored by a rationalistic mentality, was based on the furious rejection of the witch hunts, the persecutions of heretics, and the religious wards of the past centuries. And so the baby was thrown out with the bathwater."[98] Wilkinson observes, "They would rather it not be highlighted at all, in deference to more positive, life-affirming aspects of the religion."[99] Robert Orsi describes how the Catholic Church tries to monitor and control the supernatural presence from such events: "The power of the Church depends on offering access to supernatural presence while at the same time controlling who gets such access and when."[100] This force is so formidable that it is enough for Laycock to declare about the 1912 Iowa case, "Perhaps the most remarkable thing about the Earling exorcism is not that it happened, but that the story was ever told at all."[101]

So, one of the most noteworthy qualities of the Roman Catholic view of exorcism is a practical one: the church prefers not to profile these and chooses to limit and scrutinize eligible cases, all in private. This scrutiny buttresses the historicity of potential demonic activity in each case, including the 1949 exorcism. Permission is required by the archdiocese for the rite of exorcism to be applied, along certain criteria and against a popular culture that will critique their approval. At times, Malachi Martin describes, often a "blind eye" is turned without denial of the rite that can be taken as "tacit permission."[102] Such an act in turn provides support and confirmation of approval if successful but offers no support if the exorcism goes bad. Occasional dioceses staff an official exorcist.[103] An important set of criteria is seen as the church insists that priests be certain of the diagnosis of demonization before applying the rite of exorcism.

98. Amorth, *Exorcist*, 99.
99. Wilkinson, *Vatican's Exorcists*, 3.
100. Orsi, *History and Presence*, 29–30.
101. Laycock, "Secret History," 32.
102. Martin, *Hostage to the Devil*, xvii.
103. Martin, *Hostage to the Devil*, xvii.

Variations to the Ritual

While the Catholic Church employs the ritual for its exorcism practices, Taylor describes "the ritual may vary as determined by the exorcist performing the expulsion."[104] This means that the one performing the exorcism might incorporate various Scripture or prayers as a supplement without compromising the application of the rite. The introduction of additional psalms and prayers, for example, is a common variant.[105] In the end, "There is no lexicon of Exorcism," Martin remarks, "There is no guidebook or set of rules, no Baedeker of Evil Spirit to follow."[106] The rite is but a framework of structure more than an exclusive text that must be followed specifically.

Lampert describes a more extensive practice of certain protocols for exorcism, many of which are seen in the 1949 case. These are contemporary practices, an etiquette to be taken to reinforce the hesitancy not to engage in exorcism quickly or without qualification. They include a physical examination by a qualified doctor, a psychological examination by a clinician, a life history report to narrow in one the cause of demonization, an initiative to "normalize the spiritual and sacramental life of the one who is possessed," the recognition of four extraordinary signs of demonization, compliance with the processes of the diocese, with a final presentation of this material to the bishop.[107] For him, the four signs find their roots in the rite itself and they include speaking in languages unfamiliar to the victim, demonstration of unnatural strength, knowledge of unknown material, and an aversion to sacred items.[108]

However, the rite only names three such signs, with no mention of the aversion to sacred objects or holy water. Examples might include knowledge of an item as blessed, of the presence of a saintly relic, of a sacramental carried by the priest, or silent prayers. In Roman Catholicism, first-class relics are physical remnants of a saint, second-class relics are items in contact with a saint, and third-class relics are things touched by a first-class relic. All convey grace and have seen miracles supposedly

---

104. Taylor, *Devil Came to St. Louis*, 17.

105. "Rite of Exorcism" (Weller, ed., *Roman Ritual: Volume 2*, 179, 195).

106. Martin, *Hostage to the Devil*, 17. Karl Baedeker was an early nineteenth century printer of popular guidebooks for tourists.

107. Lampert, *Exorcism*, 103–5.

108. Lampert, *Exorcism*, 105.

Theology of the Rite

associated with them.[109] This aversion is also the demonic repugnance to "the detection of the holy."[110] This theology is essential for understanding the 1949 practices of the priests during the exorcism, and they become crucial for comprehending the spiritual aversion of the demon.

Lampert offers additional diocesan practices which center on the pastoral care of the victim. They include a pastoral meeting with the victim by one other than the exorcist, to cultivate discipleship to a life of faith and a plan for long-term pastoral care. Releasing information about the exorcist to the victim is prohibited, but this local parish priest can profile the case to the exorcism and receive guidance in the pastoral care process. Finally, since the bishop retains authority of the exorcism, any Catholic person should be directed to their own parish for this pastoral experience.[111] Again, each of these becomes activities recorded in the 1949 exorcist's *Diary*.

Participants in Application

It is customary for qualified assistants to be present in the application of the Catholic rite of exorcism. While the number can vary in strategy of predicted need, four is the normal number. One junior colleague is appointed by an authority in the diocese, present to assist in the rite, for accountability of the rite, to replace the exorcist should he be unable to continue, and for his own formative training. Martin describes the commonality of a medical doctor present now to support the physical pressures and dangers present for all. The Alexian Brothers Hospital venue offered that in 1949. In more remote locations, the numbers might be lower, with even exorcists going alone. Yet this is dangerous because of the common violence of the demon, warranting the strength of assistants and even carefully strapping the victim to the bed.[112] Martin further identifies three cardinal rules for the assistants: obey the exorcist upon command, take no initiative on their own, and never speak to the demon or the victim.[113]

---

109. Blai, *Hauntings*, 136, 139.
110. Blai, *Hauntings*, 71.
111. Lampert, *Exorcism*, 105–7.
112. Martin, *Hostage to the Devil*, 15–16.
113. Martin, *Hostage to the Devil*, 16.

The rite makes mention of a gender dynamic between the victim and the assisting team. "While performing the exorcism over a woman, he ought always to have assisting him several women of good repute, who will hold on to the person when she is harassed by the evil spirits."[114] This provides both discretionary accountability by witnesses of the opposite sex, as well as the safer opportunity for physical care should it arise.

The rite makes specific mention of the spiritual rather than medical sphere of exorcism when it says, "The exorcist should guard against giving or recommending any medicine to the patient, but should leave this care to physicians."[115] This recognition that the rite of exorcism is not a medical but a spiritual procedure, to be applied for spiritual healing primarily with the possibility that secondary physical effects follow this spiritual illness. In its protocol, the rite had already declared that medical diagnoses should have already been pursued and ruled out as the cause of the illness. This found fulfilment in the Georgetown phase as Robbie went to a hospital, clinic, and doctors in a way that the St. Louis Jesuits did not need to replicate as they moved ahead with approval for exorcism. However, the Alexian Brothers offered medical support during his extended stay there.

Only the priest and his assistant should wear vestments. A black cassock with a white waist surplice is expected. A purple stole should be worn around the neck.[116] This uniform of the clerical office is a symbol of the ecclesiastical authority delegated by Christ to command the demon. For readers of the *Diary*, this uniform helps to paint the picture of the event, with even clothing displaying theology.

Assistants to the exorcist provide essential support to the reading and delivery of the rite. Amorth recognizes the participation of qualified individuals of experienced faith: "With their presence and their prayers of intercession, they incarnate the living presence of the Church that gathers together and loves her children." Additionally, he says that they offer material support and strength amidst demonic disturbances.[117]

Even the assisting participants would take care to guard themselves spiritually in this process. This was described earlier in the section titled "Readiness of the Exorcist." Part of recognizing the spiritual dimension is to recognize the instrumental role of the exorcist, which required his

---

114. "Exorcism of the Possessed" (Weller, ed., *Roman Ritual: Volume 2*, 173).
115. "Exorcism of the Possessed" (Weller, ed., *Roman Ritual: Volume 2*, 173).
116. Martin, *Hostage to the Devil*, 17.
117. Amorth, *Exorcist*, 109–10.

own spiritual self-examination and preparation. Fasting was essential to this spiritual preparation. During the report of this exorcism, the demon would try to frustrate the priests by insulting and cursing them, or by alluring the exorcists into conversation by displaying intimate knowledge of their sins.[118] Thus, the value is reiterated that the assistants must not narrate the exorcism nor address the spirit but rather focus on prayer in intercession. Their own spiritual condition augments the cause.

An exorcist views this ordeal as an actual spiritual warfare—a battle framed in the larger theater of divine versus Satanic tension already depicted in biblical theology. As such, it is a dangerous and rigorous activity. On rare occasion Bowdern despairs, an act that Allen calls "the most dreadful sin, for it drained the soul of hope."[119] Allen identified how the ultimate prize for the demon would be to destroy the priest. Both Robbie and Bowdern were tormented during the process, and the exorcist had to intercede continually for the demonized, praying, fasting, and believing on God to deliver.[120] Overall, Bowdern seems to have displayed fortitude and endurance in the face of a spiritually and physically grueling exercise.

Place of Application

If possible, the rite should be applied in a church, but a private setting is allowed.[121] The exorcist should be in good mental and physical health, regularly receiving the sacraments, and relying on the authority of God. This commitment is shown outwardly by the employment of a crucifix, any relics, sacred objects, or the Holy Eucharist elements at key times. In all of this, the priest should be commanding, authoritative, confident, humble, and show fervor.[122] Like the sacramentals and the vestry, the venue strengthens the sacred effect of the exorcism.

For this reason, two episodes of the 1949 exorcism occurred as Robbie was taken to the rectory of St. Xavier College Church on the campus of Saint Louis University.[123] This was Bowdern's church, a sacred space where spiritual activities of the sacerdotal might be recognized as

---

118. See, e.g., *Diary*, "March 24."
119. Allen, *Possessed*, 125.
120. Allen, *Possessed*, 128.
121. "Rite of Exorcism" 11 (Weller, ed., *Roman Ritual: Volume 2*, 171).
122. "Exorcism of the Possessed" 16 (Weller, ed., *Roman Ritual: Volume 2*, 173).
123. *Diary*, "March 23–25"; "April 1."

potentially more efficacious. While the first occasion looked like another three days of routine exorcism in Robbie's bedroom, the second occasion was intended to be the application of the rite of baptism. The baptismal rite saw substantial resistance by the demon, not least of when the boy was asked if he renounced Satan and his ways, a normal part of the baptismal liturgy. The boy was able to consent, however, and the baptism was fulfilled.

In the Catholic mind and even among some Protestant conflict theologians, place is important for the physical connection to the demon. Amorth remarks: "In the extraordinary action of Satan, local infestation strikes places of residence and common objects of use." He insists that adaptation of the prayers of exorcism is required, but that an exorcism of place can be in order.[124] When Rev. Luther Schulze sought to change Robbie's venue, it made no alteration in manifestations. Four different venues—the Georgetown house, the St. Louis house, the St. Xavier College Church rectory, and the Alexian Brothers Hospital—suggests that space did not prevent demonic influence. However, in the Catholic mind, a sacred place might dispose the participants to faith and strengthen the spiritual power of the exorcism.

Pastoral Care

As a matter of pastoral care and exorcism strategy, "The person [victim] should be exhorted to reveal all his temptations to the exorcist." This is done in trust to the priest, as in the spirit of the sacrament of confession. Words from Scripture should be employed, especially over any personal words of the exorcist. If necessary, the resistance to this process means that assistants should be present to hold the person down, with a mention of women to restrain a female victim. Likewise, the rite continues, upon the departure of the demon, the person should be encouraged to live a holy life, lest the demon return.[125] Paul Thigpen describes how priestly prayers of exorcism represent a father's prayer for his children. A Catholic priest in care of his flock parallels that paternal love, so the major and some minor exorcism prayers are reserved for him.[126]

---

124. Amorth, *Exorcist*, 110–11.
125. "Exorcism of the Possessed" 21 (Weller, ed., *Roman Ritual: Volume 2*, 175).
126. Paul Thigpen, interview by W. Brian Shelton, July 6, 2022.

Theology of the Rite

Crucial was the pastoral approach that Bowdern made to connect personally with the boy. Allen claims that he explained the rite of exorcism to Robbie before it began. One day the *Diary* described his explanation of the institution of the Eucharist to him.[127] From the time of March 23, Father McMahon is named particularly for coaching Robbie as catechumen.[128] The Alexian Brothers community committed themselves to prayer during Robbie's stay, on April 13 alone praying for hours to complete more than fifty rounds of the rosary prayer. They also venerated the Blessed Sacrament in prayer in the days to follow. LaChance declares how the care of the clergy in the ordeal "paints a powerful picture. Their utter devotion to not only the child but to God goes without question."[129]

Kelly should not make the claim that the Alexian Brothers was not a medical environment when he declares, "At no time during the thirty-five days over which the exorcisms were performed was the boy examined by physicians."[130] As a hospital, it had an attending staff of medical professionals. While there is no available record of medical examinations for the diagnosis of Robbie's illness there, it can be recognized that he received caring medical attention in combination with the spiritual rite of exorcism. McGuire names Edmond F. Sassin as the Alexian Brothers psychiatrist overseeing the case of Robbie.[131] Meanwhile, Nicola remarks how "a great mutual affection developed between the boy and the brothers who kept a constant close watch on him," even asking and receiving instruction on the faith.[132] That they would befriend him without an eye for his physical care is unreasonable. Plus, this discipleship and camaraderie surely encouraged the boy and strengthened his optimism of the potential efficacy of the rite of exorcism. Spitzer remarks how "the priests of the Jesuit community believed that they were morally responsible for helping Robbie."[133] Father Bowdern in real life proved to be more than the "monster hunter" ideal that Wiggins attributes to Father Merritt in *The Exorcist*.[134]

---

127. *Diary*, "April 11."
128. *Diary*, "April 1."
129. LaChance, *Confrontation*, 147.
130. Kelly, *Devil*, 97.
131. McGuire, "Diary of an Exorcism," D1.
132. Nicola, *Diabolical Possession*, 112.
133. Spitzer, *Christ Versus Satan*, 162.
134. Wiggins, *Nightmares with the Bible*, 11.

Spiritual Materials

Several spiritual signs and artifacts play a role in the rite of exorcism. Consequentially, they play a significant role in the 1949 exorcism. Their power lies in their symbolic nature, as they attest to a spiritual reality that lies behind them. Each is considered here for its role in the event and its theological significance.

The Sacerdotal Culture

The Catholic Church functions under an important principle of sacerdotalism—that the church dispenses the grace and power of God. The *Roman Ritual* contains specific prayers for each rite under this premise. The sacraments on the whole contain strict formulas, while the prayers for the rite of exorcism were more lenient per the wisdom and strategy of the exorcist. Although not a formal sacrament, in the Catholic mind the spoken rite of exorcism dispenses power against a demon. The priest gives these commands by the authority of Christ through the authority of the church. These are explored below in the section titled "Christus Victor and Power over the Enemy" in the next chapter.

The rite applied this sacerdotal spirit in its general rules in description of the exorcist:

> He ought to have a crucifix at hand or somewhere in sight. If relics of the saints are available, they are to be applied in a reverent way to the breast or the head of the person possessed (the relics must be properly and securely encased and covered). One will see to it that these sacred objects are not treated improperly or that no injury is done them by the evil spirit. However, one should not hold the holy Eucharist over the head of the person or in any way apply it to his body, owing to the danger of desecration.[135]

Each of these elements related to the 1949 exorcism are analyzed here. To illustrate the sacerdotal nature of the sacraments, however, some examples here will suffice. When the boy's feet moved in a rhythm, and as Bowdern placed the blessed sacrament near one foot, it would stop. This

---

135. "Exorcism of the Possessed" 13 (Weller, ed., *Roman Ritual: Volume 2*, 171).

Theology of the Rite

led the *Diary* writer to declare, "This manifestation of the power of the Blessed Sacrament showed up time after time without fail."[136]

The sacerdotal approach is also marked the *Diary* during the occasions reaching for hope. On one day, their praying fifty rounds of the rosary "is worthy of the highest comment."[137] Ongoing adoration of the sacrament occurred by the Alexian Brothers on two earlier evenings.[138] A new statue of Our Lady of Fatima landed within the hospital as a reminder to petition for Robbie.[139]

The Faith Culture

While Catholicism places heavy weight to the significance of its sacerdotal elements, it is not without a recognition of the place of faith. This element is often overlooked by Protestants who see only the sacerdotal and associate its system with works. The Catholic Amorth claims that even the effectiveness of sacred objects in Catholicism has a place for faith: "It is necessary to specify that these objects have no value if they are not sustained by a concrete faith, based on charity."[140] However, faith receives less attention in Catholic theology compared to its emphatic significance in Protestant theology. Luther's five *sola*s of the Lutheran faith that became a Protestant hallmark includes *sola fide* which means faith alone as the instrumental means of receiving the grace of God. Yet Catholicism recognizes the place of faith several times in the *Catechism*.[141]

One of the important elements that is not fully developed in the narrative of the *Diary* is the role that Robbie's faith plays in helping to actualize the exorcism. Already named are the pastoral care of the priest to the boy, cultivating his understanding of the faith. Robbie's baptism and first Holy Communion came with instruction, including the invitation to renounce the devil. The Alexian Brothers are named for their discipleship efforts. While there are occasions where his faith is cultivated, even with the priestly expectation that his participation in faith will make more effective the spiritual force of the rite, the power of Christ is the ultimate

---

136. *Diary*, "March 18."
137. *Diary*, "April 13."
138. *Diary*, "April 13," concerning the Monday and Tuesday prior.
139. *Diary*, "April 14."
140. Amorth, *Exorcist*, 129.
141. See, e.g., *Catechism* §§186–189, 199, 815, 1190, and 1816.

source of power. Christ alone compels the demon authoritatively rather than the application of the exorcist or the participation of the victim. However, both the priest and the victim participate in belief for this work of Christ.

The Roman Catholic view of exorcism presented throughout this book has indicated a belief in the authority of the church, through the work of Christ deposited in the apostolic succession, into the liturgy of the rite of exorcism. The priest has received holy orders, making him eligible to be the spiritual descendent of the apostle Peter, able to exercise the authority given to Peter (Matt 16:18–19) and the authority of the apostles to cast out demons (Matt 10:1). He displays a form of faith when executing his office. The *Roman Ritual* states this plainly: "The power which Christ exercised over demons He passed on to the Church."[142] As a reminder, in Catholicism this authority is available to every believer, while the implementation of the rite for prayer is not. This would be akin to any believer celebrating the Eucharist with the expectation of the elements becoming the body and blood of Christ; this is reserved for the priesthood for the faithful, not to be celebrated by the faithful alone.

This authority, with its faith support, is nowhere more evident than in the stage of spiritual conflict. The biblical passages often mention the battle against spirit beings and darkness (Gal 6:10–18; Jude 9). The rite declares, "Let the priest pronounce the exorcism in a commanding and authoritative voice, and at the same time with great confidence, humility, and fervor; and when he sees that the spirit is sorely vexed, then he oppresses and threatens all the more."[143] Lampert echoes this as he exhorts his readers: "There must be no fear or hesitation in the voice of the exorcist when he confronts a demon because he is speaking, not on his own authority but, on the authority that comes from Jesus Christ."[144] When the sign of the cross is made at key times, it should be made boldly, saying these words "filled with confidence and faith: 'See the cross of the Lord; begone, you hostile powers.'"[145]

There is barely an explicit mention of the importance of faith in the rite or the *Diary*. The sacerdotal nature of Catholicism is the primary reason. A second reason is because the victim is not regularly in a position to clearly exercise full faith and sometimes cannot express even

---

142. "Exorcism" (Weller, ed., *Roman Ritual: Volume 2*, 164).

143. Weller, ed., *Roman Ritual: Volume 2*, 173.

144. Lampert, *Exorcism*, 56–57.

145. Weller, ed., *Roman Ritual: Volume 2*, 183.

Theology of the Rite

an elemental demonstration of it. Weller says in the introduction to the rite, "To be possessed can mean, at least in a broad sense, that Satan has beclouded the intellect, so that the light of faith cannot illuminate it."[146]

At the same time, the faith of the exorcist is important enough in the preparation and execution phase to show spiritual discipline such as fasting, prayer, and confession. His perseverance through the long ordeal of the exorcism can be recognized as an expression of faith. Lampert claims concerning exorcisms, "Faith is the essential ingredient in their efficacy."[147] By this, he likely means the faith of the priest performing the exorcism. The exercise of faith by the victim will be explored some more below in some of the sacramental application of the event. For now, this understanding of the place of sacerdotalism and faith can serve as foundational background to understanding how a sacrament like the Eucharist is spiritually complex, effective by itself but effective by faith.

The Sign of the Cross

While it is not a material substance, the sign of the cross is an important element. The sign of the cross is often made over the subject and against the demon as an outward expression of the authority of Christ. It is applied to the person in the air or made on the forehead or chest. For example, at the *exorcizo*, the rite reads: "Wherefore, get thee gone in the name of the Father (✠), and of the Son (✠), and of the Holy (✠) Spirit. Make way for the God the Holy Spirit through this sign of the holy (✠) Cross of our Lord Jesus Christ."[148] At each spot in the text where a cross stands, the exorcist should make the sign of the cross. This is an expression of application of the work of Christ that delivers authority to the scene. In the case of mention of members of the Trinity, three signed crosses themselves represent the Trinity. The sign of the cross is a powerful symbol during the exorcism, akin to how "the icons of the Bible are word-pictures, describing the indescribable."[149] Similarly, the rite employs the sign of the cross at the commands for expulsion based on the power of God.[150]

---

146. Weller, ed., *Roman Ritual: Volume 2*, 163.
147. Lampert, *Exorcism*, 55.
148. "Rite of Exorcism" (Weller, ed., *Roman Ritual: Volume 2*, 185).
149. West, *Outward Signs*, 31.
150. West, *Outward Signs*, 109.

Francis de Sales clarifies its usage at the turn of the seventeenth century: "The Sign of the Cross of itself has neither strength, nor power, nor any quality that merits honor... But I also know that God, in marking use of His miraculous power, very often employs signs, ceremonies, figures, and characters without attaching His power to those things." Instead, it is a representation of the passion of Christ by its shape. It represents the Trinity in its three parts. Finally, it represents the remission of sins as the Christian recognizes the purpose of the original cross.[151]

The sacerdotal spirit of this sign is viewed when the diarist once remarked, "The signs of the cross and the crucifix were very effective."[152] This gesture of faith and spiritual authority are one form of sacramental, of which there are several at work in the 1949 exorcism.

Sacramentals, Relics, and Holy Water

Sacramentals are religious signs, whether material or gestured, which "signify effects, particularly of a spiritual nature, which are obtained through the intercession of the church. By them men are disposed to receive the chief effect of the sacraments, and various occasions in life are rendered holy."[153] The Roman Catholic Church has established that certain religious material objects have spiritual authority, and the priests employed them during this event. The *Catechism* makes the claim that relics are sacramentals, alongside the rite of exorcism itself, putting this category to the forefront of our analysis. Relics are material items that were part of the life of a saint, from a bone to a piece of clothing.

Roman Catholicism uses relics as symbols of spiritual power, and the priests strategically placed them in Robbie's rooms during the exorcism. In one case, it was a clothing fragment of St. Margaret Mary, which Allen calls "too old and infinitesimal to be readily identified."[154] Here an early exorcist, Father Bishop, was invoking the spiritual intercession of a woman who supposedly experienced a moment of mystical union with Jesus. On another occasion, Father Bowdern brought a relic in velvet lining in a small glass container—a bone from Francis Xavier's

---

151. de Sales, *Sign of the Cross*, 6–10.
152. *Diary*, "April 18."
153. *Catechism* §1667.
154. Allen, *Possessed*, 59. Jesuits show special devotion to the seventeenth century nun, St. Margaret Mary Alacoque, who started devotions to the Sacred Heart of Jesus.

Theology of the Rite

right arm.[155] Father Bowdern once tried to touch Robbie with a relic during the prayers, resulting in his spitting on the priest's hand.[156] The religious medals placed around Robbie's neck reportedly caused a burning sensation.[157]

Amorth encourages the regular use of sacred objects such as images and statues in the Catholic life and home. For him, they are "a sign of our fidelity and belonging to God" as well as "a protection from the Evil One."[158] Fraune posits that images of Jesus, Mary, and the saints "powerfully convey the reality of the Person or person signified."[159] They should especially be displayed around that saints' feast day to enhance veneration and awareness. The precedent of the apostle Paul is often cited, where God did miracles through him while clothes such as handkerchiefs were the means to healing and exorcism (Acts 19:11–12). This passage makes it more difficult for Protestants to deny the work of God through spiritual materials.

When the two priests first came together to the house on Friday, March 11, Bowdern brought with him the first-class relic of St. Francis Xavier, a piece of bone from his arm. He also brought a pair of relics, that of St. Peter Canisius and that of the North American Martyrs. On this occasion, the diarist reported no shaking of the bed or scratches manifested, suggesting that the relics worked to subdue the demon.[160]

Religious medals are pieces of jewelry, often in medallion form, that represent an association of invocation to a saint, especially a patron saint. They have been blessed, making them more than simply the medal itself. For Catholics, the clergy, and to some degree the laity, can bless items as an appeal for God to sanctify them. Prayers at a meal are a sacramental familiar to most readers. Blessed medals are "an occasion of grace" according to Paul Thigpen, and, as sacramentals, they "dispose" the faithful to the holiness of life according to the *Catechism*.[161] The diarist once

---

155. Francis Xavier was the sixteenth-century founder of the Jesuit order. First class relics are pieces of the body of a saint; second-class relics are object such as pieces of wood or clothing that had touched a saint (*Diary*, "March 11"; Allen, *Possessed*, 67).

156. *Diary*, "March 18."

157. *Diary*, "April 18."

158. Amorth, *Exorcist*, 128–29.

159. Fraune, *Slaying Dragons*, 139. Here, he cautions against superstitious use of statues, such as burying the statue of St. Joseph by one's "For Sale" sign, a prisoner until the house sells.

160. *Diary*, "March 11."

161. Paul Thigpen, interview by W. Brian Shelton, July 6, 2022; *Catechism* §1667.

remarked, "The reaction to the medals and the cross was exceptional."[162] Fraune identifies the scapular as akin to a medal. The monastic version was a cloth garment draping the front and back of the monk; the devotional version can be two small rectangular dangles of wood or cloth worn over the shoulder to drape the front and back of any faithful Catholic. "Our Lady promises many spiritual benefits to those who wear the scapular in the manner she requires," declares Fraune.[163] Relics and medals cause frustration to the demon the 1949 narrative, reinforcing the Catholic view of their effect.

Holy water is frequently used, both as a blessing and as an indicator. As part of a blessing, this water is blessed by a priest who exercises sacerdotal authority over the water. In turn, this blessed water is used in purification against the spirit demonizing the person. In fact, it functions in multiple occasions in Catholic life "as a means to impart blessings upon various objects . . . and as a weapon of general spiritual warfare."[164] As an indicator, it often functions as a test to see if the person will response negatively to regular water in order to reveal that belief or superstition is at work. The 1906 case of Clara Germana Cele supposedly evidenced demonic repulsion of holy water and laughter at tap water, while the 1927 case of Emma Schmidt supposedly saw demonic repulsion of items merely sprinkled with holy water.[165] Holy water appears intermittently in the *Diary*. Once it remarks: "He writhed under the sprinkling of Holy Water. He fought and screamed in a diabolical, high-pitched voice."[166] On two occasions, the bed stopped shaking when holy water was sprinkled.[167] On one occasion, its sprinkling led to the boy emerging from a passive stage of his spell.[168] There were also violent acts of aversion to the holy water, mentioned above. Spitzer makes a theological claim when he remarks, "The liberal use of holy water and the presence of the Blessed Sacrament subdued the power within him."[169]

In Georgetown, Father Hughes sent holy water and candles to the family home as part of his act in response to the possibility of

162. *Diary*, "April 18."
163. Fraune, *Slaying Dragons*, 133–34.
164. Fraune, *Slaying Dragons*, 135.
165. Taylor, *Devil Came to St. Louis*, 22, 27.
166. *Diary*, "March 18."
167. *Diary*, "March 9"; "March 18."
168. *Diary*, "March 16."
169. Spitzer, *Christ Versus Satan*, 164.

Theology of the Rite

demonization.[170] The holy water-blessing prayer exorcises any demon that might be in the water. Candles made of beeswax are specially blessed for Mass. The stole of the priest is considered blessed and can be placed on the person during key moments of the exorcism. Fraune claims, "Blessed candles function in the same way as blessed incense, whose smoke also drives demons out of the air and the dwelling place."[171] Salt is sometimes used, offering a representation of purity and incorruptibility available to the Christian (Matt 5:13). It is associated with the making of wine that relates to the blood of Christ.[172] Fraune describes how the salt is itself first exorcised in ritual fashion.[173]

Crucifixes are crosses with Christ still suspended on them. The diarist also comments that "the signs of the Cross and the Crucifix were very effective," revealing a theological optimism of their efficacy.[174] The crucifix would be placed by the boy's bed and sometimes in his hand. The result was its unexplained movement across the length of the bed, as well as the boy's resistance and throwing of it.[175]

Eucharist

The place of the Eucharist has two distinct roles in the 1949 exorcism. While one role emphasizes the supposed inherent quality of the blessed elements, the other role looks to the place of faith around the sacrament.

Spiritual Force

The first is the use of sacramental materials as a spiritual force. Part of the ongoing drama of the event was the administration of the Lord's Supper. On Easter, the demon declared "I will not let R receive Holy Communion."[176] Keeping in mind the sacerdotal nature of the Catholic Church and its belief in the transubstantiation of the blessed elements into the real body and blood of Christ, the priest tried to administer the

---

170. *Diary*, "Witnesses"; Bishop and Saint Booth, *Exorcist Diary*, 16–17.
171. Fraune, *Slaying Dragons*, 138.
172. West, *Outward Signs*, 169; Taylor, *Devil Came to St. Louis*, 19.
173. Fraune, *Slaying Dragons*, 134–35.
174. *Diary*, "April 18."
175. *Diary*, "March 11"; "April 18."
176. *Diary*, "April 12."

Theology of a Diary

sacrament to the absolute objection of the demon. It took four tries to deliver the host into his mouth, but there was no communion nor exorcism that holy day. Once, Bowdern held a pyx (a consecrated host of bread) near the nervous foot of Robbie, which immediately calmed that leg while the other continued a marching motion.[177] Yet this is also a seeming violation of the rite instruction that it is not applied over the body for risk of its desecration. Regularly, the exorcist interpreted the demoniac's increased violence as suffering and frustration around the Eucharist, more than other sacraments and sacramentals showed an obvious irritation. The demon came to resent the sacrament and could perceive its presence even when hidden by the priest.[178] This resentment only fueled the initiative of the priests even further. Bishop remarks in the *Diary*, "This manifestation of the power of the Blessed Sacrament showed up time after time without fail."[179]

Toward the end of the exorcism period, Father Bowdern gained confidence through the boy's slow physical improvement and fewer episodes of mania. In repeated fashion, he would ask Robbie if he wanted to receive communion. He would ask Robbie if he renounced Satan and all his works, and Bowdern would listen closely between manias to hear if Robbie would utter words of profession.[180] Any confirmation would be enough validation to administer Holy Communion to Robbie, even though his arms, legs, mouth, and swallowing mechanism were controlled by the demon. Priests held the boy down while Bowdern placed a piece of the bread in Robbie's mouth. He spit it out. Bowdern would catch it on a cloth and re-administer it, time and time again until successful.[181] The struggle later led to the alternative use of a spiritual communion, where the physical elements are not used because of impossible conditions, while the desire to receive the sacrament is still present.[182] On the final day, Robbie declared that he wanted to take communion, but the demon retorted, "That isn't enough."[183] Nevertheless, the *Diary*

---

177. *Diary*, "March 18."
178. "Perception of hidden sacred objects was a traditional sign of possession" (Allen, *Possessed*, 181).
179. *Diary*, "March 18"; Allen, *Possessed*, 261.
180. Allen, *Possessed*, 161–62.
181. Allen, *Possessed*, 165–66.
182. *Diary*, "April 11"; "April 18."
183. *Diary*, "April 18."

clearly views a blessed communion host and even a forced Eucharist to be spiritually effective.

Theological analysis here centers on a Reformation-old issue of the authority of the church to dispense the grace of God and the nature of those sacraments. Of theological interest to the 1949 exorcism is the role of the participant in the effectiveness of the sacrament as a means of grace. The Protestant Reformers Luther, Calvin, and Zwingli, and the Anabaptists showed special interest in the nature of the Lord's Supper, as they sought freedom from the Catholic veneration of the sacramental elements and the doctrine of transubstantiation. Their views ranged from Christ's spiritual presence to Christ's guaranteed work, to remembrance only. For them, the faith of the recipient was an integral element of its effectiveness.

While the Catholic catechism recognizes the sign of the bread and wine as well as a memorial component, it reads, "It is by the conversion of the bread and wine into Christ's body and blood that Christ becomes present in the sacrament," and "Under the consecrated species of bread and wine Christ himself, living and glorious, is present in a true, real, and substantial manner: his Body and his Blood, with his soul and his divinity."[184] In the mind of the priests, Robbie partakes of the physical presence of Jesus, making the Eucharist an armament on the front line of battle with the demonic.

Participation in Faith

The second role is the place of the sacrament as a participation in faith. For Robbie to receive the sacraments, he must not be in a state of mortal sin. This issue does not find categorical address in the *Diary*, only the standard expectation of repentance as a part of the sacrament. While no definitive list for mortal sins exists, grievous sins such as occult practice in Catholicism might first require confession or the sacrament of penance to be eligible for communion.[185] The individual context shapes the judgment of culpability of a mortal sin. The *Catechism* offers such a qualification: "Unintentional ignorance can diminish or even remove the imputability of a grave offense."[186] For a thirteen-year-old nominally

---

184. *Catechism* §§1375, 1413.
185. *Catechism* §§1855–1861.
186. *Catechism* §1860.

Lutheran boy, coached by family members to participate in the use of a Ouija board, it might not be deemed a mortal sin because he lacks a factor of knowledge of its detriments as a sin. The exorcist would have likely made this judgment; it simply is not addressed in the *Diary*.

However, Catholicism still recognizes the faith of the recipient in the efficacy of the sacrament. This should be recognized, even as its term *ex opere operato* recognizes that the work of Christ—not the faith or faithfulness of the minister—makes the sacrament effective. The *Catechism* consistently recognizes that the liturgy seeks a participation of faith. Catholic theologian Ludwig Ott notes that, in the Eucharist, "The measure of the grace conferred *ex operato* is in proportion to the subjective disposition of the recipient."[187]

Historically, Roman Catholicism has emphasized the inherent nature of the sacrament more than the faith of the recipient. Yet Wilkinson describes the thought of Monsignor Gemma, an Italian bishop and official exorcist: "The person receiving the blessing must be open to it, must have renounced sin, and recurred to prayer and the sacraments; otherwise, the blessing might as well be an amulet."[188]

The priest called on the boy to request communion verbally, affirming faith as necessary to participate in the Lord's Supper, and for sacerdotal believers, to receive the grace of God. Before this could happen, Bowdern had to persuade the boy to convert to Catholicism so that "what Bowdern perceived as the strongest force could be brought to bear on the weakening demons," mainly the blessed host.[189] Thomas Allen insists this is not a ploy to get another convert, but a strategic battle feature: "If Robbie became a Catholic, in Bowdern's view, priest and victim would be united" against the forces of darkness.[190] In the early church, baptismal candidates, or catechumens, were theoretically exorcised at a special ceremony in which a bishop would breathe on them and hiss a command to Satan to depart.[191]

187. Ott, *Fundamentals*, 399.

188. Wilkinson, *Vatican's Exorcists*, 85.

189. Allen, *Possessed*, 137. Allen also notes, "Woven throughout the instructions and the prayers are assumptions that Satan mostly selects Catholics for his targets" (156).

190. Allen, *Possessed*, 156–57.

191. Ferguson, *Demonology*, 126–27. Ferguson's study shows that early Christian baptism came to include ritual exorcisms "in order to dramatize the driving away of demons and deliverance into the realm of Christ," while they still believed that the dedication (ownership) aspect of the baptism act itself defeats Satan.

Theology of the Rite

This is observed in the theology of the diarist on April 18. During the episodes of resisting Holy Communion, Robbie declared, "I wish to receive you." The diarist adds parenthetically: "This is all the Priest attempted to have him say, since it was sufficient."[192] However, a week earlier, Robbie could not even say the word "communion" to request it.[193] Roman Catholicism maintains that the recipient must be willing to receive the sacrament. If a barrier of resistance is offered, then there is a risk that the recipient "eats and drinks a guilt verdict into his soul" (1 Cor 11:29). Here, the priest must discern if the boy is willing despite the claim of the demon otherwise. This lands on what is called a "prudential judgment" by the priest who judges the will of the recipient as permission to receive communion. Any doubt will likely not see the administration of the sacrament.[194] Knowing the boy well by now, Bowdern is likely making a judgment about the will of the boy despite the inference of the demon.

Either by theological coincidence or in theological humor, the demon once laughed at Robbie's consent, saying, "That isn't enough. He has to say one more word, one like word, I mean one BIG word. He'll never say it. He has to make nine Communions. He'll never say that word." While the mystery of the "word" leads to a different part of the narrative, and while the "mystery of the word" is a powerful pun for the Eucharist that is likely coincidental, the quality of faith is in play in the effectiveness of the sacrament.

An evaluation of the role of the Eucharist in this event must recognize how the New Testament model for spiritual warfare is not as strongly ecclesiastical as the Catholic Church practices. Instead, it calls for a spiritual dedication through purity and faith, while calling on the power of God to be applied to the situation (Matt 17:19–21; Mark 9:29). This is the case made by many Protestant demonologists in the survey above. Furthermore, when the sacerdotal power is symbolized or represented by physical objects, it risks blurring the role of faith and can confuse the recipient of the supposed grace. Edmund Clowney puts it this way: "God does not surrender his work of grace to external symbols, controlled by the manipulation of men."[195] This becomes the basis for psychologists to

---

192. *Diary*, "April 18."

193. *Diary*, "April 11."

194. Paul Thigpen, interview by W. Brian Shelton, July 6, 2022.

195. Clowney, *Church*, 274 (see 272–76 for an explanation against the purely objective power of the sacraments). For an argument against spiritual transfer of power through objects, see Priest, et al., "Missiological Syncretism." More on the role of

see conversion disorder at work in the boy, where anxiety participates in a conversion to physical symptoms and solution. This becomes the basis for the psychological suggestion of religious powers, that the liturgy and sacraments become imagined solutions to imagined demonization by the victim. However, in the end, Catholicism sees spiritual authority and power at work by the administration of the Eucharist as part of the whole spiritual assault against the demon.

Baptism

The symbols and physical aids used in the rite of baptism are highlighted by Thomas Allen to show the spiritual strategy of the exorcist in leading the demonized Robbie to conversion.[196] Several features qualify to have possibly been a part of this event. Salt might be placed on the mouth to evoke wisdom. Holy oil might be dabbed on scratches with a blessing to impart wisdom and fortitude. Holy water could be poured on Robbie's head three times in the form of a cross to symbolize baptism in the Trinity. The forehead is understood as a site of knowledge, and the sign of the cross would be made there as "the old talisman against demons, the sign of the cross."[197] Along with the baptismal rite, Father McMahon is named particularly for coaching Robbie as catechumen since March 23.[198]

The *Diary* relates the priests' attempt to baptize Robbie on April 1. The background information recognizes a Lutheran baptism of the boy at six months, making this a conditional baptism.[199] Either the St. Louis Jesuits were unaware of a Catholic baptism in Washington, DC, by Father Hughes or they felt that baptism was somehow suspiciously incomplete. Perhaps the Georgetown baptism attempt is apocryphal, explaining why they would not have known of any such baptism there. Certainly, their own attempts to catechize and baptize Robbie seems to run counter to a prior Catholic baptism unless it were conditional. Late episodes of violence made the priests speculate later that the demon was reacting to

spiritual material objects is treated below.

196. Allen, *Possessed*, 159.
197. Allen, *Possessed*, 159.
198. *Diary*, "April 1."
199. Nicola, *Diabolical Possession*, 115. A conditional baptism follows the same rite of baptism, but such a case would recognize a possible former baptism. The Lutheran baptism would be recognized as fulfilling the form and matter of the sacrament, but the demonization of the boy warranted a fuller embrace of the Catholic faith.

Theology of the Rite

their attempt at baptism as part of Robbie's conversion to Catholicism. Allen concludes, "This would mean, theologically and theoretically, that the demon had believed he was ensconced in the body of an unbaptized person," and he dares to comment that this implies that Robbie's Lutheran baptism had no effect.[200] Nonetheless, the Catholic priests involved felt the victim's participation in baptism would strengthen the battle against the demon.

The baptism was, unsurprisingly, marked by demonic resistance. Even from the drive to the rectory, the demon declared, "So you are going to baptize me! Ha! Ha!" before Robbie grabbed the steering wheel before he was subdued. Full effort by adults in the car was required. The struggle continued from the car to the rectory. While Robbie would be engaged enough to answer the qualifying questions, "When Father Bowdern came to the Baptism proper the physical resistance exceeded any violence of the evening." The diarist even has to declare that the baptism was completed amid the drama.[201]

Conclusion

The Catholic rite of exorcism represents a comprehensive entreaty to God and a direct exercise of authority to the demon. Its contents include biblical and theological material. Embedded here is Catholic theology, including a prayer to the archangel and demands for the demand to reveal his name and time of departure. Ecclesiology lies behind the rite, and its authority is only to be administered by ordained priests with the authority of a bishop. Accusations that the rite is viewed as a magical formula are easily contradicted, as its prayerful frame and recognition of Christ as mediator are fronted and consistent. The three-part command to the demon requiring his expulsion is surrounded by appeals to God and founded on the authority of Christ. Catholicism seems to steer free of the mistake of the sons of Sceva, who merely uttered the seemingly appropriate words like an incantation that practice backfired against them (Acts 19:13–16).

Christ provides this proper model for engaging the enemy on a spiritual level at his temptation in the wilderness (Matt 4:1–11; Luke

---

200. Allen, *Possessed*, 163. He does qualify the possibility with the difficulty of dealing with the "intentions of demons" because of the theological and logical risk of believing the Prince of Lies.

201. *Diary*, "April 1."

4:1–13). The Gospels report that Christ confronted Satan using the Word of God at each point of temptation. Christ quotes the commands given by God—the same voice of authority that twice prior had condemned Satan (Gen 3:14–15; Rev 12:7–12). In fact, the brevity of the dialogue that comes to us in the Gospels between Christ and the powers of the enemy is noteworthy. Christ quickly and sharply employs God's authority without discussion or distraction.[202]

Some Protestants will find that the use of sacraments and sacramentals in complement to the rite borders on the animistic, and that using material objects to project spiritual power is biblically unapproved. Such practices are viewed as having more affinities with the occult and pagan worldviews than they do a biblical one.[203] The New Testament does not standardize the use of such physical tools in the context of his covenant people. Rather than investing in the items, God instead only uses them to point to his power, as Robert Priest and his colleagues have suggested.[204] The spiritual forces associated with physical objects deserves reconsideration, as Paul denies that idol-offered meat has demon influence (1 Cor 8:1–8) while he seems to maintain that the idol worship did (1 Cor 10:20). However, generous Protestants might view the use of symbols, including physical symbols, as means to a more deeply expressed theology.

While Catholicism recognizes faith as central to this process—from the faith of the exorcist to the discipleship of faith of the victim—it seems to be eclipsed by the ritualistic, sacerdotal dimension. The laity have no right to read the rite for exorcism and the church as the body of Christ is limited to the clergy for this prayer. The ecclesiology is too narrow and privileged for a Protestant, who sees the priesthood of all believers as eligible to cast out demons (1 Pet. 2:5). A Catholic would be hard-pressed to insist that the seventy-two sent out to see even the demons subjected to Jesus' name were ordained (Luke 10:1–20). While the priests can be viewed as legitimate members of the body of Christ, the Catholic extra-biblical elements such as sacramentals are hard-pressed to match the spoken rebuke of demons modeled in the New Testament. The one using

---

202. "For Jesus, to have found a passage in the Bible that bears on the current problem is to end all discussion" (Morris, *Gospel According to Matthew*, 74). For a critical treatment of the ancient Near Eastern and Greek senses of a hierarchy among spiritual beings with the deity at the top, see Sorensen, *Possession and Exorcism*, 144–48.

203. This is the same charge that Powlison makes again contemporary exorcism ministries that cast out demons of particular sins. Powlison, *Power Encounters*, 59.

204. Priest, et al., "Missiological Syncretism."

the Scripture ought to be subject to the message of Scripture for faith to have full effect. Perhaps the supplements distracted the spiritual efforts of exorcism; perhaps they enhanced them. Regardless, Monday, April 18, 1949, would finally see the exorcism be realized.

6

Theology of the Exorcism

"Then there were the most violent contortions of the entire period of exorcism, that is since March 16. Perhaps this was the fight to the finish. Father O'Flaherty and the Brothers were weary and sore physically from the exertion. After seven or eight minutes of violence, Robbie, in a tone of complete relief said, 'He's gone!'"

—DIARY, MONDAY, APRIL 18

WHEN FATHER WILLIAM BOWDERN first landed at Robbie's temporary home on Friday, March 11, 1949, he turned to his driver and invited him to join him in the house. Walter Halloran was only Jesuit student, explaining why he is listed as "Mr." in the *Diary*. He was assigned the duty of driving the campus pastor around St. Louis. Bowdern, standing on the sidewalk at the edge of the lawn, calmly told Halloran, "I'll be doing an exorcism."[1] It was a historical moment that would change both lives of the men. Cinema has enhanced the scene with a now iconic imprint in the American mind. The image on the cover of the 1973 film *The Exorcist* shows the exorcist standing on a sidewalk under a streetlamp facing the house. It was a showdown moment, with the protagonist arriving in town to face a former adversary from the desert sands of Iraq. He is about to enter the house to confront the devil.[2]

1. Allen, *Possessed*, 92.
2. A different but equally confrontational effect of the character's past exorcism battle is presented in the original book. The demon both wails and laughs at the priest, mockingly predicting a different outcome this time (see Blatty, *Exorcist*, 330–34).

Theology of the Exorcism

Thirty-four grueling days later, the denouement of the exorcism attempts finally arrived. The nightly struggles, writhing, prayers, blasphemies, spittle, urine, rejection, intercession, hope, and despair would suddenly end. The boy would be delivered. The priests now witnessed victory. This time was a full and genuine victory.

The delivery of a statue of Michael the archangel by an Alexian Brothers rector to Robbie's room on April 16 at first seems like the transport of another Catholic religious token into the vicinity of the demonized boy. Yet this symbol would prove instrumental. Two nights later, at 10:45 pm, days after Annunciation Day and Easter Sunday, after weeks of prayer, fasting, and reading the rite, and after emotional and physical trauma amidst shock and horror, the demon was forced to realize its hold on Robbie. Bowdern was praying the rite of exorcism, when the victim spoke with a new, clear, masterful, rich, deep voice. Declaring himself Michael the archangel, he intervened by rebuking Satan and commanding him to exit in the name of the Lord, using the name *dominus*. Bowdern then realized that Latin *dominus* ("Lord") was the necessary word yielded by the demon in mandatory confession by the rite. The violent contortions and screaming ensued before Robbie uttered the words, "He's gone."[3] Moments of deliverance from demonization are often marked by an exit sign, such as vomiting or urination. This was no exception, as the clergy testified to the delivery of a sound like the discharge of a thunderclap, reverberating through the hospital.

This chapter revisits more of the details of the account from the journal and other testimony of the witnesses. For this chapter, attention comes primarily to the activities related to Robbie's demonization leading up and culminating on the exorcism of April 18. The application of the rite and its prayers continue to be the force against the demon that leads to exorcism in this case.

Exorcism as Phases of Experience

The structure of encounter stories in conflict theology from the New Testament, from Christian history, and from ethnographic studies across other cultures and religions bear similar elements of demonization and exorcism seen in the 1949 event. From the New Testament exorcism stories, Rudolph Bultmann recognizes a typical form of exorcism encounters

---

3. *Diary*, "April 18."

which contain these parts: "meeting with the demons, description of the dangerous characteristics of affliction, the demons recognize the exorcist and put up a struggle, the exorcism, the demons demonstrably depart, and an impression is made upon the spectators."[4] Meanwhile, from the ethnographic data of exorcism stories, Witmer recognizes a similar typical form of encounters in anthropological data: its conditions, demonic detection of the exorcist, exorcist recognition of the demon, the exorcist command for the demon's identity, the command by incantation, the command for expulsion, evidence of demonic departure, and the response of the audience.[5] Joy Vaughan has collated similarities among demonization and exorcism experiences across specific numerous global cultures that parallels the event under examination here.[6] The 1949 exorcism shares similarities with the biblical episodes and the global testimony of a collective cross-cultural witness.

Catholic priest and professor Malachi Martin describes the stages that the exorcist should expect to witness during the development of the exorcism.[7] The proposed stages are insightful and clear to serve as an outline of the exorcism phase commonly represented in conflict theology testimonies. This paradigm will serve us for examination of the phases of the 1949 exorcism. This context of resistance, weariness, and perseverance during the length and experience of the exorcism is valuable to consider.

The precision offered in the summary of these phases should not suggest such a methodological approach that the phases are clean or distinguishable. However, in a general fashion, they can serve as a guide to the experience of exorcism. They clearly help to explain the application encounter of the theological proposition of demonology, exorcism, and conflict theology seen in the 1949 exorcism. They are also a medium for the introduction of Catholic theology of demonization and exorcism, as Martin is trained and practiced in this culture. They come in phased order.

---

4. Bultmann, *History*, 210.
5. Witmer, *Jesus*, 26.
6. Vaughan, *Phenomenal Phenomena*, 205–23.
7. Martin, *Hostage to the Devil*, 17–24; Taylor, *Devil Came to St. Louis*, 18–19.

Presence

An ominous presence of evil marks the room of demonization, particularly when the liturgy of the rite or any form of exorcism begins. "A peculiar feeling seems to hang in the very air. From that moment in any genuine exorcism and onward through its duration, everyone in the room is aware of some alien *Presence*." The reality that the presence is not in any specific location only magnifies the sense of terror.[8]

Among the unique features of the 1949 event, perhaps the most distinguishing is the manifestation of markings on the boy. In the Georgetown phase, the word "Louis" appeared on the boy's body. During the St. Louis exorcism phase, the word "hell" appeared, along with twenty-four other markings on the night of March 16. In a 1998 interview, Halloran remarks, "That happened a number of times. And it wasn't a case of taking a pin and scratching himself. It just appeared, and with quite a bit of pain."[9] Halloran describes how the scratchings were not the only evidenced preternatural phenomenon of presence. A resistance to religious initiatives is described: "On Holy Thursday that year, this phenomenon started occurring as I was reading the prayers. 'Don't talk about it anymore, this hurts too much,' the kid said. The markings were most visible, and there were many obscenities."[10] The *Diary* shows a consistent pattern of such conflicts of presence, as spiritual rescue confronts spiritual invasion.

In counter and competing fashion, it is noteworthy is that the power of presence and authority of the Christian is recognized by the demon. In a disclosure that might affirm the 1949 exorcist's faith, demons would sometimes "bellow and roar" in torment at the presence of a godly person, in a state of grace, upon entering the room.[11] Amorth posits how a demonized person may sense the state more acutely and the demon may manifest itself in the first presence of an intending exorcist.[12] When interpreted rightly—even in the midst of demonic distractions and power

---

8. Martin, *Hostage to the Devil*, 17–18.

9. Silvers, "Jesuit Helped."

10. Silvers, "Jesuit Helped."

11. Allen, *Possessed*, 207. Here he reports that when a physician walked in the room, the demon did not react. Bowdern, either serious or joking, told the doctor that it meant he was not in a state of grace. The flustered physician exited, went to confession, and returned to the demon greeting him with a roar of resistance. This is supported by Nicola, *Diabolical Possession*, 113, who claims it to be motivated by humor.

12. Amorth, *Exorcist*, 102.

displays—this resistance to godliness by the demon is simply a symbol of the power of Christ over the enemy. While the scene is not historical, *The Exorcist* film captures the presence of the one representing Christ in the sphere of the enemy to start the exorcism. The exorcist lands at the house, standing under a streetlight as the camera switches to the demonized child breathing heavily, about to face an historical adversary from a prior successful exorcism.

Pretense

The demon will attempt to *hide behind* the one demonized, conflating the victim and his or her demonic presence. The effort by the priest to inquire designated questions is in fact an effort to break this pretense by identifying and hearing from the demon independent of the victim. Silence, deflecting, and distractions might follow. Sometimes this takes days, Martin reports.[13] The rite itself remarks about the encounter of the priest: "He will be on his guard against the arts and subterfuges which the evil spirits are wont to use in deceiving the exorcist. For oftentimes they give deceptive answers and make it difficult to understand them."[14] Allen describes how this particular demon would display a majestic air about itself as if to counter the claim of its subjugating weakness, matching Martin's nomenclature perfectly.[15]

This phase of pretense is particularly marked by an effort to delay the exorcism from advancing. It is only natural to anticipate that a demon would resist the force of exorcism against it. "The exorcism cannot be expected to be achieved as the result of one rite outlined in the *Roman Ritual*, or without delays, frustrations, and problems," Taylor remarks.[16] Dialog, distraction, and impertinence are to be expected from the demon and through the demonized person. One possible delay is that of a feigned exit by the demon. This is confirmed by the rite, which warns the exorcist: "Once in a while, after they [demons] are already recognized, they conceal themselves and leave the body practically free from every molestation, so that the victim believes himself completely delivered. Yet

---

13. Martin, *Hostage to the Devil*, 18.
14. "Exorcism of the Possessed" (Weller, ed., *Roman Ritual: Volume 2*, 169).
15. Allen, *Possessed*, 164.
16. Taylor, *Devil Came to St. Louis*, 20.

Theology of the Exorcism

the exorcist may not desist until he sees the signs of deliverance."[17] In the 1949 case, the word "go" near the groin might have been a redirection of exit by employing a medieval expectation of demon exiting through urination. It did influence the priests' thought about departure, "An indication which might have meant that the devil would leave by way of urination or excrement," Bishop writes.[18] As has been analyzed, this message was not one of cooperation but of distraction. A clearer example is when the liturgy and prayers ensued as Robbie flailed and resisted before the demon seemed to exit: "Then in a happy, victorious mood he said sweetly, 'He's going, going' and finally, 'There he goes.'" Robbie relaxed, talked, and seemed to be himself again. The priests left at 1:30 am, but Father Bowdern was called at 3:15 am after Robbie declared about the demon, "He's coming back!"[19]

While it would be anachronistic and even irrelevant to evaluate the event from the film on the event, one moment of *The Exorcist* captures and illustrates this pretense. In particular, it shows the tempting distraction around the demon-victim personality conflation for the exorcist. Just before the first administration of the rite, the senior exorcist character, Father Merrin, shows a focus entirely independent of the demon, while the psychiatrist and assisting priest, Father Karras, seeks to integrate the victim's personalities in confrontation of the demon.

> Father Merrin: We may ask what is relevant, but anything beyond that is dangerous. Extremely. Especially, do not listen to anything he says. The demon is a liar. He will lie to confuse us; but he will also mix lies with the truth to attack us. The attack is psychological, Damien. And powerful. Do not listen. Remember that. Do not listen.
>
> Father Karras: I think it would be helpful if I gave you some background on the different personalities Regan has manifested. So far, there seems to be three.
>
> Father Merrin: There is only one.[20]

As the pretense begins to deescalate, Martin says, the behavior of the victim shows an escalation of violence and repulsion. "There is

---

17. "Exorcism of the Possessed" (Weller, ed., *Roman Ritual: Volume 2*, 169).
18. *Diary*, "March 16."
19. *Diary*, "March 18."
20. See Blatty, "First Draft of Screenplay" in Travers and Reiff, *Story*, 227; Blatty, *Exorcist*, 332.

a stream of filth and unrestrained abuse, accompanied by physical violence, writhing, gnashing of teeth, jumping around, sometimes physical attacks on the exorcist."[21]

Breakpoint

The breaking of the pretensions of the demon that hide behind the victim ends as the demon operates independently of the demonized in a display of power and its genuine character. The resistance and assault become more direct, as the agent of Satan confronts the agent of God. Here, the demon speaks of the victim in the third person for the first time. This separation is evidenced by new language in the first person, "I" and "we," with the object and possessive pronouns in tow: my, our, mine, ours.

Martin describes this phase as the most terrifying for the exorcist. Sight, smell, hearing, and tasting become mixed up:

> Each sense seems to be recording what another sense should be recording. Each nerve and sinew of onlookers and participants become rigid as they strive for control. Panic—the fear of being dissolved into insanity—runs in quick jabs through everyone there. All present experience this increasingly violent and confusing assault. But the exorcist is the one who rides the storm. He is the direct target of it all.[22]

The sudden hearing of the "voice" enters here. "An inordinately disturbing and human distressing babel," Martin describes.[23] The alien sound causes a gripping by fear, as syllables slowly frustrate the exorcist's ability to process them by running together. The exorcist must silence this voice, requiring a measure of self-control to escape and rebuke it.

In the 1949 exorcism event, the breakpoint type signs begin early but they seem to diminish for days to follow. March 18 reports a "diabolical, high-pitched voice." March 19 shows the demon speaking curses in frustration, the voice "turned hard," and bestial behavior like barking and snapping teeth. If one were to match up the *Diary* with Martin's phases a cork-screw effect might be evidenced, as the demon advances forward past Robbie in aggressive behavior but disappearing into the boy's behavior.

---

21. Martin, *Hostage to the Devil*, 19.
22. Martin, *Hostage to the Devil*, 19–20.
23. Martin, *Hostage to the Devil*, 20.

Clash

The waning of the voice leads to the most authoritative and direct confrontation between exorcist and demon: the clash. The heat of the spiritual battle is marked by strong resistance to the rite. A powerful pressure weighs on the exorcist, who Martin describes as now having the upper hand. This is a crucial moment of vulnerability for them both, where the demon might attack and overtake the exorcist, or it might be forced out of the victim. The spiritual force used against the demon to this point has led to this moment. Martin posits that if little information has been gained from the demon, this is the time to seek it: "To force as complete an identification as possible is perhaps a mark of domination of one will over another."[24] This phase can also mark an awareness by the victim that something possessed him or her and can participate with a measure of cooperation against the demon, a desire to be free of it. Yet, amidst this optimism of the completion of the exorcism, the priest's "pain is physical, emotional, mental. He has to deal with what is eerie but not enthralling; with something askew, but intelligently so; with a quality that is upside down and insight out, but significantly so. The mordant traits of nightmare are there in full regalia."[25] Every possible behavior, resistance, or distraction should be expected in this phase. After all, "The devil is fighting the intervention of the priest, resisting the expulsion, and will pull out all the stops to thwart God's work."[26]

At any time, there may be a moment of self-extraction by the demon. Perhaps more vulnerable demons temporarily disappear into withdrawal, deceiving the victim and the exorcist into a belief of departure. The Rite has already declared how demons "conceal themselves and leave the body practically free . . . so that the victim believes himself completely delivered."[27]

In the 1949 exorcism event, the clash was evident. In his resistance, the demonized boy resisted the strength of the assistants, a display of preternatural strength. The most demonstrative expression would be when the boy broke Halloran's nose and bloodied Van Roo's nose. In a 1998 interview, Halloran remarks, "The little boy would go into a seizure and get quite violent. So, Father Bowdern asked me to hold him down. Yes,

---

24. Martin, *Hostage to the Devil*, 21.
25. Martin, *Hostage to the Devil*, 23.
26. Wilkinson, *Vatican's Exorcists*, 26.
27. "Exorcism of the Possessed" 7 (Weller, ed., *Roman Ritual: Volume 2*, 169).

he did break my nose."[28] If the story of his breaking off a bedspring and slashing Hughes's arm is in fact true, this would be a resistance typical of the clash. The March 18 pseudo-exorcism could represent the clash, but in fact that would be an early progression of Martin's phases. The April 12 attempt to show control over Robbie by scripting his upcoming actions can be seen as a grasping of its hold. There the diarist writes: "One new phase was the display of the devil's power over the senses and external personality of R." Certainly the April 18 entry describes a clash, the longest entry of the *Diary* with kicking, throwing items, threats, spitting, violence, urination, and seizures. The grasp of the demon is slipping.

Expulsion

Although not named by Martin as a phase of the exorcism experience, it is worth noting the testimony of this final phase. The departure of the demon from the victim displays an evidentiary component, in this case a departure with a final bang. Loud noises, foul stenches, and precipitant material might accompany the departure. The 1928 Iowa case was marked by the deposit of dung in the room, "The stomach-churning smell of human waste that filled the room. It was the final indignity left behind by the departing spirit."[29]

Noteworthy is that this is an epic moment, a denouement to end a series of long events of struggle. It follows a significant delay, thwarted by the demon to prevent expulsion. Not available to us is the thinking of Bowdern along the lines of original expectations of the length of the exorcism. From all indicators, he would have been proud and relieved by this denouement.

In the 1949 case, reports beyond the *Diary* describe an explosion like gunshot that reverberated through the hospital as a sign for Father Bowdern.[30] Gallagher stated how the Jesuits compared it to the sound of a "thunderclap."[31] Faherty describes it, "A loud report like a gunshot was heard throughout the hospital. People came running to see what the

---

28. Silvers, "Jesuit Helped."
29. Taylor, *Devil Came to St. Louis*, 31.
30. Dobson, "Luncheon," 25; Cooper and Epperson, *Evil*, 26.
31. Gallagher, *Demonic Foes*, 25. Gallagher's testimony is linked to eyewitness Father Charles O'Hara.

trouble was."[32] Halloran commented in an interview that while he was absent that day, "I understand there was a very loud sound, a boom—sort of like a sonic boom."[33] This sign was important and even rewarding for Bowdern, who witnessed on a prior occasion how the demon seemed to depart when Robbie became calm and showed relief. In retrospect, this pseudo-exorcism intentionally withheld any manifestation in a way that misled the exorcists to desist from prayer and administration of the rite. This loud noise at the time of deliverance functioned as a credible sign of deliverance.

An interesting note is that another sign of expulsion had been pondered by the priests on another occasion. The *Diary* reports how the word "go" had appeared as a scratch mark with an arrow pointing to the Robbie's crotch. The priests thought this might mean that urination would the means and sign of demonic departure.[34] Additionally, when an exorcism seemed to be faked by the demon, Robbie was violent, pulling his clothes and convulsing in gyrations, making "as though he were trying to vomit from his stomach. His gestures moved upwards, close to his body. He seemed to try to lift the devil from his stomach to his throat."[35] These serve as other physical phenomena associated with the expulsion of the demon that also function as hopeful signs for the exorcist, even if the events proved not to be anywhere near the exorcism itself.

Post-Exorcism

Also absent from Malachi's account is the subsequent phase of spiritual activity. It is mentioned here for perspective that the goal is not merely freedom from a demon, but in fact a wholistic care for the victim. Central to this is the place of pastoral care. The rite states that upon the departure of the demon, the person should be encouraged to live a holy life, lest

---

32. Faherty, *To Rest in Charity*, 82. The source is an author of the history of the hospital and cited by Saint Booth as an eyewitness, possibly to the moment. The claim that workers also heard the sound and responded would be hard to claim if not credible.

33. Brown, "Interview." The details at this point of this interview seem scattered. Although Halloran also reports that at least six priests at St. Xavier College Church heard a boom and saw a bright light there where the exorcism had been attempted, he seems to suggest the final exorcism took place there. LaChance is right to point out that this discrepancy around Halloran's testimony has gone without commentary, but it comes second-hand regardless (*Confrontation*, 234).

34. *Diary*, "March 16."

35. *Diary*, "March 18."

the demon return.[36] This dimension of the 1949 exorcism finds minimal attention after the report of the exorcism. We only know that the parents matriculated in their Catholic devotion and one can suspect that Robbie participated. Reports of his life since then, being ever so brief anyway, do not reveal his religious long-term commitment.

On Tuesday, April 19, the *Diary* describes how Robbie was well. He was able to take communion without resistance, and he showed no manifestations of demonization. Another entry of the *Diary* is August 19, 1951, where the boy was reported as well and the family had now converted to Catholicism. A published copy of the *Diary* online shows that another entry was made, seemingly by an editor named as "K. Alford" in the *Diary*. Robbie's residential address was confirmed by a telephone operator, with an unlisted number reported.[37]

Thwarted Expectations

A tense battle develops between the exorcist and the demon. The victim is caught in the middle. For both protagonists, the desire and hope of freedom for the victim frequently finds exasperation. Expectations of a speedy or an impending deliverance are checked by the realization that the path to victory goes through suffering, as well as demonic delay and distraction.

Suffering

Suffering marked the 1949 exorcism event. The most obvious anguish comes to the demonized boy, torn emotionally, mentally, and spiritually from within. The mind is pulled back and forth in the cluster effect, as the victim tries to make sense of his or her suffering. The physical pain from wrestling against restraints, the toll of the bodily systems from irregular meals and disturbed sleep patterns, and the external manifestations like the brandings would be excruciating. The *Diary* references the pain he felt with each branding, such as "causing the boy to double up in pain" and "doubled up and uttered a rather terrifying sound."[38] On the night of

---

36. "Exorcism of the Possessed" 21 (Weller, ed., *Roman Ritual: Volume 2*, 175).
37. Small and McGonigle, "Read the St. Louis Diary."
38. *Diary*, "March 16" and "Background" respectively. Similar pain is noted from scratch marks under "March 7," "March 9," and "March 11," easily leading one to believe

Theology of the Exorcism

March 16 alone, twenty-five marks appeared on his body, and on April 7 at least twenty marks are noted in the *Diary*. Pain in his arms came from wrestling with restraints.[39] Pain came to his kidneys and groin from urination, including at the reading of the *praecipio*.[40] One researcher claims that he often could not keep down food, requiring intravenous feeding at least once.[41]

Naturally, Robbie's family also suffered. Spitzer claims that Bowdern moved the exorcism to the rectory of St. Xavier Catholic Church on campus in order to relieve the suffering health of Robbie's mother.[42] She is noted as being "beside herself" during one evening struggle.[43] Her own encounter with the demonic manifestations were surely terrifying, especially given the suffering that came to her son. The *Diary* remarks that in Georgetown, she feared disobeying what was perceived as orders from the mysterious force writing from within her son's body.[44] Nicola claims that she was on the verge of a nervous breakdown.[45] The boy's father and uncle were noted as "completely exhausted from the battle."[46]

Masters also recognizes the weariness that comes to the protagonists: "The emotions of patient and exorcist can be played upon so much that they can become inextricably tangled, and their minds can then begin to fall apart with rapid acceleration."[47] The expectation that the rite of exorcism and the power of Christ that compels the demon to depart can be discouraged by the resistance of the demon. The deflecting of the *dicas mihi* and the distracting deceit of the demon marked the 1949 exorcism. The threat that the demon might name incriminating information about someone in the room contributed to the emotional suffering. For example, an unnamed priest is told by the demon that he was seen in hell in 1956 after he was called "a big fat ass and an ox."[48] Fear was surely fostered when the demon declares, "You will die tonight" repeatedly and

---

each was painful when it is reported in the *Diary*.
39. *Diary*, "March 18."
40. *Diary*, "March 19"; "April 11."
41. Nicola, *Diabolical Possession*, 112.
42. Spitzer, *Christ Versus Satan*, 165.
43. *Diary*, "March 18."
44. *Diary*, "Background."
45. Nicola, *Diabolical Possession*, 115.
46. *Diary*, "April 1."
47. Masters, *Devil's Dominion*, 174.
48. *Diary*, "March 24."

"Dead bishop."[49] Responsible for the whole ordeal, the exorcist slowly began to accept that this exorcism would be painful to both the demoniac and the exorcist. In fact, Allen claims, "Bowdern knew that ultimately he was the prize the demon sought."[50]

It seems that discouragement set in for the exorcist of 1949. Allen notes how Bowdern became disheartened, with hope declining and self-rebuke emerging for buying into the misleading messages of the demon. After a dashed hope from the false and misleading expulsion on March 18, Allen imagines the effect for him: "Bowdern felt despair, the most dreadful sin, for it drained the soul of hope."[51] Resolve would ensue by March 24: "Bowdern would not despair again, and Bishop, though troubled, had never despaired."[52] Physically, he is reported to have lost fifty pounds from both the fasting and the stress.[53] His brother was quoted as saying, "He looked terrible," while described by his interviewer: "He looked thin and wasted, and developed styes and boils."[54]

Amidst this suffering is the threat of a demonized boy, held down only by several strong men and ready to deliver harm to the exorcist. The *Diary* entry of April 17 records the death threat by the demon against those assistants who held him down. Nicola is noted as referencing the threat of transference, that the exorcist is at risk for demonization himself. He also mentions records in other exorcisms of heart attacks, nervous breakdowns, and even death.[55] "The exorcist," he remarks, "faces the devil in all his fury."[56] Gwen Dobson notes for the exorcist: "So it is more than an occupational hazard; it can mean life or death."[57]

---

49. *Diary*, "April 3"; "March 31."

50. Allen, *Possessed*, 128.

51. Allen, *Possessed*, 125; *Diary*, "Monday, April 18." A later edition of Allen's work reads: "Bowdern had fallen. His hope for 'X' to be the annual March 25 Annunciation Day now was lost in the chaos of this room. He upbraided himself for allowing his own hopes and beliefs to undermine the regimen of the exorcism. And he rebuked himself for allowing this sheet and the pieces of paper to become a screen for the devil's work" (*Possessed*, 139).

52. Allen, *Possessed*, 141–42.

53. Nicola, *Diabolical Possession*, 115. LaChance reports that Bowdern's relative LaBarge had him for dinner during the exorcism period, when his appearance and weight loss were noticeably suffering (*Confrontation*, 176–77).

54. McGuire, "St. Louis Exorcism."

55. Dobson, "Luncheon."

56. Nicola, *Diabolical Possession*, 112.

57. Dobson, "Luncheon."

Delay

Any Christian hearer or readers of the events might show concern over the failure of the prayers to overcome their spiritual enemy. There is an echo of Jesus' disciples here: "Lord, why could we not cast it out?" (Matt 17:19; Mark 9:28). Jesus does maintain that genuine prayer bears on effectiveness in Mark 9:29 when the disciples could not understand their inability to cast out the demon: "some types only go out by prayer." Matthew 17:20–21 adds the variant phrase "by prayer and fasting." A delay in the expulsion of the demon is underway.

Bill Brinkley in the 1949 *Washington Post* article and D. R. Linson in a 1951 article claimed that it took twenty to thirty exorcism attempts to ensure success.[58] On the other hand, *The Evening Star* in 1949 cites a priest describing how the whole rite takes about an hour and a half, but the article sounds like this exorcism was quick work: "The boy become completely normal after the ritual, The Star was told."[59] However, *The Evening Star* sequel article recognized a two month process with twenty readings of the rite.[60] The majority of the length of the exorcism process is due to the resistance of the demon. It is calculatable that around thirty readings of the rite of exorcism took place. On the day before the exorcism, the diarist writes, "Everyone, including R, was becoming weary of the long performance."[61]

As often as the priest declared the *dicas mihi* in command of some sign of the name and time of departure, he received almost exclusively the scratched Roman number ten "X".[62] As noted above, this was interpreted by the priests as the Latin numeral ten. The message only frustrated them, because they never had a point of reference from which to calculate "ten." Once, Robbie told family members in a dead, unaccented voice that he would stay ten days, even while his message was couched in chiasm, riddles, and a death threat to the exorcist.[63] As already discussed, the supposed responses to the *dicas mihi* with scratchings are manifold

---

58. Brinkley, "Priest Frees Mt. Rainier Boy," 31, 34.
59. "Priest Freed Boy of Possession by Devil."
60. "New Details."
61. *Diary*, "April 17."
62. *Diary*, "March 16"; "March 31"; "April 2."
63. Allen, *Possessed*, 151. Allen also says that historically, the *Diary* takes on an irregular quality here: "The record is fragmentary. It raises more questions than it gives answers. The diary conjures up a scene of madness" (153).

Theology of a Diary

and varied. The numbers 4, 8, 10, 16, and 18 came as brandings on the boy. Sometimes the demon would not concede any departure information at all.

Bowdern tried to coordinate "ten" days with some theologically significant feast day. The notion that two upcoming days would hold meaning or even power stemmed from the victorious nature of the announcement of the Incarnation to Mary on Annunciation Day or the resurrection of Christ on Easter Day. While Bishop thought that March 24 would be the day of victor as the Feast of St. Gabriel, Bowdern thought the "X" landed on the following night on Annunciation Day.[64] However, neither would be the case.

Likewise, on Easter day, the priests came with great anticipation to administer communion to Robbie because of the significance of the day. Bowdern hoped that the demon would be expelled after four weeks of regular prayer and liturgy. Several attempts were made unsuccessfully, and Robbie could not even say the word "communion" to request it.[65] Constant adoration of the Blessed Sacrament began during Holy Week.[66] During this time, the word "exit" appeared in different places as scratches, but the voice insisted there would be no departure until the boy says one important word, which he would never say.[67] How much Bowdern reflected and analyzed this demonic statement around a key word is not known. Yet, for an exorcist seeking both victory and conclusion, one can easily imagine that he thought and prayed about the important, missing word. Clearly, he believes the theology behind the *dicas mihi* that the authority of the church could effectively demand such information. He likely thought that the command had been effective, but the compulsory message was not yet clear.

Amorth suggests that exorcisms can require a short period or many years. He reminds us that divine permission is an important variable, mysteriously allowing demonization to end or to continue, like the divine controls on Satan mentioned in the book of Job (1:12; 2:6). "A clear understanding eludes us; only many prayers and much faith can help us to accept this mystery."[68] The majority of the length of the 1949 exorcism process is due to the resistance of the demon. One operand of resistance

---

64. *Diary*, "March 24."
65. *Diary*, "April 11."
66. *Diary*, "April 13."
67. *Diary*, "April 11"; "April 18."
68. Amorth, *Exorcist*, 106.

Theology of the Exorcism

is the distraction element. One technique to delay the exorcism by the demon is to offer distractions.

Many Protestants would judge that the prayers were in fact hindered because Christ's power was fettered by theological errors of animism around physical objects or misguided prayers to saints and angels. If Catholicism is marked by these qualities, then the exorcism success was more through the mercy of God than by the systems maintained by the Catholic servant of God.

Distraction

In the application of conflict theology, standard wisdom is that direct commands to the demon are in order rather than the opportunity for distraction. The New Testament book of Jude remarks how Satan vied for the body of Moses. Yet Michael the archangel "dared not utter a slanderous condemnation against him but said, 'The Lord rebuke you'" (Jude 9). A simple, direct, undistracted rebuke came from the servant of God to the devil. However, the deflecting of the *dicas mihi* and the distracting deceit of the demon marked the 1949 exorcism.

The 1949 exorcism was marked by demonic distraction. The responses to the *dicas mihi* have already been shown to perplex the exorcists in their endeavor. Perhaps no moment of distraction was more obvious than when the exorcism seemed successful on its apparent departure in the "pretense" phase. Consistent spitting, cursing, violence, and even preternatural display of power function to cause fear and wonder to prevent the exorcist's focus on the deliverance through the reading of the rite.

Additionally, there is the risk of losing sight of the victim-centeredness of this process. While the exorcism is theologically framed as a spiritual conflict on the larger stage of a cosmic conflict contextualized in biblical theology, it is also help to the demonized victim. For example, Basham says, the identification of the demon by name is also "an exercise in honesty" for the victim, as the association between demon and sin reveals an entrance point in the secret life of the victim. "The person honest enough to pinpoint and admit his torment meets an essential prerequisite for deliverance."[69] As a matter of pastoral care and exorcism strategy, the rite reads, "The person [victim] should be exhorted to reveal

---

69. Basham, *Deliver Us from Evil*, 152.

all his temptations to the exorcist." Particularly during the answer time of the *dicas mihi*, the priest should command silence of the demon when "jesting, laughing, and nonsense" are offered. Likewise, he will instruct other participants not to listen to such talk. During this time, also, the priest will "pay attention as to what words in particular cause the evil spirits to tremble, repeating them the more frequently."[70]

Part of the strategy of Bowdern was the conversion of the boy to Catholicism to strengthen the spiritual resistance against the demonization. The April 1 entry of the *Diary* showed this resolve as well as the demonic resistance to the Catholic baptism. The March 31 entry suggests that the boy's conversion will keep the demon away. Craig Keener has documented spiritual resistance to the conversion act, as well as how this rival display of power promotes conversion and church growth in some cultures.[71] Since Bowdern thought that their own regional diocesan authorities should oversee this commitment, it led to his decision to return to Washington, DC, with Robbie. The refusal by Catholic hospitals to enroll one not diagnosed as mentally ill led to their return to St. Louis, where the catechesis process continued. This attempt to combine the boy's faith with that of the exorcist was a foremost strategy of Bowdern. At its core, conversion directs the victim's faith to the power of Christ, drawing from the *Christus Victor* imagery of Christianity.

Christus Victor and Power over the Enemy

At the final and powerful section of the rite of exorcism, the exorcist "fortifies himself and the one possessed with the sign of the cross," touching his stole to its back, and "with his right hand laid on the person's head, he says what follows with constancy and firm faith: Behold the Cross of the Lord; begone ye hostile powers!"[72] While the priest comes boldly holding forth the cross, claiming its authoritative accomplishment and application, the demon has been prone to avoid the topic. Despite the many foul and insightful sentences that a demon might offer during exorcism, Martin describes the dynamics of one thing never spoken: the name of Jesus. "The Other," "The One," "The Unmentionable," and similar references might be used, but not the name itself. This is an asset to the exorcist,

---

70. "Exorcism" 21 (Weller, ed., *Roman Ritual: Volume 2*, 173).
71. Keener, "Crooked Spirits," 358–59.
72. "Rite of Exorcism" 4 (Weller, ed., *Roman Ritual: Volume 2*, 183).

knowing that the authority of Christ named is an interpersonal weapon against this enemy.[73] "The majesty of Christ commands ✠ thee!" reads the *adjuro*.[74]

Christian thought has captured this victorious dimension of Christ's atoning work and portrayed it as *Christus Victor*. This theology is a comprehensive view of atonement that extends from Jesus' incarnation to the cross, then through his descent to the grave followed by the resurrection. Here, atonement is framed as a divine conflict with victory over the enemy, Satan, who subjected creation and humanity to suffering and subjugation. This is the basis for the power and authority that the exorcist delivers against the demon on behalf of the victim. This is the foundation for the rite of exorcism. Jon Tal Murphree describes the effect: "Satan's debauched imagination concocted another move [the crucifixion] . . . Satan played a reckless game, attempting to match wits with the eternal God. And he lost everything. Today, human sinners can appropriate the benefits of Christ's sacrifice and be rescued from Satan's bondage."[75] Matthew Emerson states: "His penal, substitutionary crucifixion provides freedom from bondage to Satan (*Christus Victor*) precisely because it solves the problem that lies at the root of humanity's imprisonment to power: enmity with God through our sinful nature and choices."[76]

This theology confronts the consequences of Robbie's own participation and invitation through occultic practices, as well as the rite of exorcism to resolve its consequences. Theologically, Satan was overcome in the 1949 exorcism by the power of the resurrected Lord. The work of the cross through prayer and the rite was aimed at defeating the Satan and the consequential effects of the fall that he helped to foster once and for all.[77] Father Bowdern engaged in spiritual warfare through prayer day in and day out because he recognized the potential triumph through the power of Christ: "The Catholic Church viewed an exorcism as a direct confrontation between Satan and Christ, with the priest summoning up the power of Christ through the prayers."[78] The prelude to the rite

---

73. Martin, *Hostage to the Devil*, 420.

74. "Rite of Exorcism" 4 (Weller, ed., *Roman Ritual: Volume 2*, 189).

75. Murphree, *God's Rescue Operation*, 71–72.

76. Emerson, "He Descended to the Dead," 170.

77. In support of the comprehensive dimension of this theology, Boyd (*God At War*, 238–68) argues that this is an instrumental goal in Christ's work and one often overshadowed in a Western, Anselmian emphasis on atoning accomplishment.

78. Allen, *Possessed*, 95.

established two theological points: that Satan and his legions existed and the coming of Jesus as Redeemer, Son, and Liberator from Satan.[79] Any Christian ought to appreciate the optimism of Justin Martyr who, only one century after Christ, declared specifically: "For the Son was made man also . . . for the destruction of the demons."[80]

One demonstration of this theology is evident when the priest makes the sign of the cross over the recipient, implying the work of Christ as spiritually efficacious in the situation. The *Ritual* contains the symbol ✠ before particular words, instructing the exorcist to make a sign of the cross at that point. Several of the places relate to the authority of God. "The majesty of Christ commands ✠ thee! God the Father commands ✠ thee! The Holy Spirit commands ✠ thee! The mystery of the Cross ✠ commands thee!"[81] In the liturgy and in rebuke, Satan is named as "accursed one" as a reminder of the authority of God over this fallen creature.[82] The forehead is understood as a site of knowledge, and the sign of the cross would be made there. In the 1949 exorcism, the cross as a symbol of this theology is an active part of the narrative. Bowdern employs it as part of the spiritual environment, bringing it to the exorcism or placing it in Robbie's hand.[83] It was also an instrumental signal to be made during the reading of the rite. Bishop would write on the day of victory: "The reaction to the medals and the cross was exceptional" and "the signs of the Cross and the Crucifix were very effective."[84] Likewise, it became a symbol for demonic aversion. They boy lunged to seize the cross for damage, he ran from the final station of the cross towards a cliff, and a cross moved by itself on the bed.[85] At several moments of the administration of the rite when Robbie resisted with violent actions and speech, it was while the sign of the cross would be made by the priest. There was also a mocking of the cross by the demon, once scratched with a cross from within and once sarcastically singing "The Old Rugged Cross."[86]

---

79. Allen, *Possessed*, 100–101.
80. Justin Martyr, 2 *Apol.* 5; Ferguson, *Demonology*, 105–6.
81. "Rite of Exorcism" 4 (Weller, ed., *Roman Ritual: Volume 2*, 189).
82. "Rite of Exorcism" 4 (Weller, ed., *Roman Ritual: Volume 2*, 193). See "Baptism of Adults" (Weller, ed., *Roman Ritual: Volume 1*, 85).
83. *Diary*, "March 11"; "March 19."
84. *Diary*, "April 18."
85. *Diary*, "April 2"; "April 13"; "March 11."
86. *Diary*, "March 11"; "March 19."

Theology of the Exorcism

As noted before, the New Testament describes Christ's authority over the enemy using "kingdom" imagery.[87] Here, kingdom authority belongs to those in the kingdom of God. Matthew 12:22–30 records Jesus declaring authority to "enter the strongman's house and spoil the goods" in a context of a Pharisaic misunderstanding of exorcism. R. T. France describes this kingdom conflict in Matt 12, insisting that it echoes Christ's victory over Satan (Matt 4:1) by direct frontal assault, unlike the Pharisaic accusation of internal trickery (Matt 4:25–26). The kingdom of God and that of Satan (Matt 4:26) are contrasted so that "Satan is powerless before the victorious incursion of God's kingdom in Jesus' ministry of deliverance." [88] Likewise, in Matt 28:18–20, Christ claims all authority in heaven and earth and commissions his disciples with it.[89] Numerous other references recognize the Christian's power over the enemy.[90] Although it was suggested above that relics, sacerdotal works, and prayers to the archangel compromise the spiritual activities of the exorcism, nonetheless the *Christus Victor* principle in this historical exorcism seems sure. Many Catholic critics would say that the exorcism occurred in spite of those Catholic ecclesiastical components.

Here also rises the theological question of where the demon goes upon its expulsion. The Gadarene demoniac begged Jesus not to send them to the abyss (Luke 8:31), suggesting that fallen angels can be "held in bondage until the day of judgment" (Jude 6). Interestingly, Jesus describes how a departing demon "goes through arid places seeking rest and does not find it" (Luke 11:24). The arid places are at least paralleled emptiness akin to some form of abyss. Certainly, there is biblical caution to beware its return to the victim after "it goes through arid places seeking rest and does not find it" (Matt 12:43–44). The intertestamental period offers a theory of insight about demons' relationship to the abyss.

---

87. For a discussion of kingdom imagery in a spiritual warfare context, see Boyd, *God at War*, 215–37.

88. France, *Matthew*, 209–10. For additional, sound exegesis of this Matt 12 passage, see Hagner, *Matthew 1–13*, 339–45.

89. France shows that in Matthew's Gospel alone, Christ has already had and displayed authority in his earthly ministry, as in 7:29; 9:6–8; 11:27; 21:23, etc. (*Matthew*, 413).

90. For example, Eph 6:10–18 instructions to "take on the whole armor of God" because of spiritual warfare; John 14:12 ("The works that I do shall he do also and greater") is declared by Jesus; see also 2 Cor 10:4–5 ("The weapons of our warfare are not of the flesh, but divinely powerful for the destruction of fortresses. We are destroying speculations and every lofty thing raised up against the knowledge of God, and we are taking every thought captive to the obedience of Christ").

The Old Testament Apocrypha book of Jubilees provides the story of Satan requesting one tenth of the demons to escape the abyss to serve him in afflicting the people of the earth (Jub 10:1–13).[91] This issue is one of the mysterious withheld in revelation, and it goes to the overall economy of the divine maintenance of fallen angels.

The Faith of the Recipient

Many Protestants might be surprised that the Catholic *Roman Ritual* recognizes the importance of human agency around demonization, not only in its cause but in its solution. Even amidst a liturgical reading marshalling ecclesiastical authority, the protocol of the rite recognizes the faith of the one praying for the demonized, and the faith of the one receiving the blessing enhances it. The *Diary* anticipates that the human agency of the victim aids in the deliverance from demonization. The Protestant will prefer to focus on the place of faith in those believing in Christ's power, whether it be the exorcist or the victim. Of course, all Christians will see the expulsion of a demon to be a demonstration of divine power that exceeds beyond the power and faith of the faithful servant praying for exorcism. It is always the Holy Spirit who liberates, but the mysterious work of God often operates through the faith of his people.

The prayer of contrition here is especially important, given the prior participation in occult activities by the now demonized. In the early part of this case, Robbie clearly and willfully "fellowships with demons" (1 Cor 10:20) in a way that would welcome demonization. He exercises faith that soothsaying connects with the dead. In corresponding fashion, the rejection of this practice as an act of obedience can allow an exercise of faith in Jesus that the consequences of the practice will cease. The faith of the demonized person functions in battle against the demon, joining the prayers of the priest and other Christians. The *Roman Ritual* recognizes this, saying that the subject should pray, fast, and engage the sacraments if he or she is able.[92]

Father Bowdern encouraged Robbie to exercise faith, by examining his conscience and making an act of contrition, or repentance of sins,

---

91. Heiser draws out the connection between their afflicting efforts with physical afflictions of illness. It represents how Second Temple Judaism linked illness with demonic activity, an influence on the culture of the New Testament era (*Demons*, 200–203).

92. "Exorcism" (Weller, ed., *Roman Ritual: Volume 2*, 167).

according to the ritual.[93] Father Bowdern prayed for the recipient, "Keep watch over his reason, rule thou over his emotions, bring cheer into his heart."[94] Such an attempt seems to keep the recipient willfully involved in the process of spiritual warfare, as well as a prayer of protection. Bowdern instructed the boy like a catechumen, and Robbie began to pray and understand the faith. Part of the solution that Bowdern sought was the conversion of the boy to Catholicism to enhance the spiritual resistance against the demonization. For example, Allen depicts the experience with spiritual activity like the acts of faith, hope, love, and contrition, seen in a first confession and first communion book common in the US during the 1930s and 1940s. These contrition prayers would be understood as armor against the enemy.[95]

As the exorcism leaguers ahead, Robbie himself struggles to keep the demon at bay. The instruction on baptism, the Eucharist, and explanation of the Catholic faith starts to take hold in the mind of the boy, functioning as a counter to the demonic hold. By the day of the expulsion, Robbie is noted as trying to learn the "Ave Maria" to sing, to learn the Latin language, and to take spiritual communion. The *Diary* describes, "He felt that he had to pray whenever he was out of his seizure . . . Whenever he became normal he reverted to prayer."[96] The next moment of the narrative sees Michael the archangel appearing in rescue.

The New Testament does not directly help us here by explaining the role of those demonized in the ministry of Jesus. On one hand, this differs from the healing episodes in which victims exercised faith toward the healing process. Scripture does not address the issue of faith by the victim, and we ought to be careful to establish precedents about the demonization of a believer from any historical passage. When faith is a variable in New Testament demonization cases it is on the part of those loved ones interceding for their demonized children: one a father (Mark 9:23–24) and one a mother (Matt 15:28), akin to the faith of the exorcist below.

On the other hand, the sample set of Gospel episodes may be too small, while the purpose of the Gospel writer to focus the reader of

---

93. Allen, *Possessed*, 93; *Diary*, "March 16."

94. *Diary*, "Monday, April 18." While he prayed it each time in the rite, the *Diary* makes specific mention of it on this day. See "Rite of Exorcism" 4 (Weller, ed., *Roman Ritual: Volume 2*, 187).

95. Allen, *Possessed*, 137–38, 317.

96. *Diary*, "April 18."

Theology of a Diary

Christ's authority through immediate exorcism might not allow the faith of the demonized to be a reported variable. More importantly, the quality or genuineness of faith translates to an effectiveness according to Scripture (Matt 17:20–21; Mark 9:29; Luke 8:50; Jas 1:6), so that the recipient participating in the belief and hope that God might work is still better than just faith of the one praying.[97]

The faith of the exorcist is also at work here, as Jesus tells his disciples that their failed exorcism was "because of your little faith." Their faith can move mountains and make things possible (Matt 17:14–21). Likewise, he comments, "This kind cannot be driven out by anything but prayer and fasting" (Matt 17:21). Catholic evidence of the place of faith is seen in the exorcist's own personal preparation of prayer and fasting.[98] Amorth comments: "The exorcist is called to a life of particular sanctity; it is essential to his ministry."[99]

The cultivation of pastoral care by the exorcist, along with the reading of the rite as his role, is intended both to defeat the demon and to strengthen the faith of the victim. Despite the demonic resistance to baptism and its mockery of the catechetical process in the 1949 exorcism, conversion by the boy was an exercise of his faith against the demonization. Progress seems to be displayed, for example, once at the prayer after the *exorcizo*, when Robbie responded by repeating the Latin after several repetitions: "Rule thou over his emotions, bring cheer into his heart." Additionally, Bishop recorded that "Robbie had expressed a real interest in Latin," perhaps showing his desire for the exorcism to work.[100]

A tension thus develops between faith and sacerdotalism that requires a theology of compatibility and cooperation for Catholicism. This means the reading of the rite alone does not have to embody the power

---

97. However, the wrong object of strong faith can be more dangerous than weak faith in God, as seen by the Israelites' "worship" in 1 Cor 10:20 and the Pharisees' "worship" in John 8:44, as well as the ongoing rejection by God of the northern kingdom's syncretistic worship (e.g., Jer 7:30). A special note of thanks is due to Robert Wetmore for helping to clarify synergistic principles and misdirected worship, as well potential idolatry and animism.

98. "Exorcism of the Possessed" 10 (Weller, ed., *Roman Ritual: Volume 2*, 171).

99. Amorth, *Exorcist*, 107.

100. *Diary*, "April 18." See Rite of Exorcism" 4 (Weller, ed., *Roman Ritual: Volume 2*, 187). The three printed versions of the *Diary* vary the Latin text, either represented by the original handwritten journal or when translated to print. The Latin reads *Tu viscera regas. Tu cor confirmes* ("Rite of Exorcism" 4 [Weller, ed., *Roman Ritual: Volume 2*, 186]; Cf. Bishop and Saint Booth, *Exorcist Diary*, 60; Rueda, *Diabolical Possession*, 66; Allen, *Possessed*, 287).

Theology of the Exorcism

for exorcism. Faith has a place, just as it did in the Gospel episodes. With a devotional spirit, Timothy Keller posits the role of faith this way: "When we discern Jesus moving toward us and encircling us with an infinite, self-giving love, we are invited to put our lives on a whole new foundation."[101] It may be no coincidence that the first time the rite of exorcism is delivered in English, that the demonic expulsion took place. The difference was not an inherent power of one language over another, but the mutual understanding between believing priest and hopeful boy found the opportunity for a significant enhancement of the faith of the boy. Spitzer's narrative reads, "As the exorcism proceeded, something very different began to happen."[102] The trance ended, and Michael appeared. The difference on this day was in fact the exercise of faith, belief, and hope by the boy. His faith entered into play with new comprehension. This can suggest—without necessarily being claimed here—that this difference illustrates the potential of faith in participating in Christian exorcism.

THE AGENCY OF THE SAINTS AND ANGELS

Roman Catholicism maintains a theology of saints and angels as part of Christ's living body, sharing a spiritual communion with believers on earth. "Invocation" is the prayer of God's people to the saints and angels, in reverence—it is not worship—for their aid. From the Reformation, Protestants have rejected the practice of praying to saints for intercessory needs, as they understand God alone as the recipient of our prayers through Christ's mediation (Heb 4:14–16). Disagreement on this theology is at work in our analysis, but the consequences of praying to the saints raises an important question of efficacy.

Saints

Catholicism recognizes that Christians are part of "the supernatural unity of the Mystical body of Christ, as in a single mystical person." The *Catechism* states that believers assist one another in the holiness process, seeing saints in heaven as part of this mystical body.[103] This spiritual

---

101. Keller, *Reason for God*, 221.
102. Spitzer, *Christ Versus Satan*, 170.
103. *Catechism* §1474.

reality agreed upon by Protestants alike advances into a new heavenly connection for Catholics. The *Catechism* continues: "A perennial link of charity exists between the faithful who have already reached their heavenly home, those who are expiating their sins in purgatory and those who are still pilgrims on earth. Between them there is, too, an abundant exchange of all good things."[104] The Second Vatican Council remarks, "By reason of the fact that those in heaven are more closely united with Christ, they establish the whole Church more firmly in holiness." Concerning the saints from heaven, "They do not cease to intercede with the Father for us."[105] Amorth insists that in the context of exorcism, invoking the saints for assistance demonstrates trust of the church and invoking the angels marshals the strength of heaven.[106]

The litany prayers of the rite summon the saints to intercede in prayer for the exorcist and the demonized. Such practice is standard across Roman Catholic liturgical doctrine, where the saints deliver the prayers to God with credibility and greater power: "The saints in heaven know the needs of the faithful and delight to aid their brethren for the sake of God's kingdom . . . the praise of [God's] glory is amplified by the joining of the prayers of the blessed in heaven to those from earth."[107] This Catholic practice of venerating and praying to saints—being careful not to ascribe worship to them—is called the "invocation of the saints." The saints intercede through prayer in heaven for the faithful on earth.

In 1949, Father Bowdern employed prayers to Our Lady of Fatima because of her past power displayed over demons.[108] These were positive moments for Robbie in the *Diary* that appear as successful spiritual exercises. The Catholic Michael Thigpen depicts the hope of saintly intercession: "The saints are veterans of spiritual war that continues to rage in the world. Their insights, born of long experience in combat with the Enemy, can make us wise and strong in battle."[109]

---

104. *Catechism* §1475.

105. See "Dogmatic Constitution of the Church" in Abbot, ed., *Documents of Vatican II*, 81.

106. Amorth, *Exorcist*, 125, 128.

107. Steeves, "Invocation of the Saints," 616.

108. *Diary*, "March 18"; "March 19"; "April 2"; "April 13"; "April 14"; "April 18." On the day after, April 19, Robbie prayed ten rosaries of thanksgiving to Our Lady of Fatima.

109. Thigpen, *Manual*, 123.

Theology of the Exorcism

Mary is particularly recognized for veneration in the exorcism process. Multiple occasions saw appealing to Mary as Virgin and Our Lady of Fatima. For example, on Holy Thursday, a statue of Our Lady of Fatima was placed in the foyer of the hospital, dedicated to the Virgin Mary for intercession on behalf of Robbie.[110] On Easter Sunday, the Office of the Virgin Mary was read to Robbie, who responded grabbing the book in resistance.[111] On the day of the exorcism, Father O'Flaherty told the story of Our Lady of Fatima and started teaching Robbie to pray the "Ave Maria" in Latin. He gave attention to the story and showed interest in the Latin.[112] At the same time, this tune and the book became a source of mockery by the demon.[113]

A reader does not see this invocation explained in the journal; a Catholic priest naturally assumes an understanding of this theological dynamic. The *Diary* shows an immense optimism around these prayers and the source of power from the saints, especially Mary with the title Our Lady of Fatima. In 1916–1917, three children at Fátima, Portugal saw a sun-brilliant lady appear who prophesied that prayer would bring an end to World War I. She held a rosary and directed them to pray to the Trinity, revealed a vision of hell, and entrusted them with spiritual secrets. Pilgrims followed, Pope Pius XII provided a decree of coronation to the Lady, and the legend has been sustained as an image of Mary's intercession. One of the secrets was that devotion to Mary herself would aid in the saving of souls and peace in the world.[114]

While the priests hoped in the intercession of Mary, most Protestant will hear echoes of Catholic dogma extending far beyond Scripture. Verses such as 1 Tim 2:5 ("There is one mediator between God and man, the man Christ Jesus") and 1 John 2:1 ("We have an advocate with the Father, Jesus Christ the righteous") emphasize Christ's sole mediation. For example, Greg Allison remarks from the Cana wedding passage in Scripture (John 2:1–11), "Protestants believe *Redemptoris Mater*'s escalation [motherly mediation] of the importance of Mary is wrong. It is the glory of Jesus—not that of Mary—that is revealed . . . Rather, she resigns herself to the fact that she does not exercise a privileged control

---

110. *Diary*, "April 14."
111. *Diary*, "April 17."
112. *Diary*, "April 18."
113. *Diary*, "April 7"; "April 8."
114. Dupré, *Full of Grace*, 240–44.

over her Son."[115] Anglicanism maintains prayers to God *for* saintly and angelic intercession along the lines of the early church writings, but not *to* them in invocation. "The Romish Doctrine concerning . . . Invocation of Saints is a fond thing, vainly invented, and ground upon no warranty of Scripture, but rather repugnant to the Word of God."[116] Lutheranism maintains that saints are remembered and serve as models of faith, but invocation is an error: "It cannot be proved from the Scriptures that we are to invoke saints or seek help from them."[117] The Calvinist tradition views the entire enterprise as idolatry. This will be considered further below, as the theology relates equally to angels.

Angels

Like saints in Catholicism, angels can receive prayers from the faithful. They join the host of the living in heaven, ready to serve God in communion to the saints on earth. The rite of exorcism contains a prayer to St. Michael the archangel: "O most illustrious prince of the heavenly hosts, holy Michael the archangel, from thy heavenly throne defend us in the battle." He is called directly to come, to intercede, to present prayers to God, to lay hold of the dragon, and cast it out.[118]

No figure is more associated with spiritual warfare in the Bible or in the Catholic system than Michael. In Scripture, Dan 10:13 describes how this angel intervened against Satan to allow Gabriel to deliver the message to Daniel the prophet. Jude 9 depicts Michael as rebuking Satan. Revelation 12:7–12 shows him as doing battle in heaven against Satan, triumphantly casting him down. In the *Catechism*, angels receive veneration by the church as they advance the work of human salvation and the church "invokes their assistance" at key junctures.[119]

Catholic exorcist Charles Fraune posits that guardian angels function defending against the influence of the demonic.[120] Thigpen depicts the hope of angelic intercession, particularly St. Michael: "In Scripture we learn that St. Michael is a great warrior who defends God's people

---

115. Allison, *40 Questions*, 257.

116. Article XXII, *Thirty-Nine Articles* (cited in Grudem, *Systematic Theology*, 1175).

117. Augsburg Confession XXI (cited in Leith, ed. *Creeds of the Churches*, 78).

118. "Rite of Exorcism" 4 (Weller, ed., *Roman Ritual: Volume 2*, 225).

119. *Catechism* §§351, 335.

120. Fraune, *Slaying Dragons*, 39.

Theology of the Exorcism

against the Devil. We should ask him daily for his protection."[121] Beginning the list of saintly heavenly intercessors in the *Rite* are the angels: Michael, Gabriel, and Raphael.[122] Beyond the rite, the Salutation of the Ninth Angelic Choir begins, "At the intercession of St. Michael . . . may God vouchsafe to grant that the heavenly angels may protect us during life."[123] Furthermore, the believer can pray this antiphon:

> Michael, glorious Prince, chief and champion of the heavenly host, guardian of the souls of men, conqueror of the rebel angels, who are set over the palace of God, our worthy captain under Jesus Christ, endowed with superhuman excellence and virtue; vouchsafe to free us from every evil, who with full confidence have recourse to thee; and by thy powerful protection enable us to make progress every day in the faithful service of our God.[124]

Thus, in Catholicism the prayers to Michael for protection and the situational defeat of Satan are many.[125] Among the many prayers offered up in the rite of exorcism is a prayer to Michael, which reflects his authority, commissioned by God to defeat Satan. Revelation contributes most strongly to this theology, as Michael the archangel's is triumphant over Satan from a seemingly prior occasion, a primordial fall of angels from heaven.[126] The rite sees exorcism as a cosmic spiritual theater that involves battling princes of the air. Francis Young relates how Pope Leo XIII ordered the addition of prayers to Mary and Michael into the rite in the *Roman Ritual* just before 1890. This figure showed deep interest in the church's resistance to demonic influence.[127] The prayer to St. Michael in the rite presents him in roles of defense, rescue, and entreaty.[128]

---

121. Thigpen, *Manual*, 264.

122. After the archangelic listing come others: holy innocents and virgins, saintly widows and martyrs, holy priests, monks and hermits, the founders of religious order such as Anthony, Benedict, Bernard Dominic, Francis, and Ignatius. "The litany produced an image of phalanxes of saints coming to the aid of the boy" (Allen, *Possessed*, 97).

123. Thigpen, *Manual*, 263.

124. Thigpen, *Manual*, 263.

125. Thigpen, *Manual*, 263–75.

126. Revelation 12:7 narrates the ancient primordial fall as an eschatological event (Osborne, *Revelation*, 469–71).

127. Young, *History of Exorcism*, 188–91.

128. "Rite of Exorcism" 3 (Weller, ed., *Roman Ritual: Volume 2*, 225). Note the millennial language of Rev 20:1–3 here. The voice of 12:9 should be understood as a divine passive, with God ultimately credited for carrying out Satan's fall.

On Holy Saturday, 1949, a statue of St. Michael the archangel was placed in the boy's room: "It should be remarked here that one of the most effective prayers of the exorcism was that dedicated to St. Michael."[129] For this exorcism narrative, this move is instrumental in enhancing the effective engagement of the protector of God's people in answer to the prayers and commands of the rite of exorcism. As Bowdern prayed, Robbie suddenly spoke with an impressive voice to declare himself Michael the archangel. He cast the demon from the boy into a cave, according to Robbie's vision. This came at the declaration of *dominus*, the name of the Lord. This moment is reminiscent of the declaration of the demon when Robbie agreed managed to agree to communion: "That isn't enough. He has to say one more word, one little word, I mean one BIG word." A final, violent fit ensued before Robbie uttered the words, "He's gone."[130]

Calling upon the name of Lord can be varied in the Christian life, from prayer to prayer, psalm to psalm, and cry to cry. It is peculiar that the declaration of the Latin word for "Lord" (*dominus*) is so authoritative here. Jesus' name had been mentioned numerous times in each reading of the rite for weeks. It had been read in Latin. While the boy might not have uttered it himself, the declaration is uttered in Latin (*dominus*) as immediately efficacious for deliverance. Our lack of justification for this secret term is not meant to detract from the efficacy of the expulsion or the history of the event. In the rhetoric of Martin Luther, one little world felled him—that name above all earthy powers, even if that name for the Lord comes as liturgical Latin. However, it points something Catholic, the language of the rite and the association with their ecclesiology.

It remains easy to affirm the role of Michael in warfare against Satan as a biblical concept, and from a theological economic view, perhaps the Lord dispatched the angel to "bind the strongman" (Matt 12:29) and so gained a demonized person for the Lord. At first glance, this Michael-centered narrative account may play down the authority of the resurrected Christ over sin, death, and Satan by glorifying the role of the archangel. A Protestant could object that *Christus Victor* and God's absolute authority over Satan were compromised through the need to somehow marshal the archangel through the "magic word." However, for the Roman Catholic, Michael functions in the agency of the Lord, and credit is still to the resurrected Son of God. However, despite the declaration of the word

---

129. *Diary*, "April 16."
130. *Diary*, "April 18."

Theology of the Exorcism

dominus, the prayers and statue of Michael shift the heroics to the archangel. Certainly, the demonization, the conflict theology, the exorcism, and angelic roles all find biblical precedence. However, the importance of a prayer to Michael in the rite, the statue of Michael in the room, and the vision of Michael as deliverer is entirely Catholic. The Protestant conclusion thus becomes that the power and grace of God visited Robbie for deliverance, despite the systematic invocation and sacramental of the archangel. After all, Rom 8:26 reminds believers that "we do not even know how to pray as we ought, but the Holy Spirit intercedes with sighs too deep for words."

Still, if the priests had directed Robbie to the one necessary word with greater frequency, the Catholic theology would be not critiqued for its prayers to God and appeal for angels. A Christ-centered rite of exorcism and spiritual counsel might draw from direct source of Christ's power. Instead, the cry to Jesus in Latin, surrounded by statuary and liturgy of the archangel, as the momentary instrument of exorcism is elusive. Of course, this theological evaluation comes easy when not faced with a grueling exorcism experience. Yet an unconditional trust of the *Diary* testimony points to the veracity of the Catholic system slightly off center from the Christ supposedly as its core.

DISCIPLESHIP TO FOLLOW

The *Roman Ritual* emphasizes the discipleship of the victim, that he or she should continue in sacramental and spiritual fidelity: "Finally, after the possessed one has been freed, let him be admonished to guard himself carefully against falling into sin, so as to afford no opportunity to the evil spirit of returning, lest the last state of that man become worse than the former."[131] Sometimes the victim is referred to as the "energumen," a term for one possessed by a spirit. Adam Blai describes how liberated victims should continue a life of faith. "Establish a solid foundation of prayer, the sacramental life, the use of sacramentals, and blessings." While victims or families seek exorcism to solve the immediate problem, failure to remain committed to God can lead back to the foundational problem leading to the exorcism, as it "only makes the problem worse in the long

---

131. "Exorcism of the Possessed" 21 (Weller, ed., *Roman Ritual: Volume 2*, 175).

run."[132] According to the rite, upon the departure of the demon, the person should be encouraged to live a holy life, lest the demon return.[133]

Some practitioners offer guidance on the post-exorcism phase for ministers and laity. Protestant Don Basham suggests five steps to post-deliverance: live by the Scriptures, learn to recognize and praise God continually, protect and guard one's thought life, cultivate right relationships, and submit to discipline. The latter includes an individual spiritual mentor or a group meeting with Christians regularly in community.[134] He sums it up this way: "Whether it's salvation, healing or deliverance, [it] is *total commitment of one's life to Jesus Christ.*"[135]

Charles Fraune provides the Catholic perspective on sanctification that follows a Catholic exorcism. "As long as we remain in a state of grace, we will be protected by Our Lord."[136] Sacerdotalism is a part of this state of grace, remaining in the practice of confession and the Eucharist. Obedience to Christ, such as prayer and study of the Word, as well as attending mass, are among the strengthening factors. At the same time, he prioritizes healing as a part of this process. He describes a demon as predator "who pursues those who are closest on its own course . . . In order to avoid this predatory behavior, one of the things we must do is allow Our Lord to heal us."[137] Similarly, Amorth remarks, "The demon keeps his distance from the one who nurtures his faith, who frequents the sacraments, and who wishes to live devoutly."[138] From a Catholic perspective, the sanctification process is marked by sacraments and the means of grace. Sacerdotalism should continue for the faithful one. In other words, Fraune says, "It is critical to lead a good Catholic life."[139] For all Christians, a commitment to the spiritual disciplines, the means of grace, and devotion to Christ all function to build up the disciple and simultaneously avoid association with demons.

Tyler Odle has described the impact of such an event on both the energumen and the exorcist, including the effect of memories, mental

---

132. Blai, *Hauntings*, 29.

133. "Exorcism of the Possessed" 21 (Weller, ed., *Roman Ritual: Volume 2*, 175).

134. Basham, *Deliver Us from Evil*, 163–67.

135. Basham, *Deliver Us from Evil*, 162 (italics original).

136. Fraune, *Slaying Dragons*, 120.

137. Fraune, *Slaying Dragons*, 121

138. Amorth, *Exorcist*, 21–22.

139. Fraune, *Slaying Dragons*, 124. His plan along these lines is comprehensive (see 119–55).

Theology of the Exorcism

and emotional challenges, internal turmoil, and their growth from the event.[140] He recognizes the community can be a support structure and important directive in the lives of those who suffered. Medical and spiritual treatments offer a healing to the longer-term personal and communal dealings with the event. Concerning the pagan fire of magical items at Ephesus following the failed Sceva exorcism in Acts 19, I. Howard Marshall remarks, "Sooner or later there must come a point when believers realize the need to confess the sinfulness of their practices; if it is possible to go further and remove the cause of the temptation, as it is in this case, so much the better."[141]

From the moment that the exorcism came to fruition, Robbie testified feeling the most relaxed since January.[142] The boy went on to live a normal life, reports always declared. The release of his name with his biography in late 2021 seems to support this. However, as already noted, there is no evidence of his religious commitments or practices in the years to follow.

Conclusion

The exorcism was a testimony to the power of God. For the participants, their faith in God and the seemingly divine sacerdotal faithfulness to the ecclesiastical process found eventual fulfilment. The journey of the exorcism experience was long, brutal, and wearying, but their endurance and perseverance in the process is commendable. For the demon, it was a reminder of the power of God in the larger theater of conflict theology with their Master and the exorcist's Master. Ultimately, the demon experienced the same outcome of defeat while the boy experienced the same victory marking the Gadarene demoniac, the epileptic boy, the Syrophoenician woman's daughter, and the Capernaum man. It was a demonstration of Christ's power over the tormenting fallen angels.

For the participants, as one test of faith, it was part of a larger journey of faith. The personal commitments of the participants to the power of Christ generally take center stage in the exorcism story. Peter Blatty remarks that he was himself on a journey of faith when he read about

---

140. Odle, "Ethnography of the Devil." He is careful to qualify that his work is not intended to claim the existence of demons or the efficacy of exorcism to expel them, only to show the value of a support structure (189).

141. Marshall, *Acts*, 312.

142. *Diary*, "April 18."

the case in the *Washington Post*, saying in an interview that he thought, "My God, if someone were to investigate this and authenticate it, what a tremendous boost to faith it would be." Like a response to faith, he admits thinking, "Someday I would like to see that happen. You know, I would like to do it."[143]

This victory through exorcism can be recognized as an evidentiary demonstration of the biblical worldview maintained by historic Christianity. At the same time, this chapter has shown an analysis of the uniquely Catholic elements that buttressed the displays of faith and ecclesiastical process. For a Catholic observer of these events seventy years later, a confidence of ecclesiology such as relics, invocation of saints and angels, priestly authority, and the rite of exorcism will likely find a justification of these elements. For a Protestant observer, these spiritual materials and roles will be viewed suspiciously, preferring to concentrate on the faith, prayer, and authority given to Christians independent of the sacerdotal potential of the church. In fact, perhaps the priestly focus on these religious elements detracted from the efficacy of the exorcism prayers. For all who believe in demonization, the power of Christ in exorcism, and the historicity of the 1949 exorcism, this story can stand as a testimony to a reality not easily sustained in a rational and scientific age.

---

143. Head, "Interview."

7

Appropriating the Event

"Highly necessary it is that we should well understand what God has revealed concerning them [demons], that they may gain no advantage over us by our ignorance; that we may know how to wrestle against them effectually."

—JOHN WESLEY, "OF EVIL ANGELS," 2.

SOME FINAL CONSIDERATIONS NOW come to this study. This chapter seeks to appropriate the theology for historicity, the historicity for reflection on the Bible, and the biblical story for the church. After reviewing the basic summary of the case presented in the book, it revisits the role of theology and the place of history around the happenings of 1949. Then, it claims a potential for belief. The hope is that this story can be found to be a modern example for the church of what is illustrated in the Gospels, that the disciples of Jesus encounter demonization and they exorcize the victims in kingdom work. This study thus hopes to fulfill what William Katerberg charges, "Historians should redefine their vocation in terms of history being useful for life."[1] In another place, Katerberg argues masterfully recognizes: "In the end, while honest accurate analysis, fidelity to one's sources, and reliable knowledge are necessary, they are not enough, and they are not the point. Applied scholarship and public issues should move to the forefront of our work if we are to love Christians outside the academy that look to history for life lessons and larger meanings."[2]

---

1. Katerberg, "'Objectivity Question,'" 102.
2. Katerberg, "'Objectivity Question,'" 113.

Theology of a Diary

Basic Narrative

Several elements of the story are universally accepted and beyond dispute that can shape a base narrative. The boy held a special affinity and affection for his aunt who practiced spiritism. Her death led to his withdrawal, as well as his attempt to contact her through a Ouija board. Strange phenomena began to manifest in the house, including scratches in the walls, footsteps in the house, and the sound of dripping water. Furniture, fruit, and haciendas moved without explanation. Investigation and an exterminator did not prove effective. The manifestations advanced to the boy in his room, including the shaking of a bed and words scratched in his flesh. Irregular and violent behavior ensued. The boy's family took medical initiatives—physiological, psychological, and psychiatric—to find a natural explanation for the condition of their son. The Lutheran family minister witnessed unexplainable behavior. A Catholic priest at least provided sacramentals and encouraged prayer. The family felt compelled to move to St. Louis in the hopes of a new venue for Robbie, although an almost unbelievable motivation to learn of hidden treasure may have marked their motivations. The manifestations and his irregular behavior continued in each place Robbie went. Father Raymond Bishop was contacted and investigated the situation, becoming convinced for further opinion from his peers. Father William Bowdern joined him in believing the boy to be demonized. The St. Louis archdiocese showed reluctance to recognize the case as a valid possession, but scientific explanations seemed futile. From March 16 to April 18, the rite of exorcism was administered on a regular basis. Manifestations expanded to more violence, profanity, sacrilege, and physical phenomena. A battle ensued with the rite of exorcism at the forefront, buttressed by prayer, fasting, sacramentals, and relics. Eventually, an expulsion was achieved. The leading priests remained silent for the rest of their lives, so that while a book and film captured the attention of a nation, the primary witnesses remained reserved in support of the anonymity of the victim. The *Diary* kept the details of their secret until it advanced to print.

Numerous additional details surround, complement, and complicate this basic narrative. Additional details are sometimes controversial, as obscure witnesses and second-hand testimonies augment the story. Most notably among them are the attempted exorcism by Father Albert Hughes with its unprecedented violence, the preternatural manifestation of speaking in a foreign language, and the levitation of a mattress

Appropriating the Event

and a boy. Likewise, some of the reported elements seem unbelievable, such as levitation, moving objects, superhuman strength, and other manifestations.

The defeat of the demon on April 18, 1949, ended a long and arduous period. So that the effect does not escape us, we should recognize this as the end of the summary and the end of the story. The words of the *Catechism* remind the faithful: "The power of Satan is, nonetheless, not infinite. He is only a creature, powerful from the fact that he is pure spirit, but still a creature. He cannot prevent the building up of God's reign . . . It is a great mystery that providence should permit diabolical activity."[3]

The reputation of the event offers a legacy that is unmatched and that almost slipped away. Francis Young calls this 1949 event "the first 'modern exorcism,' in the sense that it followed a pattern established by late nineteenth-century demonological preoccupations and set the agenda both for subsequent exorcisms and global cultural perception of the rite."[4] It is an event that almost slipped away from the public eye, however. Hallowell suggests that the case would have become entirely forgotten if not for the *Washington Post* release that same year.[5] The leak led to publications that led to public awareness, and a popular film captured the event for the mind of the masses. Before 2000, the *Diary* was successfully hidden from public view, even after a 1978 destruction worker in the Alexian Brothers Hospital discovered a copy that would later go public. Despite this documentary influence, the historicity of the event has been questioned while its theology has remained unexplored. Yet the theology can function as one measure of its historicity. Should the theology be found to be sound by orthodox and biblical Christian standards, then the case has a more viable historicity. The objective of the book was to establish a reasonability to the theory of demonization from the 1949 case. As this chapter seeks to appropriate the results of research for historicity and the church, the first appropriation of the event to summarize the case for an established and legitimate exorcism.

---

3. *Catechism* §395.
4. Young, *History of Exorcism*, 202.
5. Hallowell, *Playing with Fire*, 8.

Theology

The explanation and assessment of theology has been the focus of this study. Father Bowdern and those involved clearly held a biblical worldview that accounted for the possibility of the demonic. They held a Catholic theological worldview, celebrating a sacerdotal authority over the demonic. From the archbishop down to the witnesses of supernatural activities, those who recognized two spheres of influence—the demonic and the ecclesiological, the preternatural and the supernatural—are to be commended. Those who exercised pastoral care in and around the reading of the rite of exorcism should be recognized for the Robbie-centered approach to the ordeal. The priests and all those who prayed for the boy displayed a faith and hope in *Christus Victor* that deserves theological commendation.

Sustaining a Theological Worldview

The evaluation of the legitimacy of demonization and exorcism in this story has been delivered and finds its best explanation in a biblical and theological worldview that accounts for the preternatural work of demons and the supernatural work of God. While the Christian must work in the rational dimension and even weigh the naturalistic explanations of an event like this, the admonition to the same Christians is not to allow this worldview to be entirely disassembled by rational alternatives. While this book has avoided offering sermons to the reader against spiritual carelessness in "fellowshipping with demons," this one occasion is worth the application. In Christian thought, Satan abuses the divine gift of rational thought to counteract the biblical explanation for our world.

Even theologians are susceptible to the temptation to make figurative the theology of events like these. Influential theologian Paul Tillich erroneously reinterprets the biblical testimony of the demonic as merely "a union of form-destroying and form-creating strength" that functions as an impersonal cause that is contrary to God, the power of being. For Tillich, demons do not have ontology of their own but "they are structures within being, manifest in experience, and they bear a special relationship to the ultimate reality that is the ground of all things."[6] From this

---

6. Williams, *Demonic and the Divine*, 5.

theologically neoliberal position, Walter Wink can insist that demonic powers are systems in society that oppress and possess people.[7]

C. S. Lewis speaks of this propensity of metaphorical theology in *The Screwtape Letters*, an imaginary dialog between a master demon and a demon in training. The master offers instruction: "Our policy, for the moment, is to conceal ourselves ... When the humans disbelieve in our existence we lose all the pleasing results of direct terrorism, and we make no magicians."[8] Likewise, the mentoring demon remarks: "I have great hopes that we shall learn in due course how to emotionalise and mythologise their science to such an extent that what is, in effect, a belief in us (though not under that name) will creep in while the human mind remains closed to belief in the Enemy."[9] Even the presider of the progressive Vatican II Council, Pope Paul VI, decries the skeptical detractors of demonization:

> Evil is not merely a lack of something, but an effective agent, a living spiritual being, perverted and perverting. A terrible reality. Mysterious and frightening. It is contrary to the teaching of the Bible and the Church to refuse to recognize the existence of such a reality ... or to explain it as a pseudoreality, a conceptual and fanciful personifications of the unknown causes of our misfortunes.[10]

Such a quotation is compounded, realizing that this same pope advanced the *aggiornamento* theme of Vatican II into theological liberalism, with a rational element governing the Council. Even J. B. Rhine, the renowned parapsychologist at Duke University, who corresponded with Schulze, remarked how extraordinary this case was even for parapsychology. He called it "'the most impressive' manifestation he has heard of in the poltergeist field."[11]

At the same time, the social, psychological, medical and other theories have given voice to the interpretation of the event along natural lines; their theories have been provided to sift the data. These disciplines can be helpful in the diagnosis of the spiritual and the natural; they can also be competitive in the diagnosis of demonization. Here, they are recognized

---

7. Wink, *Powers That Be*, 1; Wink, "The World Systems Model."
8. Lewis, *Screwtape Letters*, 32.
9. Lewis, *Screwtape Letters*, 33.
10. Address delivered November 15, 1972 (cited in Travers and Reiff, *Story*, 92).
11. "Minister Tells Parapsychologists."

as unfounded alternative theories and hasty presuppositions that seek to operate without a theological worldview. Yet the theological explanation is not perfect, as Catholic theology and conflicting testimonies complicate belief. Meanwhile, digging into the topic of demonization itself is not without its complexities. Karl Barth cautions Christians along these lines: "It has never been good for anyone . . . to look too frequently and lengthily or seriously or systematically at demons . . . The very thing which the demons are waiting for, especially in theology, is that we should find them dreadfully interesting and give them our serious and perhaps systematic attention."[12]

Thus, the purpose of the book was to analyze one case on its own merits. The focus on this demonization and exorcism can offer the church a solid case of such a phenomenon, mitigating its tendency to dismiss such cases while seeking to perpetuate a worldview that theoretically maintains them. The purpose of this work is not to sensationalize or terrorize the reader. It is a theological assessment that proves to be convincing.

Conclusion to the Catholic Element

The one theological element strain that runs throughout the *Diary* is the presence of Catholic theological elements. The Catholic believer will see the sacerdotal element as essential to the success of the sacrament. The sacraments are weapons in conflict theology to fight the resistant demonic power. When Father Halloran was asked whether he feared for his life during the ordeal, he responded that he did not. His reason was a confidence in the power of faith, even while the demonized boy resisted the priest's explanation of Holy Thursday, the Blessed Sacrament, and ordination of the priests. When the interviewer Michael Brown declared these sacerdotal elements "a confirmation of the power of our faith," Halloran responded, "That's what affected me the most."[13]

Likewise, the sacramentals point to the saints and angels as sources of intercessory power against the demonic. Relics, holy water, the sign of the cross, and even the rite of exorcism itself become irritations as well as forces of power against the demonic hold over the boy. The *Diary* reports the annoyance factor: "R. spit at the relics and at the Priests' hands. He

12. Barth, *CD* 3/3:519.
13. Brown, "Interview."

writhed under the sprinkling of Holy Water. He fought and screamed in a diabolical, high-pitched voice."[14] It also reports the peaceful factor: "Father Bowdern blessed R. with the relic of St. Francis Xavier and Holy Water. The Fathers prayed the Rosary aloud and then prayed silently from 12:00 to 3:00 am. R. had a very normal sleep and there were no manifestations of an evil spirit."[15]

One Protestant judgment of this ecclesiology is that these priests operated under limiting doctrinal interpretations of the experience. The result is that we can declare a bias by the Jesuits that backfired at times. The greatest example is the expectation of ecclesiastical command over the demon by the declaration of the liturgical *dicas mihi*. Without regard to the demonic deception factor, they expected a responsive obligation in the form of an answer. This is partially what Cortés and Gatti likely have in view when they posit: "The writers of all the basic documents appear to have been very credulous, one might even say, almost to the point of gullibility."[16] However, the Jesuit engaged in the Rite of Exorcism should not be blamed for their fidelity to their Catholic faith, and their devotion does not necessarily compromise the credibility of their claims.

What remains for Protestant readers is the question of *why* about the success of the exorcism. If the theology is misplaced, why did God eventually free the boy from the demonic through the Catholic ecclesiological system of sacraments, sacramentals, liturgy, and invocation of the saints? Why did *dominus* function as the key, liberating shibboleth for the demonized boy? A Protestant critique would advance along the following lines. Perhaps the comprehensive Roman Catholic *package* applied by Father Bowdern hindered the exorcism. Conceivably, it was rendered unproductive by the interference of idolatrous and animistic type theology seen in relics, medals, transubstantiated elements, and prayers to saints and angels. Perhaps the length of the exorcism process was not due to the inability to find and utter the right term—albeit a term symbolic of the power of God over the enemy. Instead, the lack of a Christocentric focus delayed the expulsion, allowed the demon to distract the exorcist, encumbered the worship dimension, and compromised efficacy. When

---

14. *Diary*, "March 18."
15. *Diary*, "March 12."
16. Cortés and Gatti, *Case against Possessions and Exorcisms*, 79. To represent these authors fairly, the priests' Catholic devotion is only a mark of several lapses and assumptions by the priests. However, their naïve faith is called into question to compromise veracity of their claims (see 70–84).

Jesus declared that "some types only go out by prayer" (Mark 9:29), or "by prayer and fasting" with the variant reading (Matt 17:21), one cannot know whether thirty-four days represents a reasonable arduous effort or one laden with displaced theological focus.

However, no matter how critical the Protestant is of the Catholic elements that have been explained through this work, all Christians should recognize the eventual success of the exorcism. The demon was cast out. Even though the cry of *dominus* in Latin followed a prayer to St. Michael, the exorcism here still evidences that "anyone who cries out to the Lord shall be saved" (Rom 10:13).

When that final perspective is recognized, then it can be contrasted to the non-Christian, naturalistic explanations that confront the claim of demonization in the event. One realizes that the Catholic perspective on the situation at least incorporated a biblical dimension in its theory of causation. One realizes that Christ was central at times in the prayers of exorcism. It took a biblical approach by interceding with the power of Christ in service to a spiritually victimized boy. It appealed to and anticipated a *Christus Victor* principle that is foundational to Christian thought and conflict theology. Secular theories try to offer a partial explanation to certain behaviors by the boy, but they cannot convincingly encompass the whole narrative of cause and effects. Against such theories, John Nicola frames their ultimate helplessness this way: "There exists a gnawing inability to explain in purely human terms the origin of a complex web of evil which constantly seeks to engulf humanity."[17]

The theology is crucial for understanding the story. While the Catholic theology falls along traditional lines of Protestant objection, it also is a means for exorcism. The demonization and the exorcism find defeat and victory, respectively, in a way that explain and buttress the historicity of the event for the Christian.

Theological Credibility

This critique of the historical account of the 1949 exorcism has been primarily theological. The credibility of its theology in turn offers a credibility to its historicity. Father Bowden's diary account and the testimony of witnesses following the event are equally characterized by much humility without distortion. Thomas Allen's edited account also displays notable

---

17. Nicola, *Diabolical Possession*, 13.

humility and detailed research with limited exaggeration or imprecision. The historical public record is limited only by confidentiality of the sources, and then only on rare occasions such as details in Frank Bober's testimony and newspaper releases. There is genuine conflict theology at work in the sources.

This book sought to examine the Catholic theological understanding of exorcism applied in this four-and-a-half-week period because it is central to understanding and sustaining the reading of the *Diary*. Any such scrutiny has two noticeable limiting factors. First, those involved still operate under a Christian, biblical, supernatural worldview. This *bias* will surely annoy naturalistic skeptics of the events, but it does not preclude the belief by other Christians. In the words of Jack Collins, "How could a study of natural events prove that the world is shut off from the supernatural? That's a job, not for the natural sciences, but for theology."[18]

Second, a Christian analysis faces the difficulty of dealing with the *intentions of demons* because of the theological reality and the logical risk that comes with ever believing "the Prince of Lies" (John 8:44). His reputation as "the god of this world who blinds the eyes of the unbelieving" (2 Cor 4:4) is not a title we dare ignore. The primary criticism to the priests was the latitude of demonic testimony to shape their projection of the timing of the exorcism. Beyond this characteristic lies the theological differences between Catholics and non-Catholics that have been presented here: ecclesiology and means of grace, prayer to Michael the Archangel and the saints, criteria for dialoging with demons, and the animistic quality of religious artifacts. One's view on these elements determines one's confidence in their effectiveness for exorcism. As noted above, however, they do not ultimately have to be elimination criteria to this evaluation.

In a vein of theology often characterized by poor judgment, uninformed hermeneutics, and hyped encounters, this exorcism account deserves attention as arising from a time preceding our contemporary era of exorcism ministries. It is a uniquely well-documented case with firsthand details from a church branch that tends to evade such practices in the modern era. Despite the objections to Catholic theology contained

---

18. C. John Collins, *Science and Faith*, 217. This quotation is offered in response to Bultmann's quotation: "It is impossible to use the electric light and the wireless" (cited above, where Collins rejects this line of reasoning on two grounds: [1] Bultmann confuses the biblical picture and the animistic type of picture of the world; and [2] Bultmann misunderstands what science is able to prove) (see 216–20).

in the *Diary*, the events seem authentic and can offer sociological and theological insight into a biblical yet misunderstood phenomenon.

Historicity

The *Diary* and the witness testimonies chronologically precede the newspaper editorials and the second-hand witnesses that follow the event for years to come. These primary source materials that comprise the basic narrative above show a united awe and messaging that demonic manifestations best explain the phenomena they observed. Even if some initial and subsequent articles and legends reported facts beyond the evidence, that evidence offered by witnesses still provides a convincing case of demonization. Kelly relates from his interview with the exorcist: "Bowdern was dismayed that such stories [as the levitating host] were getting out, but he was not really surprised; for he recognized a strong myth-making tendency even in himself. If he did not record the events of each session of exorcism as soon as possible after it occurred, he declared, he found the details changing in his mind, becoming more 'impressive.'"[19] The *Diary* becomes the premier source for the 1949 exorcism, and its role in interpreting the events has been at the forefront of this study. Even while some details show a minimal amount of variation, there remains a collective memory, a collection of testimonies, and a recorded observation of the event.

Confirmations and Second Thoughts

Eyewitness Father Walter Halloran once remarked that Allen gave the best account of the event.[20] This is an important confirmation by an eyewitness who believed the case and a validation to a representative who expressed it as demonization. The presence of so many witnesses offers a credible constituency of support for a legitimate case of demonization and exorcism here. Yet, even among witnesses, there remains a range of interpretations. All admit to some special and unexplainable features; not a single recorded witness denies the possibility of demonization, even while one priest does not affirm all the manifestations. Not all will

---

19. Kelly, *Devil*, 95.
20. Silvers, "Jesuit Helped."

Appropriating the Event

consistently commit with assurance to call it a legitimate demonization. Tentativeness continues even among some of the witnesses.

The tension and differences around the interpretation of such an event as the 1949 exorcism can be seen in Henry Kelly's dual interviews of the exorcist William Bowdern and his assistant William Van Roo. While Bowdern admitted the limited evidence of demonization by his own witness, he was convinced by the inexplicable phenomena called "paranormal activities" and the preternatural sign of the scratching of the body.[21] He wrote to William Peter Blatty about his hope that the event would help people realize that demonic activities are real: "I can assure you of one thing: the case in which I was involved was the real thing. I had no doubt about it then and I have no doubts about it now."[22] Additionally, Father Bowdern is noted as later saying in a conversation with Father Halloran, "They will never say whether it was, or it wasn't, but you and I know it. We were there."[23]

However, William Van Roo, who entered the exorcism activities late, interviewed how some things he witnessed could have natural explanation by mental illness. For example, Kelly describes Van Roo's testimony about the same scratches: "This phenomenon could be explained naturally by dermatography, that is, hysterically or hypnotically induced skin writing."[24] Van Roo apparently was reserved to state his pessimism publicly out of respect to Bowdern.[25] Yet John Padberg once remarked about Van Roo, "He didn't believe this at all when he started. But I think he was terribly, terribly convinced by the whole thing."[26]

In an interview with a Georgetown student, Halloran seems to balk some himself. "I wouldn't be able to say if it was whether it was valid or not. I've withheld judgment. I'm not saying Father Bowdern's wrong. I was just more comfortable not coming to a decision." He further commented that some incidents could be explained by psychosomatic illness, but that cannot account for all the phenomena.[27] In another interview, Thomas Allen reflected on his own conversations with Halloran: "When we would talk about the exorcism itself, his rational mind would kick in,

21. Kelly, *Devil*, 95–96.
22. Blatty, *On The Exorcist*, 21.
23. Roland, *Complete Book of Ghosts*, 226.
24. Kelly, *Devil*, 98.
25. Kelly, *Devil*, 98–99.
26. Cooperman, "Touched by Evil."
27. Silvers, "Jesuit Helped."

Theology of a Diary

and we could discuss it as two people wondering about a phenomenon. I think he never really made up his mind."[28]

In an interview with J. B. Rhine, even Luther Schulze believed that Robbie was "possessed by some supernatural force."[29] While the Lutheran pastor showed particular interest in the paranormal and preferred to interpret many manifestations along such lines, as shown in his letters to fellow paranormalist J. B. Rhine, even he became convinced that something sinister was at work when the manifestations occurred in his own home, concentrated on the boy.

Inadequate Alternative Explanations

In the process of threshing the legitimacy of demonization, one way to further establish a case for demonization is to consider the limitations of the alternative theories. To offer hypotheses of schizophrenia, conversion disorder, or psychosomatic manifestations such as dermatographia is to avail upon the team of Jesuits an unfair diagnosis of misguided ignorance. Especially Bowdern and Bishop become uninformed in this theory, co-conspirators in forming a condition for the boy that lasted for weeks. Yet neither had an affinity to conflict theology or spiritual warfare to drive them to an overzealous interpretation or to prevail a suggestibility of demonization onto the boy.

In fact, the Jesuit culture in 1949 was marked by attempts towards rational explanations to avoid the image of superstition rather than preternatural explanations. Jesuits educators like the exorcists in this historical account of the mid-twentieth century could have found compatibility with the natural approach to understanding demonization offered by the popular T. K. Oesterreich in the chapter above. They could have stopped with the hope that more psychological testing would lead to a natural explanation. However, the St. Louis exorcists did not.

Since these Jesuits were not deeply involved in deliverance ministry nor showed deep interest in the occult or paranormal, they avoid a prejudice towards a hasty determination of supernatural and preternatural

---

28. Cooperman, "Touched by Evil."

29. Brian, *Enchanted Voyager*, 183. Rhine's biographer reported that Rhine himself did not commit to belief as one not witnessing the events. Instead, Rhine wondered if the pastor had exaggerated facts subconsciously, "As the most honest and intelligent people may do at times, especially when confronted by the unexpected and the traumatic."

Appropriating the Event

explanation for the events. They were not like the Protestant conflict theologians surveyed from the late twentieth century and they were not like the rogue Catholic exorcists populating the stories of contemporary Italy. Father Bowdern showed this neutrality when he wrote to William Peter Blatty, "It is very difficult to find authentic literature on cases of possession; at least, I could not find any when I was involved in such a case."[30] Father Halloran remarked that Bowdern read from the only case study available—the Vogl pamphlet, *Begone Satan*, from the 1928 Iowa case described above.[31]

A hypothesis worth rejecting is that of investigative reporter Mark Opsasnick that Robbie was a trickster, a practical joker. This is the basis for a fraud theory. He interviews Robbie's childhood friend in Cottage City to reveal comrades noted for their practical jokes, suggesting Robbie's exorcism experience stemmed from a shyster who orchestrated and perpetuated a prank.[32] While this testimony offers suspicion around the authenticity of the manifestations, Opsasnick overlooks two important perspectives: the parental and the priestly perspectives. The parents of a young teen jokester would be familiar with his pranks, but they did not evidence this in their own theories of Robbie's condition.[33] The manifestations were too incredible to imagine mechanical pranks. From the earliest evidence in the *Diary*, the parents are concerned: withdrawing him school, taking him to a clinic and a hospital, calling in pastors and priests, consulting a medium, relocating to St. Louis, and suffering through the experience of what Opsasnick would call only a supposed demonization. Likewise, a team of Jesuit priests would also have to be fooled. It is hard to imagine the graphic suffering of the boy in the *Diary* could be sustained if the entire ordeal were a series of pranks. It is hard to imagine such deceit would be perpetuated for four weeks and two days.

To offer a theory of fraud is to avail upon the boy a willingness to perpetuate a bag of tricks played upon the Jesuits, family, and medical professionals over a multi-month period of agony and suffering. Surely a trickster thirteen-year-old boy would have yielded to confession, not of the Catholic type but of disclosure of his pranks to escape the torture and weariness of the exorcism experience. The proposal that the boy was

30. Bowdern, "Letter to Peter Blatty," October 17, 1968 (cited in Blatty, *On The Exorcist*, 20).
31. Allen, *Possessed*, 315.
32. Opsasnick, "Haunted Boy," 20–22.
33. Dobson, "Luncheon."

committing fraud is incongruent with the suffering and endurance of the experience.

A bias in Opsasnick's report is evidenced by his choice of reporting. At first, he claims objectivity: "In setting my investigative goals it was understood that proving whether or not the boy in this case was actually possessed was not on the agenda."[34] However, by the end of his investigation, he declares, "I do not believe Rob Doe was possessed. There is too much evidence that indicates as a boy he had serious emotional problems stemming from his home life," for which he provides a list of emotional pressures, and Robbie's desire to "play his concocted game."[35] He provides quotations that center only on the boy's behavior fifty years earlier from the assessment of lay people. His interview of Halloran only quotes counterfactual material, while the priest insisted not to go on record about the state of the boy's possession.[36] As a committed fact finder, Opsasnick does not seem to factor in the extent of any of these eyewitnesses as present for all events.

Equally unfair is Opsasnick's extensive diagnosis based on speculation. He imagines a troubled home life, dysfunctional parents, emotional problems, a social outcast at school, a motivation to move to St. Louis, attention-getting behavior, and mental illness. Similarly, J. B. Rhine's interview of Luther Schulze led him to wonder if the pastor had exaggerated facts subconsciously, "As the most honest and intelligent people may do at times, especially when confronted by the unexpected and the traumatic."[37] As theories, they are worthy; presented as fact, they are presumptuous and potentially intellectually dishonest.[38] Such theories should be framed as qualified theories to the reader, although his proposal deserves consideration as a theory worth evaluating.

Kelly goes so far to claim error on the part of the archbishop: "It should have been taken as a case not of possession but of obsession or infestation." Even this is an admission of demonization, just to a lesser degree. Yet the Jesuit Kelly does not exclude the existence of demons, seeming to combine his spiritual and psychological worldviews as he

---

34. Opsasnick, "Haunted Boy," 7.
35. Opsasnick, "Haunted Boy," 26.
36. Opsasnick, "Haunted Boy," 25.
37. Brian, *Enchanted Voyager*, 183. Ruickbie also recognizes Rhine as the Director of the Parapsychology Lab at Duke University, interviewing Schulze after the events and without contact with the boy.
38. Opsasnick, "Haunted Boy," 26.

Appropriating the Event

posits that praying against the devil in private would have protected him against "bringing on a state of pseudo-possession by the power of suggestion."[39] Somehow, at the same time, he recognizes his own view as a "legitimate objection to the traditional theology of demonology."[40]

Psychological and social theories of the reason for the boy's behavior and the entire exorcism approach to the problem also find their shortfalls. The hypothesis of conversion disorder could explain the behavior, except it precedes the attempts of exorcism. The hypothesis of attachment disorder or sexual abuse could also explain some behavior, but it does not explain extreme and extensive manifestation qualities. The hypothesis of pseudo-demonization induced by the suggestibility of the priests is a safe theory, but the lack of evidence leaves it as a convenient theory. Furthermore, all these theories ascribe a disorder only to match a targeted section of the symptoms. Besides each requiring their own speculation, they also require a combination of psychological and social explanations in tandem with each other to cover all the theoretical symptoms. Likewise, medical explanations offered after the fact fall short of explaining Robbie's condition. The medical testing at the time did not yield any conclusive determination of condition to explain the events, including Robbie's own behavior. The integrity of the *Diary* reinforces this objection. It is not an edited document that provided opportunity for the diarist to redact the text to make the medical records void. The testimonies in the journal and medical summaries attest that no medical explanation was offered by the examining professionals.

In consideration of the possible sum of factors above, the theory that the explanation for a supposed demonization lies in a combination of these theories thus serves as an inadequate interpretation. The sum of alternative explanations does not combine to solve the problem. Meanwhile, the theological data points to biblical demonization instead. Sergio Rueda is an example of one who theoretically allows for the unexplainable, even demonization, but entirely dismisses strains of evidence throughout this case. In fact, he concludes that the preternatural manifestations and the exorcism were a combination of fraud to be explained by Occam's Razor, conversion disorder in the coprolalia, and poltergeist activities in the shaking bed.[41] Particularly related to the veracity of the scratches, Rueda arrives at disbelieving by ignoring the judgment of the

39. Kelly, *Devil*, 97.
40. Kelly, *Devil*, 99.
41. Rueda, *Diabolical Possession*, 237.

Jesuit testimony and the pattern of signs for potential demonization. This is particularly curious; he is like the 1970's speculators around the case, including Luther Schulze, who can attribute the unexplainable to poltergeists but is unwilling to allow for demons in this case.[42] To deepen his contradiction, all the while, he speaks of the possibility of demonization as being at work.[43] Additionally, he posits that "we cannot completely prove or deny that the Mount Rainier case was an incidence of demonic possession . . . such a possibility cannot be denied."[44] He himself employs the Hamlet principle "that all is possible."[45]

C. S. Lewis recognizes this desperate appeal of naturalism to falsify probability along exclusively naturalistic lines. It leads him to turn reason into a witness for the supernatural: "We must believe in the validity of rational thought, and we must not believe in anything inconsistent with its validity . . . Every theory of the universe which makes the human mind a result of irrational causes is inadmissible."[46] This book advances necessity even more boldly, maintaining that the reduction of physical causes consequentially strengthens the case for the miraculous.

Case for Historicity

A summative case for historicity begins with a comparison of likelihoods. The logician Pierre Simon LaPlace provides a principle in measuring probability whereby extraordinary events require extraordinary evidence. It turns against the fraud theory for the 1949 demonization event.[47] In our case study, a thirteen-year-old boy's ability to deceive adults requires an extraordinary series of hidden strings, levers, and pullies, as well as a naïve cooperation on their part. For that matter, conversion disorder does not explain the bizarre movement of objects and dermatography does not explain the lack of medical diagnosis for hysteria. Most difficult might be the necessity of each combination of social, psychological, and religious suggestive theories working in tandem to satisfy the rational mind in compounding fashion at the expense of a

---

42. Rueda, *Diabolical Possession*, 96–115.

43. Rueda, *Diabolical Possession*, 69–150, 152–57.

44. Rueda, *Diabolical Possession*, 157.

45. Rueda, *Diabolical Possession*, 159, 237.

46. Lewis, *Miracles*, 26, 28.

47. LaPlace, *Philosophical Essay*, 17. Rueda introduces and employs the LaPlace principle in his work on the 1949 exorcism (*Diabolical Possession*, 25).

more rational probability. LaPlace seems to anticipate such theoretical temptation in his philosophy of probability: "The imagination, impatient to arrive at the causes, takes pleasure in creating hypotheses, and often it changes the facts in order to adapt them to its work; then the hypotheses are dangerous."[48]

On the other hand, the *Diary* tells a story of a long chain of interconnected events that are inexplicable by natural means but can be found congruent to preternatural and supernatural criteria. Humble priests without interest in preternatural activities report such phenomena. When given the opportunity to exploit the case, they remained silent. Pastoral care for the victim was prioritized, ecclesiological values were consistently maintained, and they systematically attributed a demonic cause to the phenomena witnessed.

The witnesses augment the claims to veracity. Like the biblical reference of Heb 12:1, the 1949 case is surrounded by a great cloud of witnesses. Their voices here help to shape our understanding of historical and theological elements of the event. LaPlace's third principle of calculating probability is that a combination of combo of *independent* events, in this case testimonies, form a higher probability of likelihood.[49] Medical professionals, family, clergy, and laity offer independent and temporally fragmented testimony to preternatural manifestations. In addition to the witnesses of the 1949 event, the historical recognition of such events offers a consensus of the demonization and exorcism potential of this event. While earlier cases do not prove demonization and exorcism from any anachronistic position of testimony, they do offer precedence as prior witnesses.

These perspectives reinforce the historicity of a spiritual explanation around the event. When the foundational authority theory of integration of faith and learning—a task similar to ours—brings Scripture with its corresponding worldview to weigh this evidence, then a valid and reasonable explanation ensues. Upon returning to the inadequacy of other theories and the evidence of testimony, a theory of one, historical evidentiary demonization has a place. It becomes reasonable to permit such an explanation for the events around the 1949 exorcism. A theology of demonization accounts for the range and variety of historical activities in a way that other explanations cannot. Similarly, the effectiveness

---

48. LaPlace, *Philosophical Essay*, 183.
49. LaPlace, *Philosophical Essay*, 12.

of exorcism and the subsequent life of the victim reinforce a dramatic change. Christians realize that this is not an impossible conclusion as the historical probability of demonization and exorcism becomes increased.

At the core of this study was the question of historicity. Behan McCullagh remarks, "The probability of the conclusion is just a function of the information available to the historian, but it is normally taken to be a reliable guide to rational belief. When the probability of a conclusion is very high, historians are usually quite confident of its truth."[50] In the language of McCullah's work, we have justified the historical descriptions with the record, the testimonies, the weighing of alternative explanations, the theological litmus test, and the complementary Christian worldview considerations. In the language of William Lane Craig's work, we have posited the best or more probable explanation of the facts.[51]

Case for Belief

A case for belief in a historical exorcism is thus before us. Yes, the abounding theories about cases like the 1949 exorcism can be a stumbling block towards sustaining a Christian worldview. After all, belief in the event confronts our paradigm of thinking: even as our mind seeks a natural explanation, the comprehensive evidence is hard to dismiss when one holds a worldview that allows for demonization. While some Christians want to ignore their neighbor's claim to demonic effects, this 1949 neighbor is hard to ignore. While Christians want to dismiss fanatical conflict theologians and passionate deliverance ministers, this case does not allow for it. It thus serves as a case study in conflicting worldviews, as well as offering a solid historical case for a phenomenon to be believed.

Like one accused of being a fraud in a courtroom, this 1949 account stands in the dock while the proceedings of judgment ensue. Witnesses include philosophical naturalists, historians, social scientists, clinical psychologists, family members, and clergy. Closely akin to the latter are practical exorcists and conflict theologians. So many voices weigh in.

---

50. McCullagh, *Justifying Historical Descriptions*, 4.
51. Craig, *Reasonable Faith*, 350.

Appropriating the Event

Tension between Belief and Unbelief

The tension between believing in this demonization and rejecting it as a case study in demonization is demonstrated in the thought process of the author of *The Exorcist*, William Peter Blatty. He studied the case in depth, even seeking to understand and reinforce his own Catholic faith. This is evidenced in his own testimony: "If there were demons, there were angels and probably a God and a life everlasting . . . This case of possession which had joyfully haunted my hopes in the years since 1949 was a worthwhile subject for a novel."[52] This is also shown in his begging of Bowdern for a copy of the diary "because I am Thomas and needed to put my own fingers in the wounds."[53] In an interview he described his captivation with the 1949 story while a student at Georgetown University: "I thought, my God, if someone were to investigate this and authenticate it, what a tremendous boost to faith it would be."[54] One historian evaluates how Blatty hoped that the exorcism story "would confirm the reality of the supernatural and validate Catholic theology . . . As such, it is as much a story about faith as a horror story."[55] Until his death in 2017, he remained Catholic.[56] Meanwhile, director Friedkin was an agnostic Jew, leading to an obscuring of the theological intent of the novel in making the film. However, he showed genius in his attempt to imagine a film that confronted the horrors of demonization possibility. This frankly makes the movie a form of possibility for the Christian. As his talent sought "to make us share the fears of the characters on the screen, he was trying to achieve the deeper goal of Blatty's novel—to put us back in touch with our own fears, the ones we have shoved aside, and challenge us to take the next step."[57]

The element of faith is further evidenced in Blatty's own life. In a 1983 book *Legion: A Novel*, he drew from *The Exorcist* in a way that continues to express his curiosity of God, the problem of evil, human understanding, and demonization.[58] By bringing a fictional demon that

---

52. Blatty, *On The Exorcist*, 6.

53. Blatty, *On The Exorcist*, 21. McGuire also cites that Blatty declared, "I believe this one was the real thing" (see "St. Louis Exorcism").

54. Head, "Interview."

55. Leeder, "Blatty," 44.

56. Leeder, "Blatty," 45.

57. Travers and Reiff, *Story*, 13–14.

58. Blatty, *Legion*.

is familiar with the main character, Father Karras with his possession in *The Exorcist*, Blatty builds on that first book to perpetuate his interest in the obstacles to belief. Written from the perspective of the investigating detective, questions of the existence of God and the problem of evil are at the forefront of the character's thoughts.

One interesting response of disbelief comes from J. D. Sword, a professed member of the Church of Satan. He posits that "the sensational account of the exorcism of Roland Doe, a.k.a. Ronald Hunkeler, is more fantasy than fact," stating that "the true story is neither chilling nor likely true."[59] He reduces his rationale for this claim to Bishop's reliance to secondhand information in the "Background of the Case" in the *Diary*. John Waide, former archivist of the Saint Louis University library, is noted as remarking, "What he describes is pretty gruesome, if that's the word. I don't know what the right word is. It's pretty detailed and pretty graphic. It hits you right in the face."[60]

Interesting is the rare articulation of belief around this event by Thomas Allen himself. Besides the publication of *Possessed: Diary of a True Exorcism* that contains a narration along with the publication of Bishop's journal, his book and his career is marked by interviews and speaking engagements as an expert on the 1949 event. Yet it is not marked by expressions of belief in demonization or even God. In a rare, published comment around a truth claim, he cites no guilt or explanation from his research:

> Robbie was a normal, typical American boy of the times. What happened to him, I believe, happened without any action or provocation on his part. He seems to have been an innocent victim of horror ... He was, I believe a victim of a strange, incomprehensible event, an unearthly event whose cultural and psychological roots are deeper than Christianity's.[61]

The tension in Allen's belief and disbelief are obvious. He simply fails to recognize the spiritual dimension that is the subject of his study but cannot articulate an identified alternative. He fails to grasp the explanation offered by Christianity, whose story of creation, spirits, and the cosmic theater of conflict is subordinated to the wisdom of culture and psychology.

59. Sword, "Demoniac."
60. Holman, "Expert."
61. Allen, *Possessed*, 227.

Appropriating the Event

Reasonability for Belief

A Christian worldview confronts the skepticism of naturalistic disregard for the supernatural. It requires either a confession of faith for causes beyond the explainable or it requires a denial of faith, sometimes reinterpreting the Scriptures along natural lines. However, the Christian story is one characterized by the supernatural. For those willing, possibility of preternatural and supernatural emerges. In turn, reasonability takes hold of possibility to diminish doubt. At times, it still lingers. This is the doubt that marks Christians who hold a theoretical existence of demons but habitually dismiss individual cases of them. A diary, eyewitnesses, theologians and clergy, historians, an exorcism, and their events—explainable only as demonic in collective assessment—still combine to rise to a level of reasonable belief. It is this belief that is appropriated by the evidence of the 1949 exorcism.

A believer then realizes that an historical case of exorcism is before him or her, well-documented, to offer support to a Christian worldview that allows for such spirit beings and their power of possession. Lest that end the story, a believer also realizes—by a powerful reminder—the glorious, wondrous, and victorious grace of the living God.

FINAL PERSPECTIVE

Given the potential veracity of the 1949 event, an obligation of vocation remains. The obligation is akin to that purpose declared by Robert Tracy McKenzie: "As a Christian historian, I am called not only to speak to the academy as a Christian, but also to speak to the church as a historian."[62] It is in service to a church that this work is done, an encouragement that the biblical testimony is accurate. This book hopes to fulfill that need cited by Dietrich Bonhoeffer, "The Christian needs another Christian who speaks God's word to him. He needs him again and again when he becomes uncertain and discouraged, for by himself he cannot help himself without belying the truth."[63] It is the hope that the church is better from this book.

The body of literature continues to grow around the event as the momentum of activities about the demonic abound. Many perspectives

---

62. McKenzie, "Vocation," 4.
63. Bonhoeffer, *Life Together*, 25.

will continue to cloud this historic event. Bill Katerberg frames the burden of the historian for cases like this well: "Politicians use the past to legitimize policies, wars, and moral campaigns. Film makers use it to sell tickets. Even sociologists exploit it as raw material to produce grand theories. But historians study the past on its own terms, as objectively as possible, and for no other reason that its inherent interest."[64] For all readers, the hope is that the book is valuable for the history, the historical assessment, and the fostering of wonder about this event. Yet there is a greater conclusion to be considered, and it has been presented: belief in the demonization and exorcism of the event.

Central to any reflection is faith. How one responds is a judgment on the biblical passages that seem to promote the possibility for a case of demonization, as well as the willingness to trust the evidence. One central component to natural religious feelings, John Haldane says, is "a sense of human contingency and vulnerability: we find ourselves in our world not of our own making, in which we might not have existed and in which our existence if fragile."[65] Getting in touch with one's worldview, one's emotions, and one's wisdom becomes a hinge towards belief. When all the theories are sifted, the demonization of Ronald Hunkeler offers the most reasonable theory of belief. The great challenge of belief rests on the subject of demonization itself. Even a paranormalist recognizes the question before each Christian: "You can tell yourself that you don't believe that people can be possessed by supernatural beings, but what you believe may not matter."[66] Father John Nicola, priest and consultant to *The Exorcist*, frames it this way: "The understanding and explanation of the facts will depend on the disposition of each reader and on what criteria of truth he accepts or favors. One can respond with reliance on faith, or on science, or on both."[67]

In the end, when a Christian looks at the 1949 exorcism, a Christian should look to God. This can be done even with a measure of suspended judgment around the event, as long as the wonder and breadth of possibility that is present in Scripture mark a person's perspective. However, the Christian can also believe it and appropriate it to his or her faith. To do so would be to fall along the claims of Scripture, the great epistemology of the Christian faith. Randall Zachman helps as he articulates the place of

64. Katerberg, "'Objectivity Question,'" 101.
65. Haldane, *Reasonable Faith*, 181.
66. Taylor, *Devil Came to St. Louis*, 8.
67. Nicola, *Diabolical Possession*, 116.

Appropriating the Event

natural revelation alongside this special revelation: "All sciences should so fill us with wonder and astonishment that we are reduced to nothing, and so learn humility, as well as gratitude."[68] He insists that this experience of wonder lead to both proper piety but also a proper appreciation of genuine science established by the Creator. He echoes John Calvin in his own Genesis commentary: "This is, indeed, the proper business of the whole life, in which men should daily exercise themselves, to consider the infinite goodness, justice, power, and wisdom of God, in this magnificent theater of heaven and earth."[69] The 1949 exorcism can do just that for the believer. The Christian recognizes that some things inexplicable might eventually be explained, while some things are as inexplicable as the God who causes them. In this case, a miracle of exorcism by the mercy of God at the behest of Catholic priests.

---

68. Zachman, "Why Should Free Scientific Inquiry Matter to Faith?" 86.
69. Calvin, *Commentary on Genesis*, 105–6.

Bibliography

Abbott, Walter M., ed. *The Documents of Vatican II: In a New and Definitive Translation with Commentaries and Notes by Catholic, Protestant and Orthodox Authorities.* New York: Herder and Herder, 1966.

Alexander, T. Desmond. *From Eden to the New Jerusalem: An Introduction to Biblical Theology.* Grand Rapids: Kregel, 2008.

Allen, Thomas. *Possessed: The True Story of an Exorcism.* New York: iUniverse.com, 2000.

Allison, Gregg R. *40 Questions about Roman Catholicism.* Grand Rapids: Kregel, 2021.

———. *Historical Theology: An Introduction to Christian Doctrine.* Grand Rapids: Zondervan, 2011.

———. *Roman Catholic Theology and Practice: An Evangelical Assessment.* Wheaton, IL: Crossway, 2014.

Amorth, Gabriele. *An Exorcist Explains the Demonic: The Antics of Satan and his Army of Fallen Angels.* Bedford, NH: Sophia Institute, 2016.

Aquinas, Thomas. *Summa Theologiae.* Volume 15: The World Order. Translated by M. M. Charlesworth. New York: Blackfriars/McGraw-Hill, 1970.

Arnold, Clinton E. *3 Crucial Questions about Spiritual Warfare.* Grand Rapids: Baker, 1997.

Baglio, Matt. *The Rite: The Making of a Modern Exorcist.* New York: Image, 2010.

Basham, Don. *Deliver Us from Evil.* Washington Depot, CT: Chosen, 1972.

Beers, Stephen, and Jane Beers. "Integration of Faith and Learning." In *The Soul of a Christian University: A Field Guide for Educators*, edited by Stephen Beers, 57–60. Abilene, TX: Abilene Christian University Press, 2008.

Beilby, James K., and Paul Rhodes Eddy, eds. *Understanding Spiritual Warfare: Four Views.* Grand Rapids: Baker, 2012.

Berger, Peter. *A Far Glory: The Quest for Faith in an Age of Credulity.* New York: Free Press, 1992.

———. *A Rumor of Angels: Modern Society and the Rediscovery of the Supernatural.* Garden City, NY: Doubleday, 1969.

———. *Sacred Canopy.* New York: Doubleday, 1969.

Berkhof, Louis. *Systematic Theology.* Grand Rapids: Eerdmans, 1991.

Bibliography

Bishop, Raymond J., and Christopher Saint Booth. *The Exorcist Diary: The True Story of* The Exorcist. Granada Hill, CA: Spooked, 2015.
Blai, Adam C. *Hauntings, Possessions, and Exorcisms*. Steubenville, OH: Emmaus Road, 2017.
Blatty, William Peter. *The Exorcist*. New York: Harper, 2011.
———. *Legion: A Novel*. New York: Simon & Schuster, 1983.
———. *On* The Exorcist *from Novel to Film*. New York: Bantam, 1974.
Blumberg, Arnold T. "How 'The Exorcist' Redefined the Horror Genre." *Fandom.com* (October 25, 2016). No pages. Online: https://www.fandom.com/articles/exorcist-redefined-horror-genre.
Bonhoeffer, Dietrich. *Life Together: The Classic Exploration of Christian Community*. Translated and introduced by John W. Doberstein. New York: HarperOne, 2009.
Boyd, Gregory A. *God at War: The Bible and Spiritual Conflict*. Downers Grove, IL: InterVarsity, 1997.
———. "The Ground-Level Model." *Understanding Spiritual Warfare: Four Views*, edited by James K. Beilby and Paul Rhodes Eddy, 129–57. Grand Rapids: Baker, 2012.
———. *Satan and the Problem of Evil: Constructing a Trinitarian Warfare Theodicy*. Downers Grove, IL: IVP Academic, 2001.
Bradnick, L. David. *Evil, Spirits, and Possession: An Emergentist Theology of the Demonic*. Boston: Brill, 2017.
Brian, Denis. *The Enchanted Voyager: The Life of J. B. Rhine, an Authorized Biography*. New York: Prentice-Hall, 1982.
Brinkley, Bill. "Pastor Tells Eerie Tale of 'Haunted Boy.'" *The Washington Post*, August 10, 1949.
———. "Priest Frees Mt. Rainier Boy Reported Held in Devil's Grip." *Washington Post*, August 20, 1949.
Brisbane, Arthur S. "Youth's Bizarre Symptoms Led to 1949 Exorcism." *The Washington Post*, May 6, 1985, A10.
Brooks, James A. *Mark*. NAC 23. Nashville: Broadman, 1991.
Brown, Michael. "An Interview with the Priest Involved in the Case Behind *The Exorcist*." *Spirit Daily*. No pages. Online: https://www.spiritdaily.org/Halloran.htm.
Brown, Rebecca. *Prepare for War*. Chino, CA: Chick, 1987.
Bultmann, Rudolph. *History of the Synoptic Tradition*. Translated by John Marsh. Peabody, MA: Hendrickson, 1963.
———. "The New Testament and Mythology." In *Kerygma and Myth*, edited by Hans Werner Bartsch, 1–44. New York: Harper & Row, 1961.
Bunse, Frederick J. "The Earling Possession Case." In *Penguin Book of Exorcisms*, edited by Joseph P. Laycock, 226–28. New York: Penguin, 2020.
Cadegan, Una M. "Not All Autobiography Is Scholarship." In *Confessing History: Explorations in Christian Faith and the Historians Vocation*, edited by John Fea, Jay Green, and Eric Miller, 39–59. Notre Dame: University of Notre Dame Press, 2010.
Calvin, John. *Commentary on Genesis: Volume 1*. Edinburgh: Calvin Translation Society, 1843–1844.
Catechism of the Catholic Church. 2nd ed. New York: Doubleday, 2003.

Bibliography

Chajes, J. H. *Between Worlds: Dybbuks, Exorcists, and Early Modern Judaism*. Philadelphia: University of Pennsylvania Press, 2011.
Chirico, Leonardo di. *Same Words, Different World: What Makes Roman Catholicism Differ from the Gospel?* Downers Grove, IL: IVP, 2021.
Clowney, Edmund P. *The Church*. Contours of Christian Theology. Downers Grove, IL: InterVarsity, 1995.
The Code of Canon Law. London: Collins Liturgical, 1983.
Collingwood, R. G. *The Idea of History*. New York: Oxford University Press, 1971.
Collins, James M. *Exorcism and Deliverance Ministry in the Twentieth Century: An Analysis of the Practice and Theology of Exorcism in Modern Western Christianity*. Milton Keynes: Paternoster, 2009.
Collins, C. John. *Genesis 1–4: A Linguistic, Literary, and Theological Commentary*. Phillipsburg, NJ: P&R, 2006.
———. *The God of Miracles: An Exegetical Examination of God's Action in the World*. Wheaton, IL: Crossway, 2000.
———. *Science and Faith: Friends or Foes?* Wheaton, IL: Crossway, 2003.
Cooper, Terry D., and Cindy K. Epperson. *Evil: Satan, Sin, and Psychology*. New York: Paulist, 2008.
Cooperman, Jeannette. "Touched by Evil." *St. Louis Magazine*, March 21, 2014. No pages. Online: https://www.stlmag.com/Touched-by-Evil.
Cortés, Juan B., and Florence M. Gatti. *The Case against Possessions and Exorcisms: A Historical, Biblical, and Psychological Analysis of Demons, Devils, and Demoniacs*. New York: Vantage, 1975.
Cosgrove, Mark P. *Foundations of Christian Thought: Faith, Learning, and the Christian Worldview*. Grand Rapids: Kregel, 2006.
Craffert, Pieter F. "Medical Anthropology as an Antidote for Ethnocentrism in Jesus Research? Putting the Illness–Disease Distinction into Perspective." *HTS Teologiese Studies/Theological Studies* 67 (2001) 1–14.
Craig, William Lane. *Reasonable Faith: Christian Truth and Apologetics*. Wheaton, IL: Crossway, 2008.
Croce, Benedetto. *History: Its Theory and Practice*. New York: Russell & Russell, 1960.
Crossan, John Dominic. *Jesus: A Revolutionary Biography*. San Francisco: Harper, 1994.
Diagnostic and Statistical Manual of Mental Disorders. 5th ed. Washington, DC: American Psychiatric, 2013.
Dobson, Gwen. "Luncheon with Father John J. Nicola." *Evening Star and the Washington Daily News*, November 3, 1972, B1, B4.
Dupré, Judith. *Full of Grace: Encountering Mary in Faith, Art, and Life*. New York: Random House, 2010.
Emerson, Matthew Y. *"He Descended to the Dead": An Evangelical Theology of Holy Saturday*. Downers Grove, IL: IVP, 2019.
Erdmann, Steve. "The Truth behind *The Exorcist*." *Fate* 28.1 (1975) 50–59.
Faherty, William Barnaby. *To Rest in Charity: A History of the Alexian Brothers in Saint Louis (1869-1984)*. St. Louis: River City, 1984.
Fea, John, Jay Green, and Eric Miller, eds. *Confessing History: Explorations in Christian Faith and the Historians Vocation*. Notre Dame, IN: University of Notre Dame Press, 2010.
Fee, Gordon D. *The First Epistle to the Corinthians*. Grand Rapids: Eerdmans, 1987.

Bibliography

Ferguson, Everett. *Demonology of the Early Christian World*. SymS 12. Lewiston, NY: Edwin Mellen, 1984.

Fiske, Edward B. "'Exorcist' Adds Problems for Catholic Clergymen." *New York Times*, January 28, 1974, 1, 15.

Flood, Amelia. "SLU Legends and Lore: The 1949 St. Louis Exorcism." *Saint Louis University News*, October 30, 2019.

France, R. T. *Matthew*. TNTC. Grand Rapids: Eerdmans, 1985.

Fraune, Charles D. *Slaying Dragons: What Exorcists See and What We Should Know*. Monee, IL: Retreat Box, 2019.

Freud, Sigmund. "A Seventeenth-Century Demonological Neurosis" In *The Standard Edition of the Complete Psychological Works of Sigmund Freud: Volume 19*, edited by James Strachey, 72–105. London: Hogarth, 1968.

Gallagher, Richard. *Demonic Foes: My Twenty-Five Years as a Psychiatrist Investigating Possessions, Diabolical Attacks, and the Paranormal*. New York: HarperOne, 2020.

Garland, Amy. "Exorcism Exposé: An In-Depth Look at Saint Louis University's Part in the Most Famous Exorcism of the 20th Century." *Universita*s 40.2 (2014) 12–15.

Geisler, Norman, and Joshua M. Betancourt. *Is Rome the True Church? A Consideration of the Roman Catholic Claim*. Wheaton, IL: Crossway, 2008.

Goodman, Felicitas D. *The Exorcism of Anneliese Michel*. Searcy, AR; Resource, 2005.

———. *How about Demons? Possession and Exorcism in the Modern World*. Bloomington: Indiana University Press, 1988.

Gordon, Spencer. "*The Exorcist*: The Real Incident Involved a Mt. Rainier Priest in 1949." *Prince George's Sentinel*, February 4, 1981.

Green, Michael. *I Believe in Satan's Downfall*. London: Hodder & Stoughton, 1981.

Grudem, Wayne. *Systematic Theology: An Introduction to Biblical Doctrine*. Grand Rapids: Zondervan, 1994.

Gruenthaner, Michael J. "The Demonology of the Old Testament." *CBQ* 6 (1944) 6–27.

Hagner, Donald A. *Matthew 1–13*. WBC 33A. Nashville: Thomas Nelson, 1993.

Haldane, John. *Reasonable Faith*. New York: Routledge, 2010.

Hallowell, Billy. *Playing with Fire: A Modern Investigation into Demons, Exorcism, and Ghosts*. Nashville: Emanate, 2020.

Hamilton, Victor P. *Handbook on the Pentateuch*. Grand Rapids: Baker, 1982.

Hammond, Frank, and Ida Mae Hammond. *Pigs in the Parlor: A Practical Guide to Deliverance*. Kirkwood, MO: Impact, 1973.

Hatchman, Laura. "Conversion Disorder." In *Spirit Possession around the World: Possession, Communion, and Demonic Expulsion across Culture*, edited by Joseph P. Laycock, 86. Santa Barbara, CA: ABC-CLIO, 2015.

Head, Steve. "Interview with *The Exorcist* Writer/Producer William Peter Blatty." *IGN Film Force*, September 20, 2000 (updated May 20, 2012).

Heiser, Michael S. *Demons: What the Bible Really Says about the Powers of Darkness*. Bellingham, WA: Lexham, 2020.

Holman, Gregory J. "An Expert on the Real-Life Event That Inspired 'The Exorcist' Is Coming to Springfield." *Springfield News-Leader*, October 3, 2017.

Horsley, Richard A. *Jesus and Empire: The Kingdom of God and the New World Disorder*. Minneapolis: Fortress, 2003.

Hume, David. *An Enquiry Concerning Human Understanding*. Edited by Tom L. Beauchamp. Oxford Philosophical Texts. New York: Oxford University Press, 1999.

Bibliography

In the Grip of Evil, a film directed by Charles Vanderpool, produced by Discovery Channel Pictures, 1997.

Jenkins, Philip. *The New Anti-Catholicism: The Last Acceptable Prejudice*. New York: Oxford University Press, 2003.

Katerberg, William. "The 'Objectivity Question' and the Historian's Vocation." In *Confessing History: Explorations in Christian Faith and the Historians Vocation*, edited by John Fea et al., 101–27. Notre Dame: University of Notre Dame Press, 2010.

Keener, Craig S. "Crooked Spirits and Spiritual Identity Theft: A Keener Response to Crooks?" *Journal of Mind and Behavior* 39 (2018) 345–71.

———. *Miracles: The Credibility of the New Testament Accounts*. 2 vols. Grand Rapids: Baker, 2011.

———. *Miracles Today: The Supernatural Work of God in the Modern World*. Grand Rapids: Baker, 2021.

———. "Spiritual Possession as a Cross-Cultural Experience." *BBR* 20 (2015) 215–36.

Keller, Timothy. *The Reason for God: Belief in an Age of Skepticism*. New York: Penguin, 2008.

Kelly, Henry A. *The Devil, Demonology, and Witchcraft*. Eugene, OR: Wipf & Stock, 2004.

Kildahl, John P. *The Psychology of Speaking in Tongues*. New York: Harper & Row, 1972.

King, Susan. "Speaking of the Devil; Author Recalls It Took a Near-Miracle to Get Anyone to Notice his Thriller, *The Exorcist*." *Los Angeles Times*, October 10, 2013, D5.

Kinlaw, Dennis F. "The Demythologization of the Demonic in the Old Testament." In *The Shape of the Past: An Introduction to Philosophical Historiography*, edited by John Warwick Montgomery, 29–35. Minneapolis: Bethany Fellowship, 1976.

Klutz, Todd. *Exorcism Stories in Luke–Acts: A Sociostylistic Reading*. Cambridge: Cambridge University Press, 2004.

Kuemmerlin-McLean, Joanne K. "Demons: Old Testament." In *ABD* 2:138–40.

LaChance, Steven Allen. *Confrontation with Evil: The 1949 Saint Louis Exorcism*. Self-Published: Steven LaChance, 2018.

Ladd, George Eldon. *A Theology of the New Testament*. Grand Rapids: Eerdmans, 1974.

Lampert, Vincent P. *Exorcism: The Battle against Satan and his Demons*. Steubenville, OH: Emmaus Road, 2020.

LaPlace, Pierre Simon. *A Philosophical Essay on Probabilities*. Translated by Frederick Wilson Truscott and Frederick Lincoln Emory. New York: Dover, 1951.

Laycock, Joseph P. "Amorth, Gabriel." In *Spirit Possession around the World: Possession, Communion, and Demon Expulsion across Culture*, edited by Joseph P. Laycock, 9–10. Santa Barbara, CA: ABC-CLIO, 2015.

———. "The Secret History of the 'Earling Exorcism.'" In *The Social Scientific Study of Exorcism in Christianity*, edited by Giuseppe Giordan and Adam Possamai, 17–32. Cham: Springer, 2020.

———, ed. *The Penguin Book of Exorcisms*. New York: Penguin, 2020.

Laycock, Joseph P., and Eric Harrelson. *The Exorcist Effect: Horror, Religion, and Demonic Belief*. New York: Oxford University Press, 2024.

Leeder, Murray. "Blatty, William Peter." In *Spirit Possession around the World: Possession, Communion, and Demon Expulsion across Cultures*, edited by Joseph P. Laycock, 43–45. Santa Barbara, CA: ABC-CLIO, 2015.

Bibliography

Leith, John H., ed. *Creeds of the Churches: A Reader in Christian Doctrine from the Bible to the Present.* Atlanta: John Knox, 1982.

Levack, Brian P. *The Devil Within: Possession and Exorcism in the Christian West.* New Haven: Yale University Press, 2013.

Levine, Amy-Jill, and Ben Witherington III. *The Gospel of Luke.* New Cambridge Bible Commentary. New York: Cambridge University Press, 2018.

Lewis, C. S. *Miracles.* New York: MacMillan, 1947.

———. *The Screwtape Letters.* New York: MacMillan, 1982.

Linson, D. R. "Washington's Haunted Boy." *Fate* 4.3 (1951) 31–34.

MacLeod, Douglas. "Exorcist, The." In *Spirit Possession around the World: Possession, Communion, and Demon Expulsion across Cultures,* edited by Joseph P. Laycock, 121–24. Santa Barbara, CA: ABC-CLIO, 2015.

Marcus Minucius Felix. *The Octavius.* Translated by G. W. Clarke. ACW 39. New York: Newman, 1974.

Marshall, I. Howard. *Acts.* TNTC. Grand Rapids: Eerdmans, 1980.

Martin, Malachi. *Hostage to the Devil: The Possession and Exorcism of Five Contemporary Americans.* San Francisco: HarperSanFrancisco, 1992.

Masters, Anthony. *The Devil's Dominion: The Complete Story of Hell and Satanism in the Modern World.* Edison, NJ: Castle, 2006.

McBrien, Richard P. *Catholicism.* 2 vols. Minneapolis: Winston, 1980.

McCullagh, C. Behan. *Justifying Historical Descriptions.* Cambridge: Cambridge University Press, 1984.

McGuire, John M. "Diary of an Exorcism: A Priest's Journal Inspired Thomas Allen to Retell the Strange Event that Took Place in a St. Louis Hospital." *St. Louis Post Dispatch*, September 7, 1993, D1.

———. "The St. Louis Exorcism of 1949: The Real-Life Inspiration for 'The Exorcism.'" *St. Louis Post-Dispatch*, April 17, 1988 (republished October 28, 2019).

McKenzie, Robert Tracy. "The Vocation of the Christian Historian: Re-Envisioning our Calling, Reconnecting with the Church." *Fides et Historia* 45 (2013) 1–13.

"Minister Tells Parapsychologists Noisy 'Ghost' Plagued Family." *The Evening Star*, August 10, 1949, B7.

Morris, Leon. *The First Epistle of Paul to the Corinthians: An Introduction and Commentary.* TNTC. Grand Rapids: Eerdmans, 1988.

———. *The Gospel According to Matthew.* PNTCS. Grand Rapids: Eerdmans, 1992.

Murphree, Jon Tal. *God's Rescue Operation: A Closer Look at the Crucifixion of Jesus Christ.* Wedowee, AL: Pinnacle Point, 2020.

———. *Science's Unscientific Claim: Naturalism and Theism.* Wedowee, AL: Pinnacle Point, 2020.

Murphy, Ed. *Handbook for Spiritual Warfare.* Nashville: Thomas Nelson, 1992.

Nauman, St. Elmo, Jr. *Exorcism through the Ages.* New York: Philosophical Library, 1974.

"New Details of Boy's Exorcism In Catholic Ritual Disclosed." *The Evening Star*, August 20, 1949, A3.

Nicola, John J. *Diabolical Possession and Exorcism*: Rockford, IL: Tan, 1974.

Oberman, Hieke A. *Luther: Man between God and the Devil.* New York: Image, 1992.

Odle, J. Tyler. "Ethnography of the Devil: The Aftermath of Possession, Exorcism, and the Demonic." In *The Social Scientific Study of Exorcism in Christianity*, edited by Giuseppe Giordan and Adam Possamai, 175–89. Cham: Springer, 2020.

Bibliography

Oesterreich, T. K. *Possession: Demoniacal and Other among Primitive Races—In Antiquity, the Middle Ages, and Modern Times.* Seacaucus, NJ: University, 1966.
Opsasnick, Mark. "The Haunted Boy of Cottage City: The Cold Hard Facts behind the Story That Inspired *The Exorcist*." *Strange Magazine*, 6–27, December 1998.
——— . *The Real Story behind* The Exorcist: *A Study of the Haunted Boy and other True-Life Horror Legends from Around the Nation's Capital.* Bloomington, IN: Xlibris, 2007.
Orsi, Robert A. *History and Presence.* Cambridge, MA: Harvard University Press, 2016.
Osborne, Grant R. *Revelation.* BECNT. Grand Rapids: Baker, 2002.
Ott, Ludwig. *Fundamentals of Catholic Dogma.* St. Louis: B. Herder, 1957.
Peretti, Frank E. *This Present Darkness.* Wheaton, IL: Crossway, 1986.
Pilch, John J. *Healing in the New Testament: Insights from Medical and Mediterranean Anthropology.* Minneapolis: Fortress, 2000.
——— . "Sickness and Healing in Luke–Acts." In *The Social World of Luke–Acts: Models for Interpretation*, edited by Jerome H. Neyrey, 181–210. Peabody, MA: Hendrickson, 1991.
Plantinga, Alvin. *Where the Conflict Really Lies: Science, Religion, and Naturalism.* New York: Oxford University Press, 2011.
Possamai, Adam, and Giuseppe Giordan. "Introduction." In *The Social Scientific Study of Exorcism in Christianity*, edited by Giuseppe Giordan and Adam Possamai, 1–13. Cham: Springer, 2020.
Powlison, David. "The Classical Model." *Understanding Spiritual Warfare: Four Views*, edited by James K. Beilby and Paul Rhodes Eddy, 89–111. Grand Rapids: Baker, 2012.
——— . *Power Encounters: Reclaiming Spiritual Warfare.* Grand Rapids: Baker, 1995.
——— . "Response to Gregory Boyd." In *Understanding Spiritual Warfare: Four Views*, edited by James K. Beilby and Paul Rhodes Eddy, 165–68. Grand Rapids: Baker, 2012.
"Priest Freed Boy of Possession by Devil, Church Sources Say." *The Evening Star*, August 19, 1949, B1.
Priest, Robert, et al. "Missiological Syncretism: The New Animistic Paradigm." In *Spiritual Power and Mission: Raising the Issues*, edited by Edward Rommen, 55–64. Evangelical Missiological Society Series 3. Pasadena, CA: William Carey Library, 1995.
Reese, David George. "Demons: New Testament." In *ABD* 2:140–42.
Robinson, David C. "Introduction." In Tyconius, *Exposition of the Apocalypse*, translated by Francis X. Gumerlock, 3–26. FC 134. Washington, DC: Catholic University of America Press, 2017.
Roland, Paul. *The Complete Book of Ghosts: A Fascinating Exploration of the Spirit World, from Apparitions to Haunted Places.* London: Arcturus, 2019.
Rueda, Sergio A. *Diabolical Possession and the Case behind* The Exorcist. Jefferson, NC: McFarland, 2018.
Ruickbie, Leo. "Hunkeler, Ronald E." In *Spirit Possession around the World: Possession, Communion, and Demon Expulsion across Cultures*, edited by Joseph P. Laycock, 156–57. Santa Barbara, CA: ABC-CLIO, 2015.
Sales, Frances de. *The Sign of the Cross: The Fifteen Most Powerful Words in the English Language.* Translated by Christopher O. Blum. Manchester, NH: Sophia Institute, 2013.

Bibliography

Schulze, Luther. "Luther Schulze Case Report." In *The Penguin Book of Exorcisms*, edited by Joseph P. Laycock, 245–47. New York: Penguin, 2020.

Shelton, W. Brian. *Quest for the Historical Apostles: Tracing Their Lives and Legacies*. Grand Rapids: Baker, 2018.

———. Review of *Demons and Spirits in Biblical Theology: Reading the Biblical Text in Its Cultural and Literary Context*, by John H. Walton and J. Harvey Walton. *JGRChJ* 16 (2020) R6–R9.

Silvers, Amy Rabideau. "Jesuit Helped Inspire 'The Exorcist,' Served in Vietnam." *Milwaukee Journal Sentinel*, March 4, 2005, B7.

Small, Karen, and Pat McGonigle. "Read the St. Louis Diary that Inspired 'The Exorcist.'" *Fox 4 News Kansas City*, October 30, 2022. No pages. Online: https://fox4kc.com/news/read-the-st-louis-diary-that-inspired-the-exorcist.

Soards, Marion L. *1 Corinthians*. NIBCNT. Peabody, MA: Hendrickson, 1999.

Sorensen, Eric. *Possession and Exorcism in the New Testament and Early Christianity*. Tübingen: Mohr Siebeck, 2002.

Spitzer, Robert J. *Christ Versus Satan in our Daily Lives: The Cosmic Struggle between Good and Evil*. San Francisco: Ignatius, 2020.

Stark, Rodney. *Bearing False Witness: Debunking Centuries of Anti-Catholic History*. West Conshohocken, PA: Templeton, 2016.

Steeves, Paul D. "Invocation of the Saints." In *Evangelical Dictionary of Theology*, edited by Walter A. Elwell, 1902–70. Grand Rapids: Baker, 2001.

Stevenson, Ian. "Possession and Exorcism: An Essay Review—*Possessed: The True Story of an Exorcism by Thomas Allen*." *Journal of Parapsychology* 59.1 (1995) 59, 69–76.

Sword, J. D. "Demoniac: Who Is Roland Doe, the Boy Who Inspired *The Exorcist*?" *Skeptical Inquirer*, November/December 2021. No pages. Online: https://pocketmags.com/us/skeptical-inquirer-magazine/novdecember-2021/articles/demoniac-who-is-roland-doe-the-boy-who-inspired-the-exorcist.

Taylor, Charles. *A Secular Age*. Cambridge, MA: Harvard University Press, 2007.

Taylor, Troy. *Devil Came to St. Louis: The True Story of the 1949 Exorcism*. Decatur, IL: Whitechapel, 2006.

Thigpen, Paul. *Manual for Spiritual Warfare*. Charlotte, NC: Tan, 2014.

Thorsen, Donald. A. D. *The Wesleyan Quadrilateral: Scripture, Tradition, Reason, and Experience as a Model of Evangelical Theology*. Nappanee, IL: Francis Asbury, 1997.

Tyconius. *Exposition of the Apocalypse*. Translated by Francis X. Gumerlock. FC 134. Washington, DC: Catholic University of America Press, 2017.

Travers, Peter, and Stephanie Reiff. *The Story behind* The Exorcist. New York: Signet, 1974.

Twelftree, Graham H. *In the Name of Jesus: Exorcism among Early Christians*. Grand Rapids: Baker, 2007.

———. *Jesus the Exorcist: A Contribution to the Study of the Historical Jesus*. Eugene, OR: Wipf & Stock, 2011.

———. *Jesus the Miracle Worker*. Downers Grove, IL: IVP, 1999.

Vaughan, Joy L. *Phenomenal Phenomena: Biblical and Multicultural Accounts of Spirits and Exorcism*. Waco, TX: Baylor University Press, 2023.

Vincent, Isabel, and Jack Morphet. "What Really Happened to Ronald Hunkeler, Who Inspired 'The Exorcist.'" *The New York Times*, December 20, 2021. No pages.

Bibliography

Online: https://nypost.com/2021/12/20/is-the-exorcist-a-true-story-what-happened-to-ronald-hunkeler.

Vogl, Carl. *Begone Satan! A Soul-Stirring Account of a Diabolical Possession*. Translated by Celestine Kapsner. Charlotte, NC: Tan, 2010.

Wacker, Grant. "Understanding the Past, Using the Past: Reflections on Two Approaches to History." In *Religious Advocacy and American History*, edited by Bruce Kuklick and D. G. Hart, 159–78. Grand Rapids: Eerdmans, 1997.

Walther, Matthew. "Spiritual Lessons from 'The Exorcist.'" *New York Times*, August 23, 2023, SR5.

Walton, John H., and J. Harvey Walton. *Demons and Spirits in Biblical Theology: Reading the Biblical Text in its Cultural and Literary Context*. Eugene, OR: Cascade, 2019.

Weller, Philip T., ed. *Roman Ritual: Volume 1—Sacraments and Processions*. Gilbert, AZ: Caritas, 2017.

Weller, Philip T., ed. *Roman Ritual: Volume 2—Christian Burial, Exorcisms, Reserved Blessings, Etc.* Gilbert, AZ: Caritas, 2017.

West, Edward N. *Outward Signs: The Language of Christian Symbolism*. New York: Walker, 1989.

Wiggins, Steve A. *Nightmares with the Bible: The Good Book and Cinematic Demons*. Lanham, MD: Lexington, 2021.

Williams, Daniel Day. *The Demonic and the Divine*. Minneapolis: Fortress, 1990.

Williamson, Lamar, Jr. *Mark*. IBC. Louisville: John Knox, 1983.

Wilkinson, Tracy. *The Vatican's Exorcists: Driving Out the Devil in the 21st Century*. New York: Grand Central, 2007.

Wimber, John, and Kevin Springer. *Power Healing*. New York: HarperSanFrancisco, 1991.

Wink, Walter. *The Powers That Be: Theology for the New Millennium*. New York: Doubleday, 1999.

———. "The World Systems Model." In *Understanding Spiritual Warfare: Four Views*, edited by James K. Beilby and Paul Rhodes Eddy, 47–71. Grand Rapids: Baker, 2012.

Witmer, Amanda. *Jesus, the Galilean Exorcist: His Exorcisms in Social and Political Context*. Library of the Historical Jesus Studies. London: Bloomsbury, 2012.

Yang, May. "Boy Whose Case Inspired *The Exorcist* Is Named by US Magazine." *The Guardian*, December 20, 2021. No pages. Online: https://www.theguardian.com/us-news/2021/dec/20/the-exorcist-boy-named-magazine.

Young, Francis. *A History of Anglican Exorcism: Deliverance and Demonology in Church Ritual*. New York: T&T Clark, 2019.

———. *A History of Exorcism in Catholic Christianity*. Cambridge: Palgrave, 2016.

Zachman, Randall C. "Why Should Free Scientific Inquiry Matter to Faith? The Case of John Calvin." In *Knowing Creation: Perspectives from Theology, Philosophy, and Science*, edited by Andrew B. Torrance and Thomas H. McCall, 69–86. Grand Rapids: Zondervan, 2018.

Index of Authors

Allen, Thomas, xiii–xiv, 1–3, 5–6, 8–13, 15–24, 34, 36–37, 42, 44–46, 58, 65, 67–68, 71, 125–26, 130, 139–40, 142–43, 152, 163–66, 172–73, 187, 189, 194–95, 198, 200, 202–3, 206, 209–10, 218–19, 223–24, 227–28, 233, 246–49, 251, 258
Alexander, T. Desmond, 81
Allison, Gregg R., 80, 91, 118, 130, 231–32
Amorth, Gabriele, 40, 98, 124–25, 136, 138, 141, 153–54, 160–61, 163, 177, 183, 186, 188, 191, 195, 209, 220, 228, 230, 236
Arnold, Clinton E., 91, 97, 124

Baglio, Matt, 106
Barth, Karl, 83, 129, 244
Basham, Don, 111, 131, 134, 169–70, 221, 236
Beers, Jane, 54
Beers, Stephen, 54
Beilby, James K., 96
Berger, Peter, 49, 104, 110, 121
Berkhof, Louis, 130
Betancourt, Joshua M., 118
Blai, Adam C., 90, 124, 126, 139, 144, 152–53, 162, 182, 185, 235–36
Blatty, William Peter, xiv, xvii, 2, 18, 37–39, 44–45, 53, 68, 70, 72, 74, 105, 140, 173, 206, 211, 237, 249, 251, 257–58
Blumberg, Arnold T., 39–40
Bonhoeffer, Dietrich, 259
Boyd, Gregory A., 89–91, 97, 128–30, 223, 225
Bradnick, L. David, 93, 103–6, 112, 121
Brian, Denis, 3, 5, 8–10, 12, 19, 36, 69, 148, 171, 188, 250, 252
Brinkley, Bill, xiv, 2, 18, 148, 219
Brisbane, Arthur S., 14–16, 148
Brooks, James A., 86
Brown, Michael, 18, 22, 29, 33, 36–37, 64, 126, 145, 147, 155, 164, 170, 215, 244
Brown, Rebecca, 96–97
Bultmann, Rudolph, 104–5, 108, 207–28, 247
Bunse, Frederick J., 99, 169

Cadegan, Una M., 48–49
Calvin, John, 199, 232, 261
Chajes, J. H., 163
Chirico, Leonardo di, 118
Clowney, Edmund P., 201
Collingwood, R. G., 42–43, 49, 55, 71–74
Collins, C. John, 51, 75–77, 80, 121, 247
Collins, James M., 96–97, 127, 161, 187

Index of Authors

Cooper, Terry D., 5, 9, 13–15, 36, 107, 109, 133, 137, 177, 214
Cooperman, Jeannette, xiv, 11, 67, 70, 249–50
Cortés, Juan B., 22, 108, 131–32, 245
Cosgrove, Mark P., 54
Craffert, Pieter F., 114
Craig, William Lane, xiv, xvii–xviii, 48, 52–53, 256
Croce, Benedetto, 43
Crossan, John Dominic, 113–14

Dobson, Gwen, 15, 36, 68, 140, 144, 214, 218, 251
Dupré, Judith, 231

Eddy, Paul Rhodes, 97
Epperson, Cindy K., 5, 9, 13–15, 36, 107, 109, 133, 137 177, 214
Erdmann, Steve, 3, 15, 18, 29, 148, 155

Faherty, William Barnaby, xiii, 10, 18, 21, 32, 36, 42, 44, 67, 70, 72, 144–45, 148, 152, 214–15
Fee, Gordon D., 125
Ferguson, Everett, 93, 200, 224
Fiske, Edward B., 38, 40
Flood, Amelia, 3, 64
France, R. T., 89, 90, 225
Fraune, Charles D., 128, 133, 136, 143, 163, 195–97, 232, 236
Freud, Sigmund, 107
Friedkin, William, xiv, 37, 257

Gallagher, Richard, 18, 36, 39, 44, 124, 152, 204
Garland, Amy, xv, 24
Gatti, Florence M., 22, 108, 131–32, 245
Geisler, Norman, 118
Giordan, Giuseppe, 104, 112–13
Goodman, Felicitas D., 100, 111, 124, 136, 149–50
Green, Michael, 104
Grudem, Wayne, 130, 232
Gruenthaner, Michael J., 83

Hagner, Donald A., 225

Haldane, John, 260
Hallowell, Billy, 2–3, 43, 78, 100, 128, 162, 241
Hamilton, Victor P., 87
Hammond, Frank, 96, 110
Harrelson, Eric, 2, 38
Hatchman, Laura, 132–33
Head, Steve, 15, 18, 45, 68, 71, 238, 257
Heiser, Michael S., 78, 91, 139, 226
Holman, Gregory J., 258
Hume, David, 102–3

Jenkins, Philip, 118

Katerberg, William, 48, 239, 260
Keener, Craig S., 51, 54, 75, 80, 113, 222
Keller, Timothy, 54–55, 121, 229
Kelly, Henry A., xvi, 2, 5, 18, 31, 44, 68, 70, 74, 148, 150, 156, 181–82, 189, 248–49, 252–53
King, Susan, 39
Kinlaw, Dennis F., 47
Klutz, Todd, 87
Kuemmerlin-McLean, Joanne K., 78, 82

LaChance, Steven Allen, xiv, 13–14, 74, 127, 133, 135, 137–38, 145–48, 218, 173, 189, 215
Ladd, George Eldon, 82, 92
Lampert, Vincent P., 98, 116, 120, 124, 135–36, 138–39, 141, 144–45, 152, 159, 162–63, 172, 181–82, 184–85, 192–93
LaPlace, Pierre Simon, 52, 254–55
Laycock, Joseph P., 2–3, 8, 38, 98, 134, 169, 179, 183
Leeder, Murray, 257
Leith, John H., 232
Levack, Brian P., 96, 99–100, 111, 119–20, 124
Levine, Amy-Jill, 86, 89–91, 114–15
Lewis, C. S., 103, 120, 243, 254
Linson, D. R., 3, 8–9, 19, 148, 164, 219

MacLeod, Douglas, xv, 40

Index of Authors

Mae, Ida, 96, 110
Marshall, I. Howard, 237
Martin, Malachi, 51, 80, 95, 100, 120, 124, 134, 156, 159, 163–64, 169, 183–86, 208–14, 222–23, 234
Masters, Anthony, 2–3, 100, 107, 112, 120, 133–35, 141, 145, 153, 160, 162, 217
McBrien, Richard P., 119
McCullagh, C. Behan, xviii, 52, 78, 256
McGonigle, Pat, 216
McGuire, John M., xv–xvi, 1, 10–11, 37, 67–68, 70, 73, 145, 173, 189, 218, 257
McKenzie, Robert Tracy, 259
Morphet, Jack, 3, 12, 116, 135–36, 172, 182
Morris, Leon, 126, 204
Murphree, Jon Tal, 103, 223
Murphy, Ed, 179–80

Nicola, John J., xv, 4, 11, 14–15, 18, 32, 68, 72, 104, 130–31, 138, 140, 144, 146, 148, 152, 154, 159, 162, 173, 178, 189, 202, 209, 217–18, 246, 260

Oberman, Hieke A., 95
Odle, J. Tyler, 100, 236–37
Oesterreich, T. K., 101, 250
Opsasnick, Mark, 2–3, 9, 11–13, 15–17, 37–38, 45, 67–70, 133, 135, 150, 251–52
Orsi, Robert A., 183
Osborne, Grant R., 233
Ott, Ludwig, 200

Peretti, Frank E., 97
Plantinga, Alvin, 103–4
Possamai, Adam, 104, 112–13
Powlison, David, 97, 130, 204
Priest, Robert, 11, 18, 148, 219

Reese, David George, 78, 80
Reiff, Stephanie, 2, 12, 76, 211, 243, 257
Robinson, David C., 120
Roland, Paul, 2–3, 11, 74, 99–100, 249

Rueda, Sergio A., xiv, 2, 7–11, 14, 17–19, 21–22, 31, 37–40, 46, 68–69, 108–9, 122, 128, 131–33, 148–50, 154, 228, 253–54
Ruickbie, Leo, 1–3, 8–10, 13–14, 19, 252

Saint Booth, Christopher, 1, 3–6, 10–11, 13–14, 21–22, 46, 67, 126, 147–48, 152, 197, 215, 228
Schulze, Luther, 5, 8–11, 19, 31–32, 68–69, 108, 128, 131, 171, 252
Shelton, W. Brian, xv, 46, 93, 116, 188, 195, 201
Silvers, Amy Rabideau, 24, 67, 155, 209, 214, 248–49
Small, Karen, 216
Soards, Marion L., 126
Sorensen, Eric, 93, 124, 170, 204
Spitzer, Robert J., 4, 5, 9, 14–15, 18–20, 29, 45, 109, 125–26, 148, 189, 196, 217, 229
Springer, Kevin, 80, 97, 134–35, 141, 143, 145, 153
Stark, Rodney, 118
Steeves, Paul D., 230
Sword, J. D., 258

Taylor, Charles, 49, 103
Taylor, Troy, 2–3, 11, 14–17, 19, 29, 58, 74, 99–100, 111, 133, 142–43, 145, 148, 150, 155, 163, 182, 184, 196–97, 208, 210, 214, 260
Thigpen, Paul, 124, 130, 188, 195, 201, 230, 232–33
Thorsen, Donald, 54, 129
Travers, Peter, 2, 12, 76, 211, 243, 257
Twelftree, Graham H., xvii, 78, 83, 86, 88, 94

Vaughan, Joy L., 112–13, 138, 143, 208
Vincent, Isabel, 3, 12, 116, 135–36, 172, 182
Vogl, Carl, 99, 251

Wacker, Grant, 53, 118
Walther, Matthew, 103
Walton, John H., 78–79, 83, 115–16
Walton, J. Harvey, 78–79, 83, 115–16

Index of Authors

West, Edward N., 193, 197
Wiggins, Steve A., 2, 40, 125, 133, 189
Wilkinson, Tracy, 96, 98, 106–7, 119–20, 135, 138, 161, 165–66, 183, 200, 213
Williams, Daniel Day, 242
Williamson, Lamar, Jr., 107–8
Wimber, John, 80, 97, 134–35, 141, 143, 145, 153

Wink, Walter, 105, 243
Witherington, Ben, III, 86, 89–91, 114–15
Witmer, Amanda, 114, 208

Yang, May, 3, 12
Young, Francis, 2, 94–95, 99, 134, 170, 233, 241

Zachman, Randall C., 260–61

Index of Subjects

Alexian Brother Hospital. *See* hospital.
Allen, Thomas, xiv, 2, 12, 16, 39, 43–46, 53, 67, 70–73, 166, 246–49, 258
Aquinas, Thomas. *See* Thomas Aquinas.
Aramaic, spoken language, 14, 18, 148, 150, 180

baptism, 15, 29–30, 56, 62–63, 67, 90, 93–94, 155, 188, 191, 202–3, 222, 227–28
Basa case, 98–99
Bel-Nor, MO, 19, 58–59
Bischofberger, George, 67, 71
Bishop, Raymond J., background, 20–21
  Diary, xiv, 1, 6, 13, 16, 21–22, 31–32, 41–43, 46, 55, 57, 59, 66–67, 71, 240, 258
  exorcist, *passim*
Bober, Frank, 13, 16, 39, 68, 72, 247
Boland, Joseph, 67, 72
Bowdern, William S., appointment as exorcist, 1, 22–23, 60, 163–64, 182, 240
  background and relatives, 1, 20–21, 24, 37, 218
  calculating exorcism, 27–28, 30, 36, 61–62, 65, 166–67, 169, 172, 175–76, 179, 210–11, 214–15, 220–22
  confidentiality, 37, 53, 70–71, 240, 255
  correspondence with Blatty, xvii, 37–39, 44–45, 70, 251, 257
  exorcist, *passim*
  fatigue, 187, 206, 212, 216–18
  interaction with Hughes, 16, 31, 63, 69
  on the *Diary*, xvii, 37, 41, 46, 66
  on *The Exorcist*, 37–38
  pastoral approach, 21–24, 41–42, 60, 117, 128, 187–89, 200, 222, 226–29
Burke, Edmund, 67, 72

Canning, Father, 32, 67, 69, 71
Catechism of the Catholic Church, 91, 119–20, 129, 160–61, 182, 191, 194–95, 199–200, 229–30, 232, 241
Cele case, 99, 134, 139, 142, 196
cluster effect, 23, 64, 99, 140–43, 156–57, 216
The Code of Canon Law, 161, 181
confidentiality, 20, 24, 36–37, 45–46, 53, 67, 69–71, 73, 116, 240, 247, 255
conflict theology, 79, 89, 90–93, 96–97, 101, 105, 130, 136, 207–8, 221, 235, 237, 244–47, 250

Index of Subjects

Cottage City, MD, 2, 31, 56, 59, 63, 133, 251

demonization, contemporary cases, 23, 89, 98–101, 111, 119, 134–35, 139, 142–43, 152, 169–70, 179, 183, 196, 214, 251, 255
   difficulty as evidence, xvii–xviii, 42, 47–50, 52, 54, 75, 101–21, 180–84, 244–61
   evidence for rite approval, 13, 20, 22, 135, 160–61, 180–84, 250–51
   manifestations, *See* manifestations
   psychological association, xvii, 8, 10–11, 100–11, 113–14, 120, 132–33, 136–37, 157–58, 160–61, 182, 202, 243–44, 253–54
   possession versus oppression, 79–80
   theology, 78–92, 101, 123–58, 242–48, 256–61
Diagnostic and Statistical Manual of Mental Disorders, 132
Diary, contents, 1–39, 41–47, 55–69, 74–76, 90, 160, 167, 191, 209, 212, 228, 231, 235, 244, 246–48, 251, 255, 258–59
   history, xii–xiv, 1–2, 31, 39, 41–46, 50, 53, 55, 69–71, 73, 76–77, 240–41, 248–50, 257–58
   interpretation, xviii–xx, 42–44, 47–55, 59–60, 66–76, 117–18, 121–22, 246–50, 253, 255–61
dicas mihi, *See* Roman Ritual.
Dogmatic Constitution of the Church, 230
Donley, Ida Mae, 17–18, 68, 73, 154
Duke Parapsychology Laboratory, 8–9, 68, 128, 243, 252

Elizabeth, cousin, 20–22, 28, 68–69
Emmet, hospital worker, 32, 67, 72
Enlightenment, philosophy, 8, 10, 40, 54, 101–2, 113
The Evening Star, 17, 219
Eucharist, xx, 30, 32–34, 63–65, 69, 142, 156, 187, 189–90, 192–93, 197–202, 227, 236

exorcism, abuse association, 100–101, 111, 119–21
   faith efficacy, 47, 54, 56, 62–63, 65, 85, 87–88, 128, 142, 164, 166, 168, 185–86, 188–89, 191–94, 197–205, 209–10, 220–21, 222–23, 226–29, 230–32, 235–38, 242, 244–45, 257
   phases, 207–16
   theology, 78–92, 206–38, 242–48, 256–61
The Exorcist, film, xiv–xvii, xix, 37–40, 44–46, 53, 70, 74, 76, 96, 103, 105, 111–12, 140, 189, 206, 211, 257–58, 260

Faherty, William Barnaby, 18, 32, 67, 70, 72, 145, 152, 214–15
Felix, Marcus Minucius, 125
Flagellum Daemonum (or *The Devils Scourge*), 95–96

Gallagher, Eugene, 18, 39, 44
Georgetown University, 10–11, 14–16, 39, 44–45, 68, 257
Georgetown University Hospital, *See* hospital.
The Guardian, 3

Halloran, Walter, background, 24, 33, 206
   Diary, xiv, 44–46, 67, 70–72
   exorcism, *passim*
   The Exorcist, 37–38, 145
   interviews, xv, 23–24, 29, 33, 37, 39, 46, 60, 67, 71, 126, 145, 147, 150, 154–55, 164, 170, 209, 213–15, 244, 248–49, 251–52
Harriett, Aunt, *See* Hendricks, Mathilda.
Hendricks, Mathilda, 3–8, 19, 22, 57–60, 125–28, 146–47, 157, 178, 240
Hippolytus, 93–94
historiography, xvi–xix, 42–51, 54–55, 239–56
holy water, 13, 20–22, 24, 26, 34, 59, 61, 66, 94, 99, 118, 153–55, 161, 184, 194, 196–97, 202, 244–45

Index of Subjects

hospital, Alexian Brothers Hospital, xiii, 27, 31–32, 36, 38, 44–46, 59, 61, 63–65, 67, 72, 139, 152, 185–86, 188–89, 191, 207, 241
County Mental Hygiene Clinic, 11
Georgetown University Hospital, 10–11, 14–15, 45
Saint Louis University Hospital, 12
Hughes, Albert, 10, 12–16, 18, 31–32, 57, 63, 67–69, 71–72, 144, 150, 152, 196, 202, 214, 240
Hunkeler, Ronald Edwin, adulthood, 12, 36–37, 69, 141, 216, 236–37
childhood, 2–3, 7, 17, 36, 127–28, 106–7, 133, 251–52
diagnosis, 2, 7, 10–16, 19, 27, 31, 45–46, 55, 58, 101–2, 106–9, 120, 132, 183, 185–86, 189, 243, 250–52, 254
identity as energumen, xix, 2–3, 8, 10, 12, 19, 45, 69–71
identity as Robbie, *passim*

Iowa case, *See* Schmidt case.
Irenaeus, 81

Jenkins, Joe, 14
Justin Martyr, 93, 224

Kenny, Laurence J., 10, 20, 58, 67
Klingenberg case, *See* Michel case.

Lady of Fatima, Our, 22, 26, 30, 34, 63, 65–66, 191, 230–31
Latin, rite and reading, 28, 30, 35, 62–65, 148–51, 160, 166–69, 176, 207, 228, 234
spoken language, 14, 17–19, 28, 32, 63–65, 68, 148–51, 180, 227–28, 231, 234–35, 246
Leo XIII, Pope, 233
Lord's Prayer, 22, 165, 197, 199–200
Luther, Martin, 95, 199, 234

manifestations,
aversion to sacred, 4, 13, 21–22, 26, 28–35, 55, 58, 60–65, 85, 93, 95, 98–100, 130, 135–36, 142, 150–51, 153–58, 160, 169–70, 176, 184–85, 188, 196–99, 201, 203, 208–11, 213, 219, 220–22, 224, 227–28, 231, 244
barking, 26, 28, 33, 43, 61, 107, 135, 139, 212
bed moving, 4–9, 14, 17–20, 22, 26–28, 58–60, 62, 68–69, 105, 107, 123, 126, 130, 152–53, 195–96, 240, 253
footsteps, 4, 6–7, 21–22, 56–57, 107, 130, 152, 240
glaring, 17, 29, 100, 141, 149, 229
hissing, 139–41
knowledge, 14, 17–19, 56, 62, 65, 68, 95, 99, 134, 140, 144–51, 180, 187
languages, unfamiliar, 14, 17–19, 22, 68, 95, 98–99, 140, 145, 148–51, 180, 184, 240
levitation, xvii, 4, 6, 17–18, 68, 105, 109, 156, 240–41, 248
moving objects, xvii, 4, 6–9, 13–14, 20–22, 38, 56–57, 59–60, 152–54, 156–57, 224, 240, 254
scratches, 4–5, 7, 9–10, 12, 19–22, 24–25, 30, 32, 36, 43, 56–60, 63–64, 66, 68–69, 107–8, 123, 130–31, 142, 144, 147–48, 152, 155, 170–73, 176, 178, 181, 195, 202, 209, 215–17, 219–20, 224, 240, 249, 253
singing, 25, 28, 32–33, 35, 61, 63–64, 66, 137–38, 142, 151, 154, 227
strength, 9, 14–15, 25–28, 33, 60, 65, 85–86, 95, 98–100, 143–44, 212–14, 134, 180, 185, 203, 218, 241
voice alteration, 26–27, 29, 34–35, 61, 65, 99–100, 111, 138, 141, 157, 172–74, 176, 178, 196, 207, 212–13, 219–20, 234, 245
McMahon, Father, 67, 189, 202
mental illness, conversion disorder, 5, 11, 106, 108–10, 120, 132–33, 202, 250, 253–54

Index of Subjects

coprolalia, 12–13, 23, 25, 27–30, 32–33, 61, 63–65, 100, 132, 135–37, 146, 151, 153–55, 164, 174, 187, 207, 221–22, 253, 258
   generally, 12, 50, 83–84, 106, 109–10, 112, 132–33, 160–61, 249, 252
   obsessive-compulsive disorder, 11, 98, 135–36
Michael, church worker, 62, 67, 72
Michael, the archangel, 24, 34–35, 60–61, 65–66, 82, 117, 175, 177, 207, 221, 227, 229, 232–35, 244, 246–47
Michel case, 100–101, 111, 119, 135, 143, 152
Mt. Rainier, MD, 2

naturalism, philosophy, xv–xviii, 49–55, 75–78, 101–17, 120–21, 247, 250–56
necromancy, 3, 5–6, 19, 28, 38, 57, 59, 62, 123–28, 130, 146, 157, 170, 200, 240
New York Post, 3
Normandy, MO, 19–20, 58–59
Nicola, John, 4, 11, 15, 18, 68, 72, 104, 130, 138, 140, 144, 146, 152, 154, 162, 173, 178, 189, 208, 217–18, 246, 260

O'Boyle, Archbishop Patrick, 13
occult, xix, 3, 6–7, 38, 57, 60, 85–86, 99, 104, 124–27, 129–30, 135, 145, 147, 157, 176, 199, 204, 223, 226, 250
O'Connell, Dan, 21, 39
O'Flaherty, John, 30–31, 63, 67, 72, 154, 231
oppression, *See* demonization.
Origen, 81, 93
Ouija board, 3, 5–6, 19, 28, 38, 57, 59, 62, 125–27, 200, 240

Parapsychology Bulletin, 17
plausibility, xvi–xviii, 42, 48–50, 52–55, 70, 239–56
poltergeist, 8–10, 17, 153, 243, 253–54
possession, *See* demonization.

praecipio, *See* Roman Ritual.
Prince George's Sentinel, 15

relics, Margaret Mary, St., 20–21, 59, 154, 194
   theology, 155, 184–85, 187, 190, 194–96, 225, 238, 240, 244–45
   Xavier, St. Francis, 194–95, 245
Reinert, President Paul, 20, 58
Reppetti, William, 16, 68, 72
Rhine, J. B., 8–11, 68–69, 128, 148, 171, 243, 250, 252
Ritter, Archbishop Joseph Allen, 1, 22–23, 37, 42, 44–46, 60, 70, 117, 163, 181–82, 242, 252
Roman Ritual, *adjuro*, 167–68, 223
   approval, xix, 13–14, 22–23, 31, 60, 117, 159, 161, 163–64, 180–83, 186, 240
   contents, 162–97, 203–5
   dicas mihi, 18–19, 30, 35, 144, 148, 150, 155, 167, 169–79, 217, 219–22, 245
   exorcizo, 79, 116–17, 159, 167–68, 193, 228
   history, 97–98, 159–62, 223
   psalms, 165, 168, 184, 234
   praecipio, 24–26, 30–31, 33, 35, 60–63, 65–66, 148, 150–51, 160, 166–69, 171, 173–75, 217
Rosary, 22, 25–27, 30, 63, 66, 127, 182, 189, 191, 231, 245

Saint Louis University, xv, 1, 20, 21, 24, 27, 29, 58–59, 67, 187, 258
Sales, Frances de, 194
Sassin, Edmond F., 67, 72, 189
Schaffer, Ernest, 67, 72
Schell, Albert, 67, 72
Schmidt case (or Iowa exorcism case), 23, 89, 99, 134, 169–70, 179, 183, 196, 214, 251
Schulze, Rev. Luther, 7–10, 12–13, 17, 37, 57–59, 68, 71, 73, 108, 128, 131, 144, 148, 188, 243, 250, 252, 254
séance, 3, 19, 125, 127, 130
sign of the cross, 66, 161, 192–94, 202, 222–24, 244

Index of Subjects

Society for Parapsychology, 9
St. Francis Xavier College Church,
    1, 20, 27, 29, 59, 61–62, 67, 72,
    187–88, 215, 217
St. James Church, 12, 15
St. Louis Post-Dispatch, 11

Tertullian, 93, 174–75
Theophane, hospital worker, 67, 72
Thomas Aquinas, 95
Tillie, Aunt, *See* Hendricks, Mathilda.
Time Magazine, xiv
The Times-Herald, 17
treasure, 7, 22, 59–60, 126–27, 147,
    157, 240
Treasury of Exorcisms, 96
Trinity, 9, 29, 118, 146, 165, 168,
    193–94, 202, 224, 231

Tyconius, 79, 170–71

Van Roo, William, 31, 63, 67–68, 72,
    144, 155, 213, 249

Waide, John, xv, 46, 258
The Washington Post, xiv, 2, 17, 219,
    238, 241
Wateska case, 98
Wesley, John, 239
Wesleyan Quadrilateral, 54, 129
Widman, Father, 67, 72
witnesses, xvii–xvix, 2, 6, 22–23, 31,
    34, 37, 41–42, 46–47, 50, 53, 57,
    66–76, 108, 114, 132, 136, 148,
    150, 152–53, 180, 207, 240, 242,
    246–47, 255–56, 259

www.ingramcontent.com/pod-product-compliance
Lightning Source LLC
Chambersburg PA
CBHW071237230426
43668CB00011B/1476